Social and Economic Development in Central and Eastern Europe

The integration of post-socialist Central and Eastern Europe into the EU is one of the success stories of European development. The region has seen significant economic convergence, dramatic changes in socio-economic indicators and improvements in the natural environment. However, some challenges remain, such as political divergence, public governance issues and population demographics.

This book identifies and analyses the key post-1990 developments across the New Member States at the sub-national and national levels, with frequent country-level and regional comparisons. Careful attention is paid to drawing out commonalities in development trajectories while appreciating each country's unique context. Drawing on the academic literature and illuminating empirical material, the broad range of topics discussed in the book paints a detailed picture of both change and stability in Central and Eastern Europe.

It will be valuable reading for advanced students, researchers and policymakers in regional studies, European studies, human geography, political economy and transition economics.

Grzegorz Gorzelak is Professor of Economics at the Centre for European Regional and Local Studies (EUROREG), University of Warsaw, Poland.

Regions and Cities

Series Editor in Chief

Joan Fitzgerald, *Northeastern University, USA*

Editors

Ron Martin, *University of Cambridge, UK*
Maryann Feldman, *University of North Carolina, USA*
Gernot Grabher, *HafenCity University Hamburg, Germany*
Kieran P. Donaghy, *Cornell University, USA*

In today's globalised, knowledge-driven and networked world, regions and cities have assumed heightened significance as the interconnected nodes of economic, social and cultural production, and as sites of new modes of economic and territorial governance and policy experimentation. This book series brings together incisive and critically engaged international and interdisciplinary research on this resurgence of regions and cities, and should be of interest to geographers, economists, sociologists, political scientists and cultural scholars, as well as to policymakers involved in regional and urban development.

For more information on the Regional Studies Association visit www.regionalstudies.org

There is a **30% discount** available to RSA members on books in the *Regions and Cities* series, and other subject related Taylor and Francis books and e-books including Routledge titles. To order just e-mail Emilia Falcone, Emilia.Falcone@tandf.co.uk, or phone on +44 (0)20 3377 3369 and declare your RSA membership. You can also visit the series page at www.routledge.com/Regions-and-Cities/book-series/RSA and use the discount code: **RSA0901**

Social and Economic Development in Central and Eastern Europe
Stability and Change after 1990
Edited by Grzegorz Gorzelak

Metropolitan Economic Development
The Political Economy of Urbanisation in Mexico
Alejandra Trejo Nieto

For more information about this series, please visit: www.routledge.com/Regions-and-Cities/book-series/RSA

Social and Economic Development in Central and Eastern Europe

Stability and Change after 1990

Edited by Grzegorz Gorzelak

Routledge
Taylor & Francis Group

LONDON AND NEW YORK

First published 2020 by Routledge

2 Park Square, Milton Park, Abingdon, Oxon, OX14 4RN

605 Third Avenue, New York, NY 10017

Routledge is an imprint of the Taylor & Francis Group, an informa business

First issued in paperback 2020

British Library Cataloguing-in-Publication Data
A catalogue record for this book is available from the British Library

Library of Congress Cataloging-in-Publication Data
Names: Gorzelak, Grzegorz.
Title: Social and economic development in Central and Eastern Europe :
    stability and change after 1990 / edited by Grzegorz Gorzelak.
Description: Abingdon, Oxon ; New York, NY : Routledge, 2019. | Series:
    Regions and cities ; 137 | Includes bibliographical references and index.
Identifiers: LCCN 2019019701 (print) | LCCN 2019022002 (ebook) |
    ISBN 9780429450969 (Ebook) | ISBN 9781138324299 (hardback)
Subjects: LCSH: Europe, Eastern—Economic conditions—21st century. |
    Europe, Central—Economic conditions—21st century. | Europe,
    Eastern—Social conditions—21st century. | Europe, Central—Social
    conditions—21st century. | Post-communism—Europe, Eastern. |
    Post-communism—Europe, Central.
Classification: LCC HC244 (ebook) | LCC HC244 .S57 2019 (print) |
    DDC 338.943—dc23
LC record available at https://lccn.loc.gov/2019019701

ISBN: 978-1-138-32429-9 (hbk)
ISBN: 978-0-367-78422-5 (pbk)

Typeset in Bembo
by Apex CoVantage, LLC

Contents

Figures

Tables

Maps

Contributors

John Bachtler is Professor and Director of the European Policies Research Centre at the University of Strathclyde and at the Technical University of Delft. He has long-standing research interests in the comparative study of regional development in Europe at different spatial scales and particularly in the design, implementation and evaluation of EU Cohesion Policy. He leads a number of major EPRC research programmes in these areas and is currently developing new EPRC research on administrative capacity in regional policy.

Jerzy Bański is Professor of Human Geography and since 2018 Director of the Institute of Geography and Spatial Organization, Polish Academy of Sciences (IGSO PAS). His main research interests include geography of rural areas and agriculture, land use, regional policy, spatial organisation and local development. In 2006–12 he was president of the Polish Geographical Society. In 2017 he has been appointed chairman of the Commission of Local and Regional Development under the International Geographical Union. He is an author of over 380 publications, including 21 books. He has been co-ordinating over 40 research projects and is a member of 35 other national and international undertakings (such as FP6, FP7, Horizon, ESPON).

Roberta Capello is Professor of Regional Economics at the Politecnico of Milan, Italy, and Past President of the Regional Science Association International. She is Fellow of RSAI and Editor in Chief of Papers in Regional Science (Wiley Blackwell). She has published extensively on regional economics, innovation and technology and their role in regional development. She is a co-author of the MASST model used for socio-economic forecasting. She is author of a textbook in regional economics with several editions, also in Chinese. Winner of a carrier prize of the 50° ERSA (European Regional Science Association) anniversary (Jonkoping, 2010). Laurea Honoris Causa, West University of Timisoara, Romania (2012). Kohno Award for outstanding service to RSAI (San Antonio, Texas, 2018).

Martin Ferry, Ph.D., is a senior research fellow at EPRC. He specialises in regional economic development and policy in Central and Eastern Europe (particularly Poland) and the United Kingdom. He has a particular interest in the governance and implementation of national regional policy and Cohesion policy, and is developing a new EPRC research programme on sustainable urban development in Europe.

Agnieszka Fihel obtained her Ph.D. in economic sciences from the University of Warsaw in 2009. She has been a researcher in the Centre of Migration Research at University of Warsaw, a post-doc researcher in the *Institut national d'études démographiques* in Paris and a visiting lecturer in several Universities in France (Université Paris 1 Panthéon Sorbonne, Université Paris Nanterre, Sciences Po). Her research interests include contemporary demographic processes in Central Europe, in particular international mobility after the enlargement of European Union and mortality patterns in countries of post-communist transition.

Grzegorz Gorzelak is Professor of Economics at the Centre for European Regional and Local Studies (EUROREG), University of Warsaw, Poland.

Zbigniew M. Karaczun is Professor in the Department of Environmental Protection of Warsaw University of Life Science. He specialises in environmental management, environmental and climate policy. Author of more than 350 publications. Active in non-governmental organisations, the current Deputy President of the Polish Ecological Club, he has served as advisor to the Polish government, also negotiating the accession of Poland to the EU and was a director of Climate Action Network Central and Eastern Europe, as well as an expert of the Polish NGOs Climate Coalition.

Andrzej Kassenberg, Ph.D., is the co-founder of the Institute for Sustainable Development (ISD), and co-founder of the Polish Energy Efficiency Foundation. He has performed several advisory and managerial functions in different national and international agencies dealing with environment protection and policy. In 1991–95 and 1999–2010, he was a member of the Environmental and Social Council of the President of EBRD. He has been awarded the Scientific Award of the Polish Academy of Sciences and 'Man of the Year 2005' for Polish Ecology. He is a member of Scientific Committee of Polish Academy of Science: 'Poland in the 21st Century' and Member of Polish Ecological Club, and author or co-author of over 180 publications and reports.

Tomasz Komornicki is Professor in Geography, Head of the Department of Spatial Organization in the Institute of Geography and Spatial Organization Polish Academy of Sciences (PAS), Professor at the Faculty of Earth Sciences and Spatial Management, Maria Curie-Sklodowska University in Lublin; member of the executive body of the Committee for Spatial Economy and Regional Planning, PAS, head and participant of many Polish and international research projects, including HORIZON, ESPON and INTERREG projects). His main areas of interest are socio-economic geography, transport geography and spatial planning.

Radosław Markowski is Professor of Political Science at the Center for the Study of Democracy (Director), University of Social Sciences and Humanities and PI of the Polish National Election Study and recurring Visiting Professor at CEU, Budapest. He specialises in comparative politics, democratisation, party systems and electoral studies. He has published in peer reviewed journals including *Electoral Studies, Party Politics, Political Studies* and *West European Politics*. His books include *Post-communist Party Systems* (1999, co-author), *Europeanising Party Politics?* (2011, co-editor) and *Democratic Audit of Poland* (2015, co-author). He is an expert of the Varieties of Democracy (V-Dem), Bertelsmann SGI project and Dahrendorf Forum at the Hertie School of Governance.

Marek Okólski is Head of the Chair of International Economics at Lazarski University in Warsaw and chairs the Scientific Council of the Centre of Migration Research (CMR) at the University of Warsaw. Until September 2016 he was the Director of CMR, which he founded in 1993. Over his academic career he lectured in several renowned academic institutions in the United States, Australia and Europe. His research area includes major social transformations and their impact upon population processes, globalisation, demographic transition in Poland, migration theory, labour mobility, migration trends in Central and Eastern Europe, and health crises in the European communist states. He has served as a consultant or advisor to several of Poland's government departments and to international organisations.

Agnieszka Olechnicka, Ph.D., Associate Professor, is Director at the Centre for European Regional and Local Studies (EUROREG), University of Warsaw, Poland, and a Secretary of the Polish Section of Regional Studies Association. Her research interests concentrated on development of peripheral regions, innovation, and recently on scientometrics and geography of scientific cooperation. Currently she is also a member of the DG Regio group on smart specialisation.

Witold M. Orłowski is Professor of Economics, Rector of the Vistula University (Warsaw) and Chief Economic Advisor to PwC Polska. He is a member of the National Development Council of the president of the Republic of Poland and former economic advisor to President Aleksander Kwaśniewski, and member of the Economic Council of Prime Minister Donald Tusk, chairman of the Board of Trustees of the National Museum in Warsaw. He is the author of 12 books and 200 scientific publications, a popular economic commentator and columnist for major Polish newspapers.

Adam Płoszaj is an Assistant Professor at the University of Warsaw, Poland. Adam frequently advises national and international institutions – including the European Commission, World Bank and UNDP – on regional development and research policy. He recently co-authored *The Geography of Scientific Collaboration* published by Routledge.

Slavo Radosevic is Professor of Industry and Innovation Studies at School of Slavonic and East European Studies, University College London, where he has also been acting and deputy director. His research interests are in the area of science, technology, industry, innovation and growth in countries of Central and Eastern. He is acting as an expert for the various DGs of the European Commission, as a consultant to UN Economic Commission for Europe, OECD, World Bank, Asian Development Bank, UNESCO and several governments in CEE. He is a special advisor to the EC Commissioner for Regional and Urban Policy. Recently he has been the co-editor of *Advances in Theory and Practice of Smart Specialization* (2018).

Maciej Smętkowski, Ph.D. in Socio-economic Geography, is Associate Professor at the Centre for European Regional and Local Studies (EUROREG), University of Warsaw, and chairman of the Polish Section of the Regional Studies Association. He is the author of publications on metropolisation process, instruments of regional policy and cross-border co-operation. He has extensive experience in evaluation of public policies. He has been involved in number of research projects (FP5, FP6, FP7, HORIZON 2020, ESPON).

Paweł Swianiewicz is Professor of Economics at the University of Warsaw, Head of the Department of Local Development and Policy at the Faculty of Geography and Regional Studies. Between 2005 and 2010, he was president of the European Urban Research Association (EURA). Currently he is a member of the Steering Committee of the Standing Group on Local Government and Politics of the European Consortium for Political Research (ECPR). His teaching and research focus on local politics, local government finance and territorial administrative reforms. His recent publications include co-authorship of 'Patterns of Local Autonomy in Europe' and co-editing of 'Sub-municipal Governance in Europe: Decentralization Beyond the Municipal Tier,' and 'Inter-municipal Cooperation in Europe: Institutions and Governance'.

Peter Szewczyk is a Ph.D. candidate at the University of Warsaw, Faculty of Economics, and an economist at the Group for Research in Applied Economics (GRAPE). He holds a B.Sc. from Cornell University and an M.A. from the University of Warsaw. His research focuses around labour economics, political science, institutional economics and cultural economics. He is also a consultant at Deloitte, where he is part of the Economic Analysis Team.

Roman Szul, Professor of the University of Warsaw, Centre for European Regional and Local Studies, specialises in economics and regional studies (regional development and policy) and political sciences, recently engaged mostly in theory of nationalism, ethno-regionalism and language politics, with special reference to the linguistic history of Europe, as well as minority and regional languages in Europe.

Joanna Tyrowicz is Associate Professor at the University of Warsaw Faculty of Management, a Research Fellow at the Institute for Labor Economics (IZA), and a Research Associate at the Institute for Labor Law and Industrial Relations in the European Union, Trier University (IAAEU). She is the director of the Group for Research in Applied Economics (GRAPE). Her main research areas are labour economics, demographics and pensions with a particular focus on inequality. She has served as an economic adviser for the National Bank of Poland and as a consultant at the World Bank, OECD and the European Commission.

Deniz E. Yoruk had her Ph.D. in Innovation Management and S&T Policy at University Sussex, Science and Technology Policy Research (SPRU). She worked as a lecturer in International Business and Economics at Aston and Staffordshire Universities and as a research fellow in various research projects funded by EU, ESRC and British Academy in Staffordshire University, University of Sussex, University College London and University of Edinburgh. Her research interests include innovation and upgrading in emerging markets, GVCs and networks, and organisational learning. She has recently published in *Technological Forecasting and Social Change* on the dynamics of firm-level upgrading in Polish low-technology industries.

Esin Yoruk is Associate Professor in Business and Management at Coventry University Business School and Research Associate at International Centre for Transformational Entrepreneurship at Coventry University. Prior to that, she was a research fellow at the School of Slavonic and East European Studies, UCL – University College London. She contributed in two large-scale EUFP7 projects. Her research interests have been about the technology and innovation management, entrepreneurship and specifically the role of technology and innovation in economic growth from a systemic perspective. She has publications in international and national journals as well as chapters in edited books.

Introduction

It has been 30 years since fundamental changes occurred in Central and Eastern Europe – Bulgaria, Czechoslovakia, Hungary, Poland and Romania – as well as in the former German Democratic Republic, which was joined with (or, as some say, incorporated into) its larger and richer sister, the Federal Republic of Germany. At the beginning of the 1990s these countries emerged from was called at that time 'real socialism' and begun their path toward a market economy and pluralistic (later labelled as 'liberal' or 'procedural') democracy. These countries were later joined by the three Baltic Republics (Estonia, Latvia and Lithuania) which emerged out of the collapsed Soviet Union almost without any physical encounters. In 1991, in the southern part of the continent, Albania emerged from one of the most oppressive regimes. The bloody conflict in the former Yugoslavia spared Slovenia, which suffered only ten days of military clashes, but for most of the former Yugoslav republics this became one of the most dramatic events in their modern history, not free from genocide and war crimes.

The post-socialist transformation, leading to the economic integration of Central and Eastern Europe into the European Union, has until very recently been one of the success stories of European development after 1990. Economic convergence has been dynamic, despite some fluctuations, and in several cases more far-reaching than in Western Europe. Socio-economic changes have happened fast, though not without fluctuations in some countries, and international mobility has increased considerably. The natural environment has improved, although pollution and dependence on coal still prevail in several countries. Institutional adaptation proceeded until accession, later slowed down, and recently, in some countries, has even unexpectedly reversed.

Thus, until the middle of this third decade, the process of transition to a market economy and democratic political system has been going at an expected pace. However, assumptions about political convergence have been challenged by recent developments in Hungary and Poland, Czechia and even Slovakia, and there is a potentially broader schism between the perspectives of Central and Eastern European (CEE) countries and founding members of the EU about the future direction of European integration. There are also concerns about incomplete reforms of public administration, the quality of government and, in some countries, the prevalence of corruption. Moreover, the dependence on foreign investment and poor endogenous potential for innovation that have not been overcome in the course of transformation are considered as the main weaknesses of the CEE economies, which can remain stuck in the 'middle income trap'. Additionally, the unfavourable demographic situation and still heavily polluted natural environment continue to challenge the potential for uninterrupted economic and social development.

The number of books on Central and Eastern Europe is considerable. However, these books are now several years old and in most cases relate to specific issues. No recent publication covers as broad a scope of issues as the present book, which at the same time covers 30 years of recent history in Central and Eastern European countries – the new Member States of the European Union – and their trajectories through such different times of transformation: accession and first benefits, crisis and recovery. Moreover, only a few books have yet included the surprising turn in the political profiles of some of them, which challenges the principles of what has been called a 'liberal democracy' and the rule of law.

This book attempts to present, analyse and compare among the countries of the region – and within them – the multidimensional developments that ensued after they emerged from 'real socialism' and entered on the path of structural change which led them to the membership of the European Union and participation in as well as co-creation of policies of the EU. The chapters will present and discuss the facets of transformation in their complex internal structures and in mutual relationships.

The book is conceived as a set of topical analyses covering the most important dimensions of change that occurred in CEE over the last three decades. It presents economic developments and structural adjustment to an open market economy, both in general terms and also related to land-use and changes in rural areas; reforms of the labour markets within a broader prospective of demographic processes; and the political changes and advancement of decentralisation that have created the ideological and institutional framework for these reforms. Issues such as regionalist movements, developments in transport infrastructure and accessibility, improvements in the state of the natural environment, technological advancements as well as scientific production and research cooperation are also discussed. Regional breakdowns are applied whenever possible, and the regional dynamics and changing patterns of regional development are also presented. These reflect the direct and indirect influences of EU membership and cohesion policy on most dimensions of socio-economic processes in the last 12–15 years. The book also presents an outlook on the possible futures of the CEE countries within more general prospects for the entire European continent.

The processes and phenomena that were delayed in comparison to the developed world – due to the grip of socialist ideology and authoritarian rule shaping political life and preventing the existence of a market economy – have undergone rapid changes in the new political setting. As a result, these changes have been dramatically fast and deep but have largely followed the patterns of earlier structural reforms in more advanced countries. At the same time, the specificity of the central and eastern part of the European continent and its historical background have had a clear bearing on its economic, social, environmental, instructional and demographic structures, thus shaping in a specific way the processes of transformation. Therefore, the following theoretical question will be the main intellectual axis of the book: which dimensions of socio-economic and spatial reality are stable (undergoing the Braudelian principle of 'longue durée') and which are flexible, prone to be influenced by external impulses and the indigenous will of political elites enjoying the support of their electorates?

An important question arises: to what extent has the post-socialist transformation relied on internal, endogenous forces, and how strongly has it been induced externally? If the exogenous forces played crucial roles, then how stable are the changes that occurred in the CEE countries after 1990? The reversal of the pro-democratic political and institutional reforms would support the hypothesis that these changes, induced from the outside, were at the end of the day relatively shallow. This ties in with the inability of these countries to enter the path of innovation-driven development due to an overly strong reliance on foreign investment. On the other hand, the attachment of most CEE societies (or, at least, a large proportion of them) to the principles of the market economy, European integration and democratic institutional systems may support the theses indicating durable – though not overwhelming – changes in social attitudes and entrepreneurship. Therefore, the book will try to assess if the drive of CEE from the periphery to the centre will continue, whether it will soon stop at the stage of 'semi-periphery', or whether it will reverse its direction to put these countries back in the periphery again.

The broad scope of themes and issues discussed in the book creates a unique opportunity to provide a rich and extensive picture of both change and stability in Central and Eastern Europe. The individual chapters of the book seek commonalities between the trajectories of the post-socialist countries, at the same time exposing their heterogeneity and uniqueness. However, although prepared independently by particular authors, the chapters will draw on each other and relate their contents to considerations presented in the other sections, either by supplementing them or providing points of view from different scientific perspectives.

The chapters of the book are based on empirical material; however, frequent reference is made to the literature, including theories of development and systemic change, and these will shape the empirical analyses. Unless otherwise stated, the chapters cover the so-called New Member States: the eight countries that accessed the EU in 2004, plus Bulgaria, Romania (EU members since 2007) and, where possible, Croatia (which joined the EU in 2013).

The book consists of 15 chapters grouped into four parts. Part I is devoted to the most general issues and processes of the post-socialist transformation.

Chapter 1, written by Witold Orłowski, discusses the main trends of economic transformation in the CEE countries. The chapter begins with a short account of the starting point for the economic transition, including the historic roots of economic development and development trajectories during the second half of the 20th century, and presents the effects of the fall of the socialist system in centrally planned economies. In more detail, this chapter discusses the policies applied during the transition and relates to the hypothesis on the relationship (with a time lag) between institutional reforms and economic growth. The role of foreign investment in economic development is described. A statistical analysis presents data on economic growth and convergence with Western Europe. The chapter ends with an outlook on economic performance during the global financial crisis and prospects for future development, with a reference to the notion of the 'middle income trap'.

Chapter 2, written by Radosław Markowski, discusses the issues of political reforms and their impact on the quality of democracy – seemingly the most important recent challenges for some of the CEE countries. The chapter's goal is to depict and explain different patterns of interaction, and ultimately the outcomes, resulting from various configurations of factors such as the historical legacies of cultural and institutional systems, the mode of transition and consolidation, the economic reforms pursued as well as the political-institutional design, partly derived from a country's political culture. The emphasis of analysis is laid on interactions between culture, structure and agency. A comparison with Western European patterns serves as part of the explanation. The chapter is theoretical-speculative in nature although based on strong empirical evidence.

In Chapter 3, Paweł Swianiewicz reports on local government reforms and progress in decentralisation. Decentralisation was one of the flagships of the transformation in most of the countries of the region. However, it appears that real transfer of powers to sub-national jurisdictions was often very limited. The chapter presents the diversity and dynamism of decentralisation. It focuses on three dimensions: territorial organisation and vertical power relations according to the concept of the Local Autonomy Index are discussed to present the trajectories of central-local relations throughout the 1990–2014 period, making it possible to test the hypothesis of the European convergence of local autonomy. Finally, the horizontal power relations within local governments are documented as well as the trend towards more personal leadership, including the direct election of mayors.

Chapter 4, written by Roman Szul, is devoted to the issue of regionalism in Central and Eastern Europe. Several types of regionalism observed in the CEE countries are presented and discussed, with references to their real manifestations: multi-dimensional, genuine grass-roots regionalism based on the ethno-cultural specificity and economic interests of regions; one-dimensional, genuine regionalism based on ethno-linguistic specificity, the only aim of which is to preserve and promote a language (dialect); top-down, cultural regionalism inspired or encouraged by national authorities and addressed to populations without a clear sense of national belonging in order to inculcate a supra-local, regional identity in these populations as a step towards introducing them to the national community; and top-down pseudo-regionalism, mainly inspired by the idea of a 'Europe of regions' and the expectations of the EU, whose principal aim is the better use of EU funds and social mobilisation favouring economic development. The impacts of all these rationalistic movements on internal and external socio-economic processes are discussed. In order to better understand current issues, some historical references are also made.

Chapter 5 opens Part II, which is devoted to the challenges facing CEE countries. Agnieszka Fihel and Marek Okólski present the demographic changes that have occurred in CEE during recent decades. The severity of these changes, partly resulting from EU accession, has turned demography into one of the greatest challenges for their future development. A brief outline of population characteristics in the CEE region vis-à-vis other parts of Europe is presented. Natural demographic processes (fertility and mortality) and external migrations are documented, including regional breakdowns, and demographic prospects are discussed. The chapter concludes with an indication of the major societal and economic challenges that may stem from the emerging demographic situation.

Chapter 6, by Joanna Tyrowicz and Peter Szewczyk, is devoted to labour markets and social change. The objective of this chapter is to exploit evidence from a large collection of data to discuss the evolution of labour demand, labour market flows and earnings inequality (including the gender dimension) in CEE countries after 1990. Attention is paid to the role of demographic processes in labour market adjustments, namely the gradual entry of young cohorts and the exit of older cohorts. The empirical material comes from a study based on individual data on changes in employment structures, employment ratios, labour shares and inequality. For comparison purposes, selected Western European countries are used. Despite fairly common forecasts, the labour markets in the CEE countries have evolved in highly heterogeneous ways: some countries experienced large and protracted adverse labour demand shocks, high unemployment, a decline in the labour share and a substantial increase in poverty (e.g. Poland, Slovakia), whereas other countries saw a relatively low and short unemployment uptick, stable labour relations and a stable or much slower decline in the labour share (e.g. Czechia, Hungary, the Baltic states). The reasons for these differences are explained and related to the macroeconomic situation and labour market policies in these countries.

Chapter 7, by Agnieszka Olechnicka and Adam Płoszaj on scientific performance and patterns of scholarly networks, presents the results of scientometric analyses of scientific collaboration and the scientific performance of research and academic establishments in three CEE countries. The analyses demonstrate recent developments in the science sector in CEE by the use of data concerning research outcomes in the form of articles indexed in the Web of Science database. On the background of descriptive analysis, several reflections on factors affecting the spatial aspects of collaboration in science and causal relationships are also included. Globalisation tendencies, science specialisation, policy and politics influence the parties involved in scientific collaboration.

Chapter 8, written by Slavo Radosevic, Deniz E. Yoruk and Esin Yoruk, approaches the issue of growth in CEE countries from the perspective of technology upgrading as opposed to conventional research and development (R&D) based models of growth. The chapter explores the three dimensions of technology upgrading in CEE within the context of the EU 28 and internationally. The CEE countries show, on average, higher rankings in terms of the index of technology intensity than in the index of breadth or structural change of technology upgrading. This is quite an important feature of CEE countries, as it shows that they are not structurally dynamic economies. CEE countries are by far the lowest ranked in terms of the index of structural change, which shows the diversification of technological knowledge and changes in technology supply and demand. The key issue for their technology upgrading is whether knowledge inflows in these economies can operate as a substitute for, or complement to, their own technology activities. The chapter is concluded with policy implications.

Part III is devoted to broadly conceived territorial issues. In Chapter 9, Grzegorz Gorzelak and Maciej Smętkowski reflect on regional dynamics in the CEE countries. The hypothesis of the Williamson curve is tested against the diverse patterns and dynamics of national growth: post-socialist recession, rapid growth prior to and after EU accession, subsequent recession during the financial crisis and post-crisis recovery. The economic restructuring process is examined, and the effects of deindustrialisation patterns on regional development are analysed. The chapter also relates to metropolisation – the most important spatial phenomenon in the CEE countries after 1990 that has shaped their regional structures to the greatest extent. In particular, it refers to the special role that capital cities and other major metropolitan areas play in the CEE countries due to the rapid increase in knowledge services and technology-driven industries in these urban nodes. The statistical analyses covering all new EU Member States are conducted at the NUTS3 level, as it more closely corresponds to the functional urban regions than NUTS2 regions.

In Chapter 10, Jerzy Bański analyses changes in agricultural land-use and ownership in the CEE countries. These changes – with the exception of Poland, where private ownership of rural land was preserved – constituted one of the most dynamic structural adaptations after 1900, with all its economic, social and environmental consequences. This chapter points to the processes of (re-)privatisation affecting the agricultural sector in CEE. The analysis focuses on assessing changes in the ownership structure of agricultural land, farm size and rural land markets. The changes of ownership, above all, led to a dynamic increase in the number of individual farms. The chapter covers the Visegrád countries and Romania, for which the data is mostly available. Some general observations are also made for other CEE countries.

Tomasz Komornicki, the author of Chapter 11, presents the conditions and state of development of transport networks and changes over time, with special reference to the impact of investment carried out with help of European funds. The analysis focuses on the development of road and railway networks, changes in road traffic volumes and ongoing modal transformations. Issues related to the development of air transport will also be touched upon. In addition, the chapter refers to the debate on the impact transport infrastructure advancement on processes of national and regional development, quality of life and improvement in the state of natural environment.

In Chapter 12, Zbigniew M. Karaczun and Andrzej Kassenberg summarise the changes that took place in the years 1990–2016 in the field of environmental protection and, more broadly, in the area of sustainable development in the CEE countries. The chapter presents changes in the following spheres: environmental pressures resulting from the economic activity and structural changes that took place after 1990; pollution discharged to the environment by type and location; the state of the natural environment with its impact on human health; environmental policy and sustainable development; counteraction measures – environmental protection infrastructure and nature protection; and assessment of the environmental awareness of citizens.

Part IV contains two chapters presenting future challenges for CEE countries within an integrated Europe. In Chapter 13, John Bachtler and Martin Ferry reflect on Cohesion Policy and EU membership of the new Member States. The role of EU policies and funds in the processes of institutional and economic convergence with Western members of the EU is discussed. The chapter explores the evolution of regional development policies in terms of the conceptual thinking, objectives, spatial focus and policy instruments. In particular, it focuses on the role of EU Cohesion Policy, which is the major source of funding for economic, social and territorial cohesion and also the primary source of public investment in some countries during the recent crisis. The chapter also examines how EU funding is used and the evidence for its impact and added value.

Chapter 14, written by Roberta Capello, explores the structural changes that have taken place in Central and Eastern European countries during the crisis and post-crisis recovery which provide grounds for elaborating on the effects that such changes may have on possible future growth trajectories for these countries. In particular, trends in the major sources of productivity gains in these countries are analysed. This chapter also presents, in the form of scenarios, some future perspectives by considering the alternative paths that could evolve from such structural changes. In particular, thanks to MASST3, a macroeconomic regional growth model which has achieved its third version, two opposite scenarios are presented in the perspective of 2030: a competitiveness scenario, built on the assumption that the CEE countries will re-gain their competitive assets, and a cohesive scenario, where policies are oriented to support weak areas within these countries.

The concluding chapter wraps up the contents of the book and sets a frame for an outlook to the future of the CEE countries. The macro-perspective formulated in this chapter will be supplemented by detailed prospects of the processes dealt with in more depth in previous parts of the book.

Finally, it should be indicated that several chapters stem from research conducted within various projects, of which the 7th Framework Programme GRINCOH 'Growth – Innovation – Competitiveness: Fostering Cohesion in Central and Eastern Europe' project (coordinated by the editor of this volume), the Horizon 2020 COHESIFY 'The Impact of Cohesion Policy on EU Identification' project and several ESPON projects have been of the greatest importance.

Warsaw, January 2019

Part I

Systemic foundations of transformation

1 Trajectories of the economic transition in Central and Eastern Europe

Witold M. Orłowski

Introduction

Although the economic transition in the post-socialist countries of Central and Eastern Europe (CEE) has by and large been concluded, the topic is still of interest for scientific research. First, a change of this scale and depth has generated many thought-provoking questions and problems reaching to the very heart of market economy functioning (cf. Åslund 2007; Blanchard 1997). Second, the economic impact of the transition, depending on its trajectory, is likely to have a long-lasting effect on the society and economy of the countries affected, in total populated by 400 million people (over 5% of the global population) and producing, depending on the year, between 7% and 9% of the global output (measured in purchasing power standards (PPS)). Third, some lessons about the policies connected with this transition may still have importance for other countries undergoing deep economic change, not necessarily triggered by the removal of central planning (e.g. for developing countries, cf. EBRD 2017; Bertelsmann Stiftung 2018). Fourth, the trajectories of the transition and the economic results achieved varied so deeply that analysing factors leading to such differences still poses a challenge (cf. Havrylyshyn 2006; Åslund 2007; Orłowski 2010). And finally, even assessing the outcome of the transition in the most successful countries has provoked controversy – ranging from overall optimism (cf. e.g. Blanchard 1997; Åslund and Orłowski 2014) to much more sceptical conclusions (cf. Nölke and Vliegenthart 2009; Bátory, Cartwright and Stone 2018).

In this chapter we compare the trajectories of the transition observed in 11 countries of Central and Eastern Europe (CEE-11), which are members of the European Union (EU), and Ukraine, a country that has never had, due to internal and external reasons, any clear roadmap towards integration with the EU.

The outcome of this process varies greatly among the individual countries. In 1989, at the starting point of the transition, gross domestic product (GDP) per capita in Poland was 22% lower than in Bulgaria. However, over the last 28 years the GDP of Poland (the leader of growth among CEE-11) has increased by 145%, while the GDP of Bulgaria (one of the laggards) has increased by only 12%. As a result of this difference, the GDP per capita of Poland, measured in

PPS, increased from 78% of the Bulgarian level in 1989 to 136% in 2017.[1] An even bigger divergence can be seen in the case of Ukraine. Back in 1989, the GDP per capita of Poland and Ukraine were close to parity, while in 2017 the Polish level was equal to 340% of the Ukrainian GDP.

Obviously, numerous country-specific factors contributed to the final outcome. These included the historical heritage, the starting point of the transition, the internal and external political situation, social support for reforms, the quality of institutions, and the economic policies applied. Although no country's experience was literally copied by another, some solutions (like the Polish 'big bang' liberalization, the Czech and Slovak 'coupon privatization' or the Estonian exchange rate–based stabilization) served, to a large degree, as model policies for their followers (cf. Åslund and Orłowski 2014).

Nevertheless, some common features of the transition process can be found in all the countries undergoing the change, as well as within several groups of countries. For the sake of comparison, we have divided the group of CEE-11 into four subgroups (regions), with striking similarities in the course of the transition and in the structural and macroeconomic policies applied. The regions are:

1   Visegrád-4 countries (Czechia, Hungary, Poland, Slovakia). These four Central European countries (until 1992 Czechia and Slovakia were united within Czechoslovakia) were the early reformers that abolished the communist political system in 1989 and started their stabilization and liberalization programs in 1990–91. While bearing in mind their differences, we can point out the common features of the transition in the Visegrád region: deep social support for market reforms, a radical approach to macroeconomic and structural policies, fast development of strong links with the Western European economy and determination to join the EU. All the Visegrád-4 countries joined the EU in 2004 but, with the exception of Slovakia, still remain reluctant to adopt the euro, despite fulfilling the necessary economic criteria.

2   Baltic-3 countries (Estonia, Latvia, Lithuania). The three Baltic states were forcibly included in the Soviet Union in 1940 and only regained their independence in 1990–91. The common features of the transition in the Baltic region include a huge initial shock after separating from the Soviet Union, strong social support for independence and radical economic reforms, the similar character of the countries (small open economies), a courageous approach to liberalization and determination to join the EU. Baltic-3 countries joined the EU in 2004 and, after a few years of relentless effort, concluded the integration by adopting the euro.

3   East Balkan-2 countries (Bulgaria, Romania). Both East Balkan countries started their political and economic transformation with a considerable delay compared to the Visegrád-4 and, at least initially, implemented the reforms with less vigour and determination. The common features of the transition in the East Balkan region include weaker initial social support

for change, less clear and robust policies, a high degree of corruption and delayed efforts to build strong links with the Western European economy and join the EU. East Balkan-2 countries joined the EU in 2007 but they are still not ready to adopt the euro.

4   West Balkan-2 countries (Slovenia, Croatia). Until 1991, the West Balkan region was a part of the former Yugoslavia and enjoyed more economic freedom than any other CEE region. The dissolution of Yugoslavia, followed by war with Serbia (very short in the case of Slovenia; long and devastating in the case of Croatia), plunged the West Balkan region into a deep recession that Slovenia managed to overcome faster than the others. The common features of the transition in the West Balkan region include functioning market economy mechanisms at the starting point, a strong initial shock connected with the dissolution of Yugoslavia, less vigour in implementing structural reforms, and uneven determination to join the EU. Slovenia joined the EU in 2004 and swiftly introduced the euro, while the Croatian membership was not possible until 2013.

The historical roots of underdevelopment

In 1989, shortly before the economic transition started, the GDP per capita of all the CEE-11 countries was well below Western European levels, ranging from 36% of the German level in Poland to 65% in Slovenia and in Czechia (measured in PPS). The relative economic underdevelopment of this part of Europe had deep historical roots. Several important factors should be mentioned:

1   The first is connected with a crucial change that took place in Europe during the 16th century. In the process of creation of the early capitalist 'world economy', two different paths of development emerged (cf. Wallerstein 1974). The 'core' areas started to expand capital-intensive production, significantly increasing their labour productivity. At the same time, the 'peripheral' areas concentrated on the extensive production of food and raw materials, based on cheap labour. The borderline between two areas was the Elbe river: while Western Europe countries enjoyed intensive growth, the peripheral areas to the east of the river suffered from the phenomenon of second serfdom, which persisted until the early 19th century. The only CEE area that could be classified as a 'semi-periphery' (in between the core and the periphery), was modern-day Czechia. It should also be noted that, according to Wallerstein's definition, the majority of the CEE Balkan countries did not even constitute a part of the 16th-century European world economy but, instead, acted as a periphery of the Middle Eastern (Ottoman) world economy. As a consequence of this peripheralisation, the estimated GDP per capita of the CEE region, which in medieval times was not much below that of Western Europe, by the beginning of the 19th century had diminished to about half that of Western Europe.

2   The second important factor that contributed to the historical underde-velopment of the CEE region was its political fate. At the beginning of the industrial 'take-off' (according to Rostow's terminology) in continental Europe, in the middle of the 19th century, none of the nations of the region had its own independent state. Instead, the CEE countries belonged to external empires: the majority of the Visegrád region and the West Balkan-2 countries belonged to the Habsburg (Austrian) Empire, the remaining ter-ritories of modern-day Poland were divided between Russia and Prussia, most of the Baltic region was part of the Russian Empire, and the East Balkan-2 countries were under Ottoman rule. This situation, to a large extent, deprived the CEE countries of much-needed policies supporting the industrial revolution and modern infrastructure development, especially given that the Austrian, Russian and Ottoman Empires belonged to the most socially and economically backward parts of 19th-century Europe (cf. Wallerstein 1974; Orłowski 2010). As a result, and despite some progress towards industrializing the territories of modern-day Czechia, Poland and Hungary, the GDP per capita of the CEE region had diminished by the beginning of the 20th century to about 45% of Western European levels (ranging from 40% in Croatia to 68% in Czechia). Despite two world wars, this ratio did not change significantly until 1950.

3   The third crucial historical factor leading to the underdevelopment of the CEE region was the long period covered by an economic system of cen-tral planning. The system was imposed after World War II, together with a totalitarian (since mid-1950s in some countries authoritarian) political system, by the communist Soviet Union that liberated and then occupied the majority of the CEE region. The extent to which market mechanisms were suppressed varied: politically independent Yugoslavia enjoyed 'market socialism', Hungary and Poland tried to experiment with some elements of the market, while other CEE countries stuck to the dogmatic central planning model and the Baltic countries were fully integrated into the Soviet economy (cf. Arnason 1993). Nevertheless, the common feature of the communist economic system (i.e. the falling efficiency of resource allocation and utilization) was observed in all the CEE countries. As a result, and despite industrialization and modernization efforts, the GDP per capita of the CEE region, according to Maddison's estimates, dimin-ished well below 40% that of Western Europe in 1989 (which indicates a slower GDP growth in the CEE region, in spite of the misleading statisti-cal data published in the socialist countries; cf. Orłowski 2010). The fall of this ratio was only marginal in the case of the Balkan countries but sig-nificant in the Visegrád and Baltic regions. The economic fate of Czechia, which was downgraded from the first league of the European industrial-ized nations in 1948 to the group of Europe's poor countries in 1989, is, arguably, the most striking example of this change (the estimated Czech GDP per capita diminished from 122% of the Austrian level in 1948 to 65% in 1989).

It is also worth noting the specific spatial characteristic of the development of CEE countries connected with history. As the core of the European economy is located to the west of the region, a typically observed pattern is that the western regions are better developed than the eastern ones. Such a pattern is clearly visible in the case of the Visegrád countries (with the distinct exception of the evenly developed Czechia), Romania, Slovenia, Latvia, and Estonia (see the chapter by Gorzelak and Smętkowski in this book).

The starting point of economic transition

All the CEE-11 countries started their economic transition in 1990–91, once the decline of Soviet power and the fall of the Berlin Wall made it possible to dismantle the communist political regime and to start rebuilding the market economy. However, the starting point of transition differed significantly among the four analysed/previously defined regional subgroups as well as, despite many common features, within these groups.

First, the CEE countries had different initial political and social situations. Generally speaking, the conditions were much more favourable for deep reforms in the Visegrád and the Baltic region, where political change was greeted with enthusiasm, than in the eastern and western Balkan countries. Second, the degree of integration of various countries in the pre-transition communist economic system was different. The Baltic region was a highly integrated part of the Soviet economy, and the West Balkan countries formed part of the Yugoslav economy. Therefore, the break-up of the Soviet Union and Yugoslavia led to a drastic disruption of former cooperation links, contributing to a sharp drop in economic output. It is worth noting that the well-prepared 'velvet divorce' of Czechia and Slovakia in 1993 allowed both countries, to a great extent, to avoid such problems (cf. Blanchard 1997). Nevertheless, the evaporation of a large share of Council of Mutual Economic Assistance (COMECON) trade was a negative shock for all the CEE-11 countries, including the Visegrád and East Balkan regions (cf. WIIW 1991).

Finally, the initial economic situation of the regions and countries varied considerably. The most important differences were related to (see Table 1.1):

1   *The income level.* The highest levels of GDP per capita, measured in PPS, were observed in the West Balkan-2 countries, which had enjoyed 40 years of relatively liberal economic policies in Yugoslavia (62.5% of the German level),[2] followed by the Visegrád-4 and Baltic-3 countries that inherited stronger industrial traditions from before the communist rule (52% of the German level), and with the lowest income levels observed in East Balkan-2 countries (42% of the German level). However, the regions were not homogeneous: a notable exception to the general rule within the Visegrád region was Poland, which suffered a prolonged economic crisis from the late 1970s and saw its GDP per capita reduced from almost 50% of the German level in 1975 to 36% in 1989.

Table 1.1 Economic transition in CEE countries: the starting point (1989)

	GDP per capita in PPS (German level = 100)	CPI inflation rate	External debt to exports ratio	Military spending to GDP ratio, 1985-88	Share of the private sector in GDP (a)	EBRD transition index	
						Liberalisation (b)	Market institutions (c)
Visegrád-4	**52.1**	**67.9**	**274.3**	**7.5**	**11.3**	**1.1**	**1.5**
Czechia	65.4	1.4	143(d)	7.2(d)	5	1.0	1.0
Hungary	57.1	17.0	320	6.3	5	1.0	2.3
Poland	35.7	251.0	492	9.1	30	1.3	1.7
Slovakia	50.2	2.3	143(d)	7.2(d)	5	1.0	1.0
Baltic-3	**52.2**	**4.3**	**149.0**	**12.9**	**10.0**	**1.0**	**1.0**
Estonia	53.7	6.1	149(e)	12.9(e)	5(e)	1.0	1.0
Latvia	47.2	4.7	149(e)	12.9(e)	5(e)	1.0	1.0
Lithuania	55.8	2.1	149(e)	12.9(e)	5(e)	1.0	1.0
East Balkan-2	**42.3**	**3.8**	**151.4**	**9.7**	**10.0**	**1.0**	**1.0**
Bulgaria	45.7	6.4	293	12.8	7	1.0	1.0
Romania	38.9	1.1	10	6.6	13	1.0	1.0
West Balkan-2	**62.5**	**1, 256.0**	**165.0**	**3.8**	**25.0**	**1.5**	**2.3**
Croatia	59.2	1, 227.0	165(f)	3.8(f)	25(f)	1.5	2.3
Slovenia	65.9	1, 285.0	165(f)	3.8(f)	25(f)	1.5	2.3
Memo: Ukraine	37.6	2.2	149(e)	12.9(e)	5(e)	1.0	1.0

Notes: (a) Estimates from various sources. (b) Liberalization index: average of liberalization of prices, trade and forex system (from 1 to 4+; values over 4 indicate developed market economy standards). (c) Market institutions index: average of small and large privatization, enterprise restructuring and competition policy (from 1 to 4+; values over 4 indicate developed market economy standards). (d) Data for Czechoslovakia. (e) Data for the Soviet Union. (f) Data for Yugoslavia. *Data for the groups of countries (regions) are unweighted arithmetic means.*

Source: IMF; EBRD; Milanović (1998); US Arms Control and Disarmament Agency (1999); author's calculations.

2   *The internal economic disequilibria.* In 1989 the West Balkan-2 countries were on the brink of hyperinflation. Countries of other regions enjoyed greater stability, with the exception of Poland which suffered from both high inflation and high excess demand on the market. However, it should be remembered that in the majority of CEE-11 countries the actual levels of disequilibria were hidden by repressed inflation, typical in centrally planned economies (cf. Arnason 1993).

3   *The external economic disequilibria.* Several CEE-11 countries faced huge difficulties due to excessive external debt. Poland, with a debt-to-export ratio of 492%, was in default from 1980 (cf. WIIW 1990). A very high foreign debt burden was also recorded in Hungary and Bulgaria, while a less severe

situation was observed in Yugoslavia, the Soviet Union, and Czechoslovakia. Romania managed to reduce its foreign debt dramatically during the 1980s, at the cost of a drastic savings program that impoverished the population (cf. Orłowski 2010).

4   *The scale of military expenditure.* Due to the Soviet policies forced upon its allies, the economies of the CEE-11 countries were overloaded with military spending. The share of this expenditure in GDP, as estimated by Western intelligence sources, ranged from 3.8% in Yugoslavia, 6%–9% in the Visegrád countries and 7%–13% in the East Balkan countries to 13% of GDP in the Soviet Union (cf. US Arms Control and Disarmament Agency 1999).

5   *The quality of institutions.* The most developed market institutions that were able to ease the transition were observed in the West Balkan-2 countries (due to the Yugoslav 'market socialism' with a strong – at least verbally – role of workers and territorial self-governments), followed by Hungary and Poland (due to the pre-transition reforms, particularly in Hungary, and a relatively high share of the private sector, particularly in Poland which employed about 7% of the labour force outside agriculture; the latter sector was also predominantly private – see the chapter by Bański in this book). In the other CEE countries, the dogmatic central planning model prevented the emergence of market-friendly institutions. Although a systematic assessment of the corruption in the CEE-11 countries was not performed before the mid-1990s, the available data suggest that the level of corruption was high in all the CEE-11 countries, with a critical level observed in East Balkan-2 states, and a more favourable situation in the Visegrád-4 region.

Obviously, the differences at the starting point had a significant influence on the path of the transition: less social support for change led to delays in implementing reform programmes; serious disruption of pre-transition cooperation links deepened the decline in output; a more imbalanced economy required a tougher stabilization program; a larger share of military spending in GDP led to more severe and prolonged recession at the moment of the post-Cold War disarmament; and less developed and market-friendly institutions made the adjustment more painful.

The six phases of economic transition

Despite all the differences in the initial conditions and the policies applied, the economic transition in the CEE-11 countries can be divided into six typical phases: (1) initial decline, (2) stagnation, (3) second decline, (4) take-off, (5) global crisis and (6) new growth.

Phase 1 involved an initial fall in GDP after the liberalization and stabilization of the economy, a sharp reduction in military spending and the break-up of COMECON trade. Basic information about the course of Phase 1 of the transition in various regions is presented in Table 1.2.

Table 1.2 Economic transition in CEE countries: Phase 1 (initial decline)

	Visegrád-4	Baltic-3(a)	East Balkan-2	West Balkan-2	Memo: Ukraine
Period	1990–92	1990–94	1990–93	1990–93	1990–97
Length (in years)	3	5	4	4	8
Cumulated GDP change	−16.1	−43.4	−29.1	−29.3	−60.9
Average yearly GDP change	−5.7	−10.8	−8.2	−8.3	−11.1
Average yearly inflation	69.5	181.6	151.1	414.3	333.4
EBRD liberalization index(a)					
− at the beginning	1.5	1.0	1.0	2.3	1.0
− at the end	3.9	4.1	3.5	3.7	3.5
EBRD market institutions index(b)					
− at the beginning	1.1	1.0	1.0	1.5	1.0
− at the end	2.4	2.8	1.7	2.3	2.5

Notes: (a) During 1990–91 the Baltic states were still struggling for independence from the Soviet Union. (b) Liberalization index: average liberalization in prices, trade and forex system (from 1 to 4+; values over 4 indicate developed market economy standards). (c) Market institutions index: average level of small and large scale privatization, enterprise restructuring, and competition policy (from 1 to 4+; values over 4 indicate developed market economy standards). *Data for the groups of countries are unweighted arithmetic means.*

Source: IMF; EBRD; author's calculations.

Phase 1 started in all the CEE-11 countries in 1990. However, the length of the phase was different: the shortest occurred in the Visegrád region (three years), and lasted four to five years in the other regions. By comparison, in Ukraine the length of this phase was extended to eight years. The period was characterized by high but gradually reduced inflation, most skilfully controlled in the Visegrád countries.

The scale of the decrease in GDP, the most striking feature of this phase, was also different, ranging from a 14% fall in Poland to a 47% fall in Lithuania. The mildest recession was observed in the Visegrád region which enjoyed relatively advantageous initial conditions and carried out fast reforms; the toughest recession was witnessed in the Baltic states, which had to rapidly cut their pre-transition economic links with the Soviet Union. The West Balkan states experienced a painful drop in GDP mainly due to the dissolution of the pre-transition system, while a similar drop in the East Balkan states was due to the liberalization shock and the very weak institutions that inhibited the implementation of a skilful macroeconomic policy. However, the depth of the recession in the CEE-11 countries, even in the most extreme cases, still remains limited compared to Ukraine (for a more detailed analysis of the factors underlying the initial fall in GDP during the transition, see below).

The painful adaptation and absorption of the internal shock was accompanied by rapid structural adjustment and significant efforts to start the privatization and build market institutions. The liberalization of the economic system was fast and aggressive everywhere, except for Ukraine. Institutional change, however, was uneven: relatively fast in the Visegrád and Baltic regions, lagging behind in the East and West Balkan states, very slow in Ukraine.

Phase 2 was a period of stagnation that followed the initial fall in GDP. In contrast to Phase 1, Phase 2 was not inevitable. The stagnation following the initial decline was recorded only in the countries that failed to implement sufficiently deep structural reforms during the first years of the transition. As a consequence, the economies were institutionally unprepared for the resumption of growth, and the level of disequilibria, rather than falling as in the other countries, increased again to dangerous levels. Basic information about the course of Phase 2 of the transition in various regions is presented in Table 1.3.

In the CEE-11 region, Phase 2 was recorded only in the East Balkan-2 countries. This phase lasted for two years and was characterized by very slow GDP growth (while the other regions were already enjoying a visible recovery). Phase 2 was also observed in Ukraine, which lagged behind in reforms.

Table 1.3 Economic transition in CEE countries: Phase 2 (stagnation)

	Visegrád-4	*Baltic-3*	*East Balkan-2*	*West Balkan-2*	*Memo: Ukraine*
Period	–	–	1994–95	–	1998–99
Length (in years)	–	–	2	–	2
Cumulated GDP change	–	–	2.9	–	−2.0
Average yearly GDP change	–	–	1.4	–	−1.0
Average yearly inflation	–	–	78.5	–	16.5
EBRD liberalization index(a)					
– at the beginning	–	–	3.5	–	3.5
– at the end	–	–	3.7	–	3.5
EBRD market institutions index(b)					
– at the beginning	–	–	1.7	–	2.5
– at the end	–	–	2.1	–	2.5

Notes: (a) Liberalization index: average liberalization of prices, trade and forex system (from 1 to 4+; values over 4 indicate developed market economy standards). (b) Market institutions index: average level of small and large scale privatization, enterprise restructuring, and competition policy (from 1 to 4+; values over 4 indicate developed market economy standards). *Data for the groups of countries are unweighted arithmetic means.*

Source: IMF; EBRD; author's calculations.

The most distinctive feature of Phase 2 was very slow progress in liberalization and institutional change, connected with the continuously high level of macroeconomic disequilibria.

Phase 3 involved a second fall in GDP. Similarly to Phase 2, Phase 3 was not inevitable, and was a result of the mismanagement of reforms during the first years of the transition, in particular, slow progress in institutional reforms and the loss of the macroeconomic control over deficits. Typically, the disequilibria were accompanied by problems in the banking sector. Basic information about the course of Phase 3 of the transition in various regions is presented in Table 1.4.

Once again, this phase was recorded only in the East Balkan-2 countries, following a period of stagnation. Phase 3 lasted for three to four years, leading to the cumulative fall in GDP of 6% in Bulgaria and 12% in Romania. During this period the economies had to be stabilized once again and the structural reforms accelerated. The most distinctive feature of this phase was a deep recession, combined with a high level of disequilibria that had to be counteracted by a macroeconomic austerity policy.

It should also be noted that short episodes similar to Phase 3 were recorded in 1997–98 in Czechia and in 1996 in Hungary. However, in the Visegrád countries they were relatively mild, did not have a systemic character, and were caused by country-specific policy errors (a currency crisis in Czechia and an

Table 1.4 Economic transition in CEE countries: Phase 3 (second decline)

	Visegrád-4(a)	Baltic-3(a)	East Balkan-2	West Balkan-2	Memo: Ukraine
Period	–	–	1996–99	–	–
Length (in years)	–	–	4	–	–
Cumulated GDP change	–	–	−6.6	–	–
Average yearly GDP change	–	–	−1.7	–	–
Average yearly inflation	–	–	116.8	–	–
EBRD liberalization index(b)					
– at the beginning	–	–	3.7	–	–
– at the end	–	–	4.2	–	–
EBRD market institutions index(c)					
– at the beginning	–	–	2.1	–	–
– at the end	–	–	2.7	–	–

Notes: (a) Although the region did not experience a systemic second decline, individual countries experienced a temporary slowdown or recession due to policy errors or external factors. (b) Liberalization index: average liberalization of prices, trade and forex system (from 1 to 4+; values over 4 indicate developed market economy standards). (c) Market institutions index: average level of small and large scale privatization, enterprise restructuring, and competition policy (from 1 to 4+; values over 4 indicate developed market economy standards). *Data for the groups of countries are unweighted arithmetic means.*

Source: IMF; EBRD; author's calculations.

imprudent fiscal policy in Hungary; cf. Åslund and Orłowski 2014). Similarly, the Baltic region experienced a short recession in 1999. Nevertheless, as the problems were caused by the Russian financial crisis, they could not be assessed as a Phase 3 episode.

Phase 4 constituted the take-off stage: a long period of recovery that followed the initial and, if observed, the second fall in GDP. This period lasted from nine years in Bulgaria and Romania to 17 years in Poland, leading to a cumulative growth in GDP ranging from 60% in Hungary to 134% in Latvia. The phase coincided with the EU accession of all the CEE-11 countries except Croatia. The end of the phase was caused by the outbreak of the global financial crisis in 2007–08. Basic information about the course of Phase 4 of the transition in various regions is presented in Table 1.5.

Table 1.5 Economic transition in CEE countries: Phase 4 (take-off)

	Visegrád-4	Baltic-3	East Balkan-2	West Balkan-2	Memo: Ukraine
Period	1993–2008	1995–2007	2000–2008	1994–2008	2000–2008
Length (in years)	16	13	9	15	9
Cumulated GDP change	84.9	126.4	69.3	87.8	83.1
Average yearly GDP change	3.9	6.5	6.0	4.3	6.9
Average yearly inflation	9.2	7.2	12.2	8.1	12.6
EBRD liberalization index(a)					
– at the beginning	3.9	4.1	4.2	3.7	3.5
– at the end	4.3	4.3	4.3	4.2	4.2
EBRD market institutions index(b)					
– at the beginning	2.4	2.8	2.7	2.3	2.5
– at the end	3.8	3.7	3.3	3.3	2.8
Corruption perception index(c)					
– at the beginning	50.3	42.0	29.5	43.5	28.0
– at the end	49.9	53.7	37.0	55.5	25.0

Notes: (a) Liberalization index: average liberalization of prices, trade and forex system (from 1 to 4+; values over 4 indicate developed market economy standards). (b) Market institutions index: average level of small and large scale privatization, enterprise restructuring, and competition policy (from 1 to 4+; values over 4 indicate developed market economy standards). (c) From 0 to 100. A value of 100 indicates a corruption-free country. Available from 1996. *Data for the groups of countries are unweighted arithmetic means.*

Source: IMF; EBRD; Transparency International; author's calculations.

Phase 4 lasted for nine years in the East Balkan region and for 13–16 years in the other regions (nine years in Ukraine). The period was characterized by high GDP growth and relatively low inflation. The control over inflation was secured either by more effective monetary policy, or by opting for exchange rate stabilization under a currency board regime (in the Baltic states and Bulgaria).

The accumulated growth of GDP recorded during Phase 4 was between 70% and 90% in all the regions, with the exemption of the Baltic-3 states which recorded a very high GDP increase of 126% (and were nicknamed at that time the 'Baltic tigers'). The main engine of growth was economic integration with the EU and, in particular, the process of shifting a share of the industrial production from Western Europe to the cost-competitive new Member States. Another factor that contributed to the rapid modernization was the access to generous European development funds that helped to upgrade the infrastructure. Therefore, common phenomena observed in the CEE countries in this period were robust growth of investment, exports, and imports, rising wages and strengthening currencies. The growth was connected, in many cases, with the rapid increase of current account deficits, as many CEE countries were rapidly increasing their investment and credit-financed consumption levels without the appropriate growth of domestic savings (cf. Bakker and Gulde 2010). Particularly high deficits were recorded in the Baltic and East Balkan regions (with an average level of 16%–17% of GDP in the peak years of 2006–07).

The period of turbulent institutional change was, by and large, over at the moment of joining the EU (although in some cases, membership meant some reduction in the level of liberalization; cf. Barbone and Zalduendo 1997) and gaining the EU membership reduced the pressure for further reforms. Therefore, Phase 4 was characterized by institutional stabilization. However, a factor clearly diversifying the quality of institutions was the level of corruption: very high in the East Balkan region; moderate (showing signs of falling) in the other regions. By comparison, the corruption level in Ukraine was perceived as much higher than in the East Balkan region (and deteriorating).

Phase 5 was marked by the global crisis: a fall in GDP caused by the European recession, a sudden stopping of the capital inflows and a need to stabilize the economies and the banking sectors of the CEE-11 countries. The only country in the region (and in fact in the whole of Europe) that managed to avoid the recession was Poland, while Latvia experienced the extreme GDP fall of 21%. Basic information about the course of the Phase 5 of the transition in various regions is presented in Table 1.6.

Phase 5 lasted for just one year in the Visegrád region, two to three years in the East Balkan and Baltic regions and five years in the West Balkan-2 countries. The length of the period and the depth of the recession depended mainly on the scale of the disequilibrium generated during the previous phase and, consequently, the scale of the adjustment necessary to stabilize the economy and reduce the current account deficit (for a more detailed analysis of the factors underlying the fall in GDP during the crisis, see the next section). The currencies of the CEE-11 countries, with the exception of Slovenia and

Table 1.6 Economic transition in CEE countries: Phase 5 (global crisis)

	Visegrád-4	Baltic-3	East Balkan-2	West Balkan-2	Memo: Ukraine
Period	2009	2008–10	2009–10	2009–13	2009
Length (in years)	1	3	2	5	1
Cumulated GDP change	−3.5	−16.5	−5.5	−10.6	−15.1
Average yearly GDP change	−3.5	−5.8	−2.8	−2.2	−15.1
Average yearly inflation	2.4	5.1	4.3	2.0	15.9
EBRD liberalization index(a)					
– at the beginning	4.3	4.3	4.3	4.2	4.2
– at the end	4.3	4.3	4.3	4.2	4.0
EBRD market institutions index(b)					
– at the beginning	3.8	3.7	3.3	3.3	2.8
– at the end	3.8	3.7	3.3	3.4	2.9
Corruption perception index(c)					
– at the beginning	49.9	53.7	37.0	55.5	25.0
– at the end	48.8	52.7	36.5	52.5	22.0

Notes: (a) Liberalization index: average liberalization of prices, trade and forex system (from 1 to 4+; values over 4 indicate developed market economy standards). (b) Market institutions index: average level of small and large scale privatization, enterprise restructuring, and competition policy (from 1 to 4+; values over 4 indicate developed market economy standards). (c) From 0 to 100. A value of 100 indicates a corruption-free country. *Data for the groups of countries are unweighted arithmetic means.*

Source: IMF; EBRD; Transparency International; author's calculations.

Slovakia which adopted the euro, found themselves under strong market pressure, and several countries of the region had to ask for international financial support to avoid bankruptcy caused by the exchange rate crisis (support was granted by the International Monetary Fund (IMF), EU and groups of creditor countries). Finally, no country except for Ukraine defaulted on its obligations, but several of them had to introduce painful adjustment programs (cf. PwC 2009).

Finally, *Phase 6* was defined by the new growth recorded after the adjustment made during the global financial crisis. Moderate GDP growth was accompanied by a low level of disequilibria, and in particular by a greatly reduced demand for foreign financing. Basic information about the course of Phase 6 of the transition in various regions is presented in Table 1.7.

New growth appeared in all the CEE-11 countries after the recession caused by the global financial crisis, ranging from a yearly average of 2% GDP growth in Croatia and Hungary to 3.7% in Romania. The West Balkan region and

Table 1.7 Economic transition in CEE countries: Phase 6 (new growth)

	Visegrád-4	Baltic-3	East Balkan-2	West Balkan-2	Memo: Ukraine(a)
Period	2010–17	2011–17	2011–17	2014–17	2010–12
Length (in years)	8	7	7	4	3
Cumulated GDP change	23.2	27.7	22.3	11.2	6.0
Average yearly GDP change	2.6	3.6	2.9	2.7	2.0
Average yearly inflation	1.6	1.9	1.2	0.0	5.9
EBRD liberalization index(b)					
– at the beginning	4.3	4.3	4.3	4.2	4.0
– at the end(d)	4.2	4.3	4.3	4.2	4.0
EBRD market institutions index(c)					
– at the beginning	3.8	3.7	3.3	3.4	2.9
– at the end(d)	3.8	3.8	3.4	3.5	2.9
Corruption perception index(e)					
– at the beginning	48.8	52.7	36.5	52.5	22.0
– at the end	53.0	62.7	45.5	55.0	26.0

Notes: (a) From 2013, Ukraine suffered the next recession caused by the conflict with Russia (cumulated fall of GDP by 11.5%, average yearly inflation of 16.7%). (b) Liberalization index: average liberalization of prices, trade and forex system (from 1 to 4+; values over 4 indicate developed market economy standards). (c) Market institutions index: average level of small and large scale privatization, enterprise restructuring, and competition policy (from 1 to 4+; values over 4 indicate developed market economy standards). (d) EBRD indices available until 2014. (e) From 0 to 100. A value of 100 indicates a corruption-free country. *Data for the groups of countries are unweighted arithmetic means.*

Source: IMF; EBRD; Transparency International; author's calculations.

other countries with relatively high debt and structural problems within the banking sector (such as the high degree of foreign currency denominated mortgage loans) tended to benefit less than others from the post-crisis recovery (cf. Orłowski 2010).

The typical pattern of growth during this phase was connected with limited domestic investment, temporarily increased unemployment, low inflation (and even a lengthy periods of deflation in several countries) and either reduced current account deficits or the emergence of surpluses. A common feature during this phase was also an effort to improve the business environment, and in particular to fight corruption. It is also worth noting the worrying trend of deterioration in the quality of institutions recorded in several CEE countries during the last years of Phase 6. The most striking example is the reduced independence of the judiciary in Hungary and Poland.

The final outcome of the transition: five crucial factors

The final outcome of the transition for the regions and particular countries depended on five crucial factors. The first one was the timing of various phases, and in particular the distribution of the whole period between the years connected with growth (Phases 4 and 6) and the years connected with recession or stagnation (Phases 1, 2, 3, and 5; see Figure 1.1).

The comparison of the timing of various phases of the transition (Figure 1.2) shows quite different patterns in the four regions. In the case of the Visegrád

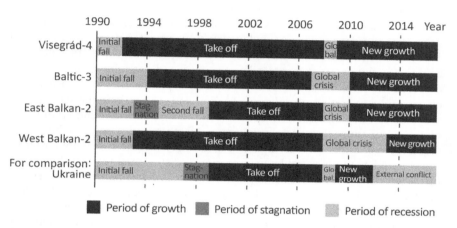

Figure 1.1 Phases of the economic transition in groups of CEE countries (1990–2017)

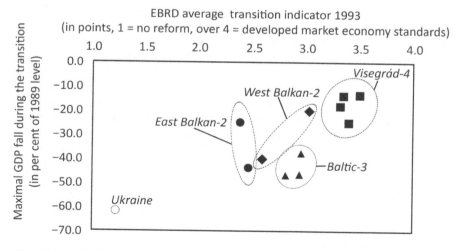

Figure 1.2 Initial GDP fall during the transition and the initial radicalism of reforms in CEE-11 countries and Ukraine

Source: Author's calculation based on IMF and EBRD data.

countries, a combination of the lengthiest periods of take-off and new growth, with the shortest periods of initial decline and global crisis, meant that growth accumulated over 24 years (out of 28 years of the transition). By contrast, in the East Balkan region, growth accumulated over just 16 years, to a large degree because of the stagnation and the second decline. In the case of the West Balkan and Baltic regions, the growth period lasted for 20 years (in Ukraine it lasted for just 12 years, partly due to the conflict with Russia that started in 2013).

The second factor that determined the final outcome of the transition was the scale of the GDP decrease during Phase 1 (initial decline).

As far as the initial decline is concerned, a number of reasons have been indicated to explain the scale of the GDP decrease during the first years of the transition. The most generally accepted explanations are (cf. Aghion and Blanchard 1993; Blanchard 1997; Gomułka 1998; Åslund 2007; Orłowski 2010) (1) limited adjustment abilities of state-owned firms combined with the limited mobility of production factors between the public and private sector; (2) Keynesian effects of the reduction of military spending and macroeconomic stabilization programmes; and (3) effects of openness to the world market and elimination of non-competitive or wasteful production. All these factors point to the crucial importance of initial conditions and of the increase in adjustment abilities (that could have been influenced by privatization and structural reforms during the first, critical years of the transition) as main factors determining the severity of the GDP fall. Indeed, as Figure 1.2 suggests, there seems to exist a close link between the radicalism of reforms, that is the speed at which structural reforms were introduced during the first four years of the transition, and the magnitude of the fall. The correlation between both variables for CEE-11 countries and Ukraine equals 0.78, while the correlation between the extent of the fall and the index of initial conditions (defined as an average of data from Table 1.1, normalized so that the more favourable the conditions, the higher the value) equals −0.48. Therefore, the data suggest that the radicalism of reforms during the first years of the transition was even more important than the starting point. This crucial finding puts the Visegrád region at the top and the East Balkan region at the bottom of the league. It should be noted, however, that even the worst results observed among the CEE-11 countries can be hardly compared with the dramatic fall of GDP recorded in Ukraine and other post-Soviet states, lagging behind in the implementation of reforms.

The third factor, observed in the East Balkan region only, was the stagnation and the second decline recorded in the countries that did not make radical enough reforms during the first years of the transition.

The fourth factor was the growth achieved during Phase 4 (take-off), after the initial fall and before the outbreak of the global financial crisis. The most commonly used explanations of the scale of this growth include (cf. Barbone and Zalduendo 1997; Buch et al. 1999; Neuhaus 2006; Åslund 2007; Orłowski 2010) (1) creating a business-friendly environment, and in particular building strong market institutions (e.g. the financial sector, regulatory bodies, competition policy, modern taxation system), fighting corruption and reducing ineffective bureaucracy; (2) enhancing political and macroeconomic stability; (3) increasing attractiveness for foreign investment; (4) exploiting opportunities created by integration with the EU; and (5) implementing policies supporting growth, in particular in the areas of education, taxation, the labour market and innovation.

Clearly, all these factors could have mattered, as well as many country-specific economic features or policy errors. However, the statistical analysis points to the crucial importance of two factors. First, a strong link exists between the pace of growth and the building of efficient institutions. The correlation between recorded growth and corruption in CEE-11 countries and Ukraine equals −0.58, and between growth and the level of the EBRD average transition indicator (reflecting mainly institutional change) equals 0.62. Second, the correlation between recorded growth and macroeconomic disequilibria (measured by the average inflation rate) equals −0.71, indicating a strong link between growth and stability. As a consequence, the East Balkan region, which suffered from the most damaging corruption and the highest inflation, recorded the weakest growth, while the least corrupt Baltic countries had the best record. Not surprisingly, the worst results were recorded in the corruption-plagued Ukraine. The data presented in Figure 1.3 support the general view that the creation of strong and business-friendly institutions, that ensure a low level of corruption and reduce the bureaucratic red tape, had crucial importance for growth. Obviously, clear links exist between this factor, and all the other factors used for explaining the growth achieved during Phase 4

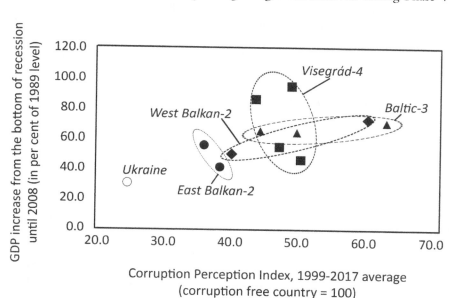

Figure 1.3 GDP growth after the initial decline, and the quality of institutions in CEE-11 countries and Ukraine

Source: Author's calculation based on IMF, EBRD and Transparency International data.

(building strong institutions and fighting corruption was a precondition for strengthening political stability and attracting foreign capital, cf. Havrylyshyn 2006, as well as one of conditions of EU membership).

The fifth factor that determined the final outcome of the transition was the scale of the recession induced by the global financial crisis. This problem was recorded worldwide and affected many emerging markets. However, in the CEE countries which had performed very well during the pre-crisis period, the shock was particularly painful. The Baltic countries, previously called the 'Baltic tigers', were immediately renamed 'subprime borrowers of Europe' (with reference to the toxic, mortgage-based securities issued by US banks that caused the outbreak of the crisis), and some of the CEE-11 countries found themselves on the brink of bankruptcy (cf. PwC 2013).

The most common explanation of the GDP fall connected with the outbreak of the global financial crisis is the scale of the credit boom recorded in the preceding period (cf. PwC 2009; Orłowski 2010; EBRD 2017). Such a boom took place, to a greater or lesser degree, in all the CEE-11 countries, leading to the emergence of sizable current account deficits that reached, in the extreme case of Latvia, over 20% of GDP. The sudden stopping of capital inflows led to huge problems in the banking sector and forced drastic austerity programs aimed at the rapid reduction of the deficit. The correlation between the scale of the credit boom in the years 2001–08 and the change of GDP during the global financial crisis in the CEE-11 countries and Ukraine equals −0.71, and the link between the two variables is presented in Figure 1.4. It should be noted that the smallest fall in GDP during the global financial crisis was recorded

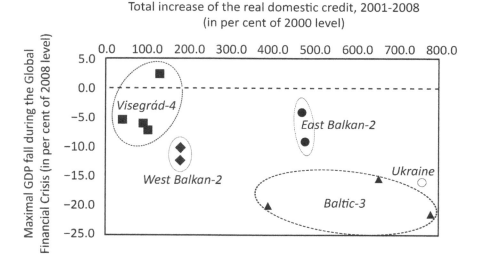

Figure 1.4 GDP fall during the global financial crisis and the pre-crisis credit expansion in CEE-11 countries and Ukraine

Source: Author's calculation based on IMF and EBRD data.

in the Visegrád countries, thanks to the cautious approach to banking sector development during the take-off phase, while the most severe recession was suffered by the Baltic region, that had experienced an extraordinarily strong credit boom financed through external borrowing (partly as a result of the 'impossible trinity' phenomenon: no control over monetary policy while running a fixed exchange rate policy in the presence of free capital flows; cf. Obstfeld, Shambaugh and Taylor 2005).

The final outcome of the transition: achievements and controversies

The final assessment of the transition in CEE-11 countries, albeit generally positive, is not free from controversy. The positive opinions are based on three main factors (cf. Åslund 2007; EBRD 2017): (1) the success in building open market economies integrated with the European and global market; (2) the dramatic enhancement of investment attractiveness and improvement of the business environment; and (3) the increase in productivity, average income and living standards.

The success, however, was not even and depended very much on the trajectory of the transition. By 2017, all the CEE-11 countries had managed to build open, functioning market economies (as measured by the EBRD transition index, cf. EBRD 2017), adjusted their laws to acquis communautaire and had become members of the EU (the last country that joined the block was Croatia in 2013), although the institutions still need enhancement and the level of corruption is still significantly higher than in the majority of western EU countries. Basic data about the outcome of the transition is presented in Table 1.8.

Table 1.8 Economic transition in CEE countries: the final outcome (2017)

	GDP per capita in PPS, (German level = 100)		Life expectancy at birth, years		Stock of inward FDI(a)	Net in-vestment position	R&D expenditure (a)	Gini coefficient (a)
	2017	Change from 1989	2017	Change from 1989	As percent of GDP			
Visegrád-4	*63.2*	*11.2*	*77.0*	*6.2*	*51.9*	*−53.6*	*1.2*	*0.27*
Czechia	70.4	5.0	78.3	6.7	58.5	−29.5	1.7	0.25
Hungary	58.5	1.4	75.6	6.1	62.8	−53.3	1.2	0.28
Poland	58.5	22.9	77.5	6.4	40.0	−66.2	1.0	0.30
Slovakia	65.5	15.3	76.6	5.5	46.5	−65.5	0.8	0.24
Baltic-3	*60.6*	*8.4*	*75.5*	*5.0*	*56.3*	*−44.0*	*0.9*	*0.35*
Estonia	63.0	9.3	77.7	7.7	84.3	−34.2	1.3	0.33
Latvia	54.8	7.6	74.5	4.4	52.1	−60.0	0.4	0.35
Lithuania	64.1	8.3	74.3	2.9	32.4	−37.7	0.9	0.37

(*Continued*)

Table 1.8 (Continued)

	GDP per capita in PPS, (German level = 100)		Life expectancy at birth, years		Stock of inward FDI(a)	Net in-vestment position	R&D expenditure (a)	Gini coefficient (a)
	2017	Change from 1989	2017	Change from 1989	As percent of GDP			
East Balkan-2	**45.8**	**3.5**	**74.8**	**4.2**	**65.0**	**−45.8**	**0.6**	**0.36**
Bulgaria	43.0	−2.7	74.6	2.9	90.1	−43.0	0.8	0.38
Romania	48.6	9.7	75.0	5.5	39.8	−48.6	0.5	0.35
West Balkan-2	**58.3**	**−4.2**	**78.7**	**6.6**	**37.2**	**−50.5**	**1.4**	**0.27**
Croatia	48.4	−10.7	76.6	5.2	45.3	−66.9	0.9	0.30
Slovenia	68.2	2.3	80.8	8.1	29.1	−34.0	2.0	0.24
Memo:								
Ukraine	17.3	−20.4	71.5	0.9	54.4	−24.3	0.6	0.26
Germany	100.0	100.0	80.6	5.6	22.5	62.7	2.9	0.30

Notes: (1) Data for 2016. *Data for the groups of countries are unweighted arithmetic means.*

Source: IMF; UNCTAD; World Bank; author's calculations.

By 2017, no CEE country had yet approached the West European level of GDP per capita (PPP), with the Czechia and Slovenia at about 70% of the German level and Bulgaria at just 43%. However, in the majority of the CEE-11 countries this ratio visibly increased during the transition. The leaders of growth, Poland and Slovakia, managed to increase the relation of their GDP per capita to the German level by 23 points and 15 points, respectively. An increase was also noticeable in the Baltic states and Romania. By contrast, this relation decreased in Bulgaria, and even more in Croatia, partly as a result of the long war with Serbia. Nevertheless, no CEE-11 country recorded as a big drop as Ukraine: the yearly average growth rate recorded in the whole period 1990–2017 in Poland was 3.4% (leading to a total GDP increase of 145%); in the slowest growing CEE-11 country, Croatia, it was 0.2% (a GDP increase of 7%); but in Ukraine there was an average annual fall of −2.5% (leading to a total GDP decrease of 44%; see Figure 1.5).

Another clear sign of improvement in living conditions was the general increase in life expectancy at birth, achieved due to the improvement of the quality of the health service (with the most visible outcome being a radical fall in infant mortality) as well as changing living habits (cf. EBRD 2017). The recorded increase in life expectancy during the transition ranged from three years in Bulgaria and Lithuania to eight years in Slovenia, bringing this indicator to 92%–100% of the German level.

The progress observed during the transition, and in particular the enhanced stability, credibility of policy, and the successful drive towards EU membership, helped the CEE-11 countries to attract sizable foreign direct investment (FDI)

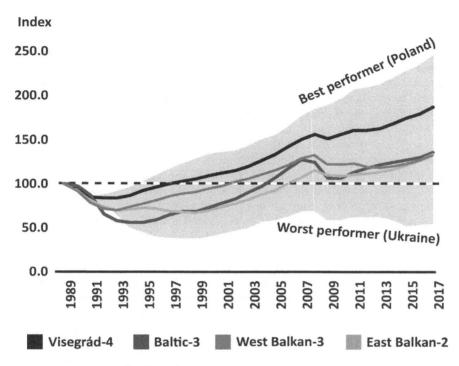

Figure 1.5 Real GDP levels in the groups of CEE countries, 1989–2017 (index, 1989
      level = 100)

Source: Author's calculation based on IMF and EBRD data

flows (cf. Buch et al. 1999; Neuhaus 2006). Although the largest FDI stock was
amassed in Poland, the leaders in attracting foreign capital, on a per capita basis,
were Estonia and Czechia followed by Hungary and Slovakia. The importance of
this phenomenon for the economies of the CEE-11 countries can be measured
by the relation of the FDI stock to GDP, ranging from 29% in Slovenia to 90% in
Bulgaria. In spite of widespread popular opinion, the data show no link between
this indicator and GDP growth during the transition: Poland and Slovakia, the
growth leaders, had a moderate FDI stock of 40%–47% of GDP, considerably less
than Czechia and Hungary, which grew at a much lower rate, not to mention
slow-growing Bulgaria. It should be noted, however, that the positive impact of
the FDI on productivity growth and technological progress, including spillover
effects, was found in the analysis on the sectoral level (cf. Neuhaus 2006). More
on this can be found in the chapter by Capello in this book.

The final assessment of the transition is also connected with some controversy.
The transition induced a deep social change, significantly increasing the level
of income inequalities. The Gini coefficient increased from an estimated level
of 0.24–0.22 during communist times to 0.24–0.30 in the Visegrád and West

Balkan regions and to 0.33–0.38 in the East Balkan and Baltic regions. (The Gini coefficient is calculated so that 0 means a theoretical state of perfectly equal distribution of income, and 1 means extreme inequality; in practice, the coefficient varies globally from 0.2 to 0.7.) Although income inequality in the CEE-11 countries remains within the limits typical for Western Europe, the scale of its increase over the transition, as well as the scale of the increase of unemployment and poverty, could have shocked those groups in society that were less successful in adjusting to the market conditions, leading to widespread social discontent (cf. Milanović 1998).

The growth model that emerged during the transition also raises some questions about its sustainability. The massive imports of foreign capital, in the form of both direct and portfolio investment, led to the significant indebtedness of the CEE-11 countries, mainly vis-à-vis Western Europe. The scale of this debt, as measured by the net international investment position, ranges from 30% of GDP in Czechia to over 66% in Croatia, Slovakia and Poland. Only a significant increase in domestic saving rates could change this pattern; however, for the time being, such a phenomenon has not taken place (cf. Orłowski 2010; EBRD 2017).

As the research and development (R&D) spending indicates, all the CEE-11 countries are lagging behind their richer Western European partners in the area of knowledge-based growth, both due to the relative attractiveness of labour-intensive investment that discourages firms from searching for innovations and to the weakness of the domestic R&D systems. Taking into account the leading role of multinational companies in production and exports, as well as the immense dependence on Western European markets, doubts have been raised about the equal position of the new CEE Member States within the EU economy (cf. Nölke and Vliegenthart 2009; see more in-depth analysis of this issue in the chapter by Radosevic, Yoruk and Yoruk in this book). As the figures in Table 1.8 demonstrate, the faster growth recorded in the region generally led to some convergence of productivity and income with Western Europe. On the other hand, with the current growth model based mainly on the competitive cost of the skilled labour, the CEE countries will be facing a growing risk of falling into the middle-income trap, a phenomenon of inability to achieve full convergence due to growing wages (cf. Agénor et al. 2012). It is obvious that further convergence will be possible only if the growth model is adapted to the new conditions: sticking to the competitive cost of labour will bring about a repetition of the 16th-century experience of the region being trapped in the role of the European periphery.

Conclusions

The transition from central planning to a market economy turned out to be a much longer and much more painful process than originally expected. At the beginning, the societies of Central and Eastern Europe experienced a dramatic fall in income connected with the emergence of undesirable increases in unemployment and poverty. The growth that came later, together with the integration into the European Union, brought about modernization and a radical increase in productivity and living standards. Although the final outcome depended on the trajectories of the transition and the way in which countries were able to manage this process, the economic transition of the region can be generally assessed as a success, albeit achieved at a high price. Nevertheless, the road towards full convergence with Western Europe still remains very long, and significant changes in the growth model are necessary to accomplish it.

Notes

1 The numbers quoted in this chapter, unless otherwise indicated, are based on data published in the IMF World Economic Outlook Database and the EBRD Macroeconomic Statistics and Transition Indicators Database. Estimates of the historic values of GDP (before 1989) are based on the well-known work by Angus Maddison (Maddison 2001; the updated version is available at: www.rug.nl/ggdc/historicaldevelopment/maddison/).
2 Data for the regions (four groups of countries) quoted in this chapter are calculated as unweighted arithmetic means.

References

Agénor, P., Canuto, O., & Jelenic, M. (2012). Avoiding middle-income growth traps. *Economic Premise*, (98).

Aghion, P., & Blanchard, O. (1993). On the Speed of Transition in Central Europe, *EBRD Working Paper* No. 6, London: EBRD.

Arnason, J. (1993). *The Future that Failed: Origins and Destinies of the Soviet Model*. London: Routledge.

Åslund, A. (2007). *How Capitalism was Built: The Transformation of Central and Eastern Europe, Russia, and Central Asia*. Cambridge: Cambridge University Press.

Åslund, A., & Orłowski, W.M. (2014). The Polish Transition in a Comparative Perspective, *mBank – CASE Seminar Proceedings* No. 133/2014, Warszawa: CASE.

Bakker, B., & Gulde, A.-M. (2010). The Credit Boom in the EU New Member States: Bad Luck or Bad Policies?, *IMF Working Paper* 10/130. Washington, DC: International Monetary Fund.

Barbone, L., & Zalduendo, J. (1997). EU Accession of Central and Eastern Europe. Bridging the Income Gap, *World Bank Policy Research Working Paper* No. 1721, Washington, DC: IBRD.

Bátory, A., Cartwright, A., & Stone, D. (eds.) (2018). *Policy Experiments, Failures and Innovations Beyond Accession in Central and Eastern Europe*. Cheltenham: Edward Elgar.

Blanchard, O. (1997). *The Economics of Post-Communist Transition*. New York: Oxford University Press.

Buch, C.M., et al. (1999). *Foreign Capital and Economic Transformation: Risks and Benefits of Free Capital Flows*. Kiel: Kieler Studien 295.

EBRD (2017). *Transition Report 2016–17*. London: EBRD.

Gomułka, S. (1998). Output: Causes of the Decline and Recovery. In: P. Boone, S. Gomułka & R. Layard (eds.) *Emerging from Communism. Lessons from Russia, China and Eastern Europe*. Cambridge, MA: MIT Press.

Havrylyshyn, O. (2006). *Diverging Paths in Post-Communist Transformation: Capitalism for All or Capitalism for the Few?* New York: Palgrave Macmillan.

Maddison, A. (2001). *The World Economy: A Millennial Perspective*. Paris: OECD.

Milanović, B. (1998). *Income, Inequality, and Poverty During the Transition from Planned to Market Economy*. Washington, DC: IBRD.

Neuhaus, M. (2006). *The Impact of FDI on Economic Growth. An Analysis for the Transition Countries of Central and Eastern Europe*. Heidelberg: Physica Verlag (Springer).

Nölke, A., & Vliegenthart, A. (2009). Enlarging the varieties of capitalism: The emergence of dependent market economies in East Central Europe. *World Politics*, 61(4).

Obstfeld, M., Shambaugh, J., & Taylor, A. (2005). The trilemma in history: Tradeoffs among exchange rates, monetary policies, and capital mobility. *The Review of Economics and Statistics*, 87(3).

Orłowski, W.M. (2010). *W pogoni za straconym czasem. Wzrost gospodarczy w Europie Środkowo-Wschodniej 1950–2030*. Warszawa: PWE.

PwC (2009). *Hard Landing. Central and Eastern Europe Facing Global Crisis*. Warszawa: PwC.

PwC (2013). *Central and Eastern Europe Economic Scorecard. A Sustainable Future in a Great Region*. Warszawa: PwC.

Stiftung, B. (2018). *Transformation Index BTI 2018. Governance in International Comparison*. Gütersloh: Verlag Bertelsmann Stiftung.

US Arms Control & Disarmament Agency (1999). *World Military Expenditures and Arms Transfers Share 1990*. Washington, DC: US Government Printing Office.

Wallerstein, I. (1974). *The Modern World-System. Capitalist Agriculture and the Origins of the European World-Economy in the Sixteenth Century*. New York–London: Academic Press.

WIIW (1991). *Comecon Data 1990*. London: Macmillan.

2 Political systems, socio-economic development and the quality of democracy in CEE countries

Radosław Markowski

Introduction

Contemporary political science is serious about at least two of its slogans: first, that *institutions matter* and second – *no parties no democracy*. Both are still important signposts, yet due to many technological and social changes they clearly call for thoughtful revisiting, equally in stable and fragile democracies.

Recent developments in the countries of Central and Eastern Europe (CEE), and in Poland and Hungary in particular, require us to reconsider our paradigmatic approaches to transitology and the assumptions on democratic consolidation. Unfortunately, a backsliding into some form of illiberal regime is evident to differing degrees in a number of CEE countries, not only in the two aforementioned. Even in countries where the interwar historical legacies seemed to be conducive to democratic quality (Czechia) or where social affluence, egalitarianism and a coordinated economic system (Slovenia) have been in place, something is missing to convincingly claim their stable 'embedded' democratic status. Political actors challenging the institutional design of liberal democratic order have emerged in all countries of the region. These changes are designed not only to radically discontinue particular policies, not even to transform selected political institutions; many are devised to convert the whole idea of an 'open access civil society' with its free media, non-governmental organization (NGO) activities, stable property rights and independent judiciary created to protect them. Briefly, developments, in Hungary and in Poland in particular, are intended to change the constitutional order of these countries.

The agenda of these new political entrepreneurs – ranging from sheer authoritarians via clientelistic/nepotistic kleptocrats to illiberal democrats – combines demands for more national sovereignty coupled at times with social traditionalism, and at times with religious fundamentalism; it is grounded in national-patriotic values aligned with an exclusivist national identity and a fear of foreigners, immigrants in particular, presenting them as a direct threat to their well-being and to labour market security (Magyar 2018; Markowski 2018a). The real conflict is clear: the CEE countries, most of whom belong to the EU, reject this institution's key policies and openly resist its more general cosmopolitan, globalist agenda, thereby also setting themselves against multinational organizations like the Council of Europe, the Court of Justice of the European Union or even the United Nations.

Numerous institutions evaluating the state of democracy and of the rule of law around the world indicate this fact. In Tables 2.1 and 2.2 and Figures 2.1 and 2.2, assessments of the quality of democracy and the rule of law in CEE countries are presented, using the renowned Bertelsmann Transformative Index (BTI) data. The data was obtained by a multistage process of detailed expert survey evaluations ending with a group comparative assessment (across countries). The entries pertain to the last dozen or so years. Briefly, save for Slovenia, which shows a slight increase in the quality of this aspect, none of the countries

Table 2.1 Mean scores of the evaluation of democracy in CEE countries across time (a 10-point scale from 1 – lowest to 10 – highest quality)

Country/year	2006	2008	2010	2012	2014	2016	2018
Poland	9.5	8.5	9	9.5	9.5	10	8
Slovenia	9.5	10	10	10	9.5	9.5	10
Slovakia	9.5	9	9.5	9	9	8.5	8
Czechia	9.5	9.5	10	10	10	9.5	9
Croatia	9.5	9	8.5	8.5	8.5	8.5	8.5
Romania	8.5	8.5	8.5	8.5	7.5	8	7.5
Hungary	9.5	9	8.5	7.5	7.5	7.6	6.5
Bulgaria	9	9	9	8.5	8.5	8	8

Source: BTI (Bertelsmann Transformative Index), www.bti-project.org/en/data/.

Please note that the years of BTI Reports are somewhat misleading due to their shift in time, for instance the BTI 2006 Report evaluates the years 2004–05 and so on.

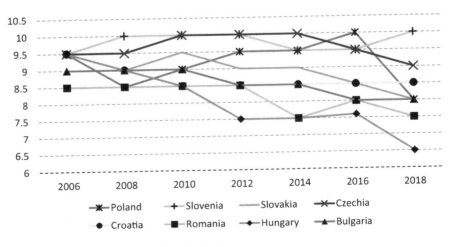

Figure 2.1 Stability of demographic institutions

Table 2.2 Mean scores of the evaluation of the rule of law in CEE countries across time (a 10-point scale from 1 – lowest to 10 – highest quality)

Country/Year	2006	2008	2010	2012	2014	2016	2018
Poland	9.3	8.8	8.8	9.3	9.3	9.3	8
Slovenia	9.5	9.8	9.8	9.5	9	9.3	9.3
Slovakia	9	9.3	9.3	8.5	8.5	8.3	8
Czechia	9	9.3	9.5	9.3	9.3	9.3	9.3
Croatia	8.3	8	7.8	7.8	8.3	8	8
Romania	7.3	8.3	8.3	8.3	7.5	8.3	8.3
Hungary	9	9.3	9	7.8	7.3	6.5	6
Bulgaria	7.8	8.5	8.3	8.5	8	7.8	7.8

Source: BTI (Bertelsmann Transformative Index), www.bti-project.org/en/data/.

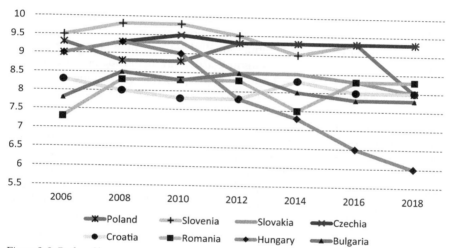

Figure 2.2 Rule of law

of the region shows an improvement in the quality of democracy, while there has been a significant decline in Hungary and Poland. A similar picture is derived from the assessment of the rule of law: no countries show an improvement except for two, one at the higher end (Czechia), as well as Romania, but from a substantially lower starting point in 2004–05.

Writing a chapter on the state of CEE polities in 2019, their democratic credentials and societal preferences is extremely difficult, because until 2010 political science and political sociology was fairly confident about determinants contributing to the given state of democracy in the CEE region. Not anymore. As of 2019, many of the acclaimed theories and empirical findings no longer hold true, yet unfortunately we are not in a position to offer convincing explanations as to why the current backsliding into authoritarianism is proceeding in the region. This is because we lack rich and reliable new data, and because the theories that would explain it are either unconvincing or brand new, thus calling for empirical testing. As a consequence, the chapter offered here is speculative and theoretical in nature, with limited empirical support, which is nonetheless given wherever possible.

Theories of transition and consolidation: the story of a failure?

The transition from communism in CEE has been treated as the last (or the third, after South European and Latin American) sub-wave of the third wave of democratization (Huntington 1991). Scholars (including the author of this chapter; see Markowski 1997; 2001; Kitschelt, Mansfeldova, Markowski and Toka 1999), experts and pundits of the transition in CEE countries have assumed too uncritically a universal development path from authoritarian regimes to democracy. To be sure, the contributions of Huntington (1991) on the three phases of transition (authoritarian exit, building of an institutional infrastructure, democratic consolidation) or Linz and Stepan's (1996) insightful proposals concerning domains of democracy and democratic consolidation are still a must when it comes to theoretical approaches aimed at explaining the current state of the new democracies in CEE. Many empirical contributions of the last dozen years or so have been devoted to explaining why CEE countries have so successfully entered the family of democratic societies and the main reasons for its (allegedly) unproblematic democratic consolidation (Ekiert and Kubik 1998; Bunce 2002; Roberts 2009; Markowski 2001; 2015; 2016a). Warnings were expressed as well, in particular about the instability of the party systems and voters' volatility (Toka 1995Bielasiak 2002Powell and Tucker 2009; Mainwaring and Zocco 2007)), the far from perfect representation and accountability mechanisms (Roberts 2008; 2009Markowski 2006; 2007), the peculiar mode of EU membership (Lewis and Markowski 2011) and the poor quality of the political elite (Higley, Kullberg, Pakulski 1996).

Before we move on to discuss particular contributions to the theme, let us start with the transition itself and its genesis. Generally, political science has done a poor job as far as this stage is concerned. There are three fundamental issues that were faultily approached and defined. First, the unfortunate supremacy of American Sovietologists studying transitions from communism have led to a dominance of *Leninist legacies* assuming an existence of a more or less similar type of communism in the CEE countries. And even if, right from the beginning, efforts were made to show that actually existing forms of socialism in Eastern Europe differed immensely (Kitschelt et al. 1999), the methods applied in the initial phase of transformation were designed as if they were similar.

Second, the prevailing political science approach had it that the mode of transition matters; the common wisdom claims superiority of *pactada* to *ruptura* as a means of exit from authoritarianism, because in the latter events are typically bloody and create new victims, which in turn destabilizes the newly established regimes. Obviously, the region experienced a plethora of modes of transition, from a clearly negotiated pact (Round Table negotiations in Poland) achieved via grass-roots, incremental process spanning the prior two decades of revolts (Poland 1970, 1976, 1980–81, 1987–89) to well-designed quasi-market economic reforms with significant political consequences (Hungary 1968, 1979). The remaining countries of the region followed the changes in these two countries, with allegedly similar results.

Third, several problems relate to the issue of choosing institutions:

1   Different levels of uncertainty of political actors in choosing particular institutions, and in particular the choices made by the first-comer to the transition (Poland), insightfully described by Lijphart (1992), compared to the challenges faced by the followers (for details see Markowski 2017).
2   Institutions have typically been treated too rationally and mechanically, as if the formal design itself were to create logically expected outcomes as a sort of transmission belt. Too little attention has been devoted to the daily operation of these institutions and the personalities fulfilling their institutional roles, along the lines proposed by Pierson (2004).
3   Hardly any serious scholar predicted that the blow to the democratic institutions of liberal democracies in CEE would come from the entrenched, institutionalised party elites; as a consequence, special attention ought to be devoted to political parties.

In what follows, I discuss selected key issues so far neglected by scholars of democratization.

1   In the search for determinants of the current decline in democratic quality in the region, far too much consideration has been given to the alleged drawbacks of communism and too little attention devoted to long term cultural-religious traditions as well as to the creative grass-roots, societal alternatives to the communist blueprint, present mostly (though not exclusively) in what we have dubbed the *national-accommodative* type of real-socialism (see Kitschelt et al. 1999). The phenomenon has been described in detail elsewhere (Markowski 2018a, 2018b, 2018c) and will be further discussed in the sections that follow.
2   Parties and institutionalized party systems are considered the fundamental factors conducive to democratic consolidation and the quality of electoral democracy in particular. The transitologist wisdom on CEE party systems unveils the following picture: the parties and party systems are clearly unconsolidated, fluid and unpredictable to the extent that Peter Mair (1997) has questioned their very 'systemness'. Unpredictable changes, weak rootedness in the social structure and voter volatility are much higher than in any other part – old or new – of European democracies (Gherghina 2014; Enyedi and Casal Bertoa 2018).

Assessment of party system institutionalization has different traditions. The most frequently used one is offered by Mainwaring and Scully (1995), who suggest we should look at several phenomena, in particular:

1   Patterns of inter-party competition and their stability.
2   The extent to which parties have strong and logical roots in society, and conversely, voters have strong attachments to parties;
3   The extent to which legitimacy is accorded to parties, irrespective of criticism expressed;
4   The extent to which party organizations are not subordinated to the interests of ambitious leaders.

I definitely opt for adding one important feature of such party systems, namely that they are autonomous and independent even from institutions that might have been instrumental in their nascence.

Party systems of the CEE countries: a general empirical overview

Available data and results of relevant analyses allow us to generalize as follows:

1   Party system volatility attests to its endurance. The latest pan-European surveys reveal that this is probably the single aspect that differs most across Europe (Ersson 2012). CEE countries manifest the highest rates of switches in voter preferences from election to election. And even if the aggregate CEE volatility has gone down slightly from the very high records in the early 1990s (approximately 40%) to the current level below 30%, the latter figure is still a lot higher than in Western Europe (about 10%–15%) or Southern Europe (15%–20%). From the first elections in the early 1990s to the second decade of the 21st century, the trend in CEE has been declining, whereas in the other two parts of Europe it has been slightly increasing. However, elections in CEE countries in the last four to five years again unveil an increase in volatility measured by the Pedersen Index,[1] irrespective of whether they come from vote switching among existing parties or from voting for new contenders, even if recent data shows that externally created volatility (i.e. springing from newcomers to the system) is on the rise (Powell and Tucker 2013).
2   Scholars of party systems have always been keen to develop a reliable measure of party organizations. Among the usual gauges are their membership (or membership ratio); the density of offices at national, regional and local levels; soundness of party structures and their internal democracy; and the transparency of party finance. On all counts, CEE parties show much less organization, lower membership and fewer internal democratic procedures and transparency than their Western European counterparts (Tavits 2013). Intra-regional variation is difficult to estimate, as many of these

indicators are hardly accessible, yet some of the more formal and mechanical indicators such as the number/ratio of members reveals that Slovenia, Czechia and Hungary demonstrate greater party organization than Poland or Lithuania. Internal democracy and party finances are also very difficult to evaluate, and they largely depend on the law that regulates both, as well as the extent to which 'leader democracy' – an increasingly popular phenomenon – dominates the proceedings within these organizations.

3   The number of competitors within a party system is important because when a party system exhibits too few or too many parties (i.e. below two or above six), it ultimately negatively affects the quality of the political culture. As Gallagher (2013) shows, apart from the very initial period of the transformation until the mid-1990s, in three countries – Poland, Latvia and Slovenia – the number of competitors exceeded six, while for most of the period afterwards the average number of parties was just above four, including these three countries. In a nutshell, the number of parties in their respective party systems does not create any reason for concern in CEE.

It is, however, another matter as to what the party competitors compete about and how they compete. In this case we can see a clear persistence of the pattern first suggested and theoretically substantiated by Kitschelt (1992) then depicted and explained by Markowski (1997), Kitschelt et al. (1999) and later on by Rovny and Edwards (2012). The essence of this pattern is that, using the universal spatial metaphor of party placements in their respective system (depicted by the classical economic 'left-right' and socio-cultural traditional/conservative vs. liberal cosmopolitan dimensions), we can see a 90-degree switch in the main axis of competition in Eastern European in comparison to Western party systems. Briefly, the CEE pattern has unveiled a clear independence of these two dimensions of competition, particularly in countries such as Poland and Hungary, with a visible difference being Czechia with its single 'left-right' economic dimension of competition and lack of socio-cultural issues contributing to party rivalry in this country, and a more fuzzy configuration in the remaining cases (Kitschelt et al. 1999). The clear difference of the CEE countries is that the economic 'left-wing' parties (favouring higher taxes, more intervention of government in the economy, focus on unemployment, rejection of privatization, etc.) were at the same time more conservative, religious and socio-culturally restrictive (family policy, abortion, public role of the church, etc.). And parties of the 'right' happened to be more economically liberal, in favour of labour market solutions with a visible preference for socio-cultural freedoms, cosmopolitan openness and separation of the state from the church – quite contrary to the Western pattern, in which the economic 'left' has always been, and still is, associated with a 'liberal' socio-cultural package of cosmopolitan features, in favour of individual freedoms, restriction of the role of the church in public life and so on. Now, as of the second decade of the 21st century, in some CEE countries the Western pattern has also started to prevail; this applies mainly to Slovenia and Slovakia as well as to Latvia and Estonia. These are countries which are either the most affluent in the region (save Latvia) or have strong Protestant foundations (the Baltic states). Nevertheless, in many CEE countries the economically 'left'/socio-culturally conservative quadrant predominate, both in terms of numbers of voters as well as in terms of the presence of a major political party (the Polish PiS party or Hungarian Fidesz party are the most obvious examples). These are usually the countries in which religion and the dominant church have been invited to play an important role in politics. What helps this strange (by Western standards) configuration is the *Catholic social teaching*, which serves as a well-elaborated ideology allowing for a plausible merger of seemingly contradictory policies.

The two dimensional space of competition is an important first step to grasp the logic of the linkage between voters and party elites, yet we need more details to understand the exact determinants of citizens' voting choice. From what we know in this respect, it is hard to generalize, although a few empirically supported observations can be offered.

1   Irrespective of the alleged universality of the economic 'left-right' dimension of competition, this should not be equated with its importance as a vote determinant. In several polities, in Poland and Hungary in particular, economic variables matter much less than the socio-cultural factors as determinants of the vote (Kotnarowski and Markowski 2014; Kreko and Enyedi 2018). One of the possible and likely mechanisms behind this is that as income inequality spreads (as in the case of the 1990s), the importance of the economic-redistributive dimension increases. If the inequality is subjectively conceived as injustice, this development is likely to benefit more left-wing than right-wing parties. Thus, a rational strategy for the latter is to divert voter attention away from economic-redistributive issues to socio-cultural ones, values, historical legacies or religious concerns. Empirically, this relationship has proved correct. Even more crucial, this phenomenon is mainly due to the appeals and programs of right-wing parties (Tavits and Letki 2014).

2   The exact meaning and content of these dimensions of competition differs across countries; in some the 'left' or 'right' has an exclusively economic meaning (e.g. the Czech case) or it comprises socio-cultural issues (e.g. Poland, Hungary).

3   Electoral studies are preoccupied with the socio-demographic roots of party support – the underlying assumption is that qualitative political representation, is possible only if logical links between major social groups and political parties exist. Knutsen (2013) offers a comparative analysis of this sort, from which a few conclusions can be submitted: first, that religiosity is by far the most important factor in the voting choice; second, that among the two variables depicting people's religiosity it is rather church attendance than denomination that matters more, suggesting indirectly that the impact on the vote is probably more of a social-communitarian phenomenon that having to do with deep religious beliefs and dogmas;

third, that it is rather the place of residence than social class that matters in the vote choice. In comparison to Western Europe, CEE party systems reveal weaker roots in society, yet religious factor matters more in structuring their party politics (Grzymala-Busse 2007; Markowski, Cześnik and Kotnarowski 2015).

Political institutions: a broader perspective on the institutional design

Parties and party systems do not feature in democratic polities alone. A federalist or unitary structure of the state is another example; in the CEE region, however, no country has a federal structure. The other key institution is (semi-) presidentialism, which in the region is a real variable. A study by Andrews and Bairett (2014), analysing 16 CEE countries, summarizes their results as follows: 'volatility is higher in countries with directly elected presidents, and [. . .] presidential strength amplifies this effect'. All in all, the presence of a president with considerable executive and veto powers creates a fertile soil for intra-executive conflicts, in particular when co-habitation occurs. In addition, the existence of a strong presidential power creates instability of the party systems because of its electoral (usually two-round) contest in which all kinds of political manoeuvres and alliances are staged, dependent on the particular configuration, sheer number and ideological leaning of the candidates (Sedelius and Mashtaler 2012; Frey 1997). In the CEE region, strong semi-presidentialism has featured almost right from the beginning of the democratic opening in Romania and Poland, with a more moderate version in Slovenia and Bulgaria. Recently Czechia has joined the family of semi-presidential systems, yet with fairly moderate executive powers (see Elgie and Moestrup 2008).

To conclude: first, institutions matter for the stability of political systems, but they matter interactively in conjunction with one another (for instance, with a bicameral structure of parliament). Second, if any message comes through the numerous analyses of the links between the quality of democracy and the chances for democratic consolidation, it is that the more simple the political system – the pure parliamentarism of the Western European configuration – the more likely are low levels of volatility, party system stability and political predictability (Fish 2006).

The impact of the EU: on elections to the European Parliament

All CEE countries under scrutiny here are members of the European Union. This fact has several consequences for their political systems. First, since 2004 all new Member States have run elections to the European Parliament (EP). In the literature, the peculiarities of these elections have been well explained and they have adequately been dubbed as 'second-order elections' (Reif and Schmitt 1980). Their essence can be summarized as follows: because citizens consider elections to the EP as much less important than to the national ones, they participate in them significantly less frequently (turnout in the EP elections is considerably lower than in the national elections). This fact leads to another key feature, namely, since they are less important, the vote choice is also less crucial and therefore a more 'sincere vote' (emotional first preference vote) takes place. Moreover, given that the stakes of this election are considered to be low, voters use this opportunity to punish the incumbents for their deeds, irrespectively of how efficient they might be. Ultimately, EP elections are an inviting political context and an opportunity for small new entrants to start competing. This very same ease with which they can organize themselves and enjoy a likely success in the low-turnout EP elections is at the same time the reason for their likely disappearance once they start competing in the 'serious' high-turnout elections. The fact that EP elections have come to provide an electoral arena which is a potentially favourable launching pad for new political parties can be interpreted both as a negative consequence of EP elections and as a positive one, by providing new opportunities for electoral entrepreneurs (for details, see van der Brug and de Vreese 2016 in Markowski 2016b). The general aggregate level message is that, as expected (Markowski 2016b) the more coherent the electorate, the more proximate it is to the parties it votes for, and the more loyal the voters are to their newly established parties, the more likely their success for a longer period. For many newly established parties, it is an open question as to whether they should present a clearly defined program aimed at attracting only a very restricted electoral base or try to invite a wide spectrum of citizens ('catch-all' model motives). It seems that the former is the more promising recipe for the establishment and socio-political rooting of a new party.

It is also interesting to note that intra-electorate cohesion and proximity matter, but more in terms of socio-demographics rather than in terms of the political and ideological message conveyed by parties (see Markowski 2016b). In other words, without vibrant social bonds in place, political/ideological appeals will not suffice. In particular, the impact of the proximity and coherence of their electorate by age groups, place of residence and class is non-trivial. Moreover, a fact that has to be emphasized is that the class factor impacts the electoral fortunes of the newly established parties in the opposite manner than expected.

It is also noteworthy that new democracies differ from stable ones: the quality of political representation and social bonds, and the religious factor in particular, matter significantly for the survival fate of a new party. One result deserves further in-depth scrutiny, namely the positive relationship between the heterogeneity or incoherence of the class factor and the survival of newly initiated parties. The interpretation at this point simply ought to emphasize that intra-electoral diversity in non-distributive socio-cultural factors like age and religiosity inhibit the chances for durable organizational effectiveness, while diversity in the economic-distributive domain – embodied here as class heterogeneity – seems to be conducive to the fortune of new parties.

The impact of the EU: on the logic and current challenges of the EU design

The conditionalities of the EU accession process nurtured convergence on a liberal–democratic model, with very few features or signs of backsliding in the pre-accession period (Ekiert, Kubik and Vachudova 2007). Nonetheless, once inside the EU structures, 'post-accession hooliganism' occurred in several countries (Ganev 2013). Much earlier, numerous studies pointed to emerging new phenomena such as weak civil societies, low social capital, distrust of the traditional institutions of liberal democracy, awkward independence of the mass media, damaging of the professionalism of the public administration and attacks on the rights of minorities. Others identified a developing conflict between the liberal rationalism of EU institutions and the populist revolt against the unaccountability of the elite, resulting (among other things) in defiant voting behaviour labelled as 'hyper-accountability', the propensity to punish any incumbents irrespective of their performance (Howard 2003; Krastev 2007; Tavits 2007; Roberts 2008; Bugaric 2008).

Still others point to the fact that, currently, CEE countries have created 'second party systems' that are filled with numerous parties of 'populist', 'Eurosceptic', 'protest' and 'extreme-right' character. 'The . . . first party systems were fragile and . . . unstable, second party systems have been overburdened by competing oligarchs, clientelism and kleptocracy' (cf. Agh 2015). The reasons are complex. There are indications that one of them might be related to the spatial distribution of EU funds in the countries of the region – favouring the western parts of countries at the expense of eastern provinces.[2] This fact – a result of CEE peripheral economies, dependent on their Western counterparts – has ultimately led to significant regional inequalities. In effect, in the eastern provinces poverty and social exclusion has been considerably higher, giving rise to political radicalism and higher support for non-mainstream parties.

The polities in the core CEE region differ, however, in their corruption and governance indicators. It is worth distinguishing between the 'party state capture' phenomenon, present in Hungary and partially in Poland, and the 'corporate state capture' demonstrated in Czechia and Slovakia. In the former, the party system seems to be dominated by a single hegemonic actor, which creates crony capitalism, with the strong support of institutionalized social actors (e.g. the church in Poland), a vibrant alternative civil society based typically on militaristic/nationalist nostalgia, and the public media. In the latter, the foundations of the system are business-driven, with oligarchs becoming politicians and fusing business with politics. Irrespective of type, these hegemonic parties, with weak social embeddedness, have been able to create an almost universally corrupt system based predominantly on EU transfers and public procurement. And even if the scope and depth of this corrupted network differs between, say Poland and Hungary (for details see Magyar 2018) the essence of the system remains as described above.

Finally, globalization and the process of EU integration have weakened domestic political actors by providing new entrants complete policy packages, elaborated typically by Western experts and policy makers. This diffusion of policy packages has resulted in limited effort being made by national parties to work on internally determined policies and has consequently reduced the opportunity to establish content links between parties and their supporters.

Backsliding towards authoritarianism and other modes of democratic decline: the theoretical context

While there are cases in the CEE region which manifest clear continuity of democratic consolidation, in other countries the quality of democracy has experienced either a relative decline or a significant decline in recent years, most notably in Hungary from 2010 onwards and in Poland after the 2015 elections. Problematic developments occurred as well after the 2018 elections in Slovenia and Czechia, even if the magnitude of the resulting challenges is qualitatively different from those of the two previous cases.

The main questions to be answered thus are: What went wrong? What are the causes of these problems? Did the differences in the institutional design of the CEE polities play a decisive role or are the determinants to be tracked rather in the deeper socio-cultural features of these societies? These questions ought to be answered empirically. The problem we are faced with, however, is that the backsliding began very recently (save in Hungary), with only a few empirical accounts, which still require retesting.

Moreover, the cases of democratic decay in the region differ ontologically. In some cases, the demand side is prominent, with the majority of voters losing faith in the liberal variant of democracy (Hungary). In other polities, we can observe examples of supply-side shifts, with part of the entrenched political elite turning its back on the liberal principles of democracies (Poland). In explaining the backsliding into authoritarianism in the CEE, scholars of the problem ought to focus on the following distinction between various forms of democratic decay: (a) a moderate decline in the quality of democracy, exemplified by deficient functioning of democracy in clearly selected domains; (b) the emergence of a 'hybrid' regime, in which a mixture of functional democratic elements are accompanied by distinctly authoritarian solutions; and (c) the total or almost complete collapse of democracy – a change of the system from democratic to non-democratic, with the establishment of a new equilibrium, new institutions and new rules of the game.

These qualitatively different degrees of backsliding are gradual. While previous theories focused on the 'authoritarian reversals' of popular or elite coups, it is worth theorizing democratic decay in a qualitatively different context. Yet, as suggested in the metaphor of backsliding, the process we are currently seeing in CEE appears to be different from the sudden ruptures and reversals certain democracies experienced during the second half of the 20th century. Instead, we can observe an erosion process in which democracy is undermined gradually by means of a sort of 'salami tactics', whereby, slice by slice, liberal ingredients are cut off from the democratic main body with no visible cut-off point. These developments follow a clear sequential pattern: first the autonomy of the judiciary and the separation of powers is taken care of, with simultaneous attempts to control public media and turn them into a party propaganda machine; then there is an assault on civil servants and erosion of non-partisan norms of public administration; next the rights of assembly and the autonomy of institutions of civil society are constrained; and finally the integrity of election laws are corrupted.

What confuses democratic citizens in the region is that the champions of the change in regime are typically not unknown new challengers from outside the polity, but well-entrenched politicians, at times previous or current incumbents who are able to claim democratic legitimacy for their actions derived from elections. Their key instruments are not military force or plain electoral fraud, but executive aggrandizement that only later on might contribute to electoral manipulation (Bermeo 2016). This is an ontologically novel form of authoritarianism: an endogenous product of CEE elites rather than an exogenous imposition from outside by occupying forces, as was the case after World War II.

Backsliding into authoritarianism – Hungary and Poland: theorizing the new phenomena

The most puzzling question of the CEE democratic decay is that it is precisely the two countries that were the grass-roots movers and first-comers to the transition and which very early on seemed to qualify as consolidated democracies that are the ones currently displaying full-blown backsliding into authoritarianism. Several factors are worth emphasizing and their consequences are worth to be empirically tested.

First, the institutional design of the two countries was as different as possible. Hungary had embarked on the simplest possible configuration: pure parliamentarism, with a single cameral parliament and a weak, indirectly elected president. Poland represented the reverse: bicameralism, with a relatively strong, directly elected president. Fairly early on, the Hungarian party system was institutionalized, with parties as the main political actors, forming two competing blocks, and in the first decade of the 21st century showing what seemed to be a party system cleavage with impressively low single-digit volatility. In fact, in both cases, the blow to democratic quality came at the time when party system stability and voter volatility were the most conducive to democratic quality. Indirectly thus, we ought to rethink the relevance of these indicators for evaluation of democratic quality and their predictive power.

Second, there were other important differences: the economic development and affluence of both societies revealed completely different dynamics, with Poland being a relative success story, overtaking Hungarian GDP per capita in 2013.[3] The Polish case – unlike its Hungarian counterpart, where a clear majority of the population supports either nationalist or clearly xenophobic political options manifested, respectively, by the governing Fidesz or the oppositional

Jobbik parties – shows that electoral accidents happen and that an evident minority of barely one-fifth of the eligible electorate can grant a majoritarian parliamentary position to a single party. In other words, in Poland, the PiS government and the subsequent anti-liberal, clientelistic, anti-constitutional changes introduced have not resulted from a 'demand' from Poles, but rather the dire developments indicate a clear case of 'supply' driven, ideologically motivated conversions that are being implemented from above.

Third, backsliding into authoritarianism in the CEE region, in Poland in particular, is often mistakenly interpreted as a manifestation of the vitality of the *Homo Sovieticus* deeply entrenched in their citizens. The Polish case and the data available show that the sources of the current democratic decay are rather to be found either in the cultural religious legacies of its pre-communist past or in its 'adaptive resourcefulness' under real existing socialism, and not in the socialist blueprint itself. In Poland, a particularly important political role is played by the Catholic Church, which is the foundation for treating the PiS party as a social-coalition based party. Moreover, *cultural lag theory* (Ogburn 1922) directs our attention to the challenges of effective familiarization with the new political and institutional inventions (democratic infrastructure) and the short-term inability of newly democratized citizens to fully adapt to the opportunities offered and their constraints (for details, see Markowski 2018c). The role of the church and the inadequacy of the political culture, its lack of deeply rooted liberal norms, has certainly played a role in both countries. Low social capital, in Poland in particular, further impacts the current democratic malfunctioning and allows the clientelistic mechanism to thrive.

Fourth, the mode of exit from authoritarianism matters. The classic assumption that 'pacted' transitions (like those in Poland and Hungary in the late 1980s) are more likely to be conducive to the successful consolidation of democracy might overlook the fact that the lack of a clear 'critical juncture' separating the *ancien régime* from the new one causes confusion among the population as to the rules of the new game. It is necessary to reiterate Poland's status as the 'first-comer' to the transition. Poland – in contrast to other CEE countries, save Hungary – saw each of these phases implemented over a prolonged period, and their overlapping. Yet, the ultimate result of this phenomenon has created a culture of rule negotiability, norm flexibility, the growth of a pragmatic instrumentalization of the political domain and – if you will – a mood of 'temporariness' of the enacted solutions, in particular because of the extremely high uncertainty as to the Kremlin's veto power. Ultimately, it seems likely that the simple answer to the question as to whether *ruptura* or *pactada* is a more promising way out of authoritarianism is complicated by the fact that average citizens need to see a clear 'critical juncture', separating the old from the new. The blurring of such political thresholds seems unconducive to the ultimate success of democratic consolidation. Both the Polish and Hungarian cases are clear indications of the problem (Markowski 2018c).

Fifth, the main question of whether the de facto coup against the constitutional order in the post-2015 period in Polish political history is to be treated ontologically more as a result of fate or choice at this point remains unanswered due to, on the one hand, contradictory developments and their likely causes, and on the other, the currently limited reliable empirical data.

Tentative conclusions on the main challenges

Among the many political challenges facing the CEE region, three deserve emphasis. First, are the CEE populist parties similar to their Western counterparts and is the democratic backsliding in the East ontologically similar to the populist challenge in the West? Second, what is the CEE countries' role in the European Union and how serious a threat are they to its goals and operations? Third, what are the likely future scenarios?

Let me address them briefly, by pointing to the key issues.

(1) The new millennium witnessed an upsurge in the popularity of populist, xenophobic, radical (mainly right-wing, but occasionally also left-wing) parties, ranging from Vlaams Blok via Dansk Folkenparti to Front National. These older radical-populist parties were entrenched in the past European nationalist politics. More recent Western parties from the same basket (Swedish Democrats, True Finns, Dutch PVV) are more liberal and democratic as well as less radical, distancing themselves from primitive biological racism or primitive border-driven identities because their roots are liberal. Their leaders (mostly) believe they are the true solution to the current problems of liberal democracies and effective correction to its (allegedly visible) democratic failures, and in particular the quality of representation.

The 'supply' of such parties in the CEE political landscape is by no means less complex. Parties that evidently resemble the old Western European xenophobic models in the CEE region are the Bulgarian Ataka, the Hungarian Jobbik (certainly until the 2018 campaign), the Slovak SNS and the PRM – the Greater Romania Party. Their program is distinctly xenophobic, at times bordering on nativism. The region was also populated by other non-liberal democratic phenomena, such as the League of Polish Families (LPR) or Self-Defence (Samoobrona), the Hungarian MIEP and the Czech Republicans, which rapidly emerged and equally swiftly disappeared (Markowski and Tucker 2010).

Were we to look at the CEE region's 'political and party supply' via fourfold taxonomy lenses (created by juxtaposing populist and nationalist dimensions), a clear dominance of the nationalist element over the populist one would be revealed. To be sure, among the anti-systemic, radical parties (uncritically labelled 'populist'), most of them share a distinct appeal to the 'nation' and a fairly horizontal view of politics, while a few of them (those whose dominant element is addressed to the 'people' en masse) are accompanied by a vertical conflicting cleavage. The Bulgarian Ataka, the Polish LPR, the Hungarian Jobbik and, earlier in the 1990s, the Polish KPN, the Hungarian MIEP and the Slovak SNS are cases in point. A caveat, however, is due here: CEE nationalism (at times closer to patriotism, at times to racial xenophobia) has moderate links to what has been the main concern of Western European 'populist, far-right' parties like Vlaams Belang, the PVV in the Netherlands, the Danish Peoples Party, which focused mainly on globalization issues, the threat of Islam and (in a way) a neoliberal approach to the economy, redistribution, and civic concerns. In short, Western counterparts are not prone to territorial nationalism and/or biological racism, which can evidently be traced in Jobbik's, Ataka's or SNS's programs and the public appearances of their leaders.

Finally, the major problem with the backsliding towards authoritarianism in CEE, in Hungary and Poland in particular, but also (though to a lesser extent) in most of the other CEE countries (save Estonia, Latvia and Slovenia) is that the widespread blow to democratic principles came from the well-established part of the incumbent elite present in the particular country's politics right from the beginning of the democratic opening in 1989. Moreover, it happened *after* their electoral success under democratic rules of the game. After installing themselves as single-party governments, their 'salami tactics' of cutting off a slice of the democratic institutional construction each week, from media pluralism, via curtailing the operation of constitutional courts, to outright violations of constitutional principles and EU norms. This process has been coupled with lip-service being paid to democratic credentials, embellished by sham ultra-legalist narrative (Markowski 2018c; Magyar 2018). Briefly, it is hard to imagine the dire developments in the CEE occurring in this form in any of the (so-far) stable Western democracies, even in those undergoing a severe economic downturn, like Portugal or Italy.

(2) The European Union itself is in crisis, without the specific additional contributions of the new entrants from CEE. Yet, once void of EU conditionalities proper, several CEE governments have decided to unveil their Eurosceptic tendencies. It is the overlap of both processes that creates the real threat. Moreover, the threat is magnified by external players: the expected ones (Putin's Russia) and surprising ones (United States). So far, and because of Brexit and other southern European negative developments – mainly economic – less attention has been paid to the CEE troublemakers. The EU's reaction to the authoritarian inclinations in Hungary and Poland is considered by many to be slow and cautious. These tendencies in the European peripheries in themselves do not create a real and present danger to the core of the EU, nonetheless the overlapping of numerous threats could destabilize the Union.

(3) The political future is always difficult to predict; the current moment of multidimensional, internal and external challenges make it even more tough. One event, however, seems to be of utmost importance for the political future and the relative importance of the CEE countries, for their policies and macrochoices. The results of the 2019 elections to the European Parliament and the likely relative gains of the Eurosceptic camp will set our political future. In this case, some kind of grand coalition of the mainstream party families (the peoples' and the socialist camp) will be needed to continue the pan-EU policies along the lines envisaged, for instance, by Emmanuel Macron, and a new logic and quality of European politics is likely to emerge. The strength of the populist contenders will further marginalize the EU's Eastern periphery, as it will force the EU core to intensify and deepen their ties.

Notes

1 The Pedersen Index is a recognized key measure of voter volatility – the shifts in support for political parties in a given party system between two consecutive elections. It measures the aggregate level volatility, not the individual one, yet it is a net change within the electoral party system resulting from individual vote transfers. The index is calculated by summing the absolute values of all gains and all losses by parties, and dividing this total by 2.

2 This description predominantly applies to the five core CEE countries: Czechia, Hungary, Slovakia, Poland and Slovenia.

3 In 1990, Poland had barely 60% of the Hungarian GDP per capita. Polish economic success has been visible during the whole quarter of a century transition and (in relative terms) even more so during the eight years of crisis (2007–15). This success was not limited to GDP growth alone; it was accompanied by a clear decline in income inequalities (GINI down from 0.36 in the early 2000s to about 0.29 in 2015, single-digit unemployment, a significant increase in life expectancy and the like; for details, see Markowski 2016c).

References

Agh, A. (2015). Radical party system changes in five East-Central European states. *Baltic Journal of Political Science*, 4, 23–49.

Andrews, J., & R. Bairett. (2014). Institutions and the stabilization of party systems in the new democracies of Central and Eastern Europe. *Electoral Studies*, 33, 307–321.

Bermeo, N. (2016). On democratic backsliding. *Journal of Democracy*, 27(1), 5–19.

Bielasiak, J. (2002). The institutionalisation of electoral and party systems in postcommunist states. *Comparative Politics*, 1.

Brug, van der W., & de Vreese, C.H. (eds.). (2016). *(Un)intended Consequences of European Parliamentary Elections*. Oxford: Oxford University Press, pp. 125–147.

Bugaric, B. (2008). Populism, liberal democracy, and the rule of law in Central and Eastern Europe. *Communist and Post-communist Studies*, 41(2), 191–203.

Bunce, V. (2002). The Return of the Left and Democratic Consolidation in Poland and Hungary. In: A. Bozoki & J. Ishiyama (eds.), *The Communist Successor Parties of Central and Eastern Europe*. New York: M.E. Sharpe, Inc.

Ekiert, G., & Kubik, J. (1998). Contentious politics in new democracies: East Germany, Hungary, Poland and Slovakia. *World Politics*, 50(4), 547–581.

Ekiert, G., Kubik, J., & Vachudova, M.A. (2007). Democracy in the Post-Communist world: An unending quest. *East European Politics and Societies*, 21(1), 7–30.

Elgie, R., & Moestrup, S. (2008). *Semi-presidentialism in Central and Eastern Europe*. Manchester: Manchester University Press.

Enyedi, Z., & Casal Bertoa, F. (2018). Institutionalization and De-institutionalization in Post-communist Party Systems. *East European Politics and Societies and Cultures*, 32(3), 422–450.

Ersson, S. (2012). Electoral Volatility in Europe. Assessments and Potential Explanations for Estimate Differences. Elections, Public opinion and Parties (EPOP) Conference Paper. Oxford University, September, pp. 7–9.

Fish, S. (2006). Stronger legislatures, stronger democracies. *Journal of Democracy*, 17(1).

Frey, T. (1997). A Politics of Institutional Choice: Post-communist Presidencies. *Comparative Political Studies*, 30, 523–552.

Gallagher, M. (2013). Election Data Indices at http://www.tcd.ie/Political Science/staff/michael_gallagher/ELSystems?index.php

Ganev, V.I. (2013). Post-accession Hooliganism: Democratic Governance in Bulgaria and Romania After 2007. *East European Politics and Societies and Cultures*, 27, 26–44.

Gherghina, S. (2014). *Party Organization and Electoral Volatility in Central and Eastern Europe: Enhancing Voter Loyalty*. London: Routledge.

Grzymala-Busse, A. (2007). *Rebuilding Leviathan: Party Competition and State Exploitation in Post-Communist Democracies*. Cambridge: Cambridge University Press.

Higley, J., Kullberg. J.S., & Pakulski, J. (1996). The persistence of postcommunist elites. *Journal of Democracy*, 7(2), 133–147.

Howard, M.M. (2003). *The Weakness of Civil Society in Post-Communist Europe*. Cambridge: Cambrige University Press.

Huntington, S. (1991). *The Third Wave: Democratization in the Late Twentieth Century*. Norman: University of Oklahoma Press.

Kitschelt, H. (1992). The formation of party systems in East Central Europe. *Politics and Society*, 20, 7–50.

Kitschelt, H. (2001). Accounting for Post-communist Regime Diversity. What Counts as a Good Cause. In: R. Markowski & E. Wnuk-Lipiński (eds.), *Transformative Paths in Central and Eastern Europe*. Warszawa: Instytut Studiów Politycznych PAN.

Kitschelt, H., Mansfeldova, Z., Markowski, R., & Toka, G. (1999). *Post-communist Party Systems: Competition, Representation and Inter-party Cooperation*. Cambridge: Cambridge University Press.

Knutsen, O. (2013). Structural Determinants of Party Choice. In: W. Mueller & H.M. Narud (eds.), *Party Governance and Party Democracy*. New York: Springer, pp. 175–204.

Kotnarowski, M., & Markowski, R. (2014). Political Preferences in times of crisis: economic voting in the Polish 2011 elections. *Acta Politica,* 49, 431–461.

Krastev, I. (2007). The strange death of the liberal consensus. *Journal of Democracy*, 18(4), 56–63.

Kreko, P., & Enyedi, Z. (2018). Explaining Eastern Europe: Orban's laboratory of illiberalism. *Journal of Democracy*, 29(3).

Lewis, P., & Markowski, R. (eds.) (2011). *Europeanising Party Politics? Comparative Perspectives on Central and Eastern Europe*. Manchester: Manchester University Press.

Lijphart, A. (1992). Democratization and constitutional choices in Czecho-Slovakia, Hungary and Poland, 1989–1991. *Journal of Theoretical Politics*, 4, 207–223.

Linz, J.J., & Stepan, A. (1996). *Problems of Democratic Transition and Consolidation. Southern Europe, South America, and Post-Communist Europe*. Baltimore: The Johns Hopkins University Press.

Magyar, B. (2018). *Węgry. Anatomia państwa mafijnego*. Warszawa: MAGAM.

Mainwaring, S., & Scully, T. (1995). *Building Democratic Institutions: Party Systems in Latin America*. Stanford, CA: Stanford University Press.

Mainwaring, S., & Zocco, E. (2007). Political sequences and the stabilization of inter-party competition. *Party Politics*, 13(2): 155–178.

Mair, P. (1997). *Party System Change: Approaches and Interpretations*. Oxford: Clarendon Press.

Markowski, R. (September 1997). Political parties and ideological spaces in East Central Europe. *Communist and Post-Communist Studies*, 30(3).

Markowski, R. (2001). Party System Institutionalization in New Democracies: Poland – a Trend-setter With No Followers. In: P.G. Lewis (ed.), *Party Development and Democratic Change in Post-Communist Europe: The First Decade*. London: Frank Cass.

Markowski, R. (2006). Political accountability and institutional design in new democracies. *International Journal of Sociology*, 36: 45–75.

Markowski, R. (2007). Political accountability and representation: Theoretical assumptions and empirical measuring. In: J. Niżnik & N. Ryabinska (eds.), *Political Accountability: Conceptual, Theoretical and Practical Orientations*. Wyd. IFiS PAN, Warsaw

Markowski, R. (2015). On Democracy: Normative and Empirical Models in Central and Eastern Europe. In: J. Zielonka (ed.), *Media and Politics in New Democracies: Europe in a Comparative Perspective*. Oxford: Oxford University Press, pp. 37–58.

Markowski, R. (2016a). Determinants of Democratic Legitimacy: Liberal Democracy and Social Justice. In: M. Ferrin & H. Kriesi (eds.), *How Europeans View and Evaluate Democracy?* Oxford: Oxford University Press, pp. 257–282.

Markowski, R. (2016b). How European elections affect national party systems: On the survival of newly established parties. In: W. van der Brug & C.H. de Vreese, (eds.), *(Un) intended Consequences of European Parliamentary Elections*. Oxford: Oxford University Press, pp. 125–147.

Markowski, R. (2016c). The Polish Parliamentary Election of 2015: A free and fair election that results in unfair political consequences. *West European Politics*, 1–12.

Markowski, R. (January 2017). Transformation Experiences in Central and Eastern Europe. The Case of Poland in Comparative Perspective, *International Policy Analysis*, Ebert Stiftung.

Markowski, R. (2018a). Populism and Nationalism in CEE: Two of a Perfect Pair? *To be published in a Report entitled When Populism meets Nationalism*. Milano: ISPI.

Markowski, R. (2018b). Wprowadzenie. In: B. Magyar Węgry (ed.), *Anatomia państwa mafijnego*. Warszawa: Magam [(in Polish) 'Introduction,' In: *Hungary. Anatomy of a Mafia State*].

Markowski, R. (2018c). Backsliding into Authoritarian Clientelism: The Case of Poland. In: P. Guasti & Z. Mansfeldova (eds.), *Democracy under Stress: Changing Perspectives on Democracy, Governance and their Measurement*. Prague: Institute of Sociology, CAS.

Markowski, R., & Tucker, J. (2010). Euroskepticism and the emergence of political parties in Poland. *Party Politics*, 16(4), 523–548.

Markowski, R., Cześnik, M., & Kotnarowski, M. (2015). *Demokracja – Gospodarka – Polityka*. Warszawa: Wydawnictwo Naukowe SCHOLAR.

Ogburn, W. (1922). *Social Change with Respect to Culture and Original Nature*. New York: B.W. Huebsch.

Pierson, P. (2004). *Politics in Time: History, Institutions, and Social Analysis*. Princeton: Princeton University Press.

Powell, E.N., & Tucker, J. (2014). Revisiting electoral volatility in post-communist countries: new data, new results, new approacher. *British Journal of Political Science*, 44(1), 123–147.

Reif, K., & Schmitt, H. (1980). Nine second-order national elections: A conceptual framework for the analysis of European election results. *European Journal of Political Research*, 8, 3–44.

Roberts, A. (2008). Hyperaccountability: Economic voting in Central and Eastern Europe. *Electoral Studies*, 27(3), 533–546.

Roberts, A. (2009). *The Quality of Democracy in Eastern Europe: Public Preferences and Policy Reforms*. Cambridge: Cambridge University Press.

Rovny, J., & Edwards, E.E. (2012). Struggle over dimensionality of party competition in Western and Eastern Europe. *East European Politics and Societies*, 26(1), 56–74.

Sedelius, T., &Mashtaler, O. (2012). Two decades of semi-presidentialism: Issues of intra-executive conflict in Central and Eastern Europe 1991–2011. *East European Politics*, 29(2), 109–134.

Tavits, M. (2007). Clarity of responsibility and corruption. *American Journal of Political Science* 51(1), 218–229.

Tavits, M. (2013). *Post-Communist Democracies and Party Organization*. Cambridge: Cambridge University Press.

Tóka, G. (1995). Parties and electoral choices in East-Central Europe. In: Pridham, G., & Lewis, P. G. (eds.), *Stabilising Fragile Democracies: Comparing New Party Systems in Southern and Eastern Europe*. New York: Routledge, pp. 100–125.

3 Local government

Progress in decentralisation

Paweł Swianiewicz

Introduction

Almost three decades ago, Jens Hesse and Jim Sharpe (1991) observed that in the first years of political transformation, decentralisation was often referred to as one of the recipes for increasing the efficiency of the public sector in most countries. Due to historical experience, it was often possible to see the 'automatic' identification of centralisation with authoritarianism. Consequently, decentralisation was almost equated with democratisation. The observation cited here in its original formulation referred to Greece, Spain and Portugal, which had (at the time the quoted study was written) relatively recently got rid of authoritarian regimes.

But their observation is also very accurate for describing the situation in the eastern part of Europe in the early 1990s. Over ten years ago, Coulson and Campbell (2006: 556) approached this issue in a similar way, saying that

> in most of the transitional countries a De Tocquevillian myth of localism had flourished in opposition circles in the years preceding the fall of Communism, in which local self-government was to be the incarnation of civil society and everything that the regime was not.

This attitude was strengthened, at least verbally, by the belief often found in academic literature (e.g. Sharpe 1973; Shah 1998; Ebel and Yilmaz 2003), that decentralisation has a direct positive impact on economic development and the effectiveness of performing public tasks.

Therefore, not surprisingly, at the beginning of political transformation in the 1990s, restoration of democratic local government was an important part of the political agenda of virtually all countries in Central and Eastern Europe. In the common opinion, the democratisation of the state and transformation towards a market economy would not be complete without deep reforms and democratisation on a local level. It is enough to mention that in Poland, the first fully democratic elections after the Second World War were the local elections on 27 May 1990. A few months later, democratic elections to the restored local governments were also organized in Czechia, Hungary and Slovakia, soon followed by other countries of the region.

But we also know that, in practice, in many countries this support for decentralisation was quite shallow and exclusively verbal in nature (Zentai and Peteri 2002), and the local government systems resulting from the changes that took place at that time are very much diversified (Swianiewicz 2014). The focus of this chapter is a more systematic analysis of this diversity and the changes taking place in this area. As is demonstrated further in this chapter, in individual countries local government has gained different levels of importance in national political systems and in the delivery of local public services. Some countries of the region have remained very centralized, while others may be classified as being some of the most decentralized in Europe. Moreover, the picture cannot always be taken for granted, nor is it always stable for longer periods. As we will see, during the last decade or so there have been examples of radical re-centralisation or deepening of decentralisation reforms.

This chapter starts with a discussion of territorial organisation, and in particular of territorial reforms at both the local and regional level, which have been a common feature for most countries of the region. Subsequently, we look at two dimensions defined by Heinelt and Hlepas (2006) as key characteristics of local government architecture: vertical and horizontal power relations. The former includes the variation and dynamics at the level of local autonomy. In the latter, we concentrate on the position of municipal mayors vis-à-vis local councils and other important actors in local politics.

The main focus is on the municipal tier of government, which is common to all of the analysed countries. However, occasionally the regional government structures are discussed as well. As in the remaining chapters, the analysis concentrates on the 11 countries of the region which have become members of the European Union, but sometimes a comparison with other Eastern European countries is necessary in order to stress the relationship between European integration and the process of decentralisation.

Territorial reforms after the 1990 political turnover

The current picture of territorial organisation in the countries of the studied region is highly diversified. The relatively small countries of Estonia, Latvia, Lithuania and Slovenia, as well as the considerably larger Bulgaria, have currently one (municipal) tier of sub-national government. The remaining countries of the region have either three-tier (Poland) or two-tier (Croatia, Czechia, Hungary, Romania and Slovakia) structures. The upper tiers of government have undergone significant changes during recent decades. In Poland, the three-tier structure, including 16 relatively large regions replacing 49 smaller semi-regional units existing before the reform, was in place by the beginning of 1999 (with all legislation completed in 1998). The issue of future integration with the EU was often used by the proponents of the 1998 reform, who argued that only large regions could be economically competitive on the future European market and become stronger partners for their Western European counterparts, especially for the German *Länder*. Some of the proponents claimed that regional reform was one of the conditions of access to EU structural funds, but this claim was not entirely justified. And, as Hughes et al. (2003: 82) notice, *the final shape of the reform should be seen as an inherently endogenous development.*

Similar reforms were soon introduced (2000) in Czechia and Slovakia, where the self-governing *kraj* level supplemented the structure of sub-national governments (14 regions in Czechia and eight in Slovakia; Illner 2011; Čapková 2011). In Bulgaria, regional reform has never been implemented, despite it being envisaged in the constitution (Kandeva 2001). In Hungary and Romania, the upper tier of sub-national government (*megye* and *judets*, respectively) has not changed its spatial shape since the 1990 turnover, although at least in Hungary its role has been marginalized (Horváth 2000).

The shape of regional reforms has had important implications for regional policies. The big difference between Polish and other countries' upper level of sub-national government is that Poland is the only country of the region in which it has been decided that the administrative region would become an European NUTS2 level region. Since NUTS2 is a basic unit for European regional policy, this has had major consequences for the regionalisation of cohesion policy implementation in Poland. It has allowed the gradually growing role of regional governments, strengthening their position in relation to both the central and the local (municipal) tiers (the latter being increasingly dependent on the region's decisions on allocation of EU funds to local projects). The process may be described as 'creeping decentralisation', in which none of the individual changes was very dramatic, but taken together they have transferred a significant share of discretion over regional policy making from the central to the regional level. In none of the remaining countries of the region has the elected regional government played any important role in the preparation and implementation of EU-funded operational programmes supporting regional development. In the 2007–13 perspective, there have been regional operational programmes in Czechia, Hungary and Slovakia (abandoned in Hungary in the 2014–20 budget), but those programmes were managed by special purpose authorities including representatives of central and regional level governments, not by the elected regional authorities. A management structure similar to the Polish model has been considered in Romania, but the relevant reform has not materialized so far.

However, the most dynamic have been territorial changes on the municipal level. Here, we can clearly distinguish between two phases.

In the first phase, after the political turnover of 1989 and the early 1990s, several countries of Central and Eastern Europe experienced considerable fragmentation reforms resulting from the bottom-up splitting of municipalities, leading to an increasing number of municipal government units. This was often a bottom-up reaction to the forced amalgamation in the earlier period of the communist regime (implemented without any democratic consultations). After 1990, decentralisation and local self-government in some countries of the region were understood as being almost synonymous with the 'right' of each (even the smallest) settlement unit to have its own, separate local government.

Attempts to sustain larger units were considered almost to be 'coups' against local autonomy. Such attitudes towards territorial fragmentation could be seen especially in Croatia, Czechia, Hungary, Slovakia and Slovenia,[1] and also to a much smaller extent in Romania and Poland, and several countries which emerged after the collapse of Yugoslavia. In subsequent years (including after 2000), individual cases of municipal splits have also been quite common in several countries in the eastern part of the continent. This is illustrated by the data in Table 3.1. In many countries, the process of fragmentation has been additionally strengthened by demographic depopulation (especially visible in Bulgaria, Romania and the Baltic states).

In the second phase, after 2000, several governments successfully implemented municipal amalgamation reforms, hoping that it would help to reduce costs of operation and increase capacity for service delivery. This has followed the more general pan-European trend (Tavares 2018; Swianiewicz 2018) but has been clearly visible in Central and Eastern Europe as well. The tendency has begun from countries beyond the focus of this volume (Macedonia in 2002, Georgia in 2006, later followed by Albania in 2015, and Ukraine as well as Armenia in 2017), but it has also appeared in the amalgamation reforms in Latvia (2009) and most recently in Estonia (2017).

Currently, territorial organisation of the municipal tier in the analysed countries is highly diversified (see Figure 3.1). On the one extreme there is Lithuania, with an average municipal population close to 50,000 residents, and on the other there are Czechia, Slovakia and Hungary with close to 80% of local governments having fewer than 1,000 residents, and several units with fewer than 100 residents, incapable of delivering any significant local public services.

In several countries (Croatia, Czechia, Hungary, Slovakia and Slovenia), territorial fragmentation is commonly seen as a significant problem, but at the

Table 3.1 The changing number of municipal governments in Central and Eastern Europe after 1990

	Number of municipal governments						
	1990	*1994*	*1998*	*2002*	*2006*	*2010*	*2014*
Bulgaria	279	255	262	264	264	264	264
Croatia	172	499	545	550	556	556	556
Czechia	4,100	6,230	6,242	6,254	6,248	6,250	6,253
Estonia	255	254	247	241	227	226	213
Hungary	1,381	3,137	3,154	3,158	3,168	3,175	3,177
Latvia	573	568	566	548	527	118	119
Lithuania	58	58	58	60	60	60	60
Poland	2,383	2,475	2,489	2,491	2,478	2,479	2,479
Romania	2,948	2,948	2,948	2,966	3,174	3,181	3,181
Slovakia	2,826	2,858	2,878	2,891	2,891	2,890	2,890
Slovenia	62	158	203	204	221	221	223

Source: Swianiewicz, Gendźwiłł, and Zardi (2017).

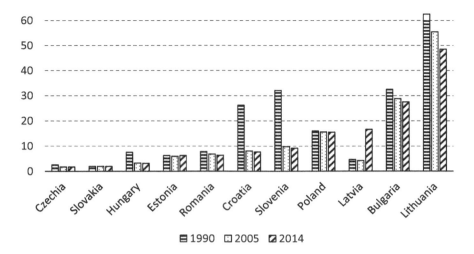

Figure 3.1 Average population size of municipalities (in thousands)
Source: Swianiewicz, Gendźwiłł, and Zardi (2017).

same time relevant reforms are not considered politically viable. There is only a system of relatively weak incentives for voluntary mergers, which only sporadically results in actual territorial changes. In most of these countries, it is expected that semi-voluntary inter-municipal cooperation may help to cope with the weaknesses related to the very small size of local government units (see, e.g. Klimovsky et al. 2014). But as recent studies suggest (e.g. Pano Puey et al. 2018 for Spain), very small local governments lack the organisational capacity to effectively enter and monitor inter-municipal arrangements. Recent reforms in Hungary (for details, see the next section of this chapter) demonstrate that territorial fragmentation may be used as a handy excuse for proponents of re-centralisation of the country.

Vertical power relations – the level of municipal autonomy

The frame for empirical analysis

This section is based on data from the Local Autonomy Index (LAI) project implemented in 2014–15 at the request of the European Commission.[2] In earlier publications, measuring the level of decentralisation was usually based on simplified indirect measures, most often related to the system of financing local governments. In this context, either the share of local government budgets in GDP or in total public expenditure was used (see, e.g. Blöchliger and King 2006). Similar measures were also used to describe the diversity of decentralisation in the countries of south-eastern Europe (e.g. Levitas 2016). Some authors used slightly more complex indicators based on the size and structure of budget revenues and expenses (e.g. Martinez-Vaques and Timofeev 2011). In some cases, the analyses were supplemented by an attempt to measure the discretion in decisions concerning delivery of individual services (Blöchliger 2011). A more sophisticated distinction of the three dimensions of central-local relations (function, discretion in decision-making and access to national policies) was made by Page and Goldsmith (1987), but their discussion did not lead to quantitative measurements. The Local Autonomy Index (LAI) refers to the municipal level and is a more complex index based on the expert measurement of 11 variables (some of them being aggregates of many detailed indicators),[3] taking into account the scope of policies local governments are responsible for, discretion in implementation of these policies, and financial autonomy (related to tax autonomy, structure of inter-governmental transfers and borrowing autonomy) as well as several measures related to organisational and political autonomy. The index has been calculated separately for each year between 1990 and 2014 in 39 European countries. The list of countries covers all 11 countries in our main focus, as well as a few other countries of Eastern Europe (Albania, Georgia, Macedonia, Moldova, Serbia, and Ukraine). Due to limited space, in this section we will consider only to a minimal extent indicators referring to individual countries. Instead, the main attention will be focused on the entire region and pre-defined clusters of countries.

The empirical analysis concerns three dimensions:

1   Differences in the level of local autonomy within and among the studied group of countries. One of the claims to be tested concerns the gradual convergence of European local government systems.
2   The relationship between the degree of decentralisation (local autonomy) and the processes of European integration. The most popular opinion is that European integration of new Member States required more radical decentralisation than in the countries less advanced in EU accession process. To some extent, this claim is confirmed by the efforts made by the countries of the region to become members of the Council of Europe and the impact of the ratification of the European Charter of Local Governments. But, as Keating and Hughes (2003) indicate, the impact of the European Union on decentralisation was much less clear than it is often assumed. It can be argued that a relationship between the process of integration with the European Union and decentralisation actually exists, but the causal relationship is rather the opposite. It was not the EU that exerted pressure in this respect, but countries implementing more radical reforms, including decentralisation reforms, were ready for membership of the European institutions earlier than the rest of the region.
3   The relationship between the size of municipalities, territorial reforms and the scope of local autonomy. There is widespread opinion that territorial consolidation (the merging of small municipalities) promotes the transfer

of a wider range of tasks to local governments and supports greater local autonomy (see e.g. Page and Goldsmith 1987; Bours 1993; Newton 1992). We will try to find empirical evidence to support this claim.

In relation to these three general theses, six detailed hypotheses were formulated:

> H1: The index of local autonomy in the countries of Central and Eastern Europe was much lower than in the 'old European Union countries' in the first years of political transformation, but later this difference gradually decreased.

This hypothesis refers, on the one hand, to the centralist heritage of the system prevailing before 1990, and on the other to a more general thesis about the convergence of European local government systems.

> H2: Changes in the value of the index were significantly faster in the countries of Central and Eastern Europe than in more stable western democracies. These differences were particularly pronounced in the nineties.
>
> H3: The trend of gradually increasing local autonomy in Central and Eastern Europe did not concern all the analysed variables equally. In particular, the difference between the eastern and western parts of the continent was visible longer with regard to financial autonomy.
>
> H4: The pace of growth of local autonomy was different in individual countries and was related to the processes of European integration.
>
> H5: The growth trend of the local autonomy index has been stopped, and sometimes even reversed, in the last decade, which was related to the global economic crisis after 2008. The tendency towards more strict control of the activities of local governments was a response to this crisis in many countries.

The claim about the relationship between the economic crisis and re-centralisation was formulated, for example, by Hlepas (2016). He points out that this shift towards reducing local autonomy appeared primarily in countries that had a long tradition of centralisation. In the more uncertain environment, with which every crisis is associated, there is a shift towards historically established forms of behaviour. Nor should we forget that tighter control of local governments was sometimes demanded by international financial institutions, in particular the International Monetary Fund (IMF).

> H6: The index of local autonomy does not show a strong correlation with the average size of municipalities in the country. Furthermore, the territorial amalgamation reforms do not have a clear impact on the increase of local autonomy.

The justification of this hypothesis refers to earlier studies, suggesting that decentralisation as a result of territorial reforms often remains solely in the sphere of verbal declarations, and that the actual level of autonomy is more determined by political will than by the objective environment supporting the transfer of new tasks (Swianiewicz and Mielczarek 2010; Swianiewicz 2015).

For the needs of empirical verification (in particular of hypothesis 4), the analysed countries were divided into the following groups:

1   New EU countries that joined the EU in 2004 (Czechia, Estonia, Lithuania, Latvia, Poland, Slovakia, Slovenia, Hungary). This group is hereinafter referred to as 'NMS 2004'.
2   Countries that joined the European Union after 2004 (Bulgaria, Croatia, Romania). This group is hereinafter referred to as 'NMS 2008–12'.

The next two 'control groups' serve as a point of reference for the countries in our main focus:

3   Central and Eastern European countries that are not members of the European Union (Albania, Georgia, Macedonia, Moldova, Serbia, Ukraine). This group is hereinafter referred to as 'Other CEE'.
4   'Old Member States' of the European Union (Austria, Belgium, Denmark, Finland, France, Germany, Greece, Ireland, Italy, Luxembourg, the Netherlands, Portugal, Spain, Sweden and the United Kingdom) as well as Switzerland and Norway. This group is hereinafter referred to as 'EU15+'.

Local government policy scope – the general picture

As elsewhere in Europe, sub-national governments in the studied region are responsible for several public services which are essential for the everyday life of citizens. First of all, municipalities deal with the major metabolic functions of cities, related for example to provision of water and sewage systems, waste management, public transport, roads, street lighting, parks and green areas. The main variation among countries is related to responsibility for social services, such as preschool and school education, health care and social protection. This variation is reflected in the simple measure of functional decentralisation, which is expressed by the share of sub-national spending in national GDP (see Table 3.2).

Empirical results

We begin our presentation of empirical results with a general picture of LAI index variation in all European countries (see Figure 3.2). The Scandinavian countries and Switzerland are 'champions of decentralisation'. As for the position of Central and Eastern European countries, it is strongly diversified. Poland is ranked eighth, with the highest level of municipal autonomy in the region. A large group of countries (Czechia, Lithuania, Bulgaria, Estonia, Slovakia, Croatia, Latvia, Romania) does not differ much from the average for the whole

Table 3.2 Sub-national government spending as a proportion of GDP in New Member States from Central and Eastern Europe

	2006	2017
Poland	13.6%	13.4%
Croatia	12.3%	11.5%
Czechia	12.2%	10.7%
Latvia	9.9%	10.1%
Estonia	9.2%	9.6%
Romania	8.6%	8.9%
Slovenia	8.6%	8.2%
Lithuania	8.4%	7.7%
Bulgaria	6.4%	7.1%
Slovakia	6.5%	6.9%
Hungary	12.7%	6.3%
EU-28 average	11.0%	10.6%

Source: Eurostat statistics. As is clear from the table, the situation in most of the countries has been fairly stable in this respect, with relatively narrow changes within the last decade. The only exception to this rule is Hungary, with a dramatic drop in the role of local governments in service provision during the last few years. This case is related to re-centralisation reforms introduced by Viktor Orbán's government, and will be discussed in more detail later on in this chapter.

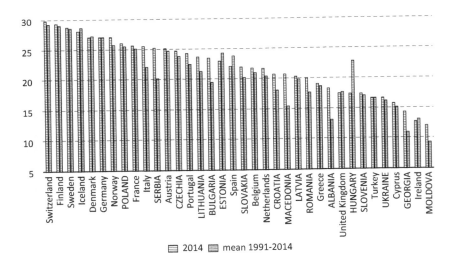

☰ 2014   ▦ mean 1991-2014

Figure 3.2 Values of Local Autonomy Index

Source: Own calculations based on LAI project data.

of Europe. However, Hungary and Slovenia, together with a group of 'non-EU' Eastern European countries, are among ten European countries with the lowest LAI values.

The situation of Hungary, which in the light of earlier publications (e.g. Swianiewicz 2014) was one of the most decentralized countries in Central and

Eastern Europe, requires special comment. The change which has taken place in this country is well illustrated by the difference between the indicator for 2014 and the average for the entire period of 1990–2014, visible in Figure 3.2. The figure suggests that the re-centralisation process in Hungary has had no equivalence in any other European country during last 25 years. Indeed, the reforms introduced by the Orbán government a few years ago deprived Hungarian municipalities of a significant part of their tasks as well as a large portion of their financial autonomy (see Palne-Kovacs et al. 2016; Hajnal and Rosta 2014). This example is a good illustration of the fact that decentralisation is not a one-way process and is not given once and for all. The direction of changes in Hungary is, however, the exception rather than the rule. As can be seen in Figure 3.2, in most other countries of the region (except Estonia), the tendency has been quite the opposite: the value of the index in the last year covered by the study was higher than the average for the whole period. This dominant trend can be seen more clearly in Figure 3.3, showing changes in the predefined groups of countries.

The data presented in Figure 3.3 confirm some of the hypotheses formulated earlier in this chapter. First of all, the difference between the countries of Western Europe and Central and Eastern Europe has decreased in the period covered by the analysis (H1), and this trend has resulted from the growing level of the index as a consequence of decentralisation reforms carried out in several Central and Eastern European countries.

Second, the pace of change has been different for individual groups of countries. The increase of the LAI index first began (back in the early 1990s) in countries that became members of the European Union in 2004 (H4). In other groups, changes started a little later, and in non-EU countries more serious decentralisation reforms did not take place until the turn of the

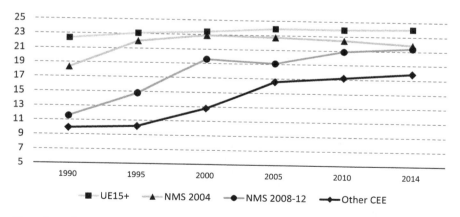

Figure 3.3 Values of LAI in groups of countries

Source: Own calculations based on LAI project data.

millennium, and their level of local autonomy is still significantly lower than in other groups. However, the data in Figure 3.3 does not confirm hypothesis 5: the crisis of 2008 did not lead to widespread decline in the autonomy index. If we look at individual countries, we can see such a drop only in Hungary, Estonia, Latvia and Czechia (apart from Hungary, the drop was relatively small), but not in other countries. Nevertheless, the relationship between the depth of the economic crisis and increasing central control over local governments can be seen more clearly if we take into account the variable measuring local autonomy in relation to borrowing policies. Among all 39 European countries covered by the LAI research, a decline of this indicator after 2008 could be observed in seven countries (including three in the eastern part of the continent: Georgia, Slovenia and Hungary). The decline occurred in more than one-third of the countries in which the GDP fell in 2008–12. Among the 22 countries recording GDP growth in this period, a decrease in the scope of autonomy in relation to local government debt took place only in one.

Tables 3.3 and 3.4 present the rate of changes in the financial autonomy index in individual groups of countries. They clearly confirm hypothesis 2. Changes in the local autonomy have been much faster in Central and Eastern Europe than in the much more stable countries of Western Europe. These differences were particularly large in the last decade of the 20th century, but they have continued to persist more recently. There have also been clear differences between particular groups of countries in the CEE region. In countries that

Table 3.3 Average pace of changes of LAI in different groups of countries

	1990–95	1995–2000	2000–2005	2005–10	2010–14
UE15+	0.78	0.45	0.73	0.43	0.35
NMS 2004	6.66	1.05	0.86	0.49	1.16
NMS 2008–12	7.43	4.80	1.50	1.80	0.50
Other CEE	0.33	2.60	4.55	1.65	0.78

Source: Own calculations based on LAI project data.

Table 3.4 Proportion (percentage) of countries in which LAI index has not changed (or the change has not exceeded 0.5)

	1990–95	1995–2000	2000–2005	2005–10	2010–14
UE15+	69	69	69	81	69
NMS 2004	25	38	50	50	50
NMS 2008–12	0	0	0	0	67
Other CEE	67	33	0	33	67

Source: Own calculations based on LAI project data.

joined the European Union, a fundamental change took place in the first half of the 1990s. In 'late member countries' these changes were extended over a whole decade. In the remaining CEE, the decentralisation reforms began only after 1995 and lasted almost until the end of the first decade of the millennium.

Figure 3.4 provides confirmation of hypothesis 3: the increase of the financial autonomy in Central and Eastern Europe has been much slower and less distinct than in the case of other dimensions of the index. This lower financial discretion compared to most Western European countries is equally apparent today. The variables used in the LAI project allow us to construct an index of financial autonomy, the value of which may vary from 0 to 13. In 2014, all 12 countries with a value below 5 were located in Central and Eastern Europe. The only two countries in the region where the value of the indicator was higher than the average for the whole group of 39 European countries were Serbia and Poland. This picture is a reflection not only of the strong tradition of an extremely centralized financial system before 1990, but also of a long-lasting reluctance towards implementing financial decentralisation in parallel with the difficult economic transformation. In general, in Central and Eastern Europe, financial decentralisation (especially in terms of discretion over local revenue policies) often lags behind the functional and other dimensions of local autonomy.

The data also confirm the hypothesis that there is no clear relationship between local autonomy and the average size of municipalities. The correlation between the two indicators is close to 0. Countries with a relatively large average size of municipalities (more than 20,000 inhabitants) may be found both among those with a relatively high level of autonomy (e.g. Serbia in second place among all CEE countries, and Lithuania fourth) and among those with the highest level of centralisation (Georgia occupies the last but one place

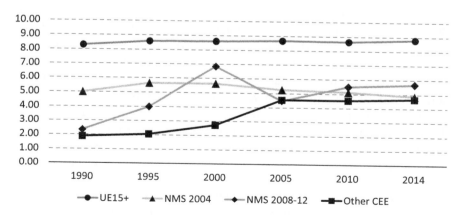

Figure 3.4 Financial autonomy index in group of European countries

Source: Own calculations based on LAI project data.

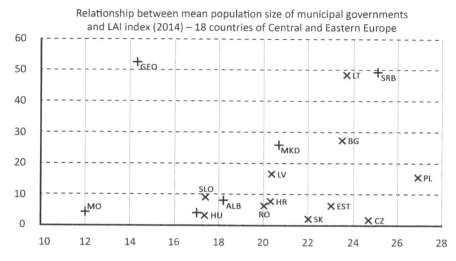

Figure 3.5 Relation between mean population size of municipalities and LAI index (2014); 18 countries of Central and Eastern Europe

in this ranking). Similarly, countries with very small municipalities are found among those with relatively high communal autonomy (e.g. Czechia in third place among CEE countries; before the recent Orbán government reforms this group would have included Hungary as well) and the group with the lowest value of the indicator (e.g. Ukraine and Moldova). The thesis about the lack of a clear relationship between the level of LAI index and the size of municipal governments is also confirmed by the data in Figure 3.5. Similarly, as regards the impact of territorial consolidation reforms, neither the Georgian reform in 2006 nor the Latvian reform in 2009 led to a significant increase in LAI over the few years following the change in territorial organisation. The exception here is the 2002 Macedonian reform, which was part of a broader decentralisation package implemented under pressure from the international community as a result of the 'Ohrid Agreement' ending the civil war in this country.

Most of the analyses conducted confirm the hypotheses formulated at the beginning of this section. Local government systems in the countries of Central and Eastern Europe are very diverse and it is difficult to find common characteristics for the whole region. Nevertheless, one can point to several regularities:

1   The difference between the level of the local autonomy index in the countries of Central and Eastern Europe and Western European countries has been gradually decreasing. This rule applies not only to the early years of the political transformation period but also to more contemporary years.

2   Changes in local government systems (including local autonomy) were, and to some extent still are, faster in Central and Eastern Europe than in more stabilized Western democracies.

3   The growth trend in local autonomy started earlier, and was faster, in the countries which became members of the European Union in 2004, while it was slowest in the group of countries which remain outside of the Union today. This may be associated with the generally higher pro-reformist determination of the Visegrád and Baltic states than in the rest of Central and Eastern Europe. In the case of Bulgaria, Romania and Croatia (countries which joined EU a few years later than the previously discussed group), the decentralisation of powers to local governments came later and was considerably slower.

4   The increase of local autonomy has not applied equally to all dimensions of the index. In particular, it has been much slower with regard to discretion over financial policies.

However, it has not been possible to clearly confirm the hypothesis about the impact of the economic crisis after 2008 on the slowdown or even reversal of decentralisation reforms. Although in countries most affected by the crisis, central control over local government debt has tightened in comparison to other countries, we can find exceptions to this rule. Moreover, the re-centralisation trend has not emerged in other dimensions of the local government autonomy index (apart from the quite exceptional case of Hungary).

The conclusions presented in the previous paragraphs suggest a trend towards the convergence of European local government systems. This claim is further confirmed by the data in Figure 3.6: the standard deviation of the scores for the local autonomy index (LAI), measured systematically for 39 countries, has been

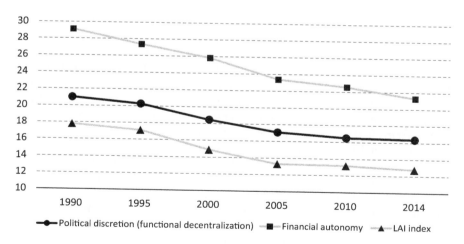

Figure 3.6 Changes in standard deviation of local autonomy indices in 39 European countries
Source: Based on Ladner et al. (2019).

systematically decreasing over the last 25 years or so. Thus, we can speak not only about the convergence Central and Eastern Europe and Western Europe, but about a wider phenomenon affecting the entire continent.

The relationship between the autonomy rate and the average size of local governments, or the impact of territorial reforms on local autonomy, has not been confirmed either. The level of municipal autonomy is determined by other factors than the objective conditions for decentralisation associated with territorial organisation.

Other, more detailed data clearly suggest that Polish municipalities are among the strongest (enjoying the greatest autonomy) in Europe. The level of the Local Autonomy Index is lower than in Switzerland or the Scandinavian countries, but higher than in all other countries of Central and Eastern Europe and many other countries of Western and southern Europe. These results confirm the observations previously formulated in earlier academic studies (see e.g. Levitas 2017). However, the case of Hungary clearly indicates that such a situation is not irreversible. The scope of empirical research and data collected in the Local Autonomy Index project ends in 2014. Some of the later changes, as well as certain reforms currently discussed in Poland, suggest that the degree of local autonomy in Poland has been slowly but systematically decreasing since then. Vertical power relations in Central and Eastern Europe are still far from being stable, and the position of the regional leader in decentralisation is not guaranteed for an undefined period.

Horizontal power relations

During the last 20 to 30 years Europe has undergone dramatic change in terms of local leadership models. Following the well-established typology by Mouritzen and Svara (2002), more and more countries have been moving towards the strong mayor system. An important (although not the only) feature of this system is the direct election of mayors by all citizens of the municipality, instead of more collective forms of leadership with a mayor or a collective board appointed by the council. In the late 1980s, the model of direct election was very rare, but later it spread, and currently well over half of European countries have adopted a more individual model of local leadership. This trend has been widely discussed in academic literature (e.g. Berg and Rao 2005; Magre and Bertrana 2007; Wollmann 2008; Copus et al. 2016; Sweeting 2017), which indicates several arguments raised by proponents of the reform. Most generally speaking, the change has been called for by both arguments relating to efficiency and to democracy deficits (Wollmann 2008). The former argument suggested that a stronger, directly elected local leader would be better equipped to implement effective development policies. In some countries, it was also stressed that the change would lead to a more stable position of local political leaders who would have better opportunity to implement their long-term strategies. In relation to the democratic dimension, the direct election of mayors was expected to contribute to the revival of popular interest in local politics, and help to increase disappointingly decreasing turnout in local elections. In several debates, the argument was raised that direct election would give 'more power to the people' instead of partisan control over mayoral nomination. All of the arguments listed above refer in one way or another to the rational choice paradigm. But there is also an alternative interpretation of the change which refers to more general cultural trends including the personalisation of politics.

Regardless of the arguments and the theoretical paradigm behind them, local governments in Central and Eastern Europe have very much followed this European trend. Among the 11 countries in our focus, only four (Bulgaria, Romania, Slovakia and Slovenia) introduced direct election of mayors right at the beginning of their decentralisation reforms following the 1990 political turnover. But Hungary followed shortly in 1994, Poland in 2002, Croatia in 2009, and most recently Lithuania in 2015. Today, only three countries (Czechia, Estonia and Latvia) retain a more collective form of leadership based on appointments made by the local councils.

The method of election is very important but constitutes only one element of the strength of the local political leader. Heinelt and Hlepas (2006) introduced an index of mayoral strength based on more complex measures which take into account not only the rules of election but also:

- Does the mayor's term in office correspond with council elections?
- Does electoral law secure a majority in the council for the mayor's party?
- Can the mayor be recalled before the end of his/her term (either through a local referendum or through the council)?
- What is the impact of the mayor on the most important nominations in the city hall?
- Does the mayor chair council meetings, and what is his/her impact on the council meeting agenda?

The index was modified in 2018 by adding different weights to individual variables (see Heinelt et al. 2018). When applied to 29 European councils, the index varied from Sweden with the weakest position to France with the strongest position of the mayor in horizontal power relations. How did the countries of Central and Eastern Europe score in that ranking? The study by Heinelt et al. (2018) gives the opportunity to check the strength of mayors in all but two countries (Estonia and Bulgaria)[4] of our region (see Figure 3.7). As with any other feature of the local government system, countries of Central and Eastern Europe are not uniform. Czechia and Latvia belong to the group of countries with the weakest position of the mayor, while Slovakia, Slovenia, Hungary and Poland are not far from the other extreme (although their strong mayors are not as strong as in France).

Another important characteristic of the position of mayor is the legal possibility of recalling him/her before the end of the regular term (see Table 3.5).

In five countries, recall is possible through popular referendum, usually after meeting certain conditions concerning minimum turnout. In three countries

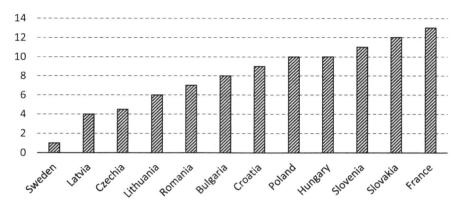

Figure 3.7 Index of mayor's strength

Note: The score for Lithuania reflects the situation before the introduction of direct mayoral elections. Sweden and France represent the two extremes of the European spectrum and are presented on the figure as reference points.

Source: Based on Heinelt et al. 2018, except for Bulgaria and Estonia; own elaboration of the author.

Table 3.5 Possibility of recalling the mayor before the end of regular term in office

Method of election/possibility of early termination	Direct election by local residents	Appointment through the local council
Possibility of recalling by council decision	Romania	Czechia, Estonia, Latvia
Possibility of recalling only by local referendum	Croatia, Poland, Slovakia	Latvia, Lithuania
No possibility for early termination	Bulgaria, Hungary, Slovenia	

Note: Lithuania – situation before the 2015 reform.

Source: Own elaboration based on POLLEADER project data (Heinelt et al. 2018).

(Czechia, Latvia and Romania), it can be done by decision of the local council. But in three other countries (Bulgaria, Hungary and Slovenia), the position of the mayor is secure till the end of the term, with no option of early termination through the political process.

As explained earlier in this section, during the last two decades several countries of the region have decided to change the type of local political leadership, opting for a strong leader, associated with direct election of the mayor. Can we say that the expectations raised by proponents of the reform have been confirmed in reality? Only to some extent. There is no proof that the change has actually contributed to an increase in citizens' participation in local elections. Nevertheless, it is true that in all these countries, the mayor is the most recognised local politician, and responsibility for local affairs is attributed directly to him or her.

The expectation that direct election would decrease the impact of political parties on local governments seems to have been verified in most of the countries (especially in Poland, but also in Slovakia; similar evidence has also been found in a number of West European countries experimenting with similar reforms; see Egner et al. 2018). In several countries of Central and Eastern Europe this is considered as a positive development, as it accords with the general anti-party mood rooted both in public opinion and among local elites. However, it is difficult to provide clear arguments as to why non-partisans are better for local governments. There is no evidence that they achieve visibly higher measurable outputs in governing municipalities than partisan mayors. And the results of strengthening independent candidates have not been uniform across the countries. Bulgaria and Croatia (as well as some other countries of the CEE region such as Albania, Armenia and Macedonia) still have local governments strongly dominated by national political parties, despite the direct election of mayors.[5]

The expectation of a stronger and more stable mayoral position has also proved to be true, at least in some of the countries. Yet, the success measured by these criteria has been so pronounced that, in Poland, the pendulum of current debate is swinging the opposite way – questioning whether mayoral power is too strong, too independent of control and too stable. This debate has led to legislative change, limiting the number of terms in office for directly elected mayors to two five-year terms. In several countries with direct election of mayors, it has become clear that strong mayors might be too strong, dominating local political arenas and limiting the role of local councils.

Summing up, neither the sometimes naïve expectations of the proponents of reforms nor the fears of opponents that are afraid of 'local dictatorships' have really materialised in any radical form.

Conclusions

There are three main lessons to be drawn from the discussion in this chapter. First, there is no single, uniform model of the local government system in Central and Eastern Europe. In contrast to what some earlier publications have suggested (e.g. Heinelt and Hlepas 2006; Loughlin et al. 2010), there are significant differences among countries which prevent us from treating the whole region as exhibiting a homogeneous type of local government (see also discussion in Swianiewicz 2014; Ladner et al. 2019). These differences are related to all the discussed dimensions: territorial organisation (from extreme territorial fragmentation in Czechia and Slovakia to radical consolidation in Lithuania), the level of local autonomy and horizontal power relations in local political systems.

Second, local government systems in this part of the continent are constantly evolving, and the pace of change is still predominantly faster than in more stable Western European democracies. Changes in the degree of local autonomy (usually aimed towards more decentralized systems, but occasionally also towards re-centralisation) are perhaps the best illustrations of this claim, but evolution can also be seen in territorial reforms (earlier in Latvia, more recently in Estonia) and in changes in the types of local leadership. Therefore, any descriptive analysis of variation in the region is just a snapshot of a given moment, which may not necessarily prevail in subsequent years.

Third, there is no doubt that in nearly all the analysed countries, the transformation after 1990 has resulted in a major shift towards more decentralized systems, in which interests expressed by local communities have much greater weight than in the highly centralized system of the pre-1990 period. As some authors argue (e.g. Levitas 2017, who sees the local government reform as an inherent element of 'state building'), decentralisation has played a very important, although sometimes underestimated, role in the more general process of political and economic transformation after the 1989 turnover. At the same time – as the example of Hungary demonstrates – the trend towards decentralisation is not irreversible. The recent shift towards populist politics and strong personal leadership on a national level makes re-centralisation tendencies almost equally as probable as the further strengthening of local governments.

Notes

1 The same process could be noted in other countries which emerged after the collapse of Yugoslavia: Bosnia and Herzegovina as well as Macedonia, but interestingly, not in Serbia or Montenegro. A similar tendency towards territorial fragmentation was also witnessed in Ukraine. Altogether, these cases confirm that territorial fragmentation of the municipal tier has been a common phenomenon in Central and Eastern Europe.

2 See http://local-autonomy.andreasladner.ch/, also Ladner et al. (2016), Ladner et al. (2019). The coordinators of the project were Andreas Ladner (University of Lausanne) and Harald Baldersheim (University of Oslo), and the author of this chapter was responsible for organizing the collection of data from 17 countries of Central and Eastern Europe.

3 See http://local-autonomy.andreasladner.ch/ for a more detailed description of the methodology.

4 In the cases of Bulgaria and Estonia, the value of the index has been additionally calculated thanks to information provided by country experts – Desislava Kalcheva and Ringa Raudla, respectively.

5 This paragraph concentrates on the municipal tier and mayors in particular. But the picture of the role of national political parties in sub-national governments is of course diversified, depending on the tier of government we look at. For example, in Poland, a country with the most non-partisan municipal government system in Europe, more than 90% of seats in regional assemblies are occupied by councillors elected from national party lists.

References

Berg, R., & Rao, N. (2005). *Transforming Local Political Leadership*. Basingstoke: Palgrave-Macmillan.

Blöchliger, H. (2011). 'What is The OECD Fiscal Network Measuring? An Overview of the Fiscal Decentralisation Database', paper presented during the conference on *Taxonomy of Grants and Measurement of Fiscal Decentralisation*, Paris, 10–11.03.2011

Blöchliger, H., & King, D. (2006). Less than you thought:The fiscal autonomy of sub-central governments. *OECD Economic Studies*, 43(2), 155–188.

Bours, A. (1993). Management, tiers, size and amalgamations of local government. In: R.J. Bennett (ed.), *Local Government in the New Europe*. London-New York: Belhaven Press.

Čapková, S. (2011). Slovakia: Local government: Establishing democracy at the grassroots. In: J. Loughlin, F. Hendriks & A. Lidström (eds.), *The Oxford Handbook of Local and Regional Democracy in Europe*. Oxford: Oxford University Press, pp. 552–575.

Copus, C., Iglesias, A., Havek, M., Illner, M., & Lidström, A. (2016). Have mayors will travel: Trends and developments in the direct election of the mayor:A five-nations study. In: S. Kuhlmann & G. Bouckaert (eds.), *Local Public Sector Reforms in Times of Crisis*. Palgrave-Macmillan.

Coulson, A., & Campbell, A. (2006). Into the mainstream: Local democracy in Central and Eastern Europe. *Local Government Studies*, 32(5), 543–562.

Ebel, R., & Yilmaz, S. (2003). On the measurement and impact of fiscal decentralisation. In: J. Martinez-Vazques (ed.), *Public Finance in Developing and Transition Countries: Essays in Honour of Richard Bird*. Cheltenham: Edward Elgar.

Egner, B., Gendźwiłł, A., Pleschberger, W., & Swianiewicz, P. (2018). Mayors and political parties. In: H. Heinelt, A. Magnier, M. Cabria & H. Reynaert (eds.), *Political Leaders and Changing Local Democracy:The European Mayor*. London: Palgrave-Macmillan, pp. 327–358.

Hajnal, G., & Rosta, M. (2014). The Illiberal State on the Local Level the Doctrinal Foundations of Subnational Governance Reforms in Hungary (2010–2014), *Paper Presented on EGPA Annual Conference*, 10–12.09, Speyer, Germany.

Heinelt, H., & Hlepas, N. (2006). Typologies of local government systems. In: H. Bäck, H. Heinelt & A. Magnier (eds.), *The European Mayor: Political Leaders in the Changing Context of Local Democracy*. Wiesbaden:Verlag für Sozialwissenschaften, pp. 21–42.

Heinelt, H., Hlepas, N., Kuhlmann, S., & Swianiewicz, P. (2018). Local government systems: Grasping the institutional environment of mayors. In: H. Heinelt, A. Magnier, M. Cabria & H. Reynaert (eds.), *Political Leaders and Changing Local Democracy: The European Mayor*. London: Palgrave-Macmillan, pp. 19–78.

Hesse, J., & Sharpe, L. (1991). Local government in international perspective: Some comparative observations. In: J. Hesse (ed.), *Local Government and Urban Affairs in International Perspective*. Analyses of Twenty Western Industrialized Countries. Baden-Baden: Nomos-Verlagsgesellschaft, pp. 603–621.

Hlepas, N. (2016). Is it the twilight of decentralisation? Testing the limits of functional reforms in the era of austerity. *International Review of Administrative Sciences*, 82(2), 273–290.

Horvath, T. (2000). *Decentralisation: Experiments and Reforms*. Budapest: Open Society Institute – LGI.

Hughes, J., Sasse, G., & Gordon, C. (2003). EU Enlargement, Europeanisation and the Dynamics of Regionalisation in the CEECs. In: M. Keating & J. Hughes (eds.), *The Regional Challenge in Central and Eastern Europe*. Bruxelles: PIE-Peter Lang.

Illner, M. (2011). The Czechia: Local government in the years after the reform. In: J. Loughlin, F. Hendriks & A. Lidström (eds.), *The Oxford Handbook of Local and Regional Democracy in Europe*. Oxford: Oxford University Press, pp. 505–527.

Kandeva, E. (ed.) (2001). *Stabilisation of Local Governments*. Budapest: Open Society Institute – LGI.

Keating, M., & Hughes, J. (2003). The Regional Challenge in Central and Eastern Europe, *Series on Regionalism and Federalism* No. 1, Presses Interuniversitaires Europeenes – Peter Lang, Brussels-Bern-Berlin-Frankfurt/M-New York-Oxford-Wien.

Klimovsky, D., Meiere, O., Mikolaityte, J., & Pinteric, U. (2014). Inter-municipal cooperation in Lithuania and Slovakia: Does size structure matter? *Lex Localis*, 12(3).

Ladner, A., Keuffer, N., & Baldersheim, H. (2016). Measuring local autonomy in 39 countries (1990–2014). *Regional & Federal Studies*, 26(3), 321–357.

Ladner, A., Keufler, N., Baldersheim, H., Hlepas, N., Swianiewiczm, P., Steyvers, K., & Navarro, C. (2019). *Patterns of local autonomy: A comparative analysis of 39 countries between 1990 and 2014 in Europe.* Houndmills: Palgrave-Macmillan.

Levitas, A. (2016). *Fiscal decentralisation indictors 2006–2014.* Skopje: NALAS.

Levitas, A. (2017). Local government reform as state building: What the polish case says about 'decentralisation'. *Studies in Comparative International Development*, 52(1), 23–44.

Loughlin, J., Hendriks, F., & Lidström, A. (2010). *The Oxford Handbook of Local and Regional Democracy in Europe.* Oxford: Oxford University Press.

Magre, J., & Bertrana, X. (2007). Exploring the limits of institutional change: The direct election of mayors in Western Europe. *Local Government Studies*, 33(2), 181–194.

Martinez-Vazques, J., & Timofeev, A. (2011). 'Decentralisation Measures Revisited', paper presented during the conference on *Taxonomy of Grants and Measurement of Fiscal Decentralisation*, Paris, 10–11.03.2011.

Mouritzen, P.E., & Svara, J. (2002). *Leadership at the Apex.* Pittsburgh: University of Pittsburgh Press.

Newton, K. (1992). Is small really so beautiful? Is big really so ugly? Size, effectiveness and democracy in local government. *Political Studies*, 30.

Page, E., & Goldsmith, M. (1987). *Central and Local Government Relations. A Comparative Analysis of West European Unitary States.* London: Sage.

Palne-Kovacs, I., Bodor, A., Finta, I., Grunbut, Z., Kacziba, P., & Zongor, G. (2016). Farewell to decentralisation: The Hungarian story and its general implications. *Croatian Comparative Public Administration*, 16(4), 789–816.

Pano Puey, E., Tejado, L.M., Mussons, C.P., & Ferran, J.M. (2018). Layer upon layer: The position of inter-municipal cooperation in the Spanish quasi-federal system – the case of Catalonia. In: F. Teles & P. Swianiewicz (eds.), *Inter-municipal Cooperation in Europe: Institutions and Governance.* Houndmills: Palgrave-Macmillan, pp. 259–278.

Shah, A. (1998). *Fiscal Federalism and Macroeconomic Governance: For Better or For Worse?* The World Bank.

Sharpe, L.J. (1973). Theories and values of local government. *Political Studies*, (2).

Sweeting, D. (2017). *Directly Elected Mayors in Urban Governance: Impact and Practice.* Bristol: Policy Press University of Bristol.

Swianiewicz, P. (2014). An empirical typology of local government systems in Eastern Europe. *Local Government Studies*, 40(2), 292–311.

Swianiewicz, P. (2015). Territorial Consolidation Reforms – European Experiences of 21st Century, *Conference Proceedings, International Conference Geobalcanica 2015*, Skopje, 379–388, 5–7 June, doi: dx.doi.org/10.18509/GBP.2015.48

Swianiewicz, P. (2018). If territorial fragmentation is a problem, is amalgamation a solution? – Ten years later. *Local Government Studies*, 44(1), 1–10.

Swianiewicz, P., Gendźwiłł, A., & Zardi, A. (2017). *Does Size Matter? Toolkit of Territorial Amalgamation Reforms in Europe.* Strasbourg: Council of Europe.

Swianiewicz, P., & Mielczarek, A. (2010). Georgian local government reform: State leviathan redraws borders?. *Local Government Studies*, 36(2), 291–311.

Tavares, A.F. (2018). Municipal amalgamations and their effects: A literature review. *Miscellanea Geographica. Regional Studies on Development*, 22(1), 5–15.

Wollmann, H. (2008). Reforming local leadership and local democracy: The cases of England, Sweden, Germany and France in comparative perspective. *Local Government Studies*, 38(1), 279–298.

Zentai, V., & Peteri, G. (2002). *Mastering Decentralisation and Public Administration Reforms in Central and Eastern Europe.* Budapest: LGI-Open Society Institute.

4   Regionalism in Central and Eastern Europe

Roman Szul

Regionalism – an introduction

The term 'regionalism' in political studies is used with two quite different meanings: (1) as the integration (cooperation) of states located in a region understood as a part of the world (e.g. European integration) and (2) as ideas and actions related to regions understood as parts of states (nation states), whose aim is to present or defend the cultural and/or economic and/or political identity and interests of such regions. Later in this chapter, the term 'regionalism' is used with the latter meaning. This kind of regionalism implies demands for the recognition, official or unofficial, of a region's distinctiveness.

There is no clear-cut distinction between regionalism and some other phenomena like nationalism (separatism, independence movements), folklorism, regional promotion or even mafia-like criminality. Each politically meaningful regionalism (regionalist movement) usually has a radical wing claiming that the population of the given region (or a part of this population) forms a separate 'ethnos' of 'nation' that has a right to autonomy or independence. Proportions within a movement between regionalists and nationalists can change in favour of the latter, thus transforming the movement into nationalism. On the other hand, weak regionalism usually confines its aims to demonstrating the folklore of the region as a sign of its specificity, often as a tourist attraction, for regional promotion. In extreme cases, regionalism-nationalism can degenerate into criminality when, for instance, forceful collection of money from local businesses for 'national purposes' becomes plain criminal extortion.

There are various actors, driving forces and inspirations of regionalism. It is important to distinguish between grass-roots, bottom-up regionalism, and top-down, externally induced or inspired regionalism. Grass-roots regionalism is a movement whose actors belong to the regional community, and the aim of this movement is somehow in opposition to the nation (nation state) as a whole and/or other regions. Top-down, induced regionalism is activity addressed to a given region and for a given region but devised, and often carried out, by external actors, for example by national authorities or leaders of nationalist movements (in the case of stateless nations). The aim of such top-down regionalism is usually to induce a sense of regional identity in a local population as the first step to introducing this population to the national community (when the distance between the local and the national is too big to be overcome in a single leap). Another type of top-down regionalism is the inducing of 'regional pride' by national authorities, as was the case with the administrative reform in Poland in the 1990s, in the hope that this 'regional pride' will strengthen the economy and democracy. Regionalism can also be inspired from outside, as was the case in recent decades in Europe, including Central and Eastern Europe, when the idea of a 'Europe of regions' and regionalisation promoted by the EU came to several countries from outside.

Summing up the preceding discussion, several types of regionalism can be distinguished in terms of the aims and driving forces of regionalism: first, 'multi-dimensional' genuine grass-roots regionalism based on the ethno-cultural specificity and economic interests of regions, and aimed at preserving and demonstrating this specificity and defending its interests; second, 'one-dimensional' genuine regionalism based on ethno-linguistic specificity whose only aim is to preserve and promote a language (or dialect); third, top-down cultural regionalism inspired or encouraged by central national authorities addressed to populations who lack a clear sense of national belonging, the purpose of this idea being to inculcate a supra-local, regional identity in these populations as a step towards introducing them into the national community; and fourth, top-down pseudo-regionalism, recently inspired mainly by the idea of a 'Europe of regions' and the expectations of the EU, whose principal aim is the better use of EU funds and to bring about the kind of social mobilisation favourable for economic development.

Regionalism and separatism in CEE in the 19th and 20th centuries

It is very difficult to understand the processes that took place after 1990 without getting a more detailed picture of the recent past, since the ethnic underpinnings of political and social phenomena have been a strong influence in several parts of the CEE. That is why we will devote part of this chapter to the processes that took place in the last two centuries.

As mentioned above, regionalism (and separatism as a more radical form of regionalism) is indissolubly related to states (nation states, empires). When analysing regionalism and separatism in Central and Eastern Europe in the 20th century, we must keep in mind the instability of states in this part of the world during this period. Most present-day states of this part of Europe are in a sense a product of separatism. The instability of states means not only the emergence (and disappearance) of states but also shifts of borders and, in some cases, of peoples. These events have strongly affected the present state of regionalism/separatism in the analysed part of Europe. Destabilisation of the geopolitical order in Central and Eastern Europe took place in three big waves ('geopolitical earthquakes'): the First World War and its aftermath, the Second World War and its aftermath, and the end of the Cold War. Each of these waves, or shocks, deserves comment.

In the first half of the 19th century, practically the whole area under consideration belonged to, or was under control of, four large empires: Prussia/Germany, the Habsburg Empire (Austria), the Russian Empire and the Ottoman Empire, existing as their geographical, political and ethno-cultural peripheries (the latter meaning that this area was populated mostly by non-dominant ethnic groups of those empires). It was a multi-ethnic area, with ethnicities in various stages of development of ethno-national consciousness and with various traditions (and memories) of own statehood, without clear-cut ethnic boundaries: core areas can be distinguished, with relatively high ethnic homogeneity and a high level of ethno-national consciousness, as well as territories without a clear majority and lacking a strong ethnic affiliation. It can be added that, out of these four empires (powers), three (except Prussia/Germany) were slow or inefficient in homogenizing their populations in accordance with the rule of nation-building (one state, one nation, one language). Prussia/Germany was more determined and successful in Germanising its population, except in the area once representing the core area of the Polish state, where the feeling of being Polish remained strong. In the second half of the 19th century, state formations – in the form of semi-independent states or autonomous regions – started to appear. The biggest geopolitical change was the transformation of the Habsburg Empire into Austria–Hungary, with Hungary, as the equal partner of Austria, stretching far beyond the ethnic Hungarian (or, in other words, Magyar) territory.

After the First World War, due to the defeat of all four empires (including the revolution in Russia) and the idea of the right of nations to self-determination, several new states emerged, while some others dramatically changed their territories. In most cases, the emergence of new states was accompanied by wars among these states or between them and the old empires. The newly established states were (1) Estonia, Latvia and Lithuania (all formed from the Russian empire); (2) Poland (parts of Russia, Austria-Hungary and Germany); (3) Czechoslovakia (with parts of Austria and of Hungary); and (4) Yugoslavia (parts of Austria, Hungary and the Ottoman Empire, including Serbia and Montenegro, which were already independent before the war). Romania considerably enlarged its territory (mostly at the expense of Hungary, but also at the expense of Russia – in the case of Bessarabia). Hungary lost half of its pre-war territory to literally all its neighbours (including Austria and the more distant Poland), leaving considerable Hungarian minorities there and creating strong resentment to the Treaty of Trianon. Bulgaria, after unsuccessful attempts to regain territories considered as historically and ethnically Bulgarian, remained practically unchanged.

All the new (or modified?) states were ethnically mixed, with large minorities, or people without a clear feeling of ethnic belonging, scattered territorially (like the Jews and Roma) or territorially concentrated, mostly in border areas. (Only Hungary did not have sizable territorial concentrations of ethnic minorities). Among these minorities were those with decisively hostile attitudes to the states they were made citizens of without or against their will, or those who initially accepted their new states but were then disillusioned. Practically all states carried out a policy of nation-building or cultural, linguistic and identity consolidation, with greater or lesser concessions for national minorities and regional communities. At the time, this policy was dominant both in Europe and elsewhere.

One of the instruments of nation-building policy, practiced for instance in Poland, was 'regionalism', understood as encouraging, supporting or tolerating cultural and social activities addressed towards populations of particular regions with a weak sense of identity other than local, in the hope that the sense of regional belonging would be a step towards adopting an all-national identity. The policy of nation-building, on the one hand, strengthened the positions of leading ethno-linguistic groups (mostly by incorporating ethnically indifferent groups, mainly peasants, as long as there were no big cultural-religious divides), and on the other hand, generated or radicalized centrifugal tendencies among minorities, often supported from abroad. The most serious clash of centripetal and centrifugal forces took place in Yugoslavia (the Kingdom of Serbs, Croats and Slovenes), where the romantic idea of unity among the linguistically close Slavic nations turned out to be an illusion when faced with the religious, cultural and economic differences and the desire of individual ethnic groups to defend their interests and identities. In this country, Serbs represented the centripetal tendency and Croats led the centrifugal trend. This clash reached a dramatic outcome during the Second World War and in inter-ethnic atrocities and slaughter.

The Second World War, with its aftermaths and post-war developments, brought about significant changes to the above picture, which are relevant from the point of view of regionalism and separatism.

First, the three Baltic states (Estonia, Latvia and Lithuania) were annexed by the Soviet Union and transformed, after some territorial changes, into Soviet Socialist Republics, members of the nominally federal Soviet state. Twenty years of independence and nation-building combined with cultural and religious distance from the rest of the USSR (western Christianity – Catholicism and Protestantism vs. Orthodox Christianity and officially promoted atheism) as well as linguistic distance (local non-Slavonic languages vs. Russian) had created in these countries a strong sense of being different and being occupied, thus generating a separatist/pro-independence mood there. The political system of the USSR meant that this mood could not be translated into political actions until Gorbachev's *perestroika* and *glasnost* in the late 1980s.

Second, the Holocaust in Poland, followed by shifts of territory and forced or voluntary cross-border transfers of national minorities (and of people without strong ethnic identity) made this country almost totally ethnically homogenous, without sizable territorial concentrations of peoples differing from the 'standard' population as regards culture, language and identity. Further developments – internal migrations, the spread of a unified national culture and standard language – also contributed to the process of homogenisation, thus considerably diminishing the possible scope for regionalism.

Third, the new, communist leadership of Yugoslavia, after the sad experience of the interwar and wartime periods, decided to transform the country into a federation (of six republics and two autonomous provinces, in many respects equal to republics), in the hope that this would satisfy the cultural and political aspirations of ethnic groups and thus assuage centrifugal tendencies. In this way, ethno-cultural differences became institutionalised. Ethnicities received institutions – republics or autonomous provinces, their communist parties, the media and so forth – through which they could express their demands and which vice versa contributed to shape ethnic cultures and identities. This system existed and functioned as long as there was a strong internal all-Yugoslav leadership (Marshal Tito), the economic situation was satisfactory and the international situation advantageous for the 'non-allied' Yugoslavia.

Fourth, in Czechoslovakia, due to the transfer of its easternmost region (Sub-Carpathia, also called Trans-Carpathia) to the USSR and the transfer of its German population to Germany, two of the three big territorial concentrations of ethnic minorities located in border areas disappeared (the third was the Hungarian minority, which was also much reduced in size due to exchange of populations with Hungary, voluntary emigration, assimilation and demographic tendencies). The ethno-cultural and linguistic affinity of the Czechs (and Moravians) and Slovaks and the idea and policy of Czechoslovakism contributed to the considerable elimination of differences between these two (or three, if one takes into account the Moravians) ethnic groups. The differences, mainly psycho-sociological, remained: a kind of inferiority complex among Slovaks and a condescending attitude attributed to Czechs (by some Slovaks). This was the reason for granting Slovakia some autonomy in 1969, thus transforming Czechoslovakia into an asymmetric federation (in which Czechia lacked its own government and parliament, their functions being fulfilled by the Czechoslovak government and parliament). Moreover, intensive industrialization of Slovakia was conceived as a remedy aimed at healing the wide differences in the level of economic development between the two parts of the federation.

Fifth, the remaining countries under consideration (Romania, Hungary and Bulgaria), after the dramatic wartime upheaval, roughly returned to their pre-war territories and populations (the main change was the loss of eastern Moldavia or Bessarabia by Romania). In Romania, a sizable Hungarian (Magyar) minority remained. Among this minority, the Székelys or Szekler (Székely in Hungarian, Secui in Romanian) distinguished themselves from both the Romanian majority and from the rest of the Hungarian minority. Their territory (in which they form the majority) is located right in the centre of Romania. In the 1950s, when Romania followed the Soviet-style ethnic policy, this territory was given autonomy as a Hungarian ethnic region. Later, this autonomy was abolished and Romanian authorities avoided giving any autonomy to its regions (ethnic Hungarians were given cultural, in other words non-territorial, autonomy).

Of course, when analysing the geopolitical consequences of the Second World War we cannot ignore the establishment of the German Democratic

Republic (GDR) from the Soviet occupation zone of Germany and the attempt to build a new, socialist German nation, but this experience has little to do with regionalism in Central and Eastern Europe.

The third of the aforementioned 'geopolitical earthquakes' in Central and Eastern Europe in the 20th century was related to the end of the Cold War, resulting from the collapse of the political system (communism/socialism) and of the broader geopolitical setting at the turn of the 1980s and 1990s. It is not the aim of this chapter to analyse the causes of this phenomenon or sequence of events. However, it can be stated that the famous fall of the Berlin Wall in November 1989, very often (especially in the West) taken as the symbol and starting point of the end of communism and of the Soviet bloc, was in fact one in a series of events which started in Poland in 1988 and 1989. These events resulted in the establishment of the first non-communist government in September 1989, then continued with changes of governments in Hungary and other countries. Such an outcome, however, could be hardly have been possible without developments in the USSR, namely the aforementioned ideas of *glasnost* ('openness') and *perestroika* ('reconstruction') propagated by the Soviet leadership as ways to mend the ever more inefficient and unpopular socialism. These ideas triggered processes which eventually led to the collapse of the communist regime.

The crisis and subsequent collapse of the system activated various movements and forces opposing this system (pro-democratic, pro-free market, pro-Western (proposing integration with the EU and NATO), nationalistic of various kinds, etc.). Among these movements and forces were regionalist and separatist/independence tendencies. The de-legitimisation of socialism brought about different results in states with a solid ethno-national basis and in states lacking such a basis. In the former states the old, socialist/communist governments were more or less smoothly replaced by new, non-communist governments (Poland, Hungary, Bulgaria, Romania, Albania). In the latter states, the end of socialism and of the Cold War undermined their very existence. In the case of the GDR, it meant its disappearing and incorporation of its territory into the Federal Republic of Germany (FRG). In the case of federal (federative) states, it meant their disintegration (USSR, Yugoslavia, Czechoslovakia).

After the smooth ('velvet') dissolution of Czechoslovakia, the less smooth but generally peaceful dissolution of the USSR and the much more painful disintegration of Yugoslavia, new states appeared on the political map of Europe (although not all of them fully recognized internationally). It can be said that many areas which used to be regions of broader states finally emerged as independent states.

The present situation of regionalism in CEE

The consecutive geopolitical shocks or 'earthquakes' of the 20th century brought about significant consequences regarding regionalism in Central and Eastern Europe. On the one hand, they brought about the political emancipation of ethno-cultural/historical regions and their transformation into separate states (nation states). On the other hand, shifts of borders, cross-border transfers of populations and internal migrations considerably levelled out ethno-cultural differences between regions within countries. As a result, in Central and Eastern Europe there are no regions such as in Scotland, Wales, Catalonia or the Basque Country – regions with a strong, distinct cultural identity and political autonomy.[1] It can be said that CEE's 'Scotlands', 'Catalonias' or 'Basque Countries' have become independent states and joined the European Union.

The above comment does not mean that the issue of sub-national regionalism has disappeared altogether in Central and Eastern Europe in countries belonging to the European Union. (Regionalism and separatism is quite strong more to the east, especially in Ukraine, but this country is outside the geographical scope of our analysis.) Two kinds of regionalism can be distinguished in CEE countries: genuine grass-roots regionalism based on cultural-linguistic and historical factors and what can termed as top-down, induced (pseudo-) regionalism.

The former, ethno-linguistic regionalism, causes a problem in definition: how should we treat the activity of territorially concentrated national minorities – as something outside the notion of regionalism or something belonging to this notion? Given that the issue of national minorities seems to be politically more relevant than 'pure' ethno-linguistic regionalism in CEE in general, and in some countries in particular, it is reasonable to include national minorities in the discussion, provided that they are meaningful in size and activity and are territorially concentrated.

At this point it seems advisable to clarify the notion of 'national minorities', for it is a notion widely used in Central and Eastern Europe, and not so much in Western Europe. This term can be used with a sociological and a legal meaning. In the sociological meaning, a national (or ethnic) minority is a community revealing cultural distance in relation to the dominant ethnic group in a given country, regardless of the characteristics of this community. In a legal sense, often applied in national legislations and international treaties, a community to be classified as a 'national minority' must fulfil additional criteria: usually its members must be citizens of this country, quite often this community must live there 'traditionally', be distinct from the majority and want to preserve this distinctiveness. Finally the decision as to whether a group of people is a national minority or not is taken by the national legislation which enumerates national minorities and, sometimes, other groups (ethnic minorities, ethno-regional groups, etc.). Classifying a group as a 'national minority' automatically means granting rights (and often funds) enabling the preservation of their identity and distinctiveness. Historically, the legal notion of national minorities relates to the decisions of the League of Nations after the First World War to grant special rights to a category of inhabitants of newly established countries in Central and Eastern Europe as a result of shifts of borders and the defeat of some countries. This category included people who became inhabitants of the new states but wanted to retain links with, and be protected by, their previous states. It was addressed primarily to ethnic Germans in Poland and Czechoslovakia. The abuse of the role of protector of German minorities in these countries by Nazi Germany meant that after the Second World War, the term 'national minority' in national and international documents lost the implication of an external protector. Now the 'protector' of national minorities is national legislation and, when concluded, multilateral international conventions and bilateral treaties.

Later in this text, the term 'national minorities' will be used with its sociological meaning (which usually overlaps with the legal meaning) unless national legislations make a distinction between national, ethnic, ethno-regional, ethno-linguistic, etc. groups.

Next, cases of ethno-regionalism including national minorities will be presented, country by country, in geographical order, starting with the north-east (i.e. the Baltic states).

Estonia, after regaining independence in 1991, made the right for citizenship conditional on one of two criteria: being a citizen or a direct descendant of a citizen of the independent interwar Estonia, or knowledge of the Estonian language. This left out the vast majority of the Russian-speaking population ('occupants') who had immigrated during the Soviet period and had not bothered to master the local language. Being a non-citizen meant that they had limited access to the labour market (especially to employment in public administration) and to privatisation schemes, let alone participation in democratic institutions (elections). This amounted to about one-third of the Estonian population. Some of them received Russian citizenship; others became expatriates. This population is spread all over the country with concentrations in big cities, mainly the capital city Tallinn and in the most north-eastern region bordering Russia, where it forms the vast majority. The status and rights of this population have constantly been a source of tension between Estonia and Russia, with Russian reproaches towards the EU, and pressure by the EU on Estonia (during the accession negotiations). The existence of this population and Russia's allegations have been, and still are, a cause of anxiety in Estonia, since they give a pretext for Russia to directly intervene in Estonia, especially after Russian engagements in Georgia (2008) and Ukraine (2014), when Russia justified its actions by its right to defend Russians abroad. It should be stated that, contrary to fears or predictions, the Russian (or Russian-speaking) population in Estonia has not revealed meaningful signs of subversive or irredentist activities. Emigration to Russia and naturalization (after passing language exams) have reduced the number of 'non-citizens', and the modus vivendi worked out by the two communities has considerably assuaged the problem of the Russian population in Estonia (an element of this modus vivendi is the practical acceptance of Russian as a working language in local administrations in areas with a high number of Russian speakers).

The situation in *Latvia* is similar to that in Estonia, in what constitutes the criteria for granting citizenship (descendants of citizens of independent Latvia, mastering of the Latvian language) and slightly different as regards the ethnic composition of the population at the moment of gaining independence.

Inhabitants belonging to non-Latvian ethnic groups amounted to as much as half the population, but these groups were more heterogeneous and there was no clear division between Latvians and non-Latvians. Some groups were highly integrated with Latvian society and thus identified Latvia as their homeland.[2] This included the Polish minority and Russian Old Believers (dissidents from the Russian Orthodox Church), who immigrated to the present territory of Latvia centuries ago, usually had a command of Latvian and revealed emotional bonds with this country. The Russian minority, the biggest non-Latvian group, was concentrated in big cities, especially in the capital Riga where it formed a majority, and in the south-eastern region called Latgalia or Latgale. In this region, likewise, other ethnic minorities are concentrated: Polish and Byelorussian, and a regional group of Latvians called Latgalians. The latter group differs from the rest of Latvians in its religion (Catholic, while most Latvians are Protestant), dialect and identity. It can be said that there is a genuine Latgalian regionalism, but its activity doesn't exceed the scope of folklore, lacking political ambitions (Ščerbinskis 2004). As regards the fate of non-citizens, similarly to Estonia, the outflow of some of them and a relatively smooth process of naturalisation by passing language exams (the linguistic barrier between Latvian and Russian is much smaller than between Estonian and Russian) has practically eliminated this phenomenon as a relevant political issue. The integration of ethnic Russians as Latvian citizens has had its political consequences – the growing political weight of this group in Latvia's politics.

In *Lithuania*, the problem of citizenship and naturalisation does not exist, as practically all inhabitants of Lithuania at the moment of (re-)gaining independence were entitled to Lithuanian citizenship.[3] This doesn't mean, however, that the problem of national minorities does not exist. Minorities, mainly Polish, Russian and Byelorussian (otherwise very similar mentally, culturally and linguistically), form up to 20% of the population and are concentrated in a strip of land along the border with Belarus (without direct contact with the territory of Poland), in the area which in the interwar period belonged to Poland (or was under Polish administration, depending on the interpretation of history (Polish or Lithuanian)). The most vocal and best organised is the Polish minority. At present, it is represented by the party called the Union of Poles in Lithuania (usually also supported by local Russians), which regularly manage to gain seats in the Lithuanian parliament although playing a rather marginal role. Since Lithuania's independence, relations between this minority and the Lithuanian state and majority has been tense. In the critical years when Lithuania was emerging from the USSR, there were separatist or centrifugal tendencies among this minority. Interestingly, these were not aimed at joining Poland but aimed at remaining in the USSR or gaining territorial autonomy, which was obviously rejected by Lithuania. There is a mutual mistrust between the Polish minority and the Lithuanian state. The minority accuses Lithuania of violating the minority's cultural and linguistic rights (in the sphere of language – Lithuanian is the only official language, even in communes where Poles form up to 90% of the population, place names in Polish in public places are banned, Polish names cannot be used in their original Polish spelling, education in Polish is being discriminated against, etc.) and economic rights (slowness in restitution of farmland to Poles, nationalised under communist regime, etc.). Lithuania, which, like Latvia and Estonia, has not signed international conventions on the protection of ethnic or national minorities (e.g. the European Charter for Regional or Minority Languages), views the existing situation of the Polish minority as sufficient (the existence of education in Polish, Polish-language private media) and regards demands for further rights as subversive activity, dangerous for national unity and the idea of nation-building. The situation of the Polish minority in Lithuania for several years after Lithuania's independence had no impact on interstate relations between Poland and Lithuania. Poland's authorities, for geopolitical considerations, supported Lithuania's independence and European aspirations, largely ignoring the grievances of Poles in Lithuania. It was hoped that the democratic and European Lithuania would respect the rights of minorities in accordance with 'European standards'. International treaties between the two states on the mutual recognition and protection of minorities seemed to support this hope. Later on, the situation deteriorated when Polish authorities realized that there was no progress in respecting the rights of the Polish minority and the treaties were ignored.

In *Poland*, two ethno-regional communities and two more or less territorially concentrated, meaningful national minorities can be distinguished, playing, however, a marginal role in the political life of the country. These two ethno-regional communities are the Kashubians and Silesians.[4] The Kashubians live in northern Poland, in the vicinity of Gdansk and Gdynia along the Baltic coast, mostly in rural areas of the Pomorskie region (voivodeship). The distinctive factor distinguishing them from the rest of Poles is their dialect (or set of dialects), which, some ten years ago (in 2005), was officially recognized as a 'regional language' (by the Law on National and Ethnic Minorities and Regional Language). As a language, it is quite close to Polish, while as a dialect is quite distant from standard Polish and other Polish dialects. Kashubians, like the majority of Poles, are mostly Roman Catholics (those Kashubians who, during centuries of German domination in this area adopted Protestantism gradually also adopted the German language, culture and identity, and most of them migrated to Germany after the Second World War). Kashubians combine their ethno-regional identity with a strong Polish identity. They are represented by an organisation called the Kashubian-Pomeranian Association and some socio-cultural institutions. The main aim of the Kashubian regionalist movement is the preservation and legal promotion of their language, otherwise strongly endangered by assimilation into standard Polish, as well as the preservation and promotion of their regional culture (folklore). In the sphere of language, it has achieved the official recognition of Kashubian as a regional language (back in the 1990s, the Ministry of Education admitted Kashubian as a subject in schools). While it has a growing presence in the public life (schools, media, church services, by no means challenging, however, the position of standard Polish) its usage is simultaneously shrinking in private life. Kashubians do not display meaningful political activity: there is no Kashubian political party (which would have gained any discernible support), and if there are members of Kashubian organisations in the regional assembly (*sejmik*) of the Pomorskie region, it is due to all-national parties which include Kashubians on their election lists.

More militant and politically significant is the Silesian community in the south of Poland, in the Silesian region (voivodeship). During the last census (2011), more than 800,000 people declared some kind of Silesian identity, with about 250,000 declaring it as their sole identity, the rest combining it with a Polish identity.[5] One of the main distinguishing factors are their dialects (not so much for their linguistic characteristics, since they are part of a linguistic continuum with other Polish dialects, as for their stronger social vitality and prestige compared with Polish dialects outside Silesia. In addition, their history and the related historical memory distinguishes them from the rest of the Polish nation. The Silesian movement is very differentiated as regards its organisational forms and aims, including political programmes. The most radical is the Movement for the Autonomy of Silesia, some years ago known for its strong anti-Polish undertones. In recent years, in attempts to gain more popularity among voters, it has avoided overt anti-Polish rhetoric. The declared aim, as its name suggests, is to gain autonomy for Silesia (for the administrative region called Silesia or for any other territorial shape of Silesia) in the future. According to this organisation, autonomy will improve the quality of regional governing and thus the quality of life for all inhabitants.[6] It also demands the official recognition of Silesian as a 'regional language', just like Kashubian. Another demand of the movement is the official recognition of Silesians as a 'nationality' and not just an 'ethno-regional group', although this demand has been rejected by Polish authorities. The Movement for the Autonomy of Silesia has gained some election success, as since 1999 (establishment of regions with their democratically elected representations) it has been regularly present in the regional assembly (*sejmik*), but support for it is not growing and cannot exceed 6%–7% of votes in the region.

The two biggest officially recognised national minorities are Byelorussians and Germans. (According to Polish law, national minorities are Polish citizens belonging (declaring adherence) to ethnic communities which have their own nation states (kin states) outside Poland, provided that these communities live in Poland 'traditionally', or for at least 100 years; the law enumerates national minorities, just like it enumerates recognised ethnic minorities.) Byelorussians live in the southern part of Podlaskie voivodeship in the vicinity of the border with Belarus. This rural population, which displays a rather weak level of national Byelorussian identity and weak bonds with the neighbouring country, is in the process of transforming itself into a religious minority – Poles of Christian Orthodox religion (Barwiński 2013). Another process underway concerning this population is a massive outflow from rural areas to urban centres, mainly to the capital of the region, the city of Bialystok, where they are undergoing assimilation. This minority is represented by a range of organisations, mainly of socio-cultural character. In politics, it always supports left-wing and liberal parties and individuals – the rivals of parties considered as representing Polish nationalism and militant Catholicism (such as the Law and Justice party). From time to time, they gain seats in Parliament, but always by starting on the lists of all-national parties. The other national minority – Germans – live mostly in two southern voivodeships: Opolskie (in its eastern part) and Śląskie (Silesia) in its central-western part, usually intermingled with ethnic Silesians (otherwise hardly distinguishable groups). Germans have 're-emerged' and were officially recognised as a minority after the transformation of 1989.[7] Earlier, after the expulsion ('resettlement') and voluntary emigration of ethnic Germans form Poland following the Second World War, the German minority was thought to be non-existent. The constitutive factor of this minority is mainly memory (of being descendants of pre-war German citizens, which gives them the right to German passports) and sentiments, as they usually don't distinguish themselves from the local 'standard' Polish or Polish-Silesian population (they speak mostly standard Polish or the Silesian dialect of Polish) and are mostly Roman Catholic. This minority forms a majority in several municipalities in Opolskie voivodeshipgoverned by organisations representing the German minority, and a sizable minority in the regional assembly (*sejmik*). Due to election privileges for national minorities (they don't need to exceed the 5% threshold nationwide to enter the national Parliament), the German minority is regularly present in Parliament. Initially after 1989, the German minority had four members of Parliament (MPs) (out of 460) and one senator (out of 100), but this number has been constantly declining – they currently have only one MP. This shrinkage is due to migration to Germany[8] (where quite often they join Polish ethnic organisations), to the change of identity (into Polish or Silesian) and to weakened political mobilisation. Apart from some minor issues (e.g. concerning bilingual place names or historical monuments) there are no serious tensions between the German minority and the Polish majority. Language is not a problem, as all people speak Polish and teaching of German (which is quite popular) is offered to the whole local population.

In terms of regionalism in *Czechia* (the Czech Republic), the Polish national minority and Moravian regionalism are of some importance. The Polish minority is concentrated in the extreme north-eastern corner of the country – Těšín Silesia (the town Těšín/Cieszyn and the whole region being divided between Czechia and Poland). This area which was once the source of serious conflicts between Czech and Polish national movements and later (but as early as just after the First World War) between independent Czechoslovakia and Poland, can now be seen as an almost exemplary case of cross-border cooperation and respect for national minority rights. The Polish minority there, numbering about 50,000 people, like many ethnic minorities in the world is shrinking in absolute numbers and share of the population (it is currently a minority even in its area of settlement) due to assimilation and outmigration to other regions of the country (Siwek 2005). Moravian regionalism, which underwent spectacular growth around 1990 (after the fall of the old regime and during the period of disintegration of Czechoslovakia) followed by almost complete disappearance ten years later, is related to Moravia, a geographical and historical region of the republic, accounting for almost one-fifth of its territory and population. The distinctiveness of Moravia in comparison to Czechia proper (Bohemia), apart from being rather weak, is related to their different histories (Moravia was usually outside the historical kingdom of Bohemia), culture and way of life (traditional, rural, Catholic Moravia vs. urban, lay, cosmopolitan Bohemia), but not to the language (there are several dialects in Moravia, similar to Czech dialects, but none which are dominant and none with sufficient social prestige to challenge standard Czech). Moravian regionalism in the early 1990s was expressed first of all in declarations of belonging to Moravian nationality during the census of 1990 (about one out of ten million in the whole Czech Republic) and in the success of Moravian parties in the Czech parliamentary election in 1990, when they gained 10% of votes. This phenomenon had to do with the general popularity (or fashion) of regionalism in Europe as well as with the emancipation and then separation of Slovakia. The absence of mobilising claims and ideas, conflicts between leaders and the general change of mood in society after the disintegration of Czechoslovakia in 1992 meant that Moravian regionalism ran out of steam in the mid-1990s. In the 2001 census, the number of people declaring Moravian nationality dropped to 380,000 from 1,362,000 ten years earlier, and since 1996 the share of votes for Moravian parties has not exceeded 1% nationwide.[9] More numerous than ethnic Poles are other ethnic groups in Czechia, first of all the Romani and Slovaks, but they mostly live dispersed. Slovaks, otherwise linguistically and culturally very close to Czechs, integrate easily with the Czech society and don't display any strong desire to retain their language and identity. The Roma people present some socio-economic problems of integration which, however, exceed the scope of this analysis. Interestingly, a new minority – the Vietnamese (quite numerous and officially recognized) can serve as a model case of integration.

One of the major political issues in *Slovakia* has been the presence of the numerous Hungarian minority (about half a million, or about 10% of the population – the number and share being in constant decline),[10] concentrated along the Slovak-Hungarian border. The main differences between the Slovak majority and Hungarian minority include the language, and especially, historical memories and the resulting symbols and emotions. During centuries of Hungarian domination in 'Upper Hungary' (as the present territory of Slovakia was called by Hungarians), the Slovaks (then called 'Toth' by Hungarians), who were mainly peasants, lived under double or triple oppression: social, political and cultural-linguistic. On the other hand, Hungarians remember discrimination against them, especially shortly after the Second World War when they were expelled from Czechoslovakia (by the so-called Beneš decrees, which however, were stopped in relation to Hungarians). Hungarians, characterised by a strong identity and pride, do not easily give up their rights, especially when they feel and obtain support from Hungary. The post-1989 history of relationships between the Hungarian minority and the Slovak state and between Slovakia and Hungary is full of larger or smaller squabbles which, nevertheless, have not taken a violent form. Among the most contentious issues is Slovakia's language policy (Škrobák 2009;Daftary and Gál 2003). The two sides are in a constant process of 'negotiation', looking – through conflicts and compromises – for forms of coexistence which would ensure the domination (control) of Slovakia (and Slovak language and administration) over the whole territory, and respect for cultural and linguistic rights of ethnic Hungarians.[11] This attitude assumes resigning from radical demands such as a ban on the public use of Hungarian or the establishment of an administrative (and autonomous) region (district) in southern Slovakia (in which Hungarians would be the majority), giving it political and cultural autonomy (like in South Tyrol in Italy). Among the most conflictive issues has been the granting of so-called Charters of Hungarian and Hungarian passports by Hungary to ethnic Hungarians living abroad. The Hungarian minority in Slovakia is represented by some political parties which often change their names, leaders and profiles. From time to time they enter Slovak Parliament and even take part in Slovak governments. It seems that as time passes, the two sides (Slovakia and its Hungarian minority) are becoming used to the situation and there are fewer and fewer outbreaks of conflict.[12] Apart from the Hungarian minority, there is a numerous Roma population with its socio-economic characteristics (poverty, low education, low employability, high unemployment, high dependence on social benefits) as well as a small Ruthenian (Rusyn, Rusnak) population in north-eastern Slovakia. This population, differing slightly from the Slovak majority in its dialect (a Ukrainian-like dialect with a Slovak component) and religion (Greek Catholics, while Slovaks are mostly Roman Catholics) is strongly integrated with the Slovak society and state. During the communist regime they were officially regarded as ethnic Ukrainians, but after 1989 they gained the freedom to choose their ethnic belonging, and the majority declare themselves as Slovaks or Ruthenians.

For the reasons described above, *Hungary* has no sizable territorially concentrated national minorities. Those existing enjoy the right to organize themselves and cultivate their traditions, languages and so forth.[13] Ethnic Hungarians are also relatively homogeneous despite the fact that they confess several Christian denominations (with Roman Catholics being the most numerous), as this differentiation is not translated into political divisions. The biggest group differing from the rest of Hungary's population are the Roma people, whose number is difficult to estimate but probably exceeds 3.6%, as recorded in the last census. As in some other central and eastern European countries, relationships between this group and the Hungarian majority is a source of tensions and problems. These tensions and problems are aggravated and exploited by radical right-wing political groups, who add them to other sources of discontent, such as illegal immigrants and the 'Trianon trauma' (the loss of half of Hungary's territory after the First World War, decided by the winning powers at the conference in Trianon near Paris).

In *Slovenia*, there are two officially recognised national minorities, Hungarian and Italian, both concentrated in respective border areas. They enjoy all the related rights for cultivating their languages, traditions and identities, and are even guaranteed seats in Parliament. It is worth mentioning that teaching of their languages is not limited to these minorities but is offered to the whole populations of these areas. Their joint number and share is, however, negligible – about 0.5% of the total population, and they are minorities even in their area of settlement. Meanwhile, immigrants from other Yugoslav republics, although more numerous – more than 10% of the population – are not regarded as national minorities.[14] Present-day Slovenians are quite homogeneous as regards language, religion, culture and identity, but two areas distinguish themselves from the rest of the country. One of them is Zagorje, bordering Croatia, which is a kind of transition zone between the two countries as regards language (dialect) and ethnicity. The other area is the Adriatic Sea coast, whose population is largely bilingual (Slovenian and Italian), has constant contact with the Italian language and culture (due to Italian TV and direct contacts) and has a mixed Slovenian-Italian identity (or 'Italianised' Slovenian identity). The ethnocultural differentiation of Slovenia has not had political repercussions (there are no significant ethnically based or regionalist political parties or movements).

Croatia distinguishes itself from the other analysed countries (as well as from most, if not all, European countries) by its peculiar territorial shape (crescent-shaped with a part of its territory separated from the rest by a strip of land belonging to another country, Bosnia and Herzegovina), expressing, in a way, the peculiarities of the formation of Croats as an ethnic nation and of Croatia as a state. It is worth mentioning that the name of the medieval kingdom, preceding present-day Croatia, was the Kingdom of Dalmatia, Croatia and Slavonia, which entered the Kingdom of Hungary (at the beginning of the 12th century) as an autonomous part. 'Croatia' in the name of that kingdom referred to the territory around Zagreb; Slavonia was, and still is, a region along the Hungarian border. The situation was further complicated by the inflow of Serbs fleeing Ottoman rule and invited as guardians of the border (the present Croatian-Bosnian border). The contemporary territorial shape was drawn during the transformation of communist Yugoslavia into a federation and reflects historical divisions. After Croatia's declaration of independence in 1991, the territories populated by Serbs (*Krajinas*) declared independence from Croatia. After several years of fighting, and the expulsion and emigration of Serbs, Croatia gained full control over its territory. In this way, the separatism of ethnic Serbs – the most serious challenge to the territorial integrity of Croatia – was destroyed. The problem now faced by Croatia is the reconciliation of the two ethnic communities. The population of Croatia, which has a common standard language, religion (Catholicism) and national Croat identity, is differentiated as regards dialects (revealing strong vitality in private and to some extent in public life), regional cultures and even anthropological characteristics. Two areas distinguish themselves by their regional cultures and identities: Istra (Istria in Italian) and Dalmatia. It can be said that these areas, due to their location, centuries of contacts with Venice (and years of belonging to Italy) and the presence of a small but influential Italian national minority belong to the Mediterranean world, while the rest of Croatia belongs to central Europe.

Istra/Istria is of special relevance owing to its quite strong regionalist movement (engaging both the local Italian minority and 'Italianised' Croats). It has
a political representation in the form of parties, the oldest and most important
being Istarski demokratski sabor/Dieta Democratica Istriana (IDS/DDI), established in Pula in 1990 (or before Croatia's independence).[15]

The aims of this organisation are: the cultivation of the Istrian regional identity resulting from 'more than two thousand years of history', including the
languages (Croatian, Slovenian and Italian) and dialects of Istria; representing
the people of Istria and its adjacent islands before the state authorities; the
decentralisation and regionalisation of Croatia including autonomy for Istria;
supporting cross-border cooperation between Croatia, Slovenia and Italy on
the Adriatic coast; supporting the idea of decentralisation and regionalism in
the EU. According to official party documents, these aims should be achieved
exclusively in a democratic way, while respecting existing state borders and
rejecting attempts to change them.[16] IDS/DDI is a significant, or even leading,
political actor at the regional level, gaining seats in regional and local representative bodies in Istria, as well as in the Croatian Parliament. At present (2018),
IDS/DDI is the biggest party with 18 seats out of 44 in the regional parliament
of Istria, and holds the position chairman and one of two vice chairpersons.
Istrian regionalism is one of the most important genuine examples of regionalism in central and eastern Europe. Apart from regional communities and the
aforementioned Serbian minority, there are some other officially recognised
national minorities in Croatia (Italian, Hungarian, Czech, Slovak – the latter
three in Slavonia), which play a marginal role in the political life of the country.

Compared to most other analysed countries, *Romania* is characterised by
relatively high regional differentiation as regards economic development, culture, language (20 officially recognised minority languages)[17] and the identity
of inhabitants. This differentiation results from its history, correlated with geography (Popa 2000). From the point of view of culture, language and identity, at
the highest level of generalisation, two types of territory can be distinguished:
the core area (or the 'old' Romania) and the peripheries ('new territories'). The
core area is the territory of the Kingdom of Romania of 1860, established by
the union of two duchies: Valahia and Moldavia. This area is located in the south
and east of the country (along the borders with Bulgaria and the Republic of
Moldavia (Moldova), largely overlapping with the Carpathian mountains, and
accounting for about two-thirds to three-quarters of the national territory. It
is almost homogeneous as regards ethnicity and identity (Romanian), language
(Romanian) and religion (Christian Orthodox). The process of cultural and linguistic unification of Valahia and Moldavia, otherwise very close communities,
started long before political unification, and so historical differences between
the two former duchies have been practically erased. 'New territories' are those
areas which were conquered/incorporated and re-incorporated later on. The
biggest and most important among them is Transylvania (in the north-west of
the country), which was incorporated after the First World War (the Treaty of
Trianon), partially lost during World War II, and regained after the war. Since

the Middle Ages it had belonged directly or indirectly to Hungary, and in terms of culture was also connected with German lands. It was settled by ethnic Valahians and Moldavians (Romanians), Saxons (Germans) and various groups of Hungarians. They confessed various Christian denominations. Germans almost entirely emigrated (or were 'sold') to Germany during the communist regime of Ceauşescu.

Hungarians remained the biggest and practically the only significant national minority (approximately 1.5 million out of about 20 million inhabitants of Romania, or about 7% of the population). There is a triple difference or barrier between the ethnic Hungarians and Romanians – linguistic, religious and emotional, resulting from different historical memories. Ethnic Hungarians enjoy minority rights regarding the cultivation of traditions, use of language and teaching in and of Hungarian at all levels of education, including university level,[18] in public administration at local and regional level and so forth, although not on the scale that they would wish. Since the change of the political system in Romania, they have been represented by political parties. The biggest of them – established just after the change – the Democratic Alliance of Hungarians in Romania, representing a rather moderate wing of the Hungarian population, is an active participant in the political scene of Romania, present in the Parliament and sometimes in the government. The most active and militant group of Hungarians in Romania are the Szeklers (Secui, Székely). They form a majority in the eastern part of Transylvania, in the area called Szeklerland. This area had territorial autonomy (although in a changing territorial shape) in 1950–68. Restoration of this autonomy, by creating the Szekler autonomous region, similar to Catalonia or South Tyrol, is the main political demand of the organisation of Szeklers – the Szekler National Council established in 2003,[19] but this has been rejected by Romanian authorities. Szeklers were especially active when Romania was negotiating its access to the EU (Romania joined the EU in 2007). They hoped that the EU would support their demands given that respecting minority rights was one of preconditions for candidate countries from central and eastern Europe to join the EU. The EU did not uphold this demand, stating that territorial autonomy is not the only way of protecting ethnic minorities. To strengthen its demand for autonomy, the Szekler National Council organized a referendum in 2006, which was ruled illegal by Romanian authorities. Szeklers, in order to demonstrate their demands, and their very existence, organize a 'march for autonomy' each year in March, combined with commemoration of Szekler heroes and martyrs. The situation of ethnic Hungarians in Romania, and the policy of the Hungarian government related to ethnic Hungarians in Romania (supporting their political rights, granting Hungarian citizenship, etc.) are a source of constant tension between the two countries.

When analysing the issue of minorities in Romania, it can be said that the largest ethnic minority, considering themselves as Romanians of different origin, culture and language are the Roma people (the similarity of names – Roma (meaning Gypsy) and Romania is coincidental, although frustrating for Romanians). Given that this population is spread all over the country, do not display political activism or demands and is better integrated into Romanian society (than, for instance, in Slovakia or Hungary), it represents a socio-economic rather than a political issue.

In *Bulgaria* therearesome ethnic groups differing from 'typical Bulgarians' (Bulgarian ethnic self-identification, Bulgarian language, Christian Orthodox religion). It should be stressed that these groups usually share some characteristics with each other and with ethnic Bulgarians, so that distinguishing them can be problematic. Of some political and socio-economic importance are Turks, Macedonians and Roma people. In Bulgaria, as in other post-Ottoman Balkan countries, the term 'Turks' may signify people speaking Turkish as their native language, but it can also signify Muslims regardless of their language and descent. In general, it points to attachment to Turkey for religious or historical reasons, which is often expressed by customs, names, dress and so forth. After forced Bulgarisation in the interwar and communist periods, Turks 'reappeared' after 1989. The first evidence of their existence was their massive cross-border migrations to Turkey and back (as some realized that in fact their homeland was Bulgaria). Then, the Bulgarian Turks organized themselves into an influential party called the 'Movement for Rights and Freedoms' (nominally a non-ethnic party). It is an indispensable and stabilizing element in the political scene of Bulgaria. Turks, forming a 8%–10% strong minority, are concentrated mainly in two areas: in the Kardzhali region close to the Bulgarian-Greek border and in the north-east of the country – in other words, quite far away from the border with Turkey, which diminishes the possible threat of separatism. Macedonians are a Slav people of Christian Orthodox religion whose relationship to Bulgarians (as a regional variety of Bulgarians or a separate ethnicity) is the subject of political interpretations and policy. They form the majority in the former Yugoslav Republic of Macedonia, where since 1945 they have been recognized as a nation (separate from Bulgarians) and their dialect was elevated to the status of a language (according to the Bulgarian stance, it is another standard variety of Bulgarian). For a short period after the Second World War (when a Yugoslav-Bulgarian federation under Soviet auspices was conceived), Bulgarian authorities recognized the inhabitants of Bulgarian Macedonia (the Blagoevgrad region in the south-west, bordering on Yugoslav Macedonia) as ethnic Macedonians. Thereafter, Bulgaria withdrew this recognition and according to its official stance there are no Macedonians (as a separate group, different from Bulgarians) in Bulgaria. Organizations claiming to represent ethnic Macedonians are banned as separatist by Bulgarian law. Nevertheless, from time to time groups and individuals appear claiming to be Macedonians (not Bulgarians) and demanding minority rights. Since the Republic of Macedonia became an independent state (1991), Bulgaria hasn't raised claims to this country, recognising de facto Macedonians from the Republic of Macedonia as a separate nation. On the other hand, the Republic of Macedonia de facto recognizes the inhabitants of Bulgarian Macedonia as Bulgarians (and not discriminated Macedonians).[20] Roma people constitute 5%–10% of the population, distinguish themselves by a lower economic status, specific way of life and by a high natural increase, which is especially important in a country like Bulgaria, whose population is shrinking due to aging and outmigration. Being scattered throughout the country and not revealing political ambitions, the Roma population by no means represents any challenge to the territorial integrity of Bulgaria.

When analysing the phenomenon of regionalism in Central and Eastern Europe after 1989, it is worth mentioning a special case which differs from the aforementioned instances of grass-roots or genuine regionalism. This special case is an attempt to generate or induce regional identity and pride by the central national authorities in Poland in the 1990s. This attempt took the form of territorial-administrative reform: the establishment in 1999 of 16 quasi-autonomous self-governed regions, introduced in place of the previous 49 territorial units of central state administration (this issue is also discussed by Swianiewicz in this book). These 49 units (called voivodeships) existed since the reform of 1975 (under the old regime) and consisted of elected bodies (councils) and executives headed by a voivode appointed by the prime minister. Given that elections were not democratic, members of these councils were in practice selected and appointed by the party in the practically one-party system. After the democratic change in 1990, the councils of voivodeships were abolished. Democratically elected bodies existed only at the central and local (commune) levels. In the 1990s, among politicians at the central level and experts dealing with territorial self-government, the concept of regional self-government gained popularity, strongly influenced by the idea of a 'Europe of regions' and by the conviction that strong regional identity helps foster economic development. It was at the time when Poland was negotiating its access to the European Union. The result was the aforementioned introduction of self-governed voivodeships, also called *regiony*(regions), equipped with democratically elected councils (*sejmik*) and executives (composed by parties or coalitions holding a majority in the *sejmik*). The ideas behind this reform were first, to help access and absorb (future) EU funds; second, to improve the management of public economic and social development at the regional level; and third, to 'complete' democracy by introducing it at the regional level. It was by no means the desire of the population to have regions. It is worth stressing that proponents of the reform wanted to generate a sense of identity and pride in the regions. It was believed that regional identity and pride would mobilize inhabitants to work hard for constructive competition among regions. This attitude echoed the then popular (but vague) idea of a 'Europe of regions' and the general positive appraisal of regionalisation in the 'old' Europe. Polish proponents of regionalism believed that the economic successes of such regions like Catalonia, the Basque Country or Bavaria were due to regional pride and identity translated into the better work of their inhabitants and leaders. To induce the sense of identity and pride they decided that the new administrative units (regions) would have historical names (referring to various periods in history, sometimes recently invented, with little connection to the historical territories denoted by these names) and thus to give regions a historical patina. To some extent, the proponents of regions succeeded in generating or awakening a regional consciousness: originally, the number of regions was to be 12 or 13, but due to grass-roots opposition and the mobilisation of local populations, the final number was 16 (with some small changes in the territories of regions, also decided by the central government).[21] In 2019, these regions will celebrate 20 years of their existence. There is no room here to evaluate their successes and failures in managing regional affairs, but one thing seems to be sure: they have not created a sense of regional identity, a real regionalism.[22] Evidence of this situation is the composition of their councils and executives: in all but two regions, councils and executives are composed exclusively by all-national parties. (Those two atypical regions are the Silesian and Opole voivodeships, with minority or symbolic representations of the regionalist Movement for Autonomy of Silesia and German minority, respectively.) The voivodeships (regions) became, from the political point of view, another 'playground' for all-national parties, and from the economic point of view, a distributor and manager of regional development funds, largely coming from the EU (Swianiewicz 2008).

Final remarks

The collapse of socialism (communism) in Central and Eastern Europe in 1989–91 deprived the countries in this part of Europe of a binding ideology and of ruling elites. This situation undermined the very existence of states without a strong ethno-national basis and led to disappearance of one of them (the GDR), which was incorporated by another state (the FRG) and the disintegration of federative states (the USSR, Yugoslavia, Czechoslovakia). In this way, the regions of these countries, characterised by a distinct identity (culture, historical memory, language) became internationally recognised independent states. Some of them joined the European Union. Transformation of former regions into independent states, together with other phenomena which took place in most countries of this part of Europe after the Second World War and afterwards (shifts of borders and populations, internal migrations, etc.) considerably reduced interregional differences within individual countries and contributed to the elimination of sub-national regionalism as an important political factor. There is practically only one regionalist movement seriously shaping the political situation of its country: this is Szekler regionalism in Romania.[23] Nevertheless, in some countries there are significant national minorities which in some way influence the political lives of their countries and relations between countries of residence and kin states – these are, first of all, the Russian minorities in Estonia and Latvia, the Hungarian minorities in Slovakia and Romania, and to a lesser extent, the Polish minority in Lithuania. In all these cases, however, a process is under way of diminishing the demographic weight and politically demobilising minorities, and this is contributing to the political stabilisation of individual countries and inter-state relations in this part of Europe. If there are some destabilising factors, these are not related to the regionalism or separatism dealt with in this chapter.

Notes

1 Of the same opinion is Czech specialist in regionalism Ladislav Cabada who wrote:'After twenty years of democracy or democratisation in this area the East European regionalism is by far not as strong as it is the case with the most visible regional, autonomist or separatist movements in Western Europe' (Cabada 2009: 20; my translation from Czech).

2 As Pascal de Rauglaudre (de Raugluadre 1999) pointed out, contrary to some fears (or hopes?) that Russian speakers in Latvia could be used by external political forces to destabilize situation of this country, this population revealed a high degree of integration and loyalty towards Latvia.

3 In November 1989 authorities of still Soviet Lithuania adopted a law guaranteeing 'the right to get Lithuanian citizenship to all permanent residents of Lithuanian SSR without regard to their nationality, length of stay and knowledge of Lithuanian language (with exception of Soviet Army personnel and their families)' (Andrlík 2009: 48, 49). Two years later, when Lithuania was fully independent, the law was changed, making conditions for getting citizenship much harder (including language test), but this new law was rather applicable to new immigrants. As a result, during the census of 2001 only 0.3% of inhabitants of Lithuania did not have Lithuanian citizenship. (Andrlík 2009: 49).

4 For more information on numbers, ethnic characteristics, identity and political demands and institutions see, e.g. Szul (2015). It should be added that the status of Kashubians and Silesians as ethno-regional communities results from Polish law, while some (many) members of these communities claim that they are national minorities, like Germans, Byelorussians and others.

5 There was a possibility to declare one (sole) identity or two identities (the main and the secondary).

6 A very detailed analysis of the Silesian regionalism/nationalism, made by sympathisers of this movement, is presented by Sekuła et al. (2012).

7 On the 're-appearing' of ethnic Germans in Poland, their characteristics, demands and organisations, there is abundant literature in Poland, see, e.g. Heffner and Solga (2003).

8 On the emigration from the area populated by German minority in the Opole region, see Heffner and Solga (2017).

9 For more details see Prokop (2001) and Hloušek (2015).

10 According to Robert Ištok (Ištok 2003), the number of ethnic Hungarians in the present territory of Slovakia dropped from nearly 900,000 and their share from 30% at the beginning of the 20th century to 521,000 and 9.7% in 2001. These numbers should be considered as approximate because of the delicate matter of one's ethnic identity and not full identification of language and ethnicity. Even in the case of Hungarians for whom language is the central element of identity there is a difference between the number of persons declaring belonging to the Hungarian ethnic group in Slovakia in 2006 (520,500) and the number of persons declaring Hungarian as their mother tongue (572,900) (Škrobák 2009). One reason of this difference may be existence of numerous Hungarian-speaking Roma (Gypsy).

11 As the most updated and comprehensive source of information on language policy and practice in Slovakia can serve the Council of Europe's report of experts (2015) on implementation by Slovakia of the European Charter for Regional or Minority Languages. This report points out to many cases of non respecting of language rights of Hungarians in education, public administration and so forth. https://rm.coe.int/CoERMPublicCommonSearchServices/DisplayDCTMContent?documentId=090000 16806dba3e (accessed 28 June 2018).

12 Regardless of changing international relations between Slovakia and Hungary, cross-border relations between the two countries develop successfully. An interesting fact is the cross-border urban sprawl of Bratislava, capital city of Slovakia, located near the border: some inhabitants of Bratislava, daily commuting to Bratislava, choose to live on the Hungarian side of the border (Hardi 2009).

13 According to the last (2011) general census, 6.5% of the population of Hungary claimed belonging to one of 13 autochthonous national minorities (Armenians, Bulgarians, Croatians, Germans, Greeks, Roma, Poles, Romanians, Ruthenians, Serbians, Slovaks, Slovenians and Ukrainians), speaking, besides Hungarian, 14 languages (one of those groups, the Roma, speaks two languages, Romani and Beás, which is a form of old Romanian). All those groups seem to be highly integrated or assimilated into the Hungarian society, as most people declaring that they belong to national minorities declare Hungarian as their mother tongue, only 1.5% declared one of those languages as their mother tongue and 3% declared using one or more of these languages in family life or with friends. It should be kept in mind that all numbers on ethnicity and language, in Hungary and elsewhere, are only tentative as they are based on personal declarations and they are highly dependent on several factors. What is sure about Hungary is that national minorities don't play a significant role. For more information, see reports of the Council of Europe on implementation of the European Charter for Regional or Minority Languages by Hungary: https://rm.coe.int/CoERMPublicCommonSearchServices/DisplayDCTM Content?documentId=09000016806d8837 (accessed 27 June 2018).

14 For more on language policy and situation in Slovenia see the Council of Europe's committee of experts from 2013 on implementation of the European Charter for Regional or Minority Languages: https://rm.coe.int/CoERMPublicCommonSearchServices/DisplayDCTMContent?documentId=09000016806dba62.

15 For more information see www.ids-ddi.com/ (accessed 15 June 2018).

16 According to Slovenian scholars Jernej Zupančič and Peter Repolusk, aacceptance of the geopolitical situation was not always characteristic of the Istrian regionalist movement (encompassing both Croatian and Slovenian parts of the peninsula). According to them, in the time of disintegration of Yugoslavia at the beginning of the 1990s, in the movement there was a significant separatist stream threatening political stability of Croatia and Slovenia (Zupančič and Repolusk 1995).

17 See https://search.coe.int/cm/Pages/result_details.aspx?ObjectID=09000016807766d3. This is the Council of Europe's report on Romania's implementation of the European Charter for Regional or Minority Languages.

18 There is no exclusively Hungarian university, but Babes-Bolyai Univesity of Cluj-Napoca offers a range of faculties with Hungarian as a language of instruction. The right to receive education in a minority language is combined with the obligation to know the official language (Romanian) to avoid socio-cultural and political isolation of minorities (Costachie 2001).

19 See http://sznt.sic.hu/en/index.php?option=com_content&view=article&id=210:the-szeklers-and-their-struggle-for-autonomy&catid=4:a-szekelyseg&Itemid=6.

20 This double recognition is a basis for the recent reconciliation between the two states confirmed in 2017 by a treaty on border and good neighbourhood relations and by some common activities undertaken by the two governments (Pieńskowski 2018).

21 Regionalisation of Poland, before and after the reform, was the subject of multiple publications. See for instance Jałowiecki et al. 2007.

22 In 2009, ten years after the start of new regions, a publication was dedicated to evaluation of their performance (Szomburg ed. 2009). The general conclusion, expressed particularly by Zarycki (Zarycki 2009) and Kleina (Kleina 2009), was that regions failed to create regionalism, regional political elites, regional pride and identity. Almost ten years after these publications, one can say that these conclusion is still valid.

23 It is not purely accidental that Hungary's prime minister, Mr. Orbán, known for his nationalistic sentiments, delivers his speeches related to 'Great Hungary' in this particular region.

References

Andrlík, J. (2009). Ethnic and language policy of the Republic of Lithuania. *Annual of Language & Politics and Politics of Identity*, III.

Barwiński, M. (2013). Geograficzno-polityczne uwarunkowania sytuacji Ukraińców, Białorusinów i Litwinów w Polsce po 1944 roku (*Geographic-political conditions of the situation of Ukrainians, Byelorussians and Lithuanians in Poland after 1944*). Łódź: Wydawnictwo Uniwersytetu Łódzkiego.

Cabada, L. (2009). Úvodem. Možnosti a limity výzkumu evropského regionalism. In: Ladislav Cabada a kolektív (ed.), *Evropa regionů*. Plzeň: Vydavatelství a nakladatelství Aleš Čeněk s.r.o.

Costachie, S. (2001). Geopolitics and Ethnic Minorities' Policy of Romania, *Revista Română de geografie politică*, Anul III No.2.

Daftary, F., & Gál, K. (2003). The 1999 Slovak Minority Language Law: Internal or External Politics? In: F. Daftary & F. Grin (eds.), *Nation-Building, Ethnicity and Language Politics in Transition Countries*. Budapest: European Centre for Minority Issues, Open Society Institute.

de Rauglaudre, P. (1999). Russophones in Latvia: A geographical approach. In: M. Koter & K. Heffner (eds.), *Multicultural Regions and Cities* [Region and Regionalism, No 4]. Lódž/Opole: University of Lódž/Silesian Institute.

Hardi, T. (2009). Changing cross-border movements in the Slovak-Hungarian border region after the EU accession. In: *Historical Regions Divided by the Borders* (ed.) Marek Sobczynski *Region and Regionalism*, No 9, vol. 1.

Heffner, K., & Solga, B. (2003). The German minority in Opole Silesia as a minority of social and cultural borderland. In: M. Koter & K. Heffner (eds.), *The Role of Ethnic Minorities in Border Regions* [Region and Regionalism, No 6 vol 1].

Heffner, K., & Solga, B. (2017). International migration and population decline in the regions with national minorities in Poland on the example of Opolskie Voivodship. In: K. Heffner & B. Soga (eds.), *Borderlands of Nations* [Nations of Borderlands Region and Regionalism, No 13 vol 2].

Hloušek, V. (2015). From region to nation and back again: Moravian parties' rhetoric and politics in the course of time. *Annual of Language & Politics and Politics of Identity*, IX.

Ištok, R. (2003). Hungarian Minority at the Southern Border of Slovakia in the Political and Geographical Contexts. In: M. Koter and K. Heffner (eds.), *The Role of Ethnic Minorities in Border Regions* [Region and Regionalism, No 6 vol 1].

Jałowiecki, B., Szczepański, M.S., & Gorzelak, G. (2007). *Rozwój lokalny i regionalny w perspektywie socjologicznej* Wydanie drugie, Tychy: Śląskie Wydawnictwa Naukowe Wyższej Szkoły Zarządzania i Nauk Społecznych w Tychach.

Kleina, K. (2009). Dziesięć lat samorządu wojewódzkiego bez regionalnej tożsamości. In: Jan Szomburg (ed.), *Jak uczynić regiony motorami rozwoju i modernizacji Polski*. Gdańsk: Polskie Forum Obywatelskie i Instytut Badań nad Gospodarką Rynkową.

Pieńkowski, J. (2018). Bulgaria's national identity policy in the Balkans. *PISM Bulletin (Polish Institute of International Affairs)* No 98 (1169), www.pism.pl/publications/bulletin/no-98-1169.

Popa, N. (2000). Elemente de unitate și alteritate în spațiul geographic românesc/Eléments d'unité et d'altétité dans l'espace géographique roumain, *Revista Română de geografie politică*, Anul II Nr 2.

Prokop, R. (2001). Identita moravské a slezské národnosti v podmínkách České republiky se nepotvrdila. In: O. Šrajerová (ed.), *Otázky národní identity – determinanty a subjektivní vnímání v podmínkách současné multietnické společnosti*. Slezský ústav, Dokumentační a informační středisko Rady Evropy. Praha: Opava.

Ščerbinskis, V. (2004). *Consolidation of Latvian Nation and Latgallian Particularity*. Warsaw Special Convention of the ASN, 18–21 VI.

Sekuła, E., Jałowiecki, A.B., Majewski, P., & Żelazny, W. (2012). *Być narodem? Ślązacy o Śląsku* (To be a nation? Silesians about Silesia) Wyższa Szkoła Psychologii Społecznej, Wydawnictwo Naukowe SCHOLAR, Warszawa.

Siwek, T. (2005). Ethnic identity versus declared nationality in the Czech part of Teschen Silesia (Zaolzie). In: M. Koter & K. Heffner (eds.), *The Role of Borderlands in United Europe* [*Region and Regionalism*, No 7 vol 2].

Škrobák, Z. (2009). Language policy of Slovak Republic. *Annual of Language & Politics and Politics of Identity*, III.

Swianiewicz, P. (2008). *Szafarze darów europejskich: kapitał społeczny a realizacja polityki regionalnej w polskich województwach*. Scholar Warszawa.

Szomburg, J. (ed.) (2009). *Jak uczynić regiony motorami rozwoju i modernizacji Polski*. Wolność i Solidarność nr 19, Gdansk 2009 ('How to make regions engines of development and modernization of Poland', in Polish).

Szul, R. (2015). Poland's language regime governing Kashubian and Silesian. In: L. Cardinal & S.K. Sonntag (eds.), *State Traditions and Language Regimes*. London, Ithaca: McGill-Queen's University Press, Montreal & Kingston.

Zarycki, T. (2009). Dlaczego potrzebujemy dobrze działających systemów komunikacji regionalnej oraz regionalnej polityki tożsamościowej. In: J. Szomburg (ed.) *Jak uczynić regiony motorami rozwoju i modernizacji Polski*. Gdańsk: Polskie Forum Obywatelskie i Instytut Badań nad Gospodarką Rynkową.

Zupančič, J., & Repolusk, P. (1995). Regionalism in Istria. In: M. Koter (ed.), *Social and Political Aspects* [*Region and Regionalism* No 2].

Part II
Reforms and challenges

5 Demographic change and challenge

Agnieszka Fihel[1] and Marek Okólski

Introduction

As a rule, due to the multitude and complexity of economic, social and political factors that condition population processes, the latter usually take place in a slow and gradual manner, whereas abrupt demographic changes are rare. Yet, in the post-1989 period, the 11 countries[2] of Central and Eastern Europe (EU11) experienced sudden and simultaneous turnabouts in all the three fundamental demographic phenomena: natality, mortality and international migration. The consequent de-population and process of population ageing, which we address in this chapter, became one of the most far-reaching changes specific to the EU11 societies undergoing the post-communist institutional and economic transition, and one of the greatest challenges for these societies in the near future.

The acceleration of unfavourable demographic changes in the EU11 originated to a great extent in the legacy of the communist system that, at least since the 1970s, hindered the modernisation of societies in many ways. Needless to say, the institutional and economic transition following the first democratic elections in Poland in 1989 and the fall of the Berlin Wall in Germany radically and rapidly changed the hitherto-prevailing determinants of population processes, forced modernisation and introduced the rules of a capitalistic economy and a highly competitive labour market. But these were not the only circumstances underlying demographic processes in the EU11 countries; the post-1989 transition itself created unique conditions, resulting in a considerable increase in unemployment, a perceptible deterioration in the living standards of large parts of society and a drastic drop in welfare expenditure (see also Boenker et al. 2002; Vihalemm et al. 2017). Some EU11 countries struggled with more severe economic conditions than others (see chapter by Orłowski in this book), but all societies under study maintained their support for the pro-Western course of change and became members of the North Atlantic Treaty Organisation (NATO) and the European Union (EU).

In this chapter, we present the most important demographic changes in EU11 countries in the post-1989 period: the lengthening of life expectancy, decreasing number of births and declining fertility rates, and the diversification of countries' migration status. We analyse the abrupt turnabouts in the three fundamental demographic phenomena: natality, mortality and international mobility, and present their impact on the process of de-population and ageing. Our objective is to study how the fundamental changes of the institutional and economic system have underlain unusual demographic change, and to highlight the uniqueness of post-communist conditioning for the population processes in the EU11. We do so by presenting demographic tendencies set against the wide European background[3] and, whenever possible, at the regional level.

Mortality

For several decades, unfavourable tendencies impeded the decline in mortality in European communist countries.[4] Before the so-called health crisis, in the first years following the end of World War II, all European countries experienced a rapid increase in life expectancy thanks to the amelioration of living conditions and food supplies, as well as the implementation of vaccination programs on a massive scale (Vallin and Lopez 1985). As a consequence, mortality among infants and young children declined radically, contributing to an overall increase in life expectancy, amounting in Europe to 5.5 years between 1950 and 1965[5] (UN 2017). However, when infant mortality was significantly reduced, that is around the mid-1960s, other epidemiologic threats emerged, posed in the first place by behaviour-related diseases: cardiovascular diseases, cancers, traffic accidents and alcohol-related diseases. At that time, the trends in mortality started to diverge between the EU11 and the western part of the continent[6] (Okólski 1993): while the latter managed to adjust their health care systems to prevent and treat man-made diseases, the former turned out to be inefficient in dealing with several dysfunctions of the socio-economic system, such as irregular supplies of food, in particular of good quality, low wages and poor working conditions, undeveloped transport organisation, deteriorating natural environment, permanent stress, the feeling of alienation and declining social morale.[7] Health indicators deteriorated in most age groups of the EU11 populations,[8] but particularly unfavourable tendencies were registered in adult groups, including men in middle age, for whom mortality due to cardiovascular diseases, neoplasm and external causes of death significantly increased. In countries such as Estonia, Hungary, Lithuania, Poland, Romania and Slovakia, male mortality rates in middle age increased by more than 50% between 1965 and 1990. In this period, life expectancy at birth[9] declined (in Bulgaria, Estonia and Latvia), stagnated (in Hungary, Lithuania, Poland and Slovakia) or marginally increased by one to two years (in Czechia, Croatia and Slovenia).

The post-communist transition brought about an improvement in public health indicators, albeit not immediate. The first to register a continuous increase in life expectancy, that is, lasting at least three consecutive years, was Czechia[10] (the increase started in 1991), followed by Poland (1992), Hungary and Slovenia (1994), Croatia (1995) and Slovakia (1996). In this group of countries, life expectancy has been rising continuously and at a relatively fast rate both for males and females during the whole post-communist period (Figure 5.1). On average, life expectancy increased in these countries by seven years between 1990 and 2016.

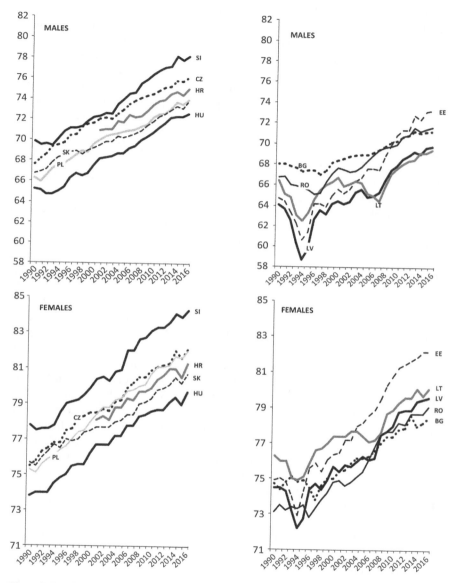

Figure 5.1 Life expectancy at birth (in years) for males (upper panel) and females (lower panel) in the EU11 countries, 1990–2016

Note: BG – Bulgaria, CZ – Czechia, EE – Estonia, HR – Croatia, HU – Hungary, LV – Latvia, LT – Lithuania, PL – Poland, RO – Romania, SI – Slovenia, SK – Slovakia.

Source: Own elaboration based on Eurostat (2018).

The other EU11 countries (the three Baltic states, Bulgaria and Romania) underwent different changes, marked by periods of life expectancy decline (1993–94 and 2006–07 in the Baltic states, 1996–97 in Bulgaria and Romania) and only since 2008 resulting in stable progress. On average, life expectancy in this group of countries increased by 5.2 years between 1990 and 2016.

Given the fact that, in the same period, the 'old' EU15 countries registered an average rise in life expectancy of 5.8 years, the distance in relation to the first above-distinguished group of EU11 countries diminished by 1.2 years, and in relation to the second group increased by 0.6 years. Thus, after several decades of divergence between the Western and Eastern Europe, life expectancy trends started to converge anew across the European continent, although some countries registered an important delay in life expectancy progress (see also Meslé and Vallin 2017).

More detailed analysis for the NUTS2 regions reveals small discrepancies in life expectancy at the regional level within countries and relatively high discrepancies between the EU11 countries. In 2016, the average life expectancy at birth in the EU11 regions was as high as 77.5 years. Estonia and all regions in Czechia, Croatia, Slovenia and 12 out of 16 regions in Poland were equal or above this value, whereas all other regions in the EU11 countries were below it. In 2005, when the average life expectancy was as low as 74.2 years, the variation of EU11 regions also ran along national borders, with Czechia, Croatia, Poland, Slovenia and one Slovak region above the average, and the three Baltic states, Bulgaria, Hungary, Romania and the rest of Slovakia below it. In 2016 and 2005, the life expectancy variation between countries was responsible, respectively, for 78% and 84% of the overall variation between the NUTS2 regions in the EU11 countries under study. The low variation within countries can be explained by the fact that the most important causes of death remain treatable through the health care systems organized at the national level. Indeed, the European atlas of cause-specific mortality shows only small intra-national differences for cardiovascular diseases, neoplasms of the digestive system or traffic accidents in the EU11 countries (European Commission 2009). In contrast, diseases determined by individual behaviours that contribute to the overall level of mortality to a limited extent, exhibit specific inequalities within these countries. Alcohol-related and smoking-related causes of death serve here as perfect examples. Large variation in mortality due to tobacco consumption can be observed in Bulgaria, Czechia, Poland and Romania, where urbanized and western regions of countries exhibit higher mortality rates.[11] The situation is more scattered in the case of alcohol abuse, with both the least developed and the most urbanized regions registering high levels of mortality.

As for the epidemiology of mortality decline in the EU11, man-made diseases have been the main drivers of life expectancy changes. On the eve of the post-communist transition, high mortality due to cardiovascular diseases contributed to approximately half of the life expectancy differential between the EU11 and the western part of the continent (Bobak and Marmot 1996). Between 1990 and 2015, cardiovascular mortality declined by approximately 48% in Croatia, Czechia, Hungary, Poland, Slovakia and Slovenia and by 34% in the Baltic states, Bulgaria and Romania. In the 1990s alone, this decline contributed the most to the increase in life expectancy, ranging from 27% of the increase in Slovakia to 72% in Estonia (Meslé 2004). Trends in malignant neoplasms, the second most important group of causes of death, remained ambiguous: between 1990 and 2015 mortality increased by 15% and 7% in Romania and Bulgaria, respectively; declined by less than 10% in Croatia, Estonia, Latvia, Lithuania, Poland and Slovakia; and declined by more than 10% in Czechia (by 35%), Hungary (14%) and Slovenia (13%). Mortality due to external causes of death, with traffic accidents constituting the most important subcategory, declined in most EU11 countries except for the Baltic states. In the latter, it increased between 1990 and 1994 by 67% on average, and decreased thereafter by 58% till 2015. In all other EU11 countries under study, it diminished by 49% on average between 1990 and 2015, ranging from 31% in Slovakia to 62% in Hungary.

Interpretation of the mortality trends in the context of political, social and economic changes taking place in the countries under study remains extremely difficult, mostly due to the fact that man-made diseases – the principal cause of death in developed countries in general and in the EU11 countries in particular – are determined by a multitude of factors, including present and past[12] health behaviours, accessibility and organisation of the health care system and the advancement of medical treatment. Except for the Baltic states, and to a lesser extent Bulgaria and Romania, the post-1989 life expectancy progress stemmed from mortality reductions for all age groups and for most groups of causes of death, which was due both to the changes in healthcare systems and the shift in lifestyles. For the most important group of cardiovascular diseases (Ischaemic Heart Diseases), the WHO Multinational Monitoring of Trends and Determinants in Cardiovascular Disease (MONICA) study[13] showed that medical treatment accounted for most of the variance in mortality in Western Europe, Czechia, Lithuania and Poland (Kuulasmaa et al. 2000). Thus, the introduction of modern medical treatment methods,[14] thanks to increased public expenditure on healthcare and the development of civic organisations,[15] improved accessibility to efficient care. According to the MONICA study, the control of hypertension in most EU11 countries improved significantly during the 1990s (e.g. Cifkova et al. 2010; Tykarski et al. 2005), and nowadays the frequency and methods of treatment of cardiovascular patients do not differ considerably from practices applied in Western European countries (Gierlotka et al. 2014).

The commercialisation of medical services could also have improved access to selected medical services, although some authors mention the growing social inequalities in the access to health services. In fact, a rise in mortality differences between socio-economic groups could be observed after 1989 in Czechia, Estonia, Hungary, Lithuania and Poland (Kalediene and Petrauskiene 2005; Leinsalu et al. 2009, 2003; Shkolnikov et al. 2006). In Czechia, Hungary and Poland, this divergence stemmed from unequal mortality reductions in all socio-economic groups, whereas in the Baltic states it was from increasing mortality in less educated groups (Leinsalu et al. 2009), mostly due to external causes of death and alcohol-related death (Jasilionis et al. 2007). This means that it was primarily differences in health behaviours, rather than health service accessibility, that underlay the growing mortality inequalities in the Baltic states.

The shift in people's health behaviours, disease awareness and individual prevention constituted the second most important determinant of life expectancy progress in the EU11. The level of risk factors was so unfavourable at the beginning of the 1990s that each modification in people's lifestyles resulted in a significant decrease in mortality. Several epidemiologic surveys proved that in most EU11 countries, except Bulgaria and the Baltic states, men started to quit smoking on a mass scale, but at the same time women increased their use of tobacco (Eurostat 2009; Ng et al. 2014; OECD 2015; Zatoński 2008). Except for the Baltic states, the consumption of alcohol has been diminishing and the structure of consumed alcoholic beverages has become less detrimental, with the increasing importance of beer and wine and decreasing importance of strong spirits (WHO 2015). Zatoński (2008) also stresses that the pattern of drinking has evolved, with irregular heavy drinking becoming more and more occasional and moderate drinking accompanying meals becoming more frequent. The Baltic states have exhibited a different pattern in this regard, similar to that observed in other ex-USSR republics, where a rise in alcohol abuse propelled alcohol-related mortality and overall mortality in the mid-1990s. Alcohol became the cause of approximately half of deaths due to external causes (Zatoński 2008) and a large share of deaths due to cardiovascular diseases.

Rising living standards in the EU11 also implied an important shift in daily diet that began to be more diversified and richer in fresh fruits and vegetables (FAOSTAT 2015). In addition, unsaturated fats started to substitute for saturated fats, which had a crucial impact on the reduction of cardiovascular mortality (Nolte et al. 2000; Rychtaříková 2002; Zatoński and Boyle 1996); for instance, intake of the former increased by 44% in Czechia and by 30% in Poland between 1993 and 2011. Bandosz et al. (2012) assessed that, in Poland, the decrease in cholesterol consumption contributed to a 39% decrease in mortality due to coronary heart diseases between 1991 and 2005, whereas favourable trends in all other risk factors contributed to an additional 15% decrease. At the same time, the improvement in treatment methods and accessibility played a secondary though still important role, contributing to a decrease in coronary heart mortality of 37%. This result proves that both factors (health behaviours and the health care system) contributed almost equally to the decrease in cardiovascular mortality that was driving the life expectancy changes in the EU11 countries.

Mortality decline in the post-1989 period had an ambiguous impact on the process of ageing in the EU11 countries. As infant mortality declined, an increasing proportion of new-borns were able to reach young age groups, which contributed to population rejuvenation. However, on the eve of the post-communist transition, infant mortality was already relatively low and, therefore, its rejuvenating effect was completely neutralised by the decline in adult and old age mortality, leading to growth in the number of old persons in EU11 societies. The study for Poland proved that the growth in the population's mean age – one of the most important indicators of population ageing – that took place between 2010 and 2015 was almost 50% determined by the mortality decline (Fihel et al. 2018). Analogical results for other EU11 countries that share Poland's demographic profiles and post-war history are likely to be similar.

Natality

In the post-1989 period, the falling number of births was one of the key components of general population trend in the EU11 countries: while back in 1950–55, 10.4 million births were recorded, on the eve of the post-communist transition in 1985–90, this figure was 8.2 million and 20 years later in 2010–15, just 5.2 million (a drop of 50.1%). Thus, in a span of 60 years, the number of births halved, despite the fact that in 2010–15 more persons (and more potential parents) lived in those countries than in 1950–55. An analogical but more moderate decrease in natality occurred in other European countries: in Western Europe,[16] 12.5 million children were born in 1950–55, 10.5 million in 1985–90 and 9.7 million in 2010–15 (a drop of 22.1%).

Changes in fertility patterns are considered as a major factor responsible for such a steep fall in the number of births in the EU11.[17] Until the early 1990s, almost all countries of CEE had lagged behind the West in the fertility transition from high and uncontrolled to low and effectively controlled. In northern and Western Europe, a broad measure of fertility levels, the so-called period total fertility rate (TFR),[18] dropped below the generation replacement level and stabilized at a record low: between 1975 and 1990 Austria and Germany reached their bottom line at around 1.5; between 1985 and 1990 other countries of Western Europe at around 1.7; between 1980 and 1985 countries of northern Europe at around 1.6. After 1995, western countries, except Austria and Germany, embarked on a slowly rising trend of TFR (Frejka and Sobotka 2008). Around 1990, when in northern and Western Europe fertility stabilized, in EU11 countries the TFR decline accelerated, hitting historically low national levels: 1.09 in Bulgaria (in 1997), 1.10 in Latvia (1998), 1.13 in Czechia (1999) and 1.19 in Slovakia (2002). In other countries, the bottom level ranged between 1.20 and 1.27 in 2002 or 2003, with the distinct exception of Croatia, where the TFR never fell below 1.3. In the middle of the first decade of the 21st century, a TFR recovery began in all EU11 countries, but the process has been rather slow and not consistent. In 2016, the TFR ranged from 1.4 (Croatia and Poland) to 1.7 (Latvia and Lithuania). Thus, as opposed to northern and Western Europe, which pioneered an almost perfect birth control and a descent of the TFR to below replacement levels, in the EU11 (except Croatia) fertility levels slipped below the threshold called the 'lowest-low fertility' (Kohler et al. 2002, 2006), that is below 1.3. This was the outcome of a number of changes in procreative and partnership behaviours,[19] which are likely to be persistent.

Figure 5.2 displays changes and regional (NUTS2) differences in TFR in two consecutive decennial periods: 1995–05 and 2005–15. It appears that no common tendency could be observed, either among the regions of different countries or among regions within a single country. In the former period, the TFR almost uniformly decreased in regions of Czechia, Hungary, Poland and Slovakia (also in Lithuania as a whole),[20] while it increased in regions of Bulgaria (and Estonia as a whole).[21] The regional differences within particular countries were generally preserved, with the exception of Poland, where the

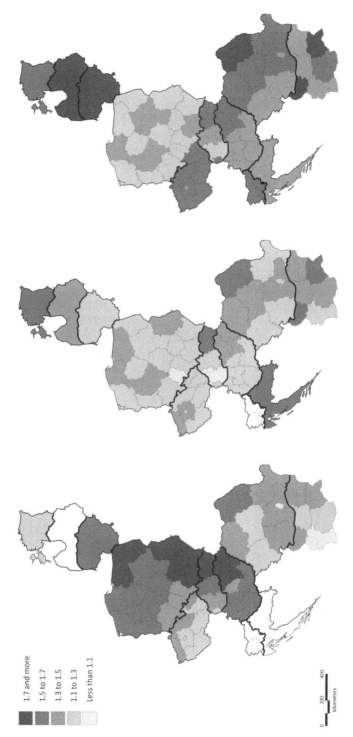

1.7 and more

1.5 to 1.7

1.3 to 1.5

1.1 to 1.3

Less than 1.1

0   200   400
kilometers

Figure 5.2 The total fertility rate (TFR) in regions (NUTS2 level) of EU11 countries, 1995 (left), 2005 (centre) and 2015 (right)

Source: Own elaboration based on Eurostat (2018).

eastern region (the least economically developed) ceased to be an area of relatively high fertility and regional differences considerably narrowed. The latter period saw increases in TFR in many countries, with the exception of Croatia (a decline) and Estonia (stability). These increases were indeed spectacular in Czechia and Romania, where they occurred in all regions. In Bulgaria, the rising tendency continued in most regions. In turn, Poland noted changes in both directions, but remained a country with only small regional differences.

Formal analysis of TFR dispersion across NUTS2 regions was limited, due to the lack of comparable data, to eight countries (all EU11 except Croatia, Latvia and Slovenia). The data suggest that regional differences in the analysed group of countries were very small over the two recent decades; the coefficient of variation between 1995 and 2005 decreased from 0.154 to 0.093 and then rose to 0.123 in 2015. However, inter-regional variation of TFR proved highly unstable; whereas in 2005 it was responsible for 52.5% of the overall variation between the NUTS2 regions, in 2005 it dropped to 41.2%, only to increase to 54.9% in 2015. Our analysis points to dynamic, but far from uniform fertility changes in EU11 regions.

The demographic technique of fertility analysis (Bongaarts and Feeney 1998) allows the separation of two principal factors that directly affect changes in TFR: 'quantum', reflecting the actual average number of children (per woman) born in the absence of any change in the average age of childbearing, and 'tempo', broadly corresponding to changes in the timing of reproduction. According to Goldstein et al. (2009), at least until 1990, changes in fertility levels in a large majority of EU11 countries[22] were almost exclusively determined by the 'quantum' component, that is a decline in age-specific fertility rates. Since then, the steep decline in period TFR (Figure 5.3) is attributed mainly to the postponement of childbearing. A tempo-adjusted TFR, a theoretical measure not allowing for postponed childbearing, would be considerably higher in the EU11 (except Bulgaria and Romania) than standard, period TFR, 1.66 vs. 1.25[23] (Frejka and Sobotka 2008). In no other group of European countries was the 'tempo' effect, reflecting a delay in motherhood, so strong as in Central Europe: −0.41 (one-third of the actual value of period TFR) as compared to −0.26 (15%) in Northern Europe and 0.17 (10%) in Western Europe.

The 'quantum' effect stems from a long-term cohort-specific tendency of declining completed (lifetime) fertility.[24] The decrease in cohort TFR in the EU11 group started with women born in the 1920s, for whom completed fertility generally exceeded 2.1. The progeny of women born in the early 1950s was still above 2 (Lithuania and Slovenia being distinct exceptions). A sharp decline took place for cohorts born at the turn of that decade, whose most intensive childbearing occurred between 1985 and 1990. The average for Central Europe as a whole fell from 2.04 (cohort 1955) to 1.88 (cohort 1965) (Frejka and Sobotka 2008) and is expected to continue the downward trend (Frejka and Gietel-Basten 2016).[25] Notwithstanding the trend in cohort fertility, there are other clear symptoms that suggest a continuation of the declining TFR or at least point to the factors preventing its considerable increase. We will mention three of them here.

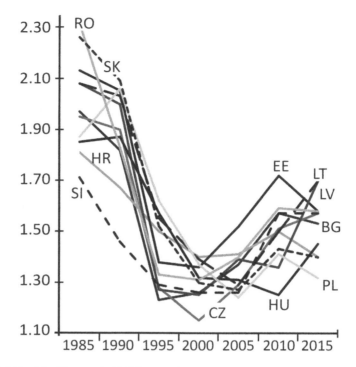

Figure 5.3 Total fertility rate in EU11 countries, 1985–2015

Note: See notes to Figure 5.1.

Source: Own elaboration based on Eurostat (2018).

First, there was an unusually rapid increase in the proportion of non-marital births (Figure 5.4), a phenomena typical for the transition period. In 1985–90, in only two countries (Estonia, and Slovenia) did the percentage of children born outside marriage exceed 15%. Between 1990 and 2016, however, the share increased extraordinarily, at least by factor two (Estonia) but in most cases by a factor of 3–5 (Bulgaria, Czechia, Hungary, Lithuania, Poland and Slovakia), with the strongest growth observed in Romania (by a factor of 6.7). In the majority of these countries, this change was by no means paralleled with an increase in the frequency of non-marital partnerships (consensual union) but often resulted in the incidence of single motherhood (Lesthaeghe and Surkyn 2002). Importantly, single mothers and women living in informal partnerships are assumed to have a lower probability of giving birth to two or more children than married women. Second, there was a rapid spread of the incidence of childless women and third, of one-child families. In six EU11 countries, the share of small-size (0 or 1 child) families increased from 22% to 28% (with one exception of 32% in Lithuania) for the cohort of women born in 1960, to 29% to 40% for the 1970 cohort (Sobotka 2015).[26]

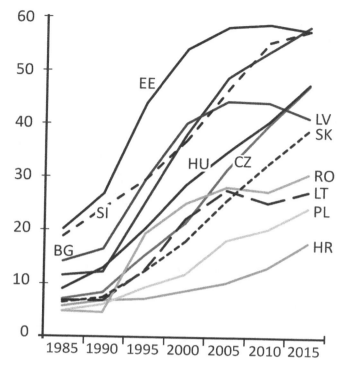

Figure 5.4 Share of non-marital births in EU11 countries, 1985–2015 (in %)

Note: See notes to Figure 5.1.

Source: Own elaboration based on Eurostat (2018).

Another tendency was the relatively high frequency of first order births: in 2016 in nine countries[27] every second childbearing woman was a primipara. A growing preference for small-size families and a strong predominance of mothers bearing their first child meant less and less room for larger families.

The 'tempo' effect (continuing delay in motherhood) seems responsible for a large part of the fertility decline in the post-1989 period. This is reflected in the rising trend of the mean age of women at the birth of their first child (Figure 5.5), which between 1990 and 2016 increased by 3.8 to 4.8 years in nine EU11 countries and by 5.1 to 5.7 in the remaining two (Bulgaria and Slovenia). The importance of this phenomenon for fertility stems not only from postponement of procreative activity but also the inability of older age groups to fully recuperate the postponed births. The rising average childbearing age clearly ensued from a decreasing propensity to contract early marital unions, which was fairly high during the two preceding decades. Until the mid-1980s, very few adults in the EU11[28] countries abstained from marriage, and marrying usually occurred early; even around 1990, the incidence of first female marriages (measured by the mean number of those unions per 1,000

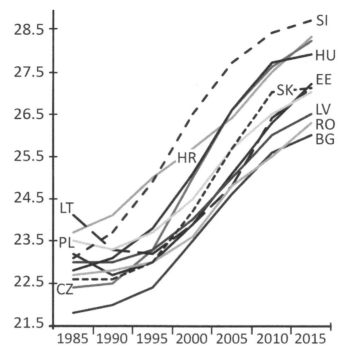

Figure 5.5 Mean age at first childbirth in EU11 countries, 1985–2015

Note: See notes to Figure 5.1.

Source: Own elaboration based on Eurostat (2018).

women at each age) exceeded 900.[29] In 2000, this rate had become only a fraction: below 500 in Czechia, Estonia, Hungary, Latvia and Slovenia, or just above 600 in Croatia, Poland and Romania (Sardon 2002), and during the next 15 years the incidence of marital unions in EU11 countries remained close to this level. Marriage as a universal experience in a person's life came to an end. A factor that might at least partly have compensated for the 'deficit' of new marital unions in family formation, the spread of consensual partnership, did not – contrary to Western and northern Europe – take place on a large scale (Hoffmann-Novotny, Fux 2001), although its incidence in several countries (notably in Bulgaria, Czechia, Hungary, Latvia and Slovenia) grew rapidly (Sobotka 2008).

What seems particularly striking, with respect to the above-described trend of decreasing fertility in the EU11, is the sharp contrast between the nearly universal 'two-child ideal' for a family (Sobotka and Beaujouan 2014) and the reality, reflected in a much lower actual number of births. Frejka and Gietel-Basten (2016) estimate the deficit of fertility in Central and Eastern Europe (i.e. the gap between the mean ideal family size and the completed cohort fertility rate) to amount to one-fourth of the 'ideal'. In other words, for some reason, young people are unable to fulfil their reproductive intentions. What might be those reasons that compel people to give up (or postpone, sometimes ad infinitum) a quarter of intended births?

The abundant literature on this issue (from Philipov 2003 to Frejka and Gietel-Basten 2016) leads us to distinguish three major groups of factors that have so drastically affected fertility trends in the EU11. The enormous strength of these factors, especially when compared with the circumstances in Western Europe, lies in their unusual coincidence. The three groups of factors include:

- The wide adoption in society, especially amongst young generations, of the Western post-modern values that prioritized personal freedoms, self-realization, individual achievement and respective specific lifestyles.
- Austerities caused by more or less deep, but in all cases painful, transition to a market-oriented and competitive economy: differentiation of incomes, deregulation of the labour market, industrial restructuring, high unemployment. Price hikes in the case of many basic commodities in the early years of the transition due to the adaptation of the prices of consumer goods to market mechanisms caused deterioration of living standards in many households. Labour surpluses and skill mismatches encouraged employers to offer workers inferior terms of employment and low remuneration. In general, after decades of relative stability and a guaranteed moderate level of living, the economic situation, for many segments of society, but especially for youth, became precarious and highly uncertain.
- The withdrawal of the state from previous paternalistic and pro-natalist social policies. While some policy measures were abandoned (e.g. prolonged child care for small children or preferential assignment of housing to young couples with children; Sobotka 2008), others waned due to inflation (Frejka and Gietel-Basten 2016).

These three groups of factors gave rise to an interplay of various social phenomena: first, economic uncertainty involved low wages and employment instability or, quite commonly, the lack of employment opportunities; second, tertiary level (university) education became very popular, particularly among women, which caused a considerable delay in entering the labour (and matrimonial) market; third, due to a lack of friendly credit arrangements and limited housing rental market, scarce opportunities existed for affordable housing, which mainly affected cohorts entering adulthood; fourth (and finally), the availability of a growing variety of fancy goods and services reinforced – despite generally low incomes – consumer aspirations, which prompted individuals to earn more money and at the same time make difficult choices between current consumption and children. On the top of these, various misgivings and meanders of the transition could and possibly did shake young people's social confidence in the possibility of improving their chances and prospects in the predictable future. In fact, many of them decided to emigrate to the West and fulfil their family building plans there.

In the course of time, all EU11 countries experienced a slackening of the austerities and hardships suffered by people due to more or less radical transition-related reforms, and the improvement of living conditions for the majority of society. However, the aforementioned transition-related complex of factors suppressed fertility rates to such low levels that any significant recovery proved extremely difficult. Indeed, many authors claim that the lowest-low fertility pattern may continue over the next several decades (e.g. Frejka and Gietel-Basten 2016; Kohler et al. 2006). Lutz et al. (2006) introduced the notion of a 'lowest-low fertility trap', which assumes a self-reinforcing mechanism: the postponement of childbearing results in a further fall in the desired number of children, which in turn brings about accelerated ageing of the population, discouraging young adults – due to growing economic hardships – from increasing their fertility. Some authors hoped that the small increases in TFR observed in the EU11 countries on the eve of the 21st century might signal a reversal of the declining trend, however, 'no widespread recovery of childbearing appears to be underway [because] cohort fertility does not appear to be increasing'[30] (Frejka and Gietel-Basten 2016: 36).

International migration

Falling fertility in EU11 countries, which accelerated shortly before the onset of the post-communist transition and quickly reached unprecedentedly low levels, did not – unlike in Western countries – coincide with a migration transition from net emigration to net immigration. Just the opposite, for almost three decades now, extremely low fertility has coexisted with a strong propensity to emigrate. This has had a devastating effect on present and future supplies of labour, and the pace of population ageing.

Having said so, we have to admit that the EU11 countries have not been uniform with respect to trends in international migration. Estimates concerning the balance of population movements published by the United Nations (UN 2012, 2017) indicate that in the immediate pre-transition period, 1985–90, six countries (Croatia, Czechia, Estonia, Latvia, Lithuania and Slovenia) displayed a positive migration balance while the remaining five (Bulgaria, Hungary, Poland, Romania and Slovakia) belonged to those with a negative balance (Figure 5.6). We should be careful with any far-reaching conclusions here; all of the net immigration countries constituted a part of larger political entities (Czechoslovakia, the USSR and Yugoslavia), and much of what was happening until 1990 that is now presented as international migration was, in fact, internal mobility. Indeed, they (especially the Baltic states and Czechia) attracted large numbers of migrants from other parts of their respective federalist states, the USSR and Czechoslovakia. It might also be mentioned in passing that official statistics did not capture a great part of the outflows from the countries under consideration (or inflows from those countries to the West) because – due to administrative restrictions particularly focused on long-term migration – many of them took the form of short-term movements, often under the guise of tourism, and as such were not included in migration statistics.

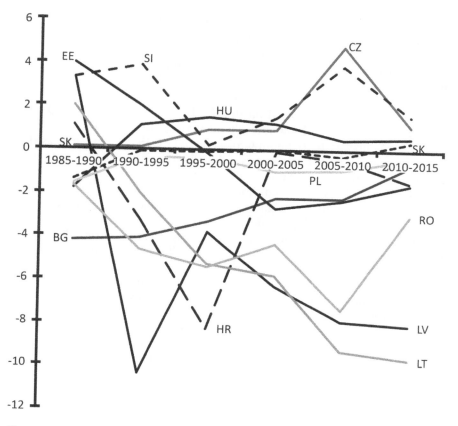

Figure 5.6 Migration balance in EU11 countries (five-year averages) per 1,000 inhabitants, 1985–1990–2010–2015

Note: See notes to Figure 5.1.

Source: Based on Eurostat (2018).

The fact that migration in the pre-transition period was heavily controlled and ultimately limited by authoritarian regimes in these countries, resulted in a large migratory potential which accumulated in many of them over several decades. A part of that potential was transformed into out-migration immediately after the dismantling of the ancien régime, which entailed the restoration of freedom to leave a country and the installation of visa-free travel to a number of western countries. In many EU11 countries, the outflow of people intensified in the course of time up until 2008, when the economic crisis severely hit labour markets in a number of destination areas. Apart from its major source in the aforementioned migratory potential, rising emigration was further propelled by an interplay of several novel factors. One of them was the relatively high, and growing, unemployment in home countries, especially among the youth. Moreover, people who ventured to migrate for work to western countries in the early 1990s gradually developed transnational communities there which attracted new migrants from their countries of origin. Those new migrants were predominantly young people seeking a better and more stable life abroad. However, the major factor conducive to growing migration turned out to be accession to the European Union and granting citizens of new member countries free access to the labour markets of the 'old' EU15 countries (Okólski 2004; King and Okólski 2018).

According to estimates based on the EU Labour Force Survey (EU LFS), between 2004 and 2014 the number of residents originating from the 'new' post-2004 EU Member States (without Croatia) in the EU15 countries increased by 5.4 times and reached approximately 6.1 million. The net increase amounted to five million, which translates to half a million per year. A particularly strong surge of those inflows was noted shortly after the accession, in 2005 and 2006, when migrants from the first eight CEE countries could freely move across EU countries, and again in 2008, when Bulgaria and Romania accessed the EU. The increase was highly differentiated across receiving countries, the highest in the United Kingdom, where it was 13-fold (Fihel et al. 2015). Holland et al. (2011) calculated the net inflow from new Member States in 1998–2009 to particular countries of the EU15, in terms of the proportion of those migrants in the 2010 host country population. It rose from close to nil to 4.0% in Ireland, 2.5% in Spain, 1.6% in Italy, 1.3% in the United Kingdom and 1.0% in Austria.

The intensity of the east-to-west flows of people also differed with respect to the countries of origin. In absolute terms, the main countries contributing to that growth were Poland and Romania (Table 5.1); by 2017, around

Table 5.1 Emigration from EU11 countries in 2009–12 and 2013–16 (annual averages)

Country	Number of emigrants (flow)	
	2009–12	*2013–16*
Bulgaria	16,615[a]	27,111
Croatia	12,737	25,552
Czechia	56,217	20,001
Estonia	5,622	9,543
Hungary	15,457	40,004
Latvia	33,333	20,568
Lithuania	54,155	42,576
Poland	247,212	260,006
Romania	202,587	182,230
Slovakia	1,933	3,521
Slovenia	15,282	14,551
EU11[b]	661,150	645,663

[a] Based on the 2012 data only.
[b] Due to the varying degree of accuracy of outflow estimates across the EU11 countries, the total number of emigrants in both periods should be treated with caution.

Source: Own elaboration based on Eurostat (2018).

2.4 million and 3.1 million citizens of those countries, respectively, became residents of other EU (or European Economic Area) countries (Eurostat database: migr_pop1ctz).[31] Data extracted from the EU LFS for the period 1998–2009 indicate that the strongest outflows measured as a percent of the resident population in the respective home country were noted in Romania (8.9%), Lithuania (4.8%), Czechia (4.7%) and Bulgaria (3.7%), while in other EU11 countries the total loss of population due to outmigration did not exceed 3% (Holland et al. 2011).

During the post-communist transition, all EU11 countries, irrespective of whether their migration balance was positive or negative, were subject to sizable outflows of people. However, reasonably reliable data on emigration, in particular conforming to the common definition recommended by Eurostat, are available only since 2008 or 2009.[32] The data indicate that the estimated official emigration from these countries was indeed consistently massive: 661,000 annually in 2009–12 and 646,000 annually in 2013–16, of which 68% was from Poland and Romania (Table 5.1). The main destinations were countries of the EU15 and in some of them, the EU11 citizens became leading nationalities either in migration flow or stock statistics, even though before 1990 their presence had been hardly noticeable in official records. For instance, regarding the contribution to inflows in 2005–14 of the top five origin countries, in Austria three (Romania, Hungary and Poland) belonged to the EU11 group, in Belgium and Denmark two (Poland and Romania), in Finland one (Estonia), in Germany four (Poland, Romania, Bulgaria and Hungary), in Italy, Portugal and Spain one (Romania), in the Netherlands two (Poland and Bulgaria), and in Sweden and the United Kingdom one (Poland). In this period, Polish migrants constituted the main (most numerous) foreign nationality in Denmark, Germany and the Netherlands (also in Iceland and Norway), while Romanians were the main migrants in Italy and Spain, and Estonians in Finland (OECD 2017).

The elevated east-to-west migration observed after the eastern enlargements of the EU was strongly related to imbalances in the EU labour market. Since 2004, CEE countries have increasingly played the role of a worker reservoir for EU15 economies. As a consequence of intensive east-west flows of people in an enlarged common economic area, this intra-EU mobility has replaced mobility from the third countries as the main source of foreign labour[33] (Riso et al. 2014).

It could be argued that the outflow of people from EU11 countries during the post-communist transition strongly affected population processes in those countries in several ways. First of all, this outflow contributed (besides the sub-replacement fertility) to severe depopulation. In the period 1990–2017, the population of Lithuania decreased by almost a quarter, Bulgaria by one-fifth, Estonia and Romania by nearly one-sixth, and Croatia and Latvia by over one-eighth.[34] Bearing even more heavily on the population was the selectivity of the outflow, a characteristic feature of any migration. In the discussed cases, selectivity related to the place of residence prior to emigration, migrants' sex, age and human capital. Since, as satisfactorily evidenced (Fihel et al. 2015), the outflow in the period of the post-communist transition was particularly intense for young and well-educated people and especially, in some countries (e.g. Poland), those living in peripheral areas, this resulted in a number of actual or potential (future) consequences, above all, shrinking populations of various under-developed (mostly agricultural) areas or micro-regions, and a changing age composition of these populations.[35] The importance of the latter effect was a disproportionate loss of people of childbearing age and school graduates entering the labour market. Clearly, under persistent mass emigration, this kind of selectivity must have reinforced the ageing of the population, aggravating its social and economic consequences.

It follows from Figure 5.6 that, since 1990, a long-lasting divide has arisen between net immigration and net emigration countries, the former including Czechia, Hungary and Slovenia, and the latter, the remaining eight countries (including Slovakia with a migration balance oscillating around zero). In addition, Latvia, Lithuania and Romania have continuously suffered from relatively heavy population losses due to migration. In the case of Latvia and Lithuania, these losses have been growing in the course of time.

As we noted, some EU11 countries have recently attained net immigration status, and growing inflows can also be observed in other countries in this group. Quite frequently, however, a predominant share of people participating in these movements consists of returning migrants. Meanwhile, foreign citizens who migrate to those countries originate largely from non-EU countries, and their inflow – due to difficulty in obtaining resident status – is often not adequately reflected in official statistics. Nevertheless, the cumulative effect of immigration to EU11 countries, even to those which have already achieved a positive migration balance, is still relatively insignificant when compared to western countries. On 1 January 2018, in just two countries (Czechia and Slovenia), the share of foreign citizens amongst all residents amounted to 5%; in all others[36] it ranged between 0.6% (Poland and Romania) and 1.5% (Hungary).[37]

Immigration, however, should not be neglected as far as its present and future impact on population change and demographic composition are concerned. We will highlight here the case of Poland, a 'traditional' net emigration country with presently the lowest share in the EU11 of foreign citizens in the total resident population. However, over the last decade Poland has witnessed a growing inflow of foreign citizens under a rich variety of categories, mostly perfectly regular: permanent residents, temporary residents, students and trainees, people granted a work permit and seasonal workers who are admitted without a work permit. In addition, a considerable number of incoming foreigners arrive legally as visitors (tourists), but while in Poland they resort to clandestine employment. Most of these foreigners stay on a more or less temporary basis,[38] but many of them strike roots. This has given rise, in a newly published population projection, to predicting the completion of the migration transition in the coming decade or two, and turning Poland into a net immigration area (Janicka and Anacka 2018).

Demographic prospects: depopulation and rapid ageing

In 1989, the EU11 countries numbered 110.9 million inhabitants, including 37.9 million (34%) in Poland and 23.1 million (21%) in Romania (Table 5.2). In 2017, the EU11 population decreased to 104.9 million, that is by 5.4%, but if we allow for our alternative estimates of the population of Poland, accounting for unregistered emigration occurring since the late 1980s,[39] the depopulation of the EU11 region seems more pronounced: a decrease to 101.2 million in 2017, that is by 8.8%. The process of de-population in Europe occurred exclusively in the post-communist countries (the EU11 and the former USSR), whereas the old EU15 countries registered an increase in population size from 361.9 million in 1989 to 407.3 million in 2017, that is by 12.5%. Among the EU11 countries, only Czechia, Poland, Slovakia and Slovenia registered an overall increase in population size, but only in the two latter countries did this increase occur relatively evenly in all sub-regions (Figure 5.7). In turn, in Czechia, Hungary and Poland population changes remained very diversified spatially, with some peripheral regions registering a decrease in the number of inhabitants and other regions, especially those with large cities – an increase. Nonetheless, the scale of depopulation in some regions in the EU11, notably the Baltic states, Bulgaria and Romania, exceeded 15%.

In the EU15 both components of population change: the migration balance and natural increase, prompted growth in population size (Figure 5.8). Meanwhile, in the EU11 both the negative migration balance and negative natural increase contributed to de-population, the former being more important (68%

Table 5.2 Registered and projected[a] population, in thousands, in selected European countries, 1989, 2017, 2040, 2050

Country	1989	2017	2040[a]	2050[a]	Change as compared to 1989 in %		
					2017	2040[a]	2050[a]
EU15	**361,934**	**407,343**	**431,760**	**435,335**	**12.5**	**19.3**	**20.3**
EU11	**110,860**	**104,865**	**95,137**	**91,736**	**−5.4**	**−14.2**	**−17.3**
Bulgaria	8,987	7,102	5,934	5,564	−21.0	−34.0	−38.1
Croatia	4,762	4,154	3,820	3,675	−12.8	−19.8	−22.8
Czechia	10,360	10,579	10,552	10,478	2.1	1.9	1.1
Estonia	1,566	1,316	1,284	1,257	−16.0	−18.0	−19.7
Hungary	10,589	9,798	9,471	9,287	−7.5	−10.6	−12.3
Latvia	2,666	1,950	1,599	1,506	−26.9	−40.0	−43.5
Lithuania	3,675	2,848	2,129	1,957	−22.5	−42.1	−46.7
Poland	37,885	39,973	35,840	34,373	5.5	−5.4	−9.3
Romania	23,112	19,644	17,070	16,331	−15.0	−26.1	−29.3
Slovakia	5,264	5,434	5,373	5,262	3.2	2.1	0.0
Slovenia	1,996	2,066	2,066	2,045	3.5	3.5	2.5

[a] Based on the Eurostat baseline projection EUROPOP 2015–80.

Source: Own elaboration based on Eurostat (2018).

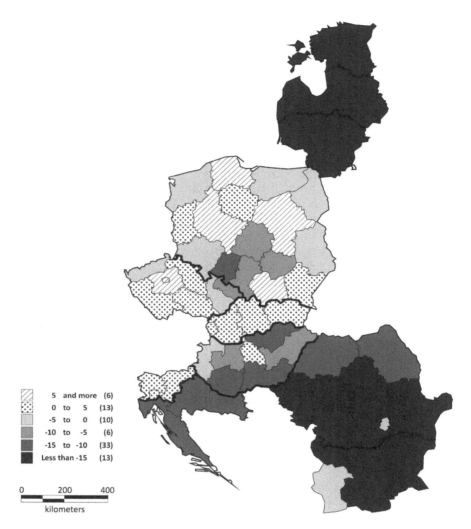

Figure 5.7 The change in population size in EU11 regions (NUTS2) between 1990 and
2017 (in %)

Source: Own elaboration based on Eurostat (2018).

of the population change) than the latter (32%). Only in three countries did the
positive migration balance counteract the population decline (Czechia, Hungary and Slovenia)[40] whereas in other EU11 states the opposite was observed,
either due to ethnically driven outflow straight after the collapse of communism (the case of the Baltic states and Bulgaria) or due to the labour emigration
occurring in the 1990s and after the eastward EU enlargements. As for natural
increase, it counteracted the process of de-population only in Poland, Slovakia
and Slovenia, but while in Slovenia the natural increase fluctuated between positive and negative values from year to year, in Poland and Slovakia it remained

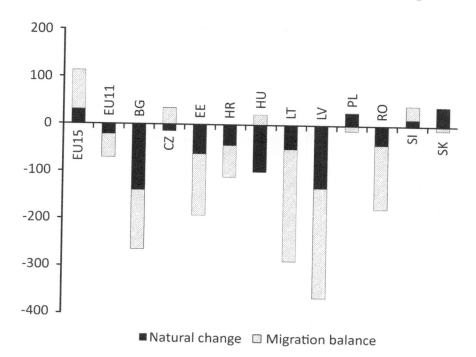

Figure 5.8 Population change per 1,000 population between 1989 and 2016 decomposed between natural change and migration balance, selected European countries

Note: BG – Bulgaria, CZ – Czechia, EE – Estonia, EU11 – 'new' member states of the European Union: Bulgaria, Czechia, Estonia, Croatia, Hungary, Latvia, Lithuania, Poland, Romania, Slovenia, Slovakia, EU15 – 'old' member states of the European Union: Austria, Belgium, Denmark, Finland, France, Germany, Greece, Ireland, Italy, Luxembourg, the Netherlands, Portugal, Spain, Sweden, the United Kingdom, HR – Croatia, HU – Hungary, LT – Lithuania, LV – Latvia, PL – Poland, RO – Romania, SI – Slovenia, SK – Slovakia.

Source: Own elaboration based on Eurostat (2018).

positive only in the 1990s due to the favourable demographic structure. Indeed, the population of Europe and the population of the EU11 in particular, have been affected by the recurrence of baby booms and baby busts originating in the First and Second World Wars; due to the baby boom occurring at the turn of the 1940s and 1950s, a relatively large number of people reached their peak reproductive age (that is aged 25–34) at the turn of the 1970s and 1980s and at the turn of the 1990s and 2000s.

On the eve of the post-communist transition, the EU11 populations were significantly younger than those of the old EU15. In 1989, 23.7% of EU11 inhabitants were aged under 15 years as compared to 18.5% in the western part of the continent, and 10.8% were aged 65 years or over as compared to 14.3% (Figure 5.9). This situation changed in 2017, when the proportion of youngest population segment diminished by 8.6 percentage points (p.p.) in the EU11 (and only by 0.7 p.p. in the old EU15) and that of the oldest segment increased by 7 p.p. (8.3 p.p.). In 2017 the share of children under 14 years became lower

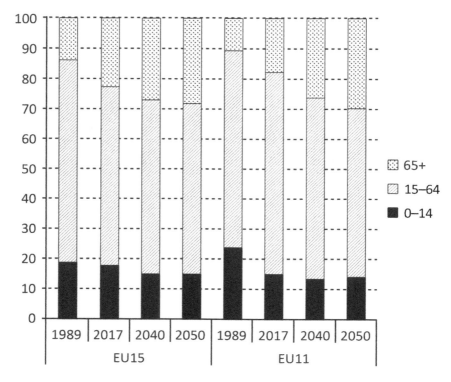

Figure 5.9 Registered and projected population structure by age in the old EU15 and EU11
    countries, 1989, 2017, 2040 and 2050 (in %)

Note: Based on the Eurostat baseline projection EUROPOP 2015–2080.

Source: Own elaboration based on Eurostat (2018).

in the EU11 than in the old EU15 and, as the Eurostat population projection
shows,[41] this tendency will persist in the decades to come. According to the
Eurostat projection, the demographic prospects of EU11 remain indeed pessi-
mistic, with a progressive drop in population size of 17% in 2050 (as compared
to 1989, Table 5.2), and more advanced ageing, implying a lower share of children and a larger share of older persons than in the old EU15 (Figure 5.10).
Consequently, by 2050 the EU11 Member States will dominate among European countries, with the highest shares of older persons in the population.
    Population ageing is taking place all over the world, that is, in the great
majority of countries that have been undergoing the fertility decline crucial for this process. Nonetheless, the particularly unfavourable demographic
trend observed in the EU11 countries has resulted in the reversal of proportions between the main age groups: under 15, 15–64 and 65 and over. Until the
beginning of the 21st century, the share of persons at a reproductive age (15–64)
increased gradually, from 63% in 1960 to 70% in 2009. Since then, this proportion
started to decline (to 67% in 2017), whereas the decline in the proportion of the

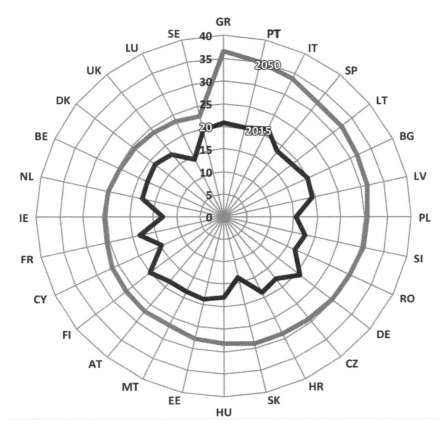

Figure 5.10 Registered and projected share of persons aged 65 years and over in EU member states, 2015 and 2050 (in %)

Note: Based on the Eurostat baseline projection EUROPOP 2015–2080. AT – Austria, BE – Belgium, BG – Bulgaria, CY – Cyprus, CZ – Czechia, DE – Germany, DK – Denmark, EE – Estonia, FI – Finland, FR – France, GR – Greece, HR – Croatia, HU – Hungary, IE – Ireland, IT – Italy, LV – Latvia, LT – Lithuania, LU – Luxembourg, MT – Malta, NL – the Netherlands, PL – Poland, PT – Portugal, RO – Romania, SE – Sweden, SI – Slovenia, SK – Slovakia, SP – Spain, UK – United Kingdom.

Source: Own elaboration based on Eurostat (2018).

young and the increase in the proportion of the oldest visibly accelerated. In general, a growing (or at least stable) proportion of population at a reproductive age constitutes a so-called demographic dividend, which, when taking place in favourable economic and institutional conditions and properly managed, fosters economic growth, capital accumulation and investments. In the case of the EU11 countries, this opportunity was not fully used, as a large part of the demographic dividend occurred at a time when the effectiveness of state systems was limited, that is, under communism. In turn, the period from 1989 to 2009 (which marked the end of the demographic dividend) was far too short to entirely eliminate the economic differentials between the EU11 and the western part of the European continent.

The radical decline in natality registered in the EU11 in the post-communist period is likely to have far-reaching consequences for future demographic processes: it implies a lower share of persons at reproductive age in the future and incites a further decline in number of births, thus accelerating the process of ageing. This mechanism is called fertility-driven ageing, or 'ageing from the bottom' of the age structure.[42] Similarly to Western European countries, the EU11 has been simultaneously experiencing a mortality decline that translates into a rise in life expectancy and a growth in the share of older persons in the population, that is, so-called mortality-driven ageing ('ageing from the top'). But what distinguishes most EU11 countries from what can be observed in the old EU15, is the interrelation between international migration and the process of ageing: while in Western European countries the positive migration balance implies a growth in population size and reinforces, at least temporarily, the younger segments of the population, the opposite can be observed in the EU11. Indeed, emigration from the EU11 involves mostly young adults and according to Eurostat data concerning migrants who de-registered from the place of permanent stay in the EU11 countries, as many as 70% of persons who settled down abroad between 1998 and 2016 were aged below 40. Although in most EU11 countries emigration remains quantitatively small in relation to the size of the entire population, it implies certain population losses of young adults, a decline in the share of adults in the population and, consequently, an increase in the share of the elderly. This mechanism, which we could call migration-driven ageing ('ageing from the middle'), also has an indirect effect consisting of an additional drop in natality: since young adults are characterized by highest fertility rates, their emigration implies displacing their children or forming a family abroad. In Poland, this indirect effect of adult migration has been estimated at a loss of 10% births between 2005 and 2014 (Fihel et al. 2018). Thus, migration-driven ageing further reinforces natality decline in the EU11 region and contributes to the low-fertility trap.

The process of ageing can be observed in most countries of the world and is most advanced in Europe and selected Asian countries. Nevertheless, what distinguishes the situation in the EU11 is the fact that the simultaneous fertility decrease, mortality decrease and emigration increase has intensified unfavourable trends: it has prompted de-population and accelerated the process of ageing. While the inflow from abroad to some extent neutralised the process of ageing in the EU15, the post-communist reality of the EU11 failed to encourage a massive inflow that could have had relevant demographic consequences.

Conclusions

In the EU11 countries, the post-1989 period brought unique circumstances resulting in abrupt and radical turnabouts in demographic trends: after decades of ambiguous tendencies, life expectancy started to rapidly increase, early and high fertility was replaced by postponed and low fertility, while family patterns and reproductive behaviours became more diversified. Moreover, new political circumstances freed a massive migration potential, resulting in intense outmigration. In the course of our discussion, we have distinguished three types of social and economic factors characteristic of the post-1989 reality responsible for these demographic processes: (1) the spread of Western attitudes in the domain of health and procreative behaviours; (2) the austerities of economic transition intensifying labour migration and implying the postponement of reproductive plans; and (3) the weakening of public policies, in particular family support programmes. As we argued, contrary to previous trends in Western Europe, these rapid demographic changes occurred in the EU11 simultaneously, which resulted in de-population and intensified the ageing process.

Due to the low fertility levels observed in the 1990s onwards, increasing longevity and the outflow of young adults and their offspring, the EU11 countries are expected to become some of the most advanced in the process of ageing in Europe in the near future. This, in turn, constitutes several important challenges with far-reaching consequences for the economic, political and social systems of EU11 societies. In the domain of public health, the increasing number and proportion of older persons will necessitate higher expenditures on health care, assistance and convalescence of the elderly, the disabled and/or persons with chronic illnesses. Alternative solutions, such as non-governmental organisations (NGOs), volunteering, social and neighbourhood networks will be required to complement the support provided by families and institutionalised health care systems and to counteract the social alienation of elderly people. The growing share of older consumers will also imply a change in the economic demand structure, favouring goods and services related to health and long-term care. Rapidly ageing societies will need to re-orient their public finances, including retirement and welfare systems, as these will become overburdened by the growing number of beneficiaries and decreasing number of contributors. And this can happen in circumstances of slow economic growth, given the fact that a 'silver society' is, as a rule, less dynamic, innovative and enterprising than a young one. There is also a growing need for labour market policies favouring the economic activity of older and/or disabled persons, including re-training and changing their qualifications. All these challenges will require a holistic change in public policies, incorporation of new priorities and adjustment of public institutions to the needs of older people. This means that the interests of other social groups, such as young families, may be marginalised.

Notes

1 Agnieszka Fihel received funding from National Science Centre, Poland (UMO-2017/26/M/HS4/00441).
2 Bulgaria, Croatia, Czechia, Estonia, Hungary, Latvia, Lithuania, Poland, Romania, Slovakia and Slovenia.
3 That is, so-called old EU15 Member States (Austria, Belgium, Denmark, Finland, France, Germany, Greece, Ireland, Italy, Luxembourg, the Netherlands, Portugal, Spain, Sweden and the United Kingdom), or referring to the United Nations' terminology of northern Europe (Denmark, Estonia, Finland, Iceland, Ireland, Latvia, Lithuania, Norway, Sweden and the United Kingdom), southern Europe (Albania, Andorra, Bosnia and Herzegovina, Croatia, Gibraltar, Greece, Italy, Malta, Montenegro, Portugal, San Marino, Serbia, Slovenia, Spain and TFYR Macedonia), and Western Europe (Austria, Belgium, France, Germany, Liechtenstein, Luxembourg, Monaco, the Netherlands and Switzerland).

4 In this chapter we refer exclusively to EU11 countries; however, the health crisis was particularly pronounced in the USSR and, after 1991, selected former USSR republics: Belarus, Russia, Ukraine (Meslé 1991). For the most recent literature on these three countries, see Grigoriev et al. (2012, 2013, 2014), McKee and Nolte (2004), Meslé (2004), Nolte et al. (2004, 2002), Shkolnikov et al. (2004).

5 That is by 0.4 years annually. Such a rapid rate has never been registered for Europe (as a whole) since then.

6 To illustrate, in 1965 the life expectancy at birth was equal in Czechia, England and Wales, France and two other Western but non-European countries (Japan and the United States (around 71 years for both sexes)). In 1990, after years of stagnation in Czechia and continuous progress in the other aforementioned countries, life expectancy in the latter outpaced that in Czechia by three to seven years.

7 In each country the course and determinants of the health crisis were very complex. For more on this, see for instance Bobak and Marmot (1996), Cockerham (1997), McKee and Nolte (2004), Nolte et al. (2004), Okólski (1985, 1987), Shkolnikov et al. (2004).

8 Including infants, whose average birth weight declined in some EU11 countries.

9 Life expectancy at birth is a broad measure of mortality and should be interpreted inversely, that is the higher the mortality, the lower the life expectancy and vice versa. It is based on the age-specific mortality rates for a given period (usually a calendar year) and expresses the average number of years a newly born child is expected to live if he or she experiences mortality at each age corresponding to the rates of a given period.

10 And the former East Germany.

11 Fihel and Muszyńska (2015) discuss the determinants of such geographical patterns of smoking-related mortality in Poland.

12 Like in the case of malignant neoplasms of the upper respiratory tract, to a great extent determined by past smoking habits.

13 The MONICA study, conducted in many countries on relatively large samples, focused on cardiovascular diseases, their prevention, treatment and impact on overall mortality levels. See WHO (1988) for more details.

14 See also Rychtaříková (2004) on Czechia.

15 The most striking example is the non-governmental organization Great Christmas Orchestra Charity, established in 1993 in Poland, which has so far donated as many as 30,000 medical devices to public hospitals, paid for by fundraising concerts and income tax transfers.

16 According to the United Nations breakdown of countries.

17 For instance, Sobotka et al. (2005) quantified the impact of generation size and fertility on the number of births after 1990 for Czechia and Poland. The authors found out that changes in the number of women at reproductive age systematically mitigated a decline in the number of births, which clearly indicates that the latter was the sole factor of the natality collapse in those countries (30% and 35% fewer births, respectively, in 2002 relative to 1990).

18 TFR is calculated as the sum of the age-specific fertility rates for a given period (usually a calendar year) and interpreted as the average number of children born per woman during her lifetime if she were to experience fertility at each age corresponding to the rates of a given period.

19 Kohler et al. (2006: 99) argued that this pattern is, among others, 'characterized by a rapid shift to delayed childbearing, a low probability of progression after the first child (but not particularly low levels of first-birth childbearing, [and] a "falling behind" in cohort fertility at relatively late ages'.

20 No NUTS2 data for Lithuania TFR are available.

21 No NUTS2 data for Estonia TFR are available.

22 The Baltic states, Czechia, Hungary, Poland, Romania and Slovakia.

23 An alternative computation performed for the group of EU12 countries (EU11 without Croatia but with Cyprus and Malta) resulted in very similar findings. The 'tempo' effect in those countries was −0.39 (31% of period TFR).

24 Otherwise named cohort TFR; it denotes the real average number of children born by a woman in a given cohort (year of her birth) over her life span.

25 At least for five EU11 countries (Czechia, Hungary, Poland, Romania and Slovakia), whereas in four countries (Bulgaria, Estonia, Lithuania and Slovenia) increasing fertility is predicted (Myrskyla et al. 2013). However, the data for cohorts born in the mid-1970s and later are meaningless, since women representing those cohorts are still at a fertile age and many of them may consider motherhood.

26 The inter-cohort rise in the incidence of childlessness was especially surprising. For instance, in Poland, for the cohort born between 1945 and 1955 it was 8%, whereas for the cohort born in 1965 it was almost twice that figure (15.5%) (Matysiak 2012).

27 In Estonia and Latvia the frequency was lower (41%). After it reached 50% (Estonia) or passed that threshold (Latvia) in the early transition years, both countries began a downward trend.

28 In Croatia, however, marriage already ceased to be a common social practice in the early 1970s, whereas in Slovenia, in the late 1970s.

29 With four exceptions (Croatia, Estonia, Hungary and Slovenia), where it had already fallen to a much lower level.

30 This view was contested by a claim that it was the economic crisis of 2008 which hampered the apparent reversal (Matysiak et al. 2018). This, however, is not fully consistent with the empirical evidence. For instance, although Poland was not affected by the crisis, it experienced only a minor and short-lived reversal of fertility recovery.

31 Accessed on 5 June 2018.

32 Before 2008, practically the only method of outflow measurement was based on the obligatory administrative cancellations of residence in a home country which, however, did not account for the outflow of people who failed to comply with that obligation. Since such 'irregular' emigration was relatively large and changed over time, and because it differed between EU11 countries, this led to an underestimation of that flow on an unknown scale, but certainly quite severe in some countries and in certain periods.

33 As Riso et al. claim (2014: 18), 'In an enlarged EU, and largely as a result of strong east-west flows, intra-EU mobility has replaced mobility from non-EU countries as the main source of migrant workers in the EU'.

34 In contrast to those countries, Czechia, Slovakia and Slovenia recorded a tiny (2%–3%) increase in their population size. Hungary and Poland experienced a relatively small population decline, not exceeding 5%.

35 For instance, it follows from EU LFS data, that the share of the 15- to 34-year-olds amongst all migrants from the new Member States/new accession countries usually far exceeded 50%; in the peak years in the UK it was as high as 70%, and in Spain 60%, whereas the respective share in domestic populations hardly reached 40% in migrants' home countries (Fihel et al. 2015). It was found in a special study on the post-accession outflow from Poland that in 2004–08, 72% of emigrants were 15- to 34-year-olds, while in the resident population only 32% (in 2004) reached that age (Grabowska-Lusińska and Okólski 2009).

36 We omit here two Baltic states (Estonia and Latvia), where the official estimate of the share of foreign residents in the total population was 15% and 14%, respectively. Both countries are highly specific in this respect. In Estonia, over 80% of the foreigners were born in Belarus, Russia and Ukraine (64% in Russia); most of those people settled in Estonia when the country was still one of the SSRs, and their arrival at that time was in fact internal migration. By the same token, 82% foreign residents in Latvia who were born in the same three countries became residents as a result of internal migration within the ex-USSR.

37 Based on Eurostat databases (migr_pop1ctz, migr_pop2ctz and migr_pop3ctb), accessed on 5 June 2018.

38 Officially, on 1 January 2017 Poland hosted only 150,000 foreign residents (Eurostat database migr_pop1ctz), but in the same year – besides a few hundred thousand

foreigners staying as temporary residents – around 2 million foreigners were admitted as seasonal workers.

39 The phenomenon of unregistered emigration refers to Poland in the first place, while the other EU11 countries either experience less numerous outflows, or apply modern administrative measures tracking international mobility in an efficient way (i.e. Lithuania). In our previous study concerning Poland, we established population estimates for Poland accounting for long-term emigrants who did not de-register from the place of permanent residence in their origin country. Between 1980 and 2009, approximately 3,070,000 persons left and did not come back by 2011, of whom 2,315,000 migrated without deregistering from their place of permanent residence in Poland. The study was based on data from the passport traffic recoding system used in the 1980s, and population censuses conducted in 1988, 2002 and 2011. For more details, see Fihel et al. (2018).

40 Apart from return migration, the inflows to these three countries took place from other countries of Central and Eastern Europe (republics of the former Yugoslavia, Belarus, Moldova, Russia, Ukraine) and, to a lesser extent, remote Asian countries (China and Vietnam). In the case of Hungary, important inflows also occurred from Germany, Romania and Slovakia.

41 And still, the Eurostat projection is based on the very optimistic assumption that whenever a drop in the number of working age population occurs, it is compensated by an identical positive net migration.

42 The population pyramid illustrating the age structure includes the youngest groups of the population at the bottom and the oldest at the top. A decline in natality implies narrowing the bottom of the population structure, while increasing longevity – extending the top of population structure.

References

Bandosz, P., O'Flaherty, M., Drygas, W., Rutkowski, M., Koziarek, J., Wyrzykowski, B., Bennett, K., Zdrojewski, T., & Capewell, S. (2012). Decline in mortality from coronary heart disease in Poland after socioeconomic transformation: Modelling study. *British Medical Journal*, 344. http://dx.doi.org/10.1136/bmj.d8136

Bobak, M., & Marmot, M. (1996). East-west mortality divide and its potential explanations: Proposed research agenda. *British Medical Journal*, 312, 421–425.

Boenker, F., Mueller, K., & Pickel, A. (eds.) (2002). *Postcommunist Transformation and the Social Sciences*. Lanham, MD: Rowman & Littlefield Publishers Inc.

Bongaarts, J., & Feeney, G. (1998). On the quantum and tempo of fertility. *Population and Development Review*, 24(2), 271–291.

Cifkova, R., Skodova, Z., Bruthans, J., Adamkova, V., Jozifova, M., Galovcova, M. (2010). Longitudinal trends in major cardiovascular risk factors in the Czech population between 1985 and 2007/8. Czech MONICA and Czech post-MONICA. *Atherosclerosis*, 211, 676–681.

Cockerham, W. (1997). The social determinants of the decline of life expectancy in Russia and Eastern Europe: A lifestyle explanation. *Journal of Health and Social Behavior*, 38, 117–130.

European Commission (2009). Health statistics – Atlas on mortality in the European Union, Eurostat – statistical books. Eurostat, Luxembourg.

Eurostat (2018). Population database, electronic resource, Accessed on 25 May 2018.

Eurostat (2009). The European Health Interview Survey. Eurostat.

FAOSTAT (2015). 2013 Food Balance Sheets for 42 selected countries. United Nations, New York.

Fihel, A., Janicka, A., Kaczmarczyk, P., & Nestorowicz, J. (2015). Free Movement of Workers and Transitional Arrangements: Lessons from the 2004 and 2007 Enlargements, Warsaw: Centre of Migration Studies; unpublished report to the European Commission.

Fihel, A., Janicka, A., & Kloc-Nowak, W. (2018). The direct and indirect impact of international migration on the population ageing process: A formal analysis and its application to Poland. *Demographic Research*, 38, 1303–1338. https://doi.org/10.4054/DemRes.2018.38.43

Fihel, A., & Muszyńska, M. (2015). The regional variation in tobacco smoking – attributable mortality in Poland, 2006–2010. *Przegląd Epidemiologiczny*, 69, 87–92.

Frejka, T., & Gietel-Basten, S. (2016). Fertility and family policies in Central and Eastern Europe after 1990. *Comparative Population Studies*, 41(1), 3–56.

Frejka, T., & Sobotka, T. (2008). Fertility in Europe: Diverse, delayed and below replacement. *Demographic Research*, 19, 15–46.

Gierlotka, M., Zdrojewski, T., Wojtyniak, B., Poloński, L., Stokwiszewski, J., Gąsior, M., Kozierkiewicz, A., Kalarus, Z. (2014). Incidence, treatment, in-hospital and one-year outcomes of acute myocardial infarction in Poland in 2009–2012 – nationwide database AMI-PL. *Kardiologia Polska (Polish Heart Journal)*, 73(3), 142–158.

Goldstein, J. R., Sobotka, T., & Jasilioniene, A. (2009). The end of 'lowest-low' fertility? *Population and Development Review*, 35(4), 663–699.

Grabowska-Lusińska, I., & Okólski, M. (2009). *Emigracja ostatnia?* Warsaw: Wydawnictwo Naukowe Scholar.

Grigoriev, P., Doblhammer-Reiter, G., & Shkolnikov, V. (2013). Trends, patterns and determinants of regional mortality in Belarus, 1990–2007. *Population Studies: A Journal of Demography*, 67, 61–81.

Grigoriev, P., Mesle, F., Shkolnikov, V., Andreev, E., Fihel, A., Pechholdova, M., & Vallin, J. (2014). The recent mortality decline in Russia: Beginning of the cardiovascular revolution? *Population and Development Review*, 40, 107–129. https://doi.org/10.1111/j.1728-4457.2014.00652.x

Grigoriev, P., Meslé, F., & Vallin, J. (2012). Reconstruction of continuous time series of mortality by cause of death in Belarus, 1965–2010. Demographic Research.

Hoffmann-Novotny, H. J., & Fux, B. (2001). Sociological analysis. In: A. Pinelli, H. J. Hoffmann-Novotny, & B. Fux (eds.), *Fertility and New Types of Households and Family Formation in Europe*. Strasbourg: Council of Europe Publishing, pp. 19–45.

Holland, D., Fic, T., Rincon-Aznar, A., Stokes, L., Paluchowski, P. (2011). Labour Mobility within the EU. The Impact of Enlargement and the Functioning of the Transitional Arrangements. Final report. London: National Institute of Economic and Social Research.

Janicka, A., & Anacka, M. (2018). Starzenie się populacji w warunkach dopełniającego się przejścia migracyjnego. In: M. Okólski (ed.), *Wyzwania starzejącego się społeczeństwa*. Warsaw: Wydawnictwa Uniwersytetu Warszawskiego, pp. 334–354.

Jasilionis, D., Shkolnikov, V. M., Andreev, E. M., Jdanov, D. A., Ambrozaitiene, D., Stankuniene, V., Meslé, F., Vallin, J., Rogers, G. (2007). Sociocultural mortality differentials in Lithuania: Results obtained by matching vital records with the 2001 census data. *Population*, 62, 597–646.

Kalediene, R., & Petrauskiene, J. (2005). Inequalities in mortality by education and socio-economic transition in Lithuania: Equal opportunities? *Public Health*, 119, 808–815.

King, R., & Okólski, M. (2018). Diverse, fragile and fragmented: The new map of European Migration. *Central and Eastern European Migration Review*, online first, 1–24, doi: 10.17467/ceemr.2018.08.

Kohler, H-P., Bilari, F. C., & Ortega, J. A. (2002). The emergence of lowest-low fertility in Europe during the 1990s. *Population and Development Review*, 28(4), 641–680.

Kohler, H-P., Bilari, F. C., & Ortega, J. A. (2006). Low fertility in Europe: Causes, implications and policy options. In: F. R. Harris (ed.), *The Baby Bust: Who Will Do the Work? Who Will Pay the Taxes?* Lanham, MD: Rowman & Littlefield Publishers, pp. 48–109.

Kuulasmaa, K., Tunstall-Pedoe, H., Dobson, A., Fortmann, S., Sans, S., Tolonen, H., Evans, A., Ferrario, M., & Tuomilehto, J. (2000). Estimation of contribution of changes in classic risk factors to trends in coronary-event rates across the WHO MONICA project populations. *Lancet*, 355, 675–687.

Leinsalu, M., Stirbu, I., Vagero, D., Kalediene, R., Kovacs, K., Wojtyniak, B., Wróblewska, W., Mackenbach, J.P., & Kunst, A. (2009). Educational inequalities in mortality in four Eastern European countries: Divergence in trends during the post-communist transition from 1990 to 2000. *International Journal of Epidemiology*, 38, 512–525.

Leinsalu, M., Vagero, D., & Kunst, A. (2003). Estonia 1989–2000: Enormous increase in mortality differences by education. *International Journal of Epidemiology*, 23, 1081–87.

Lesthaeghe, R., & Surkyn, J. (2002). New Forms of Household Formation in Central and Eastern Europe: Are they related to newly emerging Value Orientation? Interuniversity Papers in Demography, IPD-WP 2002–2 (Vrije Universiteit Brussel and Universiteit Gent).

Lutz, W., Skirbekk, V., & Testa, M.R. (2006). The low-fertility trap hypothesis: Forces that may lead to further postponement and fewer births in Europe. *Vienna Yearbook of Population Research*, 167–192.

Matysiak, A. (2012). Fertility development in Central and Eastern Europe: The role of family tensions, *Institute of Statistics and Demography Working Papers (Warsaw School of Economics)*, (22).

Matysiak, A., Sobotka, T., & Vignoli. (2018). The Great Recession and Fertility in Europe: A Sub-national Analysis, *Vienna Institute of Demography Working Papers*, 02/2018.

McKee, M., & Nolte, E. (2004). Health sector reforms in central and eastern Europe: How well are health services responding to changing patterns of health? *Demographic Research Special Collection*, 2, 163–182.

Meslé, F. (1991). La mortalité dans les pays d'Europe de l'Est. *Population*, 46, 599–649.

Meslé, F. (2004). Mortality in Central and Eastern Europe: Long-term trends and recent upturns. *Demographic Research Special Collection*, 2, 45–70.

Meslé, F., & Vallin, J. (2017). The end of east – west divergence in European life expectancies? An introduction to the special issue. *European Journal of Population*, 33, 615–627. https://doi.org/10.1007/s10680-017-9452-2

Myrskylä, M., Goldstein, J.R., & Cheng, Y.A. (2013). New cohort fertility forecasts for the developed world. *Population and Development Review*, 39(1), 31–56.

Ng, M., Freeman, M., Fleming, T., Robinson, M., & Dwyer-Lindgren, L. (2014). Smoking prevalence and cigarette consumption in 187 countries, 1980–2012. *The Journal of the American Medical Association*, 311, 183–192.

Nolte, E., Scholz, R., & McKee, M. (2004). Progress in health care, progress in health? Patterns of amenable mortality in central and eastern Europe before and after political transition. *Demographic Research Special Collection*, 2, 139–162.

Nolte, E., Scholz, R., Shkolnikov, V., & McKee, M. (2002). The contribution of medical care to changing life expectancy in Germany and Poland. *Social Science & Medicine*, 55, 1905–1921.

Nolte, E., Shkolnikov, V., & McKee, M. (2000). Changing mortality patterns in East and West Germany and Poland. I: Long term trends (1960–1997). *Journal of Epidemiology and Community Health*, 54, 890–898.

OECD (2017). *International Migration Outlook*. Paris: OECD Publishing.

OECD (2015). *OECD Health Statistics*. Paris: OECD Publishing.

Okólski, M. (1985). The case of Poland. In: J. Vallin & A. Lopez (eds.), *Health Policy, Social Policy and Mortality Prospects*. Paris: INED, IUSSP, pp. 445–464.

Okólski, M. (1987). Umieralność mężczyzn w Europie Wschodniej i w Europie Zachodniej. *Studia Demograficzne*, 89, 3–28.

Okólski, M. (1993). East–West mortality differentials. In:A. Blum & J.-L. Rallu (eds.), *Demographie Europeenne. II. Dynamiques Demographiques*. Paris: John Libbey, INED, pp. 165–189.

Okólski, M. (2004). The effects of political and economic transition on international migration in Central and Eastern Europe. In: D.S. Massey & J.E. Taylor (eds.), *International Migration: Prospects and Policies in a Global Market*. Oxford: Oxford University Press, pp. 35–58.

Philipov, D. (2003). Fertility in times of discontinuous social change. In: I.E. Kotowska & J. Jóźwiak (eds.), *Population of Central and Eastern Europe. Challenges and Opportunities*. Warsaw: Statistical Publishing Establishment, pp. 665–689.

Riso, S., Secher, J.E., & Andersen, T. (2014). *Labour Migration in the EU: Recent Trends and Policies*. Luxembourg: Publications Office of the European Union, 'Eurofound' Report.

Rychtaříková, J. (2002). Czech mortality patterns:The past, the present, and regional dissimilarities. *Geografie – Sbornik Ceske geograficke spolecnosti* 107, 156–170.

Rychtaříková, J. (2004). The case of the Czech Republic. Determinants of the recent favourable turnover in mortality. *Demographic Research Special Collection, 2*, 105–138.

Sardon, P. (2002). Recent Demographic Trends in the Developed Countries. *Population*, English Edition 1 (January –February), 111–154.

Shkolnikov, V., Andreev, E., Jasilionis, D., Leinsalu, M., Antonova, O., & McKee, M. (2006). The changing relation between education and life expectancy in central and eastern Europe in the 1990s. *Journal of Epidemiology and Community Health*, 60, 875–881.

Shkolnikov, V., Chervyakov, V., McKee, M., & Leon, D. (2004). Russian mortality beyond vital statistics: Effects of social status and behaviours on deaths from circulatory disease and external causes – a case-control study of men aged 20–55 years in Udmurtia, 1998–99. *Demographic Research Special Collection, 2*, 71–104.

Sobotka, T. (2008). The diverse faces of the second demographic transition in Europe. *Demographic Research*, 19(8), 171–224.

Sobotka, T. (2015). Demographic change in Central and Eastern Europe – European trends and national diversity, *Conference 'Demographic Change in Central and Eastern Europe'*, JPI More Years, Better Lives, Vienna, 24 March 2015.

Sobotka, T., & Beaujouan, E. (2014). Two is best? The persistence of a two-child family ideal in Europe. *Population and Development Review*, 40(3), 391–419.

Sobotka, T., Lutz, W., & Philipov, D. (2005). 'Missing births': Decomposing the declining numbers of births in Europe into tempo, quantum and age structure components, Vienna Institute of Demography, Friday Lunch Seminar, 24 June.

Tykarski, A., Posadzy-Małaczyńska, A., Wyrzykowski, B., Kwaśniewska, M., Pająk, A., Kozakiewicz, K., Rywik, S., & Broda, G. (2005). Rozpowszechnienie nadciśnienia tętniczego oraz skuteczność jego leczenia u dorosłych mieszkańców naszego kraju. Wyniki programu WOBASZ. *Kardiologia Polska (Polish Heart Journal)*, 63, 1–6.

UN (2012). *World Population Prospects. The 2012 Revision*. New York: United Nations.

UN (2017). *World Population Prospects. The 2017 Revision*. Volume II: Demographic Profiles. New York: United Nations.

Vallin, J., & Lopez, A. (eds.) (1985). *Health Policy, Social Policy and Mortality Prospects*. Paris: INED, IUSSP.

Vihalemm, P., Masso, A., & Opermann, S. (eds.) (2017). *The Routledge international handbook of European social transformations*. London: Routledge.

WHO (1988). The World Health Organisation MONICA project (monitoring trends and determinants in cardiovascular disease): A major international collaboration. *Journal of Clinical Epidemiology*, 41(2), 105–114.

WHO (2015). World Health Statistics 2015. Geneva: WHO.

Zatoński, W. (ed.) (2008). *Closing the Health Gap in European Union*. Warszawa: Cancer Center and Institute of Oncology.

Zatoński, W., & Boyle, P. (1996). Health transformations in Poland after 1988. *Journal of Epidemiology and Biostatistics*, 4, 183–197.

6   Labour markets

Joanna Tyrowicz and Peter Szewczyk

Introduction

The collapse of the Soviet Bloc and political liberation of countries in Central and Eastern Europe triggered a series of economic reforms, which together are often described as a transition from a centrally planned system to a market economy. This transition process had a fairly similar starting point in terms of institutional design: absolute prices were centrally fixed, which caused relative prices and incentives to be distorted. This was particularly relevant for the labour markets, as in many firms the combination of labour input and capital input was inappropriate, while workers were not compensated according to their actual productivity. This double misalignment in the labour market caused many researchers and advisors at the time to place particular emphasis on the phenomenon of unemployment. Thus, policy and academic research at the time focused primarily on how structural changes brought about unemployment, rather than the resultant worker flows that also characterized transition.

Indeed, for many of the transition countries, the unemployment rate rose sharply at the beginning of transformation, raising the costs of social safety nets and undermining political support for the economic reforms (see Figure 6.1). The focus on unemployment was observed also among the academics and among the international financial institutions (IFIs) advising and partially financing the transition processes: the World Bank, the International Monetary Fund and the European Bank for Reconstruction and Development. For scholars and policymakers alike, key to combating the vast unemployment was identification of the optimal transition process. The academic interest in unemployment was catalyzed and reinforced by the influential work of Philippe Aghion and Olivier Blanchard, who proposed a framework relating the speed of privatization to the unemployment rate and wage growth. This workhorse model for a large share of subsequent empirical and theoretical work – the so-called optimal speed of transition (OST) – postulated that the government could control the rate of demise of the (inefficient) public sector by picking the optimal rate of privatization and thus achieve labour market equilibrium. Privatization deemed too fast or too slow in this framework resulted in an unstable equilibrium of relatively high unemployment (Aghion and Blanchard 1994).

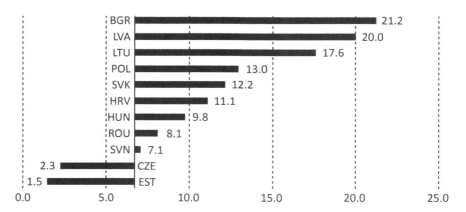

Figure 6.1 Unemployment rates in 1991

The OST framework has received considerable attention from the academic community and has frequently been used as an explanation for the rapid growth of unemployment in many transition countries: privatization that was deemed 'too fast' or 'too slow' was believed to explain the immediate hikes in unemployment in Bulgaria, Poland and Slovakia. By contrast, synchronization between layoffs and job creation in the private sector were to explain the relatively good performance of Czechia and Estonia.

However, the process of transition did not have to reflect the assumptions or the mechanics of the OST model. Privatization alone was not the only way to increase efficiency. Among others, Czechoslovakia, over the 1990–91 period, implemented firm fragmentation: large state-owned enterprises were spun off into smaller firms, sometimes at the level of specific plants. This process is analysed by Lizal et al. (2001), who show that such breakups of large state-owned enterprises (SOEs) boosted efficiency and improved allocation without substantial adjustments in total employment over this period. Moreover, in many of the transition countries, workers did not actually reallocate from SOEs to private firms, as postulated by the Aghion and Blanchard (1994) OST model. As Tyrowicz and van der Velde (2018) demonstrate, worker flows were, in general, rarely to a different type of employer than previously, even if mediated by a spell of unemployment. Rather, the shift of workers from SOEs to private firms was due to cohort entry and exit, as well as demography-based employment decisions.

In this chapter, we describe the findings of the empirical literature related to labour reallocation in the process of economic transition and discuss the nature of these flows. The structure of the chapter is as follows. First, we discuss insights from the earlier literature with the objective of emphasising the narrative concerning labour adjustments during transition. Second, we exploit a novel source of data to document the actual patterns of worker flows. These patterns were mainly driven by demographic processes rather than economic forces. Given the paramount role of demographics, in the third section we focus on the special role of adjustments in the employment of women, whose decline in labour force participation largely explains the overall decline in employment in the transition countries. Again, there are important differences across the birth cohorts, which further emphasizes the role of demographic processes. Finally, we discuss the evolution of wages and wage dispersion during the economic transition. This chapter is concluded by suggestions for the future research agenda in the interests of better guiding major transitions in other countries.

Insights from the empirical literature

In the centrally planned economy, overemployment was prevalent. The consensus estimate of labour redundancy ranged between 20% and 30% of total employment in Central and Eastern European countries (Svejnar 1991; Wellisz 1991). While these estimates were obtained without actual insights from firm level data, they were considered reliable at both policy and academic level. Indeed, some countries in Central and Eastern Europe still recognized a degree of labour redundancy in the 1980s. The generally poor economic performance in the region during this period led some firms to reduce labour demand. In order to avoid unemployment, which was non-reconcilable with the socialist ideology, older workers were often offered an opportunity to retire early. While such policies were implemented in some large enterprises, smaller enterprises and most notably the service sector could not afford to implement them, since plants were much smaller and labour was indivisible.

Industrial production (or output) declined in the 1980s, but then plummeted throughout the transition economies as of 1989–90. The trajectories were originally similar, with declines of roughly 20% within the first year of transformation (Aghion and Blanchard 1994; Boeri and Terrell 2002). With such a fall in output, subsequent decline in employment was to be expected, regardless of the redundancies prior to the beginning of transition. While this may explain the rapid increase in unemployment in some countries, in the majority of transition countries the adjustment in employment was much smaller than the decline in output. This wide discrepancy in the behaviour of unemployment is puzzling to say the least, and hints that the labour adjustment did not have to mechanically follow the adjustments in output.

Indeed, employment adjustment followed differentiated patterns, as shown in Figures 6.2 and 6.3. Large downward adjustment in the early years of transition appears to have been common, although countries such as Estonia observed only a negligible decline in employment, and countries generally troubled by high unemployment throughout the transition period (Poland or Slovakia) were characterized by a relatively mild adjustment in employment. Meanwhile, the transition country characterized by low unemployment (Czechia) observed a total reduction in employment of nearly 30% over the two decades of

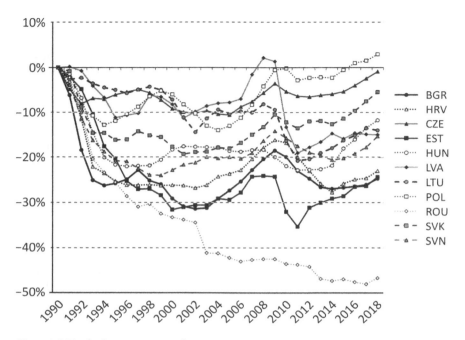

Figure 6.2 Total adjustment in employment since 1989

transition. These patterns cannot be explained by the intensive margin adjustments in hours worked per worker (see Figure 6.3).

In principle, the mechanics of the economic transition from a centrally
planned to a market economy are as follows: presumably inefficient public sector firms need to dissolve and a vibrant, efficient new private sector needs to
emerge. Job flows may come in two different forms: privatization, when workers stay in the firm, but the ownership structure changes to private hands; or
worker flows between different jobs in different companies, possibly with a
spell of unemployment between the two.

The optimal speed of transition theory posits that these simple mechanics
are subject to two forces. The first of these forces stems from the fact that non-
employment (possibly transitory) usually happens with state support, while at
the same time the collapse of the public sector limits the options to raise the
funds necessary to intensify social safety net expenditure. This particular type
of relationship was emphasized in the model by Aghion and Blanchard (1994).
The state raises funds to finance safety nets by taxing labour, which pushes
the non-wage cost of labour up. If the tax wedge becomes too high, job creation lags behind job destruction. The accumulating non-employment pushes
wage claims down, but the tax wedge prevents significant job creation, deepening the social costs of public-to-private sector reallocation. If the speed of job

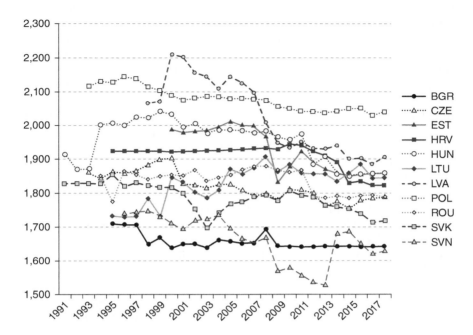

Figure 6.3 Hours worked

destruction is synchronized with the capacity of the emerging private sector to create new jobs, the non-employment pool is low, fiscal needs are small, levied taxes are less distortionary and an economy may find a fairly efficient equilibrium. Otherwise, an unstable high non-employment equilibrium emerges, and consequently, the relation between job creation and unemployment has an inverse U shape. Garibaldi (1998) arrived at the same conclusion using a search and matching model, though the transmission channel was different: unemployment benefits increase the reservation wages of employees and decrease the value of a match, which discourages job creation.

Clearly, both the 'non-employment' and the 'taxes' should be taken figuratively, not literally. Benefits may include pre-retirement benefits made available to individuals aged between 45 and the retirement age to discourage them from participating in the labour market and increase their support for the reforms, as has frequently been the policy in the transition economies (see Fox 1997). Moreover, taxes should be viewed in a broad sense, as they may encompass the opportunity costs of expanding productivity-enhancing infrastructure.

The second force is associated with the extent to which labour is a specific input, as highlighted by Cabaillero and Hammour (1996a, 1996b, 1998, 2000). In a series of models, Caballero and Hammour developed a family of models of structural change. In a series of papers, the authors analysed the cases of a restructuring impulse coming from cyclical factors, technological innovation, and inter-sectoral shift with two particular features: capital specificity and incomplete contracts. Capital specificity leads to the generation of quasirents (a surplus over the value of the match) which can be partially appropriated by workers, even though they are firm specific, due to the incompleteness of employment contracts. With considerable adjustment costs, the impulse to reallocate labour may yield excessive job destruction and insufficient job creation. Different characteristics and institutional arrangements associated with an employment contract imply a different scope of appropriation for the workers, which changes the bargaining balance between workers and employers. In a simple model, where all sectors have the same productivity, it produces a desynchronization of job creation and destruction, which eventually generates an inefficient equilibrium of excessive unemployment. If two sectors differ in productivity (as in the Aghion and Blanchard model), appropriation leads to sudden increases in unemployment and slow job creation. A consequence of such sclerosis is that, if appropriation is close to complete, no transition will occur at all, even if it would be socially optimal to do so. Unlike the Aghion and Blanchard (1994) model, the reallocation is a private process (i.e. the state cannot directly decide on the flow of people to unemployment). In the extreme, employers create little or no jobs at all, despite actual demand for the final product.

Both of these forces have been subjected to empirical testing in abundant literature. The countries that are most frequently analysed in earlier studies (Czechia, Estonia, Poland and Slovenia) all come from one region, while southern Europe, most of the Baltic states and central Asia are rarely the subject of analyses. Moreover, only few of the earlier studies cover the period of the early 1990s.

Three main stylized facts emerge from the empirical literature on labour reallocation during the transition. First, the patterns of job creation and job destruction changed as the transition ensued. Haltiwanger and Vodopivec (2002) show that in Estonia, job destruction initially exceeded 10%, with job creation lagging, but as of 1995 they were fairly at par, making gross reallocation rates in Estonia close to those observed in the United States. Gradual synchronization of job destruction and creation was also confirmed for a number of other countries by Faggio and Konings (2003) and by Jurajda and Terrell (2008), but the time period covered in these studies makes it likely that the cyclicality of job flows caused this result. Second, determinants of worker flows also changed with the progress of the transition. In the first stage they were predominantly a consequence of job terminations, whereas in later stages wage differences appear to have encouraged worker flows (Konings et al. 1996; Bilsen and Konings 1998). In principle, the net changes were initially much faster in Central and Eastern Europe (see e.g. Boeri and Terrell 2002; Earle and Sabrianova 2002; Svejnar 2002). With the exception of Czechia, Estonia and Slovenia, little is known about the synchronization of job destruction and job creation processes (see Sorm and Terrell 2000; Jurajda and Terrell 2003; Haltiwanger and Vodopivec 2003; or Orazem et al. 2005).

When it comes to testing the assumptions of the Aghion and Blanchard (1994) and the Caballero and Hammour (1996a, 1996b, 1998, 2000) models, the empirical evidence so far is inconclusive and rather country specific. De Loecker and Konings (2006) measured factor productivity in Slovenia between 1995 and 2000 and decomposed the changes into their possible causes. They showed that productivity increased more in private firms than in public firms, and that the main drivers of the increment were downsizing (job destruction) in privatized firms and pronounced productivity growth in newly created firms. However, Orazem and Vodopivec (2009) showed that the overall productivity growth was a universal pattern, unrelated to industry or ownership. Dimova (2008) also contested the claim on transition-driven productivity with data from Bulgaria: even though jobs and workers clearly reallocated to more efficient industries, the impact of this process on factor productivity was overshadowed by industry specific changes, such as market competition and import penetration.

In general, the narrative from transition economies suggests that job destruction occurred in the sections of the public sector that fell into bankruptcy or were privatized, mostly in the manufacturing industry; meanwhile job creation was most intense in de novo private firms, mostly in the service sector. Previous analyses also indicate that the proportions between these processes were different across time and countries (Boeri 2000). These general tendencies were confirmed in the Baltic and Central European countries, whereas Russia, Ukraine and southern Europe provide much weaker or sometimes even contradictory evidence (Acquisti and Lehmann 2000). On the other hand, mostly due to data shortages, not many studies have been able to explicitly identify the flow of workers from 'old' (state-owned, manufacturing) sectors to 'new' (private, services) ones. Studies show that employment grew rapidly in construction and trade, while it dropped in manufacturing, but these analyses rely on net changes in employment rather than gross worker flows. In the next section we describe the actual adjustments in workers across transition countries.

Worker flows, demographics and economic adjustment

In this chapter, we present evidence that the majority of labour market flows in the transition countries did not follow the patterns posited in the theoretical models. While the earlier empirical literature suggested that the mechanics of the Aghion and Blanchard (1994) model operate, data shortage made it impossible to verify if these proposed patterns did indeed define the labour market adjustments in the transition countries. Exploiting novel data from the Living in Transitions Survey (LiTS) provided by the European Bank for Reconstruction and Development (EBRD) made it possible to analyze the actual adjustment in the labour force over the transition process.

The optimal speed of transition model neglects four potentially important flows: (1) movement towards permanent non-employment and movements into job-seeking from non-employment; (2) flows out of employment from the *private/emerging* sector as well as into employment in the *public/disappearing* sector and direct job-to-job transitions from one sector to the other. A few models include destruction in the private sector (Tichit 2006) as well as emigration flows (Papapanagos and Sanfey 2003), but no serious attempt has been made to account for demographic processes. Think of the following example: if five birth cohorts leave the labour market (e.g. the jobs in a declining sector), and five birth cohorts enter the labour market (e.g. jobs in the growing sector), the overall change in the structure of employment will be approximately 12.5% in net terms and as much as 25% in gross terms without a single worker flow between the sectors. If roughly 10% of the active population is without a job and actively seeking work, the arrival of one new young cohort already constitutes a 25% increase in the number of job seekers, ceteris paribus. On the other hand, the exit of an additional cohort improves the bargaining position of the remaining workers, potentially reducing the size of the pool of job seekers whose skills are partially or fully outdated. With these examples, it appears paramount that the demographic transition could play an important role, with empirical evidence provided by Tyrowicz and van der Velde (2018).

The data behind Tyrowicz and van der Velde (2018) is the retrospective Life in Transition Survey (henceforth LiTS), launched by the European Bank for Reconstruction and Development in 2006. This data covers 27 countries from Europe and central Asia between 1989 and 2006 and is based on a representative sample from the population. In addition to basic socio-economic variables (age, gender, education, household size), respondents also provide a complete list of all previous jobs held between 1989 and 2006. For each job, workers report the starting and ending year, as well as other relevant characteristics, such as the type of industry and the form of ownership. This characterization of jobs enables the direct identification of worker flows, which is unique for such a long period of time and wide selection of countries. This data well matches the features observed in alternative data sources for the available countries and years.

The Tyrowicz and van der Velde (2018) study provides two important findings concerning worker flows during the transition from a centrally planned to a market economy, as they identify patterns which surface strongly despite the substantial heterogeneity in transition paths as well as the different starting points of these economies. First, they show that the flows attracting the greatest interest in the previous literature – from SOEs to private sector and from manufacturing to services – in fact represent but a minority of all flows. This is portrayed in Figure 6.4, which plots the intensity of all types of flows, averaged over time, in each country. In fact, labour market entries and exits were by far the most numerous in all countries considered. Across all countries, between-industry reallocation is of minor importance, while ownership flows are larger, but still remain substantially smaller than flows within groups of the same type of worker and actually even flows opposite to those posited by transition theories. The patterns persist if shorter periods are analysed (e.g. early transition).

Second, Tyrowicz and van der Velde (2018) show that, even though the flows analysed in the literature were relevant for overall labour reallocation, a vast

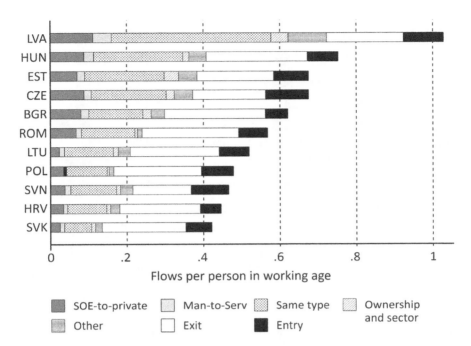

Figure 6.4 Structure of labour market flows during transition

part of the adjustment in the employment structure occurred via demographic flows (i.e. the entry of the youth and the exit of the elderly). This is portrayed in Figure 6.5, which plots the contribution of each type of flow to the total change in employment. These analyses comprise flows mitigated by periods of non-employment (such as unemployment). In fact, flows into the private sector from SOE were smaller in all the countries than exits to retirement, and in some countries substantially smaller. A similar pattern holds for the manufacturing industry, where virtually all the adjustment occurred via retirements, and few workers actually changed their industry of employment to services (market or non-market).

The paramount role of demographic trends was not noticed in the earlier literature, partly because the exits of the elderly and entries of youth are difficult to measure without the panel dimension of data, and most of the previously analyzed sources were not panel data. These findings shed new light on the understanding of labour market adjustments in transition: while it was previously acknowledged that job destruction may be the main driver of the unemployment surge, it appears that the firings and bankruptcies made, at best, a minor contribution to the total decline in employment and the rise in unemployment. Furthermore, job creation was particularly relevant for the labour

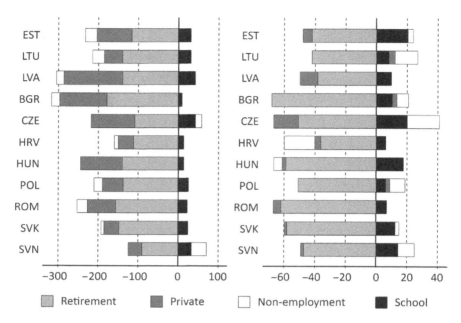

Figure 6.5 Labour market adjustment: public sector (left) and manufacturing (right)

market entrants, as labour market participants – if they changed jobs at all – would typically search employment with the same type of employer both in terms of industry and in terms of ownership. This suggests that a particularly relevant aspect of labour market adjustments in transition, in addition to job creation, is job brokering and the facilitation of school-to-work transition.

A specific type of the labour market flow concerns international mobility. Indeed, historically speaking, the countries of Central and Eastern Europe have been traditionally sending regions, with long migration traditions including both overseas flows to North America and mobility within Europe. The transition period was no different in this respect. In fact, international labour mobility was not a significant component of the transition worker flows (Fidrmuc 2004). On aggregate, throughout the region, migration flows decreased during the transition decades. There were notable exceptions to this rule (the migration wave from Bulgaria, the so-called accession migration in the aftermath of the EU labour market opening as of 2004, etc.). However, these flows rarely concerned individuals unemployed prior to migrating (Iglicka 2000; Kupiszewski 2005; Kaczmarczyk and Okulski 2008) and hence remained unrelated to aggregate employment and unemployment trends, even if they had severe local or sectoral consequences. Therefore, while migration is a notable trend describing the region and the transition period in general, the process of migration had little influence over the structure of the labour markets.

Employment of women

Female labour force participation, especially after accounting for individual characteristics, was high in the socialist states, when compared to market economies. First, socialist states had a functional school-to-work transition mechanism, with all school graduates obtaining a *work order*. Second, although enforced on a differentiated scale over time and across countries, people able to work were obliged to work, hence labour force participation was not entirely voluntary. These two policies coerced high labour force participation from women, in relative terms. Employment typically came with an employment guarantee, which made job transitions possible in principle, but not very frequent or necessary. With the onset of transition, both these mechanisms were dismantled immediately: work orders disappeared and so did the employment guarantee. A decline in female employment ensued, and this decline in fact explains a substantial share of overall employment reduction. The gender gaps in employment, once adjusting for individual characteristics, make it possible to disentangle the sources of employment decline into those attributable to changes in preferences and those attributable to changes in labour market conditions.

Many studies confirm that labour market differences based on gender emerged as a result of transition (e.g. Trapido 2007 for Estonia, Latvia and Russia; Adamchick and Bedi 2003 for Poland; Campos and Jolliffe 2002 for Hungary). However, the decline in female employment is not explained by unemployment per se, in a sense that the scale of employment decline among women was much larger than the extent of gender-related unemployment risk across the transition countries.

Another potential explanation consists in exploiting institutional change: labour force participation was not entirely voluntary prior to the transition and thus, if the institutional setup forced the employment of women above their preferred levels, then with the elimination of this legal requirement women could give up their professional careers and align the hours of market work to their preferences. For this hypothesis to be true, we should observe the labour market exits among women of working age and the lower labour market entries among young women (relative to older cohorts). This type of analysis requires both a long individual panel (for changes within birth cohorts) and enough time (to observe the changes between birth cohorts). Using a novel collection of individual data, Tyrowicz et al. (2018) show that in the older birth cohorts there were virtually no withdrawals from the labour market of working age women and only some labour market exits (see Figure 6.6). Labour market entries among the young cohorts were lower in transition countries.

The drop in the employment rates of young women in transition economies was associated with higher tertiary enrolment. This process was coupled with another striking phenomenon: the youngest cohorts were exposed to substantially lower gender employment gaps relative to youngest cohorts of men. The reduction in employment among the youngest cohorts hints that the cost of working may indeed be an important factor. The opportunity costs of

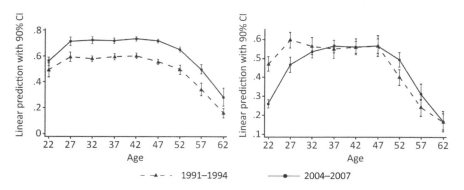

Figure 6.6 Age profiles of employment in advanced economies (left) and in CEECs (right)

working stem from care-giving, which usually burdens women asymmetrically. Thus, it may be proxied by fertility rates and access to institutionalized care. Indeed, Tyrowicz et al. (2018) find that these factors are related to higher gender employment gaps, after accounting for the educational attainment of women. However, this relation holds mostly in advanced economies. In transition economies, these effects are weaker or even non-existent. By contrast, the opportunity cost of not working stems from forgone earnings, and it is especially high for those that have invested in human capital. Thus, proxies for this cost include, for example, tertiary education among women. Although returns to human capital reduced the adjusted gender employment gaps in advanced economies, this was not the case in transition countries. In fact, gender employment gaps increased with labour productivity in transition countries. Even more strikingly, while in advanced economies the higher labour force participation of women was associated with a decrease in adjusted gender employment gaps – a sort of 'goodwill effect' – this effect was substantially less important in transition economies.

Eventually, towards the third decade of transition, gender employment gaps, once accounting for differences in individual characteristics between men and women, became equal in Western and CEE countries, on average. This change was achieved through a great increase in the labour market activity of women in Western Europe and a substantial decline in CEE. Effective policies to advance further equality in employment in Europe as a whole still have to be tested in practice, as evidence suggests that the instruments used so far work only up to a point. It is also important to emphasize that gender *wage* gaps remain higher in CEE than in Western Europe, which discourages labour force participation among women in the former group of countries.

Earnings in transition

An important driver of the labour market adjustments were adjustments in compensations. Notably, existing literature documents a large increase in inequality during the transition, but a large part of this literature exploits household-level income data, typically equivalized and post-transfer (Estrin and Svejnar 1993; Basu et al. 2005). Meanwhile, the interest is actually in individual earnings data, but the analyses could rarely be done on a large scale or comparatively, because individual earnings data are scarce.

Theory and policy debate in the early transition emphasized three important processes. First, markets offer more earnings dispersion than central planners, who tend to compress compensations, especially for high-skilled workers. Second, trade liberalization and entry to global value chains was likely to produce winners and losers, furthering earnings inequality. Third, with foreign direct investment and overall global trends, CEE countries were to swiftly experience skill-biased technological change, a process which took place gradually over several decades in advanced market economies due to the equally gradual invention and adoption of new technologies. CEE countries were to catch up rapidly, whereas it was already proven in advanced market economies that skill biased technological change contributes to greater income inequality, particularly through increasing returns to high-level skills. These structural changes were expected to reinforce the initial push towards greater earnings inequality.

Exploiting a new collection of data, Tyrowicz and Smyk (2019) document changes in earnings inequality, disentangling them into changes attributable to the varying structure of the labour force and changes attributable to how market economies rewarded individual characteristics. The findings are quite striking. First, raw levels of inequality were quite similar for the transition countries and advanced economies of Western Europe prior to the transition. Second, the raw inequality of earnings increased rapidly and, as of 1995, there were no further adjustments in raw wage dispersion. The initial shock to wage distribution was essentially instantaneous, and countries experiencing rapid structural change did not return to the initial levels of wage compression. Third, with wages fixed, the earnings dispersion was much lower in transition countries and continues to be so, despite a rapid increase in the early years of transition. This third finding is especially important, as it has two important policy implications: the labour force remains more homogeneous in terms of characteristics in CEE than in Western Europe, and the majority of the adjustment in earnings dispersion occurred via rewards for individual characteristics (i.e. how the market priced workers) and not via adjustment in the structure of workers.

Tyrowicz and Smyk (2019) also provide an evaluation of whether the changes in inequality – raw or adjusted – can be accounted for by trade liberalization, globalization and skill-biased technological change, as postulated by the common theory. The indicators of structural change correlate mostly with the decompression in the lower half of the wage distribution. Most indicators of structural change exhibit a negative correlation, which implies that more compressed wage distributions and greater structural change coexist, not vice versa. Since some changes have been more rapid in transition economies, some of the interaction terms provide significant estimates, but these usually make the negative correlations stronger, not weaker. In particular, the technology intensity of exports is only significant for the transition countries, whereas the compression for the share of R&D expenditures in GDP is twice as strong in transition countries as in advanced market economies. For the top of the distribution, most correlations become insignificant once we take away the effects of prices. The only exception is the share of high-skilled workers in the economy, which is also associated with lower wage compression. Hence, these results suggest that structural shocks correlate mostly with changes in prices, but not changes of individual characteristics.

Clearly, the correlations discussed above cannot be indicative of causality. Rather, they document that, despite controlling for country-level heterogeneity, there seems to be a significant correlation between the level of structural change and changes in wage compression. A common trend identified is the initial rapid increase in wage dispersion during early transition and subsequent reactionary adjustment. Increases in wage inequality in these countries stemmed mostly from the disappearance of the middle of the wage distribution. The degree to which such polarization occurred was subject to the institutional setting of a given country. What is confirmed by the rich data exploited in Tyrowicz and Smyk (2019) is that the driver of inequality was the changes in the bottom half of the wage distribution. Individuals without the adequate skills to function in a market setting drove down the left tail of the income distribution, thus widening the dispersion of wages in the economy. However, this only describes the early stages of transition. As shown in Figure 6.7, the earning dispersion that accounts for worker characteristics shows that, following the initial phase of transition, wage inequalities according to skills stabilized. This would imply that adequately skilled individuals were able to transfer into employment matching their skill set following an initial phase of employment mismatch, as confirmed by the massive labour reallocation during this period. Therefore, earnings in transition can

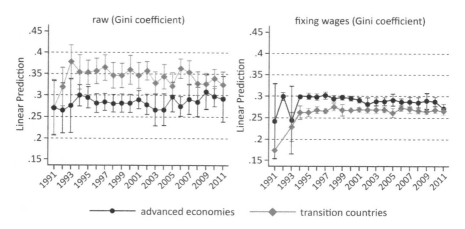

Figure 6.7 Earnings dispersion: raw (up) and accounting for wage schemes (down)

be ultimately characterized by an initial shock in demand and increased wage dispersion, initiated by inequality 'from below' that was swiftly absorbed by market forces.

Conclusions

Literature on the labour markets of CEE countries during their transition into market economies has been largely fixated on the effects of privatization, which is believed to have been a driver of the massive labour reallocation from unproductive state-owned firms into productive private firms. The emphasis has been placed on the speed of transition as an indicator of the friction caused by the necessary labour adjustments. Through the examples of labour flows and the growing gender employment gap, we have shown nuances that prove the process was to a large extent driven by demographic process, rather than change of ownership. First, we showed that the entering cohorts were the driving force for job creation and flows into private firms and more productive sectors, with cohorts already in the labour market prior to transition moving less frequently between sectors or into newly formed firms. Second, we showed that women entering the labour market after the onset of transition explain the changes in the gender employment rate, with few working-age women withdrawing from the labour market. Last, we showed that, while wage dispersion widened during the early phase of transition due to the way market mechanisms valued individual characteristics, neither the opening to international trade, nor the adoption of modern technologies is to blame.

The demographic-based explanation of labour market adjustment during transition in CEECs offsets the existing policy implications. It has been argued that policies lowering the cost of working and increasing the cost of not working (i.e. investment in human capital) are effective in reducing adjusted gender employment gaps. However, the experience of transition countries adds some caveats on this matter: higher employment rates under central planning reflected lower institutional barriers to women working rather than involuntary, coerced labour force participation. Moreover, high employment rates among older cohorts already in the course of transition hint that there may be some room for habit formation, although it does not seem to have been fully transmitted inter-generationally. With the substantial increase in labour market frictions, family-friendly institutions – despite the fiscal cost as well as burden to employers, hence hindering job creation – have so far proven to be insufficient in reducing gender employment gaps in this part of the world. Transition countries continue to respond only weakly to changes in the opportunity costs of employment. Thus, policies lowering the costs of working and increasing the costs of not working may not be highly effective in the future. Indeed, improvement in the employment rates in advanced European economies has been achieved mostly by reducing the unemployment and prolonging the activity of older cohorts, none of which was likely to be affected by pro-family or educational policies.

Furthermore, the demographic-based explanations undermine the validity of active labour market policies, such as retraining, as an effective tool to foster labour market restructuring. While such policies may be of value on their own, the key processes occur via generational exchange. On the one hand, it could be that the active labour market policies were simply not on a scale to match the scope of labour market restructuring. On the other hand, the data clearly show that job seekers generally look for employment not only in a similar industry but also in a firm with a similar form of ownership, which is rational (rewards to employer-specific human capital will be higher with a similar employer) and cost-effective. Early retirement schemes, popular in some of the CEE countries contributed to speeding up the labour market restructuring, but at a high fiscal cost. Perhaps, the optimal speed of transition model, rather than concentrating on the rate of privatization, should rather focus on the optimal rate of generational exchange.

Finally, the scope to which transition (a general trend) turned out to be gender-specific is striking. In nearly all CEE countries, growing gender employment gaps reduced the available labour force, hence slowing down the per capita growth rate and raising the scale of resource underutilization. Enabling the human capital embodied in unemployed women to reach their potential remains a challenge throughout the world, but it appears that the last three decades brought about a reversal from a more gender-equal society towards a less gender-equal one. Better understanding of the drivers of this process is needed: central planners, as inefficient as they were, ensured smooth school-to-work transitions for both genders, whereas after the introduction of the market-based system this aspect of gender equality appears to have permanently disappeared.

References

Acquisti, A., & Lehmann, H. (2000). *Job Creation and Job Destruction in the Russian Federation.* Trinity College Dublin, Economics Department.

Adamchik, V.A., & Bedi, A.S. (2003). Gender pay differentials during the transition in Poland. *Economics of Transition*, 11(4), 697–726.

Aghion, P., & Blanchard, O.J. (1994). On the speed of transition in Central Europe. *NBER Macroeconomics Annual*, 9, 283–320.

Basu, S., Estrin, S., & Svejnar, J. (2005). Employment determination in enterprises under communism and in transition: Evidence from Central Europe. *ILR Review*, 58(3), 353–369.

Bilsen, V., & Konings, J. (1998). Job creation, job destruction, and growth of newly established, privatized, and state-owned enterprises in transition economies: Survey evidence from Bulgaria, Hungary, and Romania. *Journal of Comparative Economics*, 26(3), 429–445.

Boeri, T. (2000). *Structural Change, Welfare Systems, and Labour Reallocation: Lessons from the Transition of Formerly Planned Economies.* Oxford: Oxford University Press.

Boeri, T., & Terrell, K. (2002). Institutional determinants of labour reallocation in transition. *Journal of Economic Perspectives*, 16(1), 51–76.

Caballero, R.J., & Hammour, M.L. (1996a). On the ills of adjustment. *Journal of Development Economics*, 51(1), 161–192

Caballero, R.J., & Hammour, M.L. (1996b). On the timing and efficiency of creative destruction. *The Quarterly Journal of Economics,* 111(3), 805–852

Caballero, R.J., & Hammour, M. L. (1998). Jobless growth: Approrpriability, factor substation and unemployment. *Carnegie-Rochester Conference Series on Public Policy*. Vol. 48. Elsevier, pp. 51–94

Caballero, R.J., & Hammour, M.L., 2000. Creative destruction and development: Institutions, crises, and restructuring. *NBER Working Paper*, 7849, National Bureau of Economic Research.

Campos, N.F., & Jolliffe, D. (2002). After, before and during: Returns to education in the Hungarian transition. *William Davidson Institute Working Papers Series*, 475. William Davidson Institute at the University of Michigan Stephen M. Ross Business School.

De Loecker, J., & Konings, J. (2006). Job reallocation and productivity growth in a post-socialist economy: Evidence from Slovenian manufacturing. *European Journal of Political Economy*, 22(2), 388–408.

Dimova, R. (2008). The impact of labour reallocation and competitive pressure on TFP growth: Firm-level evidence from crisis and transition ridden Bulgaria. *International Review of Applied Economics*, 22(3), 321–338.

Earle, J.S., & Sabirianova, K.Z. (2002). How late to pay? Understanding wage arrears in Russia. *Journal of Labour Economics*, 20(3), 661–707.

Estrin, S., & Svejnar, J. (1993). Wage determination in labour-managed firms under market-oriented reforms: Estimates of static and dynamic models. *Journal of Comparative Economics*, 17(3), 687–700.

Faggio, G., & Konings, J. (2003). Job creation, job destruction and employment growth in transition countries in the 90s. *Economic Systems*, 27(2), 129–154.

Fidrmuc, J. (2004). Migration and regional adjustment to asymmetric shocks in transition economies. *Journal of Comparative Economics*, 32(2), 230–247.

Garibaldi, P. (1998). Job flow dynamics and firm restrictions. *European Economic Review*, 42(2), 245–275.

Fox, L. (1997). Pension reform in the post-communist transition economies. In J.M. Nelson, C. Tilly, L. Walker (Eds.), *Transforming post-Communist Political Economies*, 370–384. Washington, D.C.: National Academy Press.

Haltiwanger, J.C., & Vodopivec, M. (2002). Gross worker and job flows in a transition economy: An analysis of Estonia. *Labour Economics*, 9(5), 601–630.

Haltiwanger, J., & Vodopivec, M. (2003). Worker flows, job flows and firm wage policies: An analysis of Slovenia. *Economics of Transition*, 11(2), 253–290.

Iglicka, K. (2000). Mechanisms of migration from Poland before and doing the transition period. *Journal of Ethnic and Migration Studies*. 26(1), 61–73.

Jurajda, Š., & Terrell, K. (2003). Job growth in early transition: Comparing two paths. *Economics of Transition*, 11(2), 291–320.

Jurajda, Š., & Terrell, K. (2008). Job reallocation in two cases of massive adjustment in Eastern Europe. *World Development*, 36(11), 2144–2169.

Kaczmarczyk, P., & Okólski, M. (2008). Demographic and labor-market impacts of migration on Poland. *Oxford Review of Economic Policy*, 24(3), 599–624.

Konings, J., Lehmann, H., & Schaffer, M. (1996). Job creation and job destruction in a transition economy: Ownership, firm size and gross job flows in polish manufacturing 1988–1991. *Labour Economics*, 299–317.

Kupiszewski, M. (2005). Migration in Poland in the Period of Transition: The Adjustment to the Labour Market Change. *PIE Discussion Paper Series*. Insitute of Economic Research, Hitotsubashi University.

Lizal, L., Singer, M., & Svejnar, J. (2001). Enterprise breakups and performance during the transition from plan to market. *Review of Economics and Statistics*, 83(1), 92–99.

Orazem, P.F., Vodopivec, M., & Wu, R. (2005). Worker displacement during the transition: Experience from Slovenia 1. *Economics of Transition*, 13(2), 311–340.

Orazem, P.F., & Vodopivec, M. (2009). Do market pressures induce economic efficiency? The case of Slovenian manufacturing, 1994–2001. *Southern Economic Journal*, 76(2), 553–576.

Papapanagos, H., & Sanfey, P. (2003). Emigration and the optimal speed of transition. *Review of International Economics*, 11(3), 541–554.

Sorm, V., & Terrell, K. (2000). Sectoral restructuring and labour mobility: A comparative look at the Czech Republic. *Journal of Comparative Economics*, 3(28), 431–455.

Svejnar, J. (1991). Microeconomic issues in the transition to a market economy. *Journal of Economic Perspectives*, 5(4), 123–138.

Svejnar, J. (2002). Transition economies: Performance and challenges. *Journal of Economic Perspectives*, 16(1), 3–28.

Tichit, A. (2006). The optimal speed of transition revisited. *European Journal of Political Economy*, 22(2), 349–369.

Trapido, D. (2007). Gendered transition: Post-Soviet trends in gender wage inequality among young Full-Time workers. *European Sociological Review*, 23(2), 223–237.

Tyrowicz, J., & Smyk, M. (2019). Wage inequality and structural change. *Social Indicators Research*, 141(2), 503–538.

Tyrowicz, J., & Van der Velde, L. (2018). Labour reallocation and demographics. *Journal of Comparative Economics*, 46(1), 381–412.

Tyrowicz, J., Van der Velde, L., & Goraus, K. (2018). How (not) to make women work? *Social Science Research*, 75, 154–167.

Wellisz, S. (1991). Poland under 'solidarity' rule. *Journal of Economic Perspectives*, 5(4), 211–217.

7 Running faster or measuring better?

How Central and Eastern European science is catching up with Western Europe[1]

Agnieszka Olechnicka and Adam Płoszaj

Introduction

Central and Eastern Europe (CEE) is often portrayed in contrast to Western Europe. Due to a wide variety of economic, social, institutional and historical factors, this region exhibits a lower level of socio-economic development, lower levels of innovation as well as a less advanced information society and so forth. The successive entry of CEE countries to the EU and their adoption of cohesion policy instruments brought positive economic consequences – we can talk about economic convergence on a European level. This optimistic picture of convergence on the European scale is undermined by the internal divergence that can be observed within countries – that is, the increasing difference among regions of CEE countries (see the chapter by Gorzelak and Smętkowski in this volume).

One of the elements allowing CEE countries to catch up with Western Europe in socio-economic terms is the development of science and innovation. However, we cannot talk about a simple relationship here (see the chapter by Radosevic, Yoruk and Yoruk in this volume). In the area of scientific performance, CEE countries stand out visibly from their western neighbours, although even here we can observe a (slow) process of convergence (Vinkler 2008; Must 2006; EC 2018; Abbott and Schiermeier 2014; Radosevic and Yoruk 2014; Kozak et al. 2015; Jurajda et al. 2017). On one hand, this is the consequence of economic growth, and on the other, it is the result of EU policy and closely related national policies. We would expect that incorporating CEE countries into EU structures and thereby allowing them to make use of EU instruments to support science sector development, including Framework Programme grants, should help reduce the distance dividing CEE from Western Europe in terms of both expenditure as well as research outcomes, including the number of articles and citations.

In this chapter we pay further attention to this issue by drawing on seldom used data concerning research outcomes in the form of research articles indexed in the Web of Science database (WoS).[2] For the purposes of this study, data on research articles derived from WoS has been elaborated to show not only the number of publications in specific years but also their citations, language, country of publication of the journal in which they appear and declared international collaboration with authors from various countries. The presentation of data from different perspectives allows for a better understanding of the dynamics of emerging processes in the science sector in CEE and to differentiate among countries in the region.

Our analysis serves to show a phenomenon that has till now been largely overlooked with regard to CEE countries: the way in which modifications to the coverage of bibliometric databases influence the process of scientific convergence of CEE countries with Western Europe. The question of how accounting for a greater number of journals on a local or national scale in international bibliometric databases influences the publication results of individual economies has been addressed, among others, with reference to Latin America (Collazo-Reyes 2014), India (Pandita and Singh 2017) and China (Liu et al. 2015). Basu (2010), using data from 90 countries, demonstrated that their scientific productivity, to a significant degree, depended less on the number of journals indexed in WoS but rather on the number of articles they contained. Meanwhile, Shelton et al. (2009) showed that changes in the WoS database consisting in the addition of new journals did not significantly influence the global structure of publications worldwide.

In order to conduct such an analysis for the CEE, we make use of detailed data from the Web of Science database. The usual analyses conducted are based on the overall number of articles attributed to a given country. From this angle, the growth and convergence of CEE countries are as clear as day. However, this approach ignores the fact that the list of journals in the WoS database is not permanent but, quite the contrary, changes significantly in some periods. We put forward the hypothesis that changes in the list of journals, particularly in the number of periodicals published in specific CEE countries, have a significant impact on bibliometric indicators and, consequently, on the convergence levels they are used to measure. In a broader sense, our analysis aims to show that observed trends in scientific output sometimes result not only from intensified research activity, but may also be the effect of elements being accounted for which were not previously included – in short, they derive from more precise (or simply different) measures. This viewpoint is also important because data on the number of publications and citations in the Web of Science are increasingly used as development indicators of national R&D sectors (EC 2018). By showing how modifications in these databases influence the results obtained, we can better understand and thus make better use of data from these sources.

Data

The spatial scope of the study was defined as the ten countries of Central and Eastern Europe (EU10) which acceded to the EU as part of expansion in 2004 and 2007. These are Bulgaria, Czechia, Estonia, Hungary, Lithuania, Latvia, Poland, Romania, Slovakia and Slovenia. In this chapter, their situation is outlined against the background of the so-called old Member States, also referred to as 'the fifteen' (EU15) as well as in reference to the situation of the whole European Union (EU27, i.e. without Croatia, which entered the EU on 1 July 2013).

In the study, alongside widely available data concerning expenditure and employment in research and development, bibliometric data was used that was generated from the Web of Science database. Detailed data, on the level of individual articles, was retrieved from the database in June 2014. The sample created from this source contains in total 547,050 articles affiliated to Central and Eastern Europe (EU10) published in the years 2000–2013. These constitute 10.9% of articles affiliated to EU27 countries (5,034,893).

The EU10 group of countries is very diverse in terms of the size and structure of publication output due to the disparate sizes of individual economies as well as the specificity of their scientific sectors (Figure 7.1). Almost 40% of all the publications in the region published in the years 2000–2013 are affiliated to Poland (217,288), 18% to Czechia (97,012), 13% to Hungary (68,713) and 11% to Romania (59,175). It is interesting that the share of Czechia and Hungary in the EU15 citation pool is higher than in the publication pool, which is the reverse in the case of Romania. This means that the publications affiliated to this country are cited much less often. For our analysis it is important that the

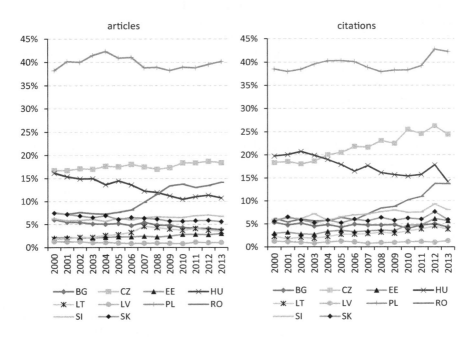

Figure 7.1 Countries' share in articles and citations of EU10

Source: Own study based on data from the Web of Science.

dominant role of Polish publications in the publication output and citations of the EU10 means that processes affecting Poland determine the results obtained for the whole group of CEE countries.

The share of individual countries in the joint publication output of CEE countries hardly changed during the analyzed period; the greatest change took place in Hungary, whose share fell from 16% in 2000 to 11% in 2013, as well as Romania, where there was a fourfold increase in the number of articles and whose share rose from 8% to 14% in the study period. Meanwhile, Romania came in third place among the EU10 in terms of its share in the general publication pool. Only Lithuania noted a higher uninterrupted growth in the number of articles affiliated there, although due to the small scale this did not translate into a spectacular rise in its share in EU10 output (by 2 percentage points) (Figure 7.1).

Results

Expenditure on R&D and employment in R&D

Convergence of the scientific systems of the EU10 and EU15 is visible in terms of expenditure as well as outcomes of R&D activity. The basic indicators which can be traced in this respect are the level of expenditure on R&D with reference to GDP as well as the indicator of employment in R&D relative to population size. In order to be consistent with the scientific output data presented in the following parts of the paper, we restrict the analysed period to the years 2010–13 (Figure 7.2). Data on R&D expenditures for the following three available years (until 2016) are presented in the chapter by Radosevic, Yoruk and Yoruk in this volume.

Data on R&D expenditure and employment (Figure 7.3) lead us to several conclusions. First, in the years 2000–2013 both groups of countries display an increase in expenditure on R&D measured in relation to GDP as well as growth in the indicator of employment in science in relation to population size. Interestingly, during the crisis period (starting in 2009), there was no fall in the level of investment in research and development in relation to GDP; quite the contrary, a growth in the value of this indicator was noted.

Second, there are important differences among the EU10 countries. In recent years, Slovenia and Estonia achieved a level of expenditure exceeding the EU15 average. In Slovenia this was a permanent upward trend as from 2011, while in Estonia spectacular growth in the years 2010–12 was followed by a dramatic drop in value of the said indicator. Besides the aforementioned countries, only Czechia and Hungary achieved a level of expenditure exceeding the EU10 average. Slovenia confirmed its strong position equally in terms of employment in R&D – after 2011 this indicator reached levels exceeding the EU15 average. However, Czechia, Estonia and Lithuania noted higher levels of employment in R&D than the EU10 average in the study period. Romania and Bulgaria are in the weakest position in this respect, and Poland is marked out by weak values for this indicator in relation to its population size.

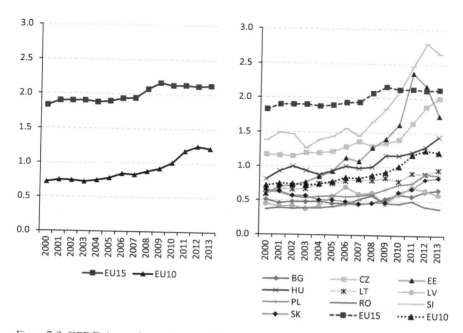

Figure 7.2 GERD (gross domestic expenditure on research and development) as % of GDP
Source: Own study based on data from the Web of Science.

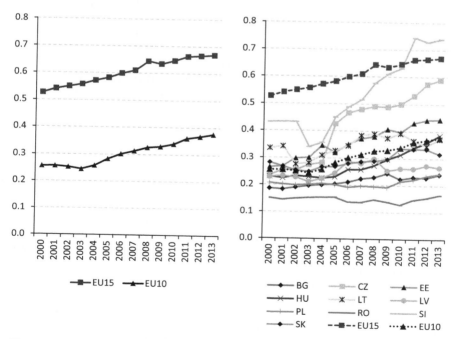

Figure 7.3 Employment in R&D as % of population
Source: Own study based on data from the Web of Science.

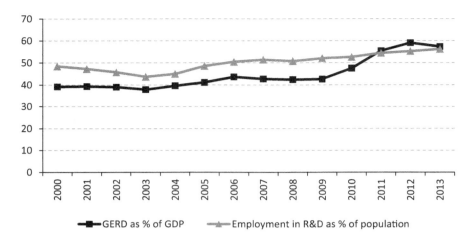

Figure 7.4 GERD in % of GDP and employment in R&D as % of population in EU10 in
relation to EU15 (EU15 = 100)

Source: Own study based on data from the Web of Science.

Third, as we might have anticipated, the gap in values for expenditure and
employment between CEE countries and the 'fifteen' is significant. In 2000,
expenditure on R&D as % GDP in the EU10 came to only 39% of that in the
EU15, rising to 57% in 2013. Meanwhile, employment taken as % inhabitants
in EU10 countries was 48% in 2000, rising to 56% at the end of the study
period. All things considered, despite the significant disproportion between the
EU10 and EU15, a visible convergence of results can be seen to take place on
the European scale (Figure 7.4). More and more resources in the science sector
can contribute to subsequent growth in the scientific output of CEE countries
(Vinkler 2008; Lin et al. 2014).

Journals published in CEE

The Web of Science contains only articles from selected journals. In principle, the choice of journals is meant to be content based – the intention is to
include the most prominent (the best) periodicals. However, other factors also
play a role. One of these is the desire to achieve a spatially balanced database,
by including journals that are not only important on the world scale, but also
those whose scope is more regional (i.e. a group of countries) or even national
(Testa 2011). This approach is particularly important in the case of periodicals
in the field of social science and humanities, as the research problems they
deal with are often of a national, linguistic or even local nature. However,
journals relating to the exact sciences which are clearly of a national character

(supported by the fact that they are published in non-congress languages) can also be included in WoS, such as the journal *Przemysł Chemiczny* ('Chemical Industry'), which is published in Poland and mostly in the Polish language (there is a fraction of articles in English).

Inclusion in the database is not indefinite. If a journal does not fulfil the criteria determined by WoS, it is simply removed. The criteria include formal requirements (e.g. regular issue) as well as content requirements (a suitably high impact factor).[3] When a given journal is removed from the index, the 'space' becomes available to new titles. The scope for considering new titles depends both on the engagement of publishers who apply for entry, as well as of the database administrators who, apart from respecting the overriding principle of listing the most important journals, must to some extent be guided by business sense. We should also remember that WoS is a commercial product, and its creators (owners) are guided by economic outcomes. Moreover, an important question remains unanswered as to whether the owners' selection criteria are consistent and rigorous or whether some countries are favoured and overrepresented in WoS (Kosanovic and Sipka 2013).

In recent years, we have witnessed a fairly important expansion in the spatial range of the WoS database. This growth has been markedly more intense than in previous decades. In the years 1980–90, the number of journals in the database rose from 6,130 by 654 titles (10.7%). In the decade 1990–2000, a further 1,444 journals were added (21.3%). In the years 2000–2010 the increase was visibly steeper: in 2000 there were 8,228 titles, and as many as 11,793 in 2010. The increase of 3,511 journals meant that the list of titles grew by 42.7%. This radical expansion of the database is described by Thomson Reuters as 'The Globalisation of the Web of Science' (Testa 2011). Apart from the routine analysis of journals for inclusion in the database – in recent years around 2,500 applications annually, of which around 10% are accepted – in the years 2007–09 action was undertaken to increase the database's representation of journals outside the 'centre' of world research:

> from 2007 to 2009 the Editorial Development Department at Thomson Reuters focused on a collection of more than 10,000 regional journals (these are journals published outside the US or UK that contain the scholarship of authors from a particular region or country, and cover topics of regional interest or topics studied from a regional perspective). Sixteen hundred (1,600) of these 10,000 journals met Thomson Reuters standards and were selected for coverage.
>
> (Testa 2011, s. 2)

In consequence, the number of journals published in some countries and listed in WoS grew significantly between 2005 and 2010. The steepest growth in absolute numbers was recorded in Spain (112 new titles; growth of 207%), Brazil (105; 389%), Australia (97; 105%), Poland (85; 149%), Turkey (68; 971%), Italy (68; 56%), France (62; 28%), China (62; 75%),

South Korea (62; 168%), Japan (61; 35%), India (60; 113%), Romania (52; 650%), Croatia (47; 336%) and South Africa (41; 152%) (Testa 2011: 4). The increase in the number of journals naturally leads to an increased number of indexed articles in WoS. This should be remembered when performing time analyses. The growth in the number of articles are, after all, not only the result of increased research activity but also the effect of more extensive monitoring of scientific production – in this case, the greater number of journals included in WoS.

The greater openness of WoS to journals outside the global research centre is clearly visible in Central and Eastern Europe. In the years 2000–2006, published titles in CEE constituted barely more than 3% of all journals published in the entire EU27. As a consequence of the database's expansion, in the years 2007–09 this percentage rose by around 3.5% and in subsequent years (2010–13) maintained a level of around 7.5% (see Figure 7.5, left). This growth in the number of journals affected all the CEE countries analyzed (see Figure 7.5, right), although the scale varied due partly to the size of the country as well as to the number of journals from a given country that were listed in WoS before the 'global expansion' of 2007–09. When we compare figures for 2000 and 2013, the greatest growth in journal numbers in WoS was noted in Romania and Estonia – where the number of titles increased tenfold. To a large

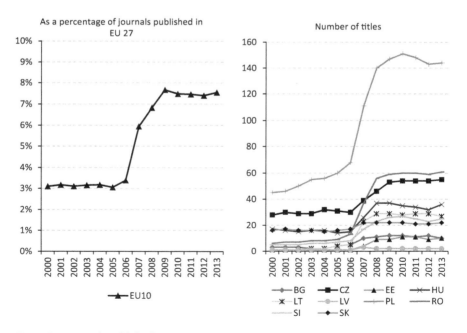

Figure 7.5 Journals published in EU10 countries and indexed in WoS

Source: Own study based on data from the Web of Science.

extent this results from the low starting point (i.e. a low number of journals from these countries in 2000). A spectacular fivefold increase was recorded in Slovenia. In the case of Poland and Bulgaria, growth was just over threefold. Meanwhile Poland is the clear leader in the group of countries analysed in terms of absolute numbers of titles – one in three journals from the EU10 in the database is a journal published in Poland. Hungary, Lithuania and Czechia doubled the number of journals in WoS and Slovakia increased its share by 140%. Meanwhile, Latvia is a very unusual case, as in 2013 only two journals from this country were present in WoS, and its entire growth is attributed to the addition of just one title in 2007. Another specific case is Lithuania: in the years 2000–2001, not a single journal published in this country appeared in WoS while, as a result of the expansion, as many as 29 titles had been included by the end of the decade.

Analysis of the number of articles appearing in journals published in EU10 countries and included in WoS results in a similar picture to that given by analysis of the number of journal titles. Equally in this case, there is a clear leap in the years 2007–08 (Figure 7.6).

One of the effects of including such a large number of national journals in WoS is the noticeable increase in the percentage of articles affiliated to EU10 countries and appearing in journals published by institutions in this part of

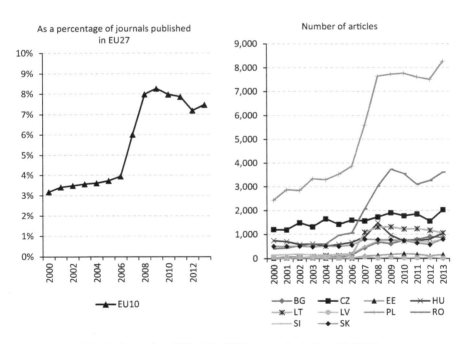

Figure 7.6 Articles in journals published in EU10 countries indexed in WoS

Source: Own study based on data from the Web of Science.

Europe. In the years 2000–2006 these constituted 17%–18% of all articles affiliated to these countries and indexed in WoS. However, in the years 2008–09 this percentage increased to 31%. Subsequent years saw a fall in numbers, and in the years 2012 and 2013 only around one in four articles from the EU10 in WoS came from journals published in this region. Despite this drop, the figure is still higher than a decade earlier. The significance of national journals in the number of articles is very diverse in CEE. In the case of Lithuania and Romania, in the years directly following the expansion of WoS to include a large number of titles from these countries, more than half the articles in WoS came from journals published in the EU10 (which is almost equal to the number of journals from these countries – it is very rare that articles affiliated to the EU10 appear in journals published in other countries). However, Czechia presents a completely different scenario. In this country, despite the number of journals in WoS doubling, the percentage of articles appearing in journals published in the EU in the years 2000–2013 (this also differs from national journals) remained at a level of 20% (see Figure 7.7).

The difference in the share of articles appearing in journals published in countries in the region could testify to the differing levels of internationalization of publishing activity. A high percentage of publications in journals of a particular country (region) can be interpreted as indicating a lower level of internationalization in the science sector of this country. Meanwhile, a

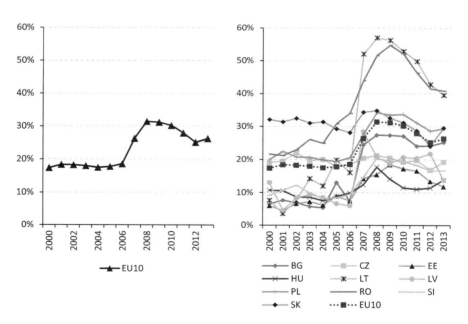

Figure 7.7 Percentage of articles affiliated to EU10 appearing in journals published in EU10

Source: Own study based on data from the Web of Science.

dominance of articles published in journals outside the country (region) in question indicates a greater presence in international research circles.

Citations

Information on citations from scientific journals are often used to gauge the quality of these publications and/or their impact factor (see Hoekman et al. 2008; van Raan 2004). However, citations are not a perfect measure, as they do not allow for context, that is, they assign weight to a given publication, even if the citation is negative – for example to show misconceptions or incorrect methods. Moreover, the most recent studies are often cited in preference to earlier ones which relate to a given issue (citation amnesia) or overlook studies included in the canon of research because their influence is regarded as obvious (oversight due to incorporation). This measure also fails because studies are produced by large teams of researchers recruited to study new, popular issues (see de Bells 2009; Moed 2005; Andrès 2009; Kamińska-Włodarczyk and Siwiec-Kurczab 2003). The size and extent of an author's collaboration network may also affect the number of citations, which may therefore attest more to collaboration than to research impact (Olechnicka et al. 2019). The weakness of citations is the fact that they are derived from (imperfect) bibliometric databases which do not encompass all citations appearing in all publications worldwide, but only those indexed in a given database. Moreover, in researching citations we should allow for the time lapse in relation to publication (Schneider 2009; Moed 2005).

This analysis of 'citability' is based on the normalized citations, that is, the number of citations from articles affiliated to a given country and published in a given year is compared with the average number of citations from articles in the EU15 in that year. This allows us to compare citability over time. This is essential, as information on article citations is obtained at the moment of retrieving data from the WoS database (i.e. mid-2014). Therefore more recent articles have decidedly fewer citations than older articles, not because they are of inferior quality, but above all because the more time passes, the greater likelihood of a larger number of citations. This is also the reason why the data presented here relates to the period 2000–2011 (as opposed to the remaining analyses in this article which relate to the period 2000–2013). Information on article citations where only a short time has lapsed since publication is less reliable than articles published some distance in the past (Research Evaluation and Policy Project 2005). This stems from the fact that usually, from the moment of publication to the moment of citations appearing, at least a few or several months pass, or often even many years.[4]

Analyses relativized to the EU27 values for average article citation shows that publications affiliated to EU10 countries are much less frequently cited than those affiliated to the EU15, although this difference can be seen to be lessening over time. The average number of citations per publication affiliated to the EU10 constituted 56.3% of the EU average in 2000, while in 2011, 63.3% – a growth of 6.9 percentage points (Figure 7.8, left). However, as with

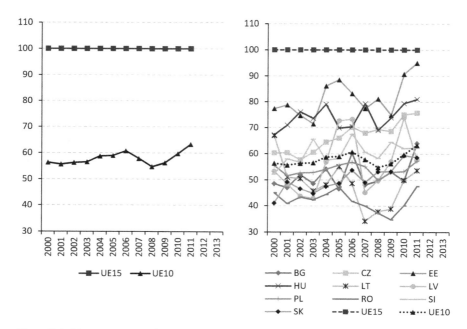

Figure 7.8 Citations per article in EU10 and EU15 in relation to EU27 (EU27 = 100) – all journals

Source: Own study based on data from the Web of Science.

the number of articles, convergence can be seen to be much stronger when we exclude from the publication sample those titles which were published in CEE countries. The relative increase in normalised citations in the EU10 for this newly defined sample of articles is 16 percentage points (from 64.9% in 2000 to 80.9% in 2013) (Figure 7.8, left). This means that publications which appeared in CEE journals are generally less often cited and the normalized citations of these articles increases on average at a slower rate.

The EU10 group is diverse in terms of the indicators discussed above. In both respects (all articles and only those published outside CEE), values above the EU average are achieved by Czechia, Hungary and Estonia. In 2010 and 2011 this last country exceeded even the EU15 average in the case of articles published in journals outside CEE. Poland and Slovenia noted values close to the EU10 average or slightly below it (although the trend observed in Poland reflects the EU10 average – Poland, as the country with the largest number of articles in the region, has the greatest influence on this average). On the other hand, Romania and Lithuania are countries which fall furthest below the EU10 average (with considerable fluctuation from year to year). The values for Latvia are the most unstable; this is due to the relatively small number of articles affiliated to this country (see Figure 7.8, right; Figure 7.9, right).

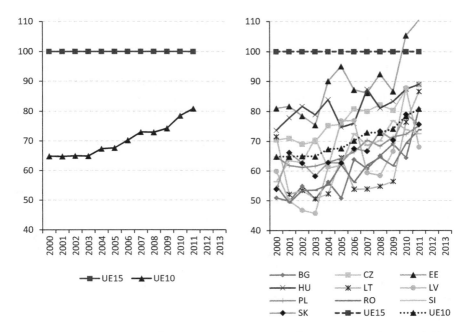

Figure 7.9 Citations per article in EU10 and EU15 in relation to EU27 (EU27 = 100) – journals published outside EU10

Source: Own study based on data from the Web of Science.

International collaboration

Modern-day science is increasingly globalized. This is evidenced by the grow-ing intensity of international collaboration among researchers from different countries and continents. The scale of this phenomenon is so impressive that the process can be called a 'collaborative turn' (Olechnicka et al. 2019). In terms of scientific publications, this has led to a growing number of articles with multiple authors from various institutions and countries (Glänzel et al. 1999; Glänzel and Schubert 2004; Wagner and Leydesdorff 2005; Tijssen 2008). A synthetic indicator of the internationalization of publications can be the percentage of articles affiliated to a given country which have at least one foreign author, in the overall number of publications from that country. In 2013 over half the publications from the EU15 were produced in cooperation with co-authors from abroad. Moreover, the value of the discussed indicator has grown in recent years. In 2000, international articles constituted 37.6% of those published in the EU15, with as many as 54.8% in 2013. In this context, Central and Eastern European countries give a different picture. In the years 2000–2006, the share of international articles in the overall publication output of the EU10 maintained a fairly stable level of between 44.5% and 46.7%. In the years 2007–08 there was a noticeable drop to a level of 40%. In subsequent years the value of this indicator gradually rose but did not exceed the level of 2000–2006. Thus, despite the fact that in the first half of the analyzed period the share of international publications in the EU10 was greater than in the EU15, in subsequent years Western European countries began to noticeably overtake CEE countries in this respect (Figure 7.10, left). Poorer achievements of the EU10 countries are also visible at the regional level, since most of the regions with the lowest internationalization scores (below 33%) are located at the EU eastern peripheries – in Bulgaria, Lithuania, Poland and Romania (Olechnicka et al. 2019).

As with other aspects discussed in this article, the group of CEE countries is diversified in terms of the share of articles with foreign co-authors. In many cases we can also see major changes in the values of this indicator. Generally speaking, we can distinguish three groups of countries. The first group is formed of countries in which the share of international articles in the period 2000–2013 noticeably fell. The steepest drop was noted in Lithuania (−16.9%), while it was slightly less steep in Romania (−9.6%) and in Poland (−6.3%). Finally, at the end of the analyzed period, only these three countries had a share of international articles below the EU10 average. The second group constitutes countries with a clear growth in the share of international articles. The most spectacular growth was witnessed in Slovenia (13.7 pp) and Slovakia (11.8 pp). Significant growth could also be observed in Bulgaria (9.5 pp), Estonia (8.2 pp),

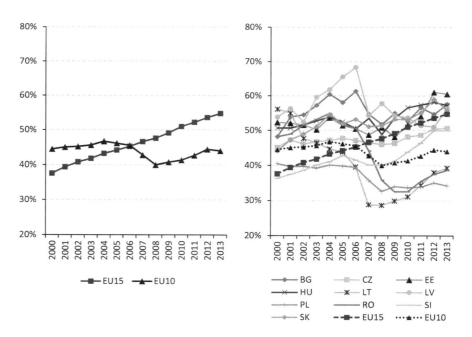

Figure 7.10 Percentage of articles with at least one foreign affiliation – all journals

Source: Own study based on data from the Web of Science.

Hungary (6.7 pp), as well as in Czechia (5.6 pp). A distinct case is represented by Latvia, in which the indicator began to rise dramatically, from 53.9% in 2000 to 68.3%, and then subsequently fell dramatically. Thus at the end of the discussed period, Latvia noted only insignificant growth in the share of international articles (2.5%). This dramatic fluctuation in Latvia's case is the result of the relatively small number of articles affiliated to this country (Figure 7.10, right).

We can presume that changes in the share of international articles in the EU10 were influenced by the expansion of the WoS database to include journals published in these countries. This is shown by the fall in the number of international publications produced in the years 2007–08, exactly when WoS started to index a large number of journals published in CEE countries (see above). This presumption is further supported by analysis of the share of international articles appearing only in journals published outside Central and Eastern Europe. From this angle we do not see a fall in the value of the indicator, but quite the contrary, we can observe constant – although slight – growth (see Figure 7.11, left). Moreover, it appears that the share of international articles appearing in journals published outside CEE in the case of the EU10 was noticeably higher for many years than in the case of articles from the EU15. However, considering the much more dynamic growth of the indicator in the EU15 than in the EU10, the levels for both these groups of countries at the end

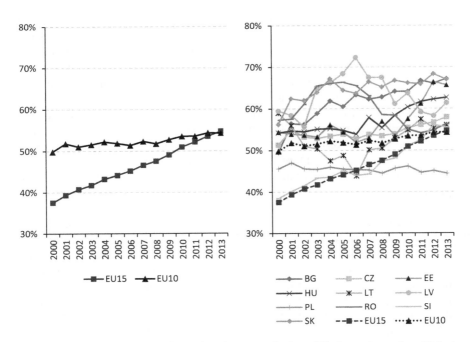

Figure 7.11 Percentage of articles with at least one foreign affiliation – journals published outside EU10

Source: Own study based on data from the Web of Science.

of the period balanced out. On a national level, Poland stands out noticeably. This is the only country which experienced a constant fall in the number of international articles appearing in journals published outside CEE. Thus Poland is clearly falling behind the EU10 and EU15 averages, and in 2013 was the only CEE country which came in below these averages (see Figure 7.11, right).

Productivity and effectiveness

Comparing information on articles and their citations to data regarding expenditure on scientific activity and human resources in science allows us to estimate the scientific productivity and effectiveness of individual countries. The average number of articles and average number of citations per researcher can be used as a productivity indicator (generally understood as the relationship between output volume to the level of resource input). Meanwhile, the level of expenditure per article or citation is an indicator of effectiveness (the relationship of outcomes achieved to costs incurred).

The advantage of this approach is that it is a relatively simple way of achieving a general comparison of countries. However, this method of presenting data also has limitations, which should be remembered when interpreting results. The fundamental drawback is the fact that, in order to calculate these indicators, information is used on the total employment in research and development as well as data on the total expenditure on R&D in a given country. Thus, this type of calculation is not sufficient to claim that the costs of 'production' of scientific articles in a given country are 'X', or that the number of articles per researcher is 'Y'. Nevertheless, the proposed approach allows us to spot some interesting differences among countries and between groups of countries.

First, the convergence of EU10 countries is stronger in terms of productivity indicators than effectiveness measures. While the indicator for the number of articles per researcher at the end of the analyzed period came close to the EU15 average (in the years 2008–09 it even exceeded it slightly) and the citation indicator per R&D worker reached 60% of the EU average, at the same time expenditure on R&D per article or citation oscillated between 53% and 34% of the EU15 average. This phenomenon is linked to the aforementioned greater convergence of CEE in employment in R&D than in expenditure on research and development activity (see Figure 7.12).

Among the indicators of effectiveness, the disparity between the scale of convergence calculated for the whole publication pool and for the sample of publications appearing in Western European journals is three times greater in the case of the cost of articles compared to the cost of citations (60% vs. 20%). This means that the rate of growth in the cost absorption of articles published in foreign journals is greater than for those published in CEE. A similar conclusion can be drawn from the indicator of citations, with the exception that here, differences relating to the place of publication are less significant. Meanwhile, in the case of citations per researcher, the disparity is also visible, but decidedly less pronounced. This may indicate that the inclusion of journals from the EU10 in WoS had an impact on the number of publications from this region indexed in WoS, but did

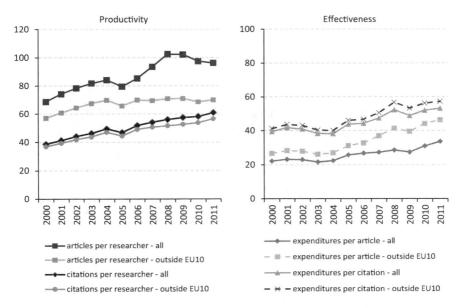

Figure 7.12 Productivity and effectiveness measures in EU10 in relation to EU15 (EU15 = 100)

Source: Own study based on data from the Web of Science.

not influence (at least for the time being) growth in the normalized citations of researchers from Central and Eastern Europe (see Figure 7.12, left).

Diversity among CEE countries regarding output, measured as the number of articles per researcher, is very great. We only need to notice that while many countries with the highest level of convergence, such as Estonia, Slovenia, Poland and Romania, achieved values that exceed the EU15, countries such as Bulgaria and Latvia achieved levels of no more than 50%–60% of the EU15 average. This disparity is visible in both the levels and rates of convergence. The clear leader is Romania, where the index of articles per researcher in relation to the EU15 grew in the study period from a level of one-third to a level exceeding the EU15 average. This fast rate of convergence also distinguishes Estonia, Lithuania and Poland. However, Czechia and Hungary show a fall in productivity measures in terms of articles. As a result, while starting at a high level – close to the EU15 average – at the beginning of the study period, they have clearly lost ground in recent years, distancing themselves both from the EU15 and even the EU10 average (Figure 7.13, left). However, by limiting the pool of articles and citations to journals published outside CEE, we arrive at significantly revised values for the discussed indicators. The observed convergence is decidedly less pronounced (e.g. Estonia, Lithuania, Romania) or non-existent, and we can even notice a departure from the EU15 (Bulgaria). In the case of Czechia and Hungary, this divergence is plainly visible (Figure 7.13, right).

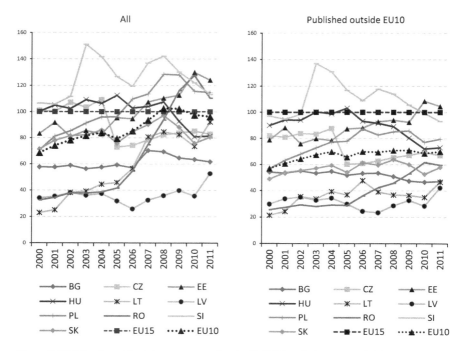

Figure 7.13 Number of articles per researcher in EU10 in relation to EU15 (EU15 = 100)
Source: Own study based on data from the Web of Science.

While in the case of articles per researcher some CEE countries achieved the EU15 average or even significantly exceeded it, in the case of citations per researcher the distance dividing EU10 countries from the EU15 average is still enormous. Apart from a few exceptions (Slovenia in 2003 and Estonia in 2010 and 2011), none of the analyzed countries came close to the EU15 average. However, we should point out that certain countries noted constant improvement (e.g. Poland, Romania, Slovakia and Lithuania). Meanwhile, Czechia and Hungary, which also began in a relatively high position in this respect, did not achieve significant convergence (Figure 7.14, left). It is interesting to note that in the case of citations, the inclusion of articles appearing in journals published outside CEE in the citation sample analyzed has little influence on the shape of these trends (Figure 7.14, right). This may stem from the fact that articles published in journals outside CEE are cited more often than those from CEE.

The situation looks completely different regarding effectiveness within the region (Figures 7.15 and 7.16). First, none of the CEE countries in the entire study period noted output levels that exceeded the EU15 average. In the case of Latvia, the EU15 average was exceeded incidentally in 2007 in terms of the average expenditure on citations. Second, the scale of diversity among CEE countries

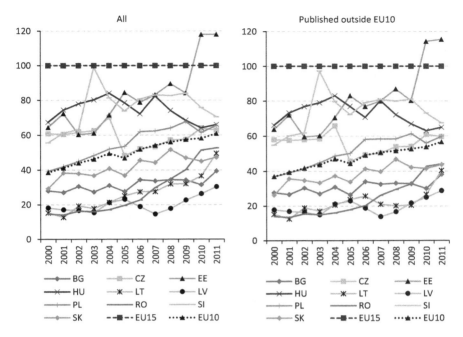

Figure 7.14 Number of citations per researcher in EU10 in relation to EU15 (EU15 = 100)
Source: Own study based on data from the Web of Science.

is decidedly less than in the case of productivity (around 30 pp versus 100 pp). Moreover, the group of countries which stand out in terms of convergence levels is also somewhat distinct. Countries with a cost absorption indicator exceeding the EU10 average are Czechia, Slovenia, Hungary and Latvia. However, the countries with the lowest cost absorption of articles in relation to the EU15 average are Romania and Bulgaria, thus the economies which have the lowest level of GERD in % GDP. Third, the rate of convergence is weaker than that for output levels. The cost of articles is growing fastest in Estonia, Latvia, Czechia and Hungary, while the slowest in Lithuania, Poland and Romania. Similar tendencies affect expenditure relative to citation numbers (Figure 7.16, left).

Comparison of trends calculated for all journals, as well as for a sample excluding journals published in the EU10, generally gives similar results. Of course, the average cost of an article in all the countries appears greater than when we include all articles, which is a natural consequence of excluding a group of articles (e.g. those appearing in journals published CEE). The differences in the case of expenditure on citations are less pronounced, due to the aforementioned fact that articles from journals published in CEE are much less often cited (i.e. citations from these articles constitute a sufficiently small

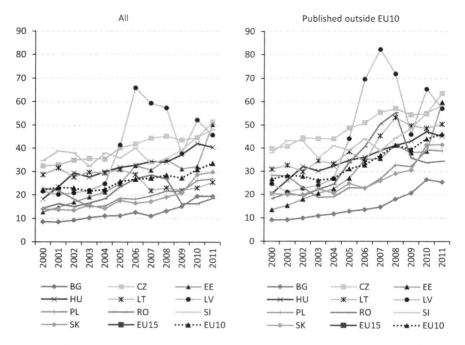

Figure 7.15 R&D expenditures per article in EU10 in relation to EU15 (EU15 = 100)
Source: Own study based on data from the Web of Science.

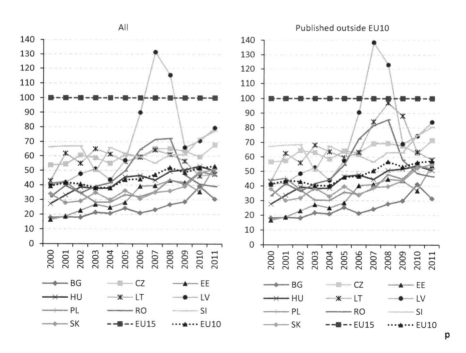

p

Figure 7.16 R&D expenditures per citation in EU10 in relation to EU15 (EU15 = 100)
Source: Own study based on data from the Web of Science.

proportion of total citations that their exclusion from the analysis does not significantly influence results, since they combine the same level of expenditure with a slightly lower number of citations).

Discussion

The analyses presented in this chapter support the argument that countries from Central and Eastern Europe, despite showing fairly consistent convergence trends, achieve noticeably weaker results than Western Europe in terms of research and development and scientific activity. The best runners up behind Western Europe are Estonia, Slovenia, Czechia and Hungary. The first two of these countries are relatively small economies which in recent years took up a comprehensive, knowledge-based approach to economic growth. Meanwhile, Czechia and Hungary possess a strong scientific tradition, which in recent years they have been able to maintain and even develop. The middle of the Central European league table for science and R&D is taken by Lithuania, Latvia, Poland and Slovakia. The weakest results are shown by Romania and Bulgaria (see Table 7.1). We can see here quite a clear (two-way) relationship between the level of economic growth of a country (measured e.g. by GDP per capita), or the wider level of socio-economic development (assessed using e.g. the Human Development Index created by UNDP), and indicators of R&D development.

Traditional measures of research and development activity – expenditure on R&D relative to GDP as well as employment in R&D as a percentage of the population – show that, in 2013, the EU10 average reached over half the

Table 7.1 R&D in EU10 in relation to EU15 average

		UE10	BG	CZ	EE	HU	LT	LV	PL	RO	SI	SK
GERD as % of GDP (2013)		57	31	94	82	68	45	28	41	18	125	40
Employment in R&D as % of population (2013)		56	36	88	66	58	56	40	36	25	110	47
Articles per inhabitants (2013)	*All*	48	23	78	102	48	52	24	46	31	146	46
	Non-EU10	35	18	63	90	42	32	21	33	19	122	33
Citations per article (2011)	*All*	63	64	76	95	81	54	58	57	48	62	59
	Non-EU10	81	81	89	110	89	87	68	75	74	73	76
Share of international articles (2013)	*All*	80	105	93	110	105	72	103	63	70	91	102
	Non-EU10	99	123	106	120	114	102	112	81	103	102	122
Articles per researcher (2011)	*All*	96	62	83	124	82	92	53	115	110	113	81
	Non-EU10	70	47	67	105	73	47	42	80	60	93	58
Citations per researcher (2011)	*All*	61	40	63	118	66	49	30	66	53	71	47
	Non-EU10	57	38	60	115	65	40	29	60	44	68	44
Expenditures per article (2011)	*All*	34	19	51	50	40	26	46	27	19	48	30
	Non-EU10	46	26	64	60	45	50	57	39	34	58	42
Expenditures per citation (2011)	*All*	53	30	68	53	50	48	79	47	39	77	51
	Non-EU10	57	32	71	54	51	58	84	52	47	81	55

Source: Own study based on data from the Web of Science and EUROSTAT.

EU15 average (57% and 56% of the average, respectively). In terms of the number of articles listed in WoS per inhabitant, this distance is somewhat greater: the EU10 attained a level of 48% of the EU15 average. However, if we set the number of publications against the number of researchers, it turns out that the EU10 comes up equal with the EU15 average. Thus we can assume that further growth in the number of publications in the EU10 is unlikely without an increase in human resources in science. Scientists from Central and Eastern Europe have similar levels of output to their Western European colleagues, but there are proportionately less of them (relative to population potential). They have decidedly less funds at their disposal with which to finance research. This is also the reason why the relationship between expenditure on R&D and the number of articles and citations differs to such an extent between the EU10 and EU15. In the EU10 this amounts to 34% (expenditure per article) and 53% (expenditure per citation) of the EU15 average. It can be attributed to the fact that less costly research areas are dealt with, but also to the fact that remuneration for research in CEE countries is significantly less.

While in terms of articles per researcher, Central and Eastern Europe has caught up with the EU15 average, as regards the average number of citations per article as well as the number of citations per researcher, this convergence is decidedly less pronounced. The average number of citations from articles affiliated to the EU10 in 2011 amounted to 63% of the EU15 average, and the number of citations per researcher constituted 61% of this average. This shows that convergence in science is taking place to a greater degree in terms of quantitative outcomes (number of articles) than in qualitative terms (citations). Scientists from CEE publish increasingly more articles which are listed on WoS, but they are still much less often cited than their Western European colleagues. The reasons for this are complex. We certainly cannot ignore the significance of lower expenditure on science in comparison to the West, the lesser importance of CEE languages for scientific communication and the generally weaker scientific traditions of these countries resulting from their isolation in finding themselves on the 'wrong' side of the Iron Curtain following World War II (Kozak et al. 2015). Moreover the characteristic focus on quantity (as opposed to quality) in the EU10 may be related to prevailing deficiencies in public governance related to scientific evaluation and funding mechanisms in the post-communist countries (Jonkers and Zacharewicz 2016). Another interconnected reason is the lower level of international collaboration of CEE countries, which distracts their limited resources away from internationally more competitive research, and as a result diminishes the probability of higher citations (Olechnicka et al. 2019).

Nonetheless, the chapter proved that the place in which journals are published also plays a role. If we exclude from our analysis those journals published in CEE, then the average number of citations from articles written by authors from EU10 countries comes much closer to the EU15 average, attaining a level of 81% – that is 18 percentage points more than if we include journals published in CEE. This suggests that reasons for the weaker citability of CEE scientists should also be sought in the characteristics of journals published in these countries. This finding is in line with that of Pajić (2015), who analyzed the impact of national journals on citations in humanities and social sciences. The weaker citability of articles published in local journals is confirmed by analyses performed on other peripheral regions in the world (e.g. in Brazil), the growth in the number of publications brought about by the expansion of WoS only slightly increased the citability, due to the inclusion of national journals (Collazo-Reyes 2014). For some reason, the articles publish by CEE scholars (or more generally, scholars from peripheries) are less likely to be cited. This partly stems from the national language they are published in. However, this factor does not have great impact since only 6% of articles in the years 2000–2013 affiliated in the EU10 were published in a language other than English. Therefore, we can assume that a major role is played by factors which are hard to capture, such as the prestige of a journal, its international recognition, its availability on the internet in full-length form and finally – even harder to assess – the quality of the articles published. For authors affiliated to EU10 countries it may be easier to publish articles in national journals (even English-language ones), than in international titles. A whole range of factors contribute to this situation including, among others, poorer knowledge of publication standards and publication strategies as well as inadequate levels of proficiency in English, but also perhaps poorer standards of research resulting, inter alia, from weaker international collaboration (Olechnicka et al. 2019). We can suppose that publishing in CEE journals, even for authors of the region, is a second choice, particularly if the article has valuable content. This aspect requires further detailed analysis based on the experiences and opinions of scientists in this part of Europe.

Conclusions

The development of scientific and R&D activity in Central and Eastern European countries, and consequently their progressing convergence towards the old EU Member States, is easily observable. Even basic data from EUROSTAT testifies to this phenomenon and it is also quite easy to explain. On one hand, convergence has been caused by the opening of borders, the incorporation into EU structures, the growing wealth of society, the implementation of scientific policies, and also to the substantial EU funding designated to support the research and development sector and innovation in general in these countries. On the other hand, the purely statistical aspect is also important, that is the so-called low-base effect. It is easier to achieve a high rate of development if you start from a low ceiling.

The aim of this chapter is to confirm that there is also a third factor which influences the observable (but real?) convergence in terms of research and development outcomes, in the form of publications in scientific journals. This factor is the wider inclusion of research articles from journals published in Central and Eastern European countries in worldwide bibliometric databases.

To illustrate this we used the Web of Science, which has for decades been the main reference source for international bibliometric comparisons. The evident impact made by inclusion, in 2007–08, of numerous CEE journals in WoS on the values of the indicator analyzed, directly supports the argument put forward in this article. The growth in the number of articles from individual countries in WoS thus not only testifies to the organic growth of the science sector in these countries, but also results from decisions made by the managing bodies of these commercial databases. Changes in the database are doubtless content driven and are prompted, for example, by the desire to better reflect the state of world research. But we cannot reject other, non-content-related motives, such as the wish to make the database more attractive to potential clients in countries with 'developing' science sectors and who have a great need to evaluate their research achievements (which in many countries goes hand in hand with reforms in higher education and science). However, irrespective of the reasons for expanding the database, it has led to better visibility in the European arena (Vanecek 2014) and easier access to the research outcomes of CEE countries. And in the context of scientometric studies and international comparisons, we can say that the state of research in CEE countries is also being better measured.

Without a doubt, this chapter has many limitations and – thanks to these limitations – possibilities for furthering and deepening selected themes. First, the analyses conducted are based on a single bibliometric source. Conducting similar analyses on other source materials would help verify our theories. An obvious line of research would be to investigate data from the SCOPUS database, as the main rival database for bibliometric analyses. The unquestionable advantage of SCOPUS over WoS is its wider inclusion of publications from the social sciences and the arts. Second, this chapter is based only on descriptive and comparative statistical analyses. More detailed analyses using more advanced statistical instruments could help give a more precise understanding of the nature and scale of differences as well as the incidence of co-variance and causal relationships. Third, we can point to several content-related areas for pursuing the given approach: (a) an important area would be to analyze more precisely the influence of the language of publication on the normalized citations of articles; and (b) a very important factor – completely overlooked in this chapter – is the differentiation of research fields. This is important because, in certain countries, the range of research fields in the publication pool varies, and each field has a very different approach to publishing, internationalization, the number of co-authors, the average number of citations and the speed at which (citations of) articles are included into intellectual circulation in a given field (see van Raan 2004). Initial analysis shows that the field structure of articles in the EU10 countries differs significantly to that in the EU15. In particular, there is a much higher percentage of publications from natural science fields, while the share of articles from medical sciences is much less. These preliminary findings are in line with available results for Czechia, Hungary, Poland, Slovakia, Slovenia and Croatia in the years 2010–14 – they perform better in natural sciences, engineering and technology than in social or medical sciences

(Jurajda et al. 2017). This is largely a result of their historical legacy (Kozlowski et al. 1999). Fourth, a potentially interesting aspect for further analysis would be to analyze in detail international collaboration, taking into consideration not only the share of articles from foreign authors, but also the directions of this collaboration (from national and regional perspectives), as well as national collaboration. Fifth, it would be worth carefully analyzing indicators of productivity and effectiveness (e.g. paying attention to division of expenditure on public and private R&D, employment in R&D in government and enterprise sectors), as well as taking into account the differences in average salaries of R&D employees in both groups of countries (by using PPPs).

Notes

1 This chapter is based on the results of empirical analyses prepared by Agnieszka Olechnicka and Adam Ploszaj within the FP7 GRINCOH project: 'Growth – Innovation – Competitiveness: Fostering Cohesion in Central and Eastern Europe' ((2012-2015), and Polish National Science Centre grant: 'Polish science centres in the European Collaboration network – characteristics, determinants, mechanisms' (2011/03/B/HS4/05737).

2 WoS is a bibliographic database containing bibliographic descriptions and indexes of citations from scientific publications. This database is one of the products created and made available by the Institute of Scientific Information, later maintained by Clarivate Analytics (previously the Intellectual Property and Science business of Thomson Reuters). WoS (Core Collection), from among many databases of this kind, boasts extensive coverage with a total file count of 71 million records, which includes over a billion cited references (see https://clarivate.libguides.com/webofscienceplatform/coverage; accessed 29 January 2019).

3 http://wokinfo.com/essays/journal-selection-process/.

4 In order for an article to be cited it must first be read, then the citation must be included in an article submitted for publication; this is then followed by a review process that may last several months or even years leading to amendment or further review, etc.

References

Abbott, A., & Schiermeier, Q. (November 2014). After the Berlin Wall: Central Europe up close. *Nature*, 515, 5.

Andrès, A. (2009). *Measuring Academic Research. How to undertake a Bibliometric Study*. Oxford: Chandos Publishing.

Basu, A. (2010). Does a country's scientific 'productivity' depend critically on the number of country journals indexed? *Scientometrics*, 82(3), 507–516.

de Bells, N. (2009). *Bibliometrics and citation analysis. From the Science Citation Index to Cybermetrics*. Plymouth: The Scarecrow Press, Inc.

Collazo-Reyes, F. (2014). Growth of the number of indexed journals of Latin America and the Caribbean: The effect on the impact of each country. *Scientometrics*, 98(1), 197–209.

European Commission. (2018). *European Innovation Scoreboard 2018*. Retrieved from https://ec.europa.eu/docsroom/documents/30281

Glänzel, W., Schubert, A., & Czerwon, H.J. (1999). A bibliometric analysis of international scientific cooperation of the European Union (1985–1995). *Scientometrics*, 45, 185–202.

Glänzel, W., & Schubert, A. (2004). Analysing scientific networks through co-authorship. In: F.H. Moed, W. Glänzel & U. Schmoch (eds.), *Handbook of Quantitative Science and Technology*

Research. The Use of Publications and Patent Statistics in Studies of S&T Systems. Dordrecht: Kluwer Academic Publishers, pp. 257–276.

Hoekman, J., Frenken, K., & Oort, F. van. (2008). Collaboration networks as carriers of knowledge spillovers: Evidence from EU27 regions, *KITeS Working Papers* No 222, KITeS, Centre for Knowledge, Internationalization and Technology Studies, Universita' Bocconi, Milano, Italy.

Jonkers, K., & Zacharewicz, T. (2016). Research performance based funding systems: A comparative assessment (No. JRC101043). Institute for Prospective Technological Studies, Joint Research Centre.

Jurajda, Š., Kozubek, S., Münich, D., & Škoda, S. (2017). Scientific publication performance in post-communist countries: Still lagging far behind. *Scientometrics*, 112(1), 315–328.

Kamińska-Włodarczyk, R., & Siwiec-Kurczab, B. (2003). Problemy oceny dorobku naukowego w Polsce. Biuletyn Informacyjny Biblioteki Głównej Akademii Wychowania Fizycznego w Krakowie [on-line].

Kosanovic, B., & Sipka, P. (2013). Output in WoS vs. representation in JCR of SEE Nations: Does mother Thomson cherish all her children equally (pp. 125–137). *Presented at the Fifth Belgrade International Open Access Conference 2012*, 18–19 May, Belgrade: CEES, doi: 10.5937/BIOAC-111.

Kozlowski, J., Radosevic, S., & Ircha, D. (1999). History matters: The inherited disciplinary structure of the post-communist science in countries of Central and Eastern Europe and its restructuring. *Scientometrics*, 45(1), 137–166.

Kozak, M., Bornmann, L., & Leydesdorff, L. (2015). How have the Eastern European countries of the former Warsaw Pact developed since 1990? A bibliometric study. *Scientometrics*, 102(2), 1101–1117, February.

Lin, P.H., Chen, J.R., & Yang, C.H. (2014). Academic research resources and academic quality: A cross-country analysis. *Scientometrics*, 101(1), 109–123.

Liu, W., Hu, G., Tang, L., & Wang, Y. (2015). China's global growth in social science research: Uncovering evidence from bibliometric analyses of SSCI publications (1978–2013). *Journal of Informetrics*, 9(3), 555–569.

Moed, H.F. (2005). *Citation Analysis in Research Evaluation*. Springer, Dordrecht.

Must, Ü. (2006). 'New' countries in Europe-Research, development and innovation strategies vs bibliometric data. *Scientometrics*, 66(2), 241–248.

Olechnicka, A., Płoszaj, A., & Celinska-Janowicz, D. (2019). *The Geography of Scientific Collaboration: Theory, Evidence and Policy*. London and New York: Routledge.

Pajić, D. (2014). Globalization of the social sciences in Eastern Europe: Genuine breakthrough or a slippery slope of the research evaluation practice? *Scientometrics*, 1–20.

Pandita, R., & Singh, S. (2017). Journal packing density across subject disciplines at the global level: A study. *Information and Learning Science*, 118(11/12), 642–659.

Płoszaj, A., & Agnieszka, O. (2015). Running Faster or Measuring Better? How is the R&D Sector in Central and Eastern Europe Catching Up with Western Europe? *GRINCOH Working Paper Series*, Paper No. 3.06.

Radosevic, S., & Yoruk, E. (2014). Are there global shifts in the world science base? Analysing the catching up and falling behind of world regions. *Scientometrics*, 101(3), 1897–1924.

Research Evaluation and Policy Project. (2005). Quantitative indicators for research assessment – A literature review (REPP discussion paper 05/1). Canberra, Australia: Research Evaluation and Policy Project, Research School of Social Sciences, The Australian National University.

Schneider, J.W. (2009). An outline of the bibliometric indicator used for performance-based funding of research institutions in Norway. *European Political Science*, (8), 364–378.

Shelton, R.D., Foland, P., & Gorelskyy, R. (2009). Do new SCI journals have a different national bias? *Scientometrics*, 79(2), 351–363.

Testa, J. (2011). *The Globalisation of Web of Science: 2005–2010.* Thomson Reuters.

Tijssen, R.J.W. (2008). Are we moving towards an integrated European research area? *Collnet Journal of Scientometrics and Information Management*, 2(1), 19–25.

van Raan, A.F.J. (2004). Measuring science. In: F.H. Moed, W. Glänzel & U. Schmoch (eds.), *Handbook of Quantitative Science and Technology Research. The Use of Publications and Patent Statistics in Studies of S&T Systems.* Dordrecht: Kluwer Academic Publishers, pp. 19–50.

Vanecek, J. (2014). The effect of performance-based research funding on output of R&D results in the Czech Republic. *Scientometrics*, 98(1), 657–681, doi: 10.1007/s11192-013-1061-1.

Vinkler, P. (2008). Correlation between the structure of scientific research, scientometric indicators and GDP in EU and non-EU countries. Scientometrics, 74(2), 237–254.

Wagner, C.S., & Leydesdorff, L. (2005). Network structure, self-organization and the growth of international collaboration in science. *Research Policy*, 34(10), 1608–1618.

8 Technology upgrading and growth in Central and Eastern Europe

Slavo Radosevic, Deniz E. Yoruk and Esin Yoruk

Introduction

The economies of Central and Eastern Europe (CEE) grew rapidly at the beginning of the 21st century until the 2008 global financial crisis, which hit this region very badly, with some exceptions (e.g. Poland). Since 2008 growth has resumed, but at much lower levels, and the process of convergence that was very strong before 2008 has slowed down substantially. This raises issues about the foundations of the pre-2008 growth, as well as the basis of future long-term growth.

With the benefit of hindsight, pre-2008 growth in CEE could be characterised as finance-dependent and debt-intensive growth, based on externally financed consumption (consumer durables) (in most of the CEE) (Labaye et al. 2013). The post-2008 challenge is how to shift towards growth driven by investments and improvements in productivity. The issue of the basis of growth is quite important, as growth before 2008 was driven by total factor productivity, or what is conventionally defined as technological progress, or by improvements in efficiency.[1] Moreover, labour productivity in CEE countries was visibly higher before 2008 when compared to the recent period. On average, after 2008 we observe weak convergence between CEE and old Member States, but this de facto is hiding a pattern of polarisation within both old EU15 and CEE. This suggests that drivers of growth or decline have become more diverse within the EU, which as a region has shown declining growth dynamics from the early 2000s.

We consider the technology upgrading approach to be relevant for monitoring technology upgrading in catching-up economies like CEE. Gereffi (1999: 51–52) defines it as 'a process of improving the ability of a firm or an economy to move to more profitable and/or technologically sophisticated capital and skill-intensive economic niches'. Technology upgrading is 'a shift to higher value-added products and production stages through increasing specialization'.

The technology upgrading framework shows what is behind the lack of convergence in technology and innovation capability, and the very weak dynamics, of the EU25.[2] First, we point to the disjunction between production capability, R&D and technological capability. We consider this to be a direct effect of EU policy, which favours R&D but does relatively less to support production capability and innovation implementation. Second, the lack of progress in production capabilities in the EU is striking in relation to the strong policy drive and improvements regarding science and technology (S&T) and innovation infrastructure which suggest that there is a disjunction between R&D/innovation and industrial policy in the EU. Finally, we show that the intensity of knowledge exchange in the EU25 is unrelated to technology upgrading and structural changes, except possibly for the German-led Central European manufacturing cluster. This suggests that there is a disjunction between foreign direct investment (FDI)/value chains policy and national and EU level innovation policies.

This chapter is organised as follows. First, we explain the differences between the R&D-driven approach to growth and indexes of technology upgrading conceptualised in a more comprehensive setting. Second, we rank EU economies based on our indexes. We present the main results of analysis based on indexes of technology upgrading and conduct a descriptive analysis of each of the three sub-indexes of technology upgrading which point to the three major insights outlined above. We further elaborate on sub-indexes of the main indexes to compare macro-regions of CEE with other macro regions of the EU in the north and south. We conclude by drawing policy challenges that our analysis has generated.

The narrow (R&D) and broad (ITU) approach to assessing technology accumulation in CEE

Metrices of innovation dynamics explicitly or implicitly assume a specific understanding on how technology and innovation impacts growth. For example, a conventional policy model of technology upgrading assumes that R&D is the major source of growth. This model is the basis of the new (endogenous) growth theory (Romer 1990; Lucas 1988). Endogenous growth models assume that R&D is essentially a probabilistic process with a partly public nature, and thus brings technology spillovers which in turn lead to increasing returns to scale. A strong focus in innovation metrics on R&D reflects the generally accepted view that R&D and innovation are among the main drivers of sustained economic growth.[3] However, the linear logic by which more R&D should lead to more economic growth is a somewhat simplified picture of reality. Innovation literature does not actually support such a narrow approach to the relationship between innovation and growth. Ultimately, an extensive literature on innovation systems has emerged as counterevidence to the simplified view that R&D suffices for innovation and growth. This literature, as well as the Schumpeterian growth theory, have shown that R&D does not play an identical role in economies at different levels of development. For example, middle-income economies tend to grow more on imitation activities, while transition towards the high-income group requires a shift towards technology frontier activities, where R&D plays a more important role (see Aghion et al. 2013; Aghion et al. 2010). For example, this has been recognised by the WEF Global Competiveness Reports, which classify CEE countries in terms of driving factors of growth as efficiency driven (Bulgaria and Romania); in transition (other CEE countries); and innovation driven (Slovenia, Estonia).

Our approach is based on the premise that the CEE countries are predominantly technology users; hence the pattern of their technology upgrading is different, and thus they require appropriately amended metrics.

R&D investments and outputs in Central and Eastern Europe

After the 'transition recession' during the 1990s, R&D systems in CEE started to recover during the first decade of the 21st century. GERD/GDP ratios for EU CEE countries increased from below 0.8% until 2006 to 1.16% in 2012, or by 0.4 percentage points of GDP. It is important to recognise that on average GERD/GDP did not increase during the period of economic growth or before 2008, but only in 2008–2012 period when GDP had fallen in many CEECs (except Romania and Croatia). (Table 1). The picture after 2012 until 2016 is somewhat mixed, with some countries experiencing a continuing increase, while some others a decrease in their GERD/GDP. In 2016, all countries showed a considerable decline in their GERD/GDP, except Croatia.

Table 8.1 shows that increases of GERD/GDP in Slovenia, Czechia, Estonia and Poland have been quite dramatic or well above the regional average increase of 0.4 percentage points. In other CEE countries these increases ranged between 0.2 and 0.4 percentage points (see Figure 8.1).

Where do changes in the CEE GERD/GDP funding stand in the broader EU context? Figure 8.2 shows that changes in CEE are within the EU28 range. The most significant improvements in R&D intensity among the EU28 countries have taken place in Austria, followed by Belgium, Czechia, Estonia, Slovenia, Portugal and Germany. Other CEE countries are scattered across the EU28 spectrum including countries with relative declines in R&D intensity (Croatia with Finland and Iceland) or marginal increases (Romania with France and the UK).

Changes in the 2002–16 period show very strong effects of the 2008 crisis until 2012, with a turnaround from 2012 to 2016. More precisely, they show quite a different role of R&D which was used either as an anti-cyclical instrument to stimulate demand for technology or as expenditure that shared the impact of austerity policies targeting not directly productive expenses.

Table 8.1 Gross domestic expenditures on R&D in GDP (GERD/GDP) in CEECs

	2002	2003	2004	2005	2006	2007	2008	2009	2010	2011	2012	2013	2014	2015	2016
Slovenia	1.44	1.25	1.37	1.41	1.53	1.42	1.63	1.82	2.06	2.42	2.57	2.58	2.37	2.2	2
Czechia	1.1	1.15	1.15	1.17	1.23	1.3	1.24	1.29	1.34	1.56	1.78	1.9	1.97	1.93	1.68
Estonia	0.72	0.77	0.85	0.92	1.12	1.07	1.26	1.4	1.58	2.31	2.12	1.72	1.45	1.49	1.28
Hungary	0.98	0.92	0.86	0.92	0.98	0.96	0.98	1.13	1.14	1.19	1.26	1.39	1.35	1.36	1.21
Poland	0.56	0.54	0.55	0.56	0.55	0.56	0.6	0.66	0.72	0.75	0.88	0.87	0.94	1	0.97
Croatia	0.95	0.95	1.03	0.86	0.74	0.79	0.88	0.84	0.74	0.75	0.75	0.81	0.78	0.84	0.85
Lithuania	0.66	0.66	0.75	0.75	0.79	0.8	0.79	0.83	0.78	0.9	0.89	0.95	1.03	1.04	0.85
Slovakia	0.56	0.56	0.5	0.49	0.48	0.45	0.46	0.47	0.62	0.66	0.8	0.82	0.88	1.18	0.79
Bulgaria	0.47	0.48	0.47	0.45	0.45	0.43	0.45	0.49	0.56	0.53	0.6	0.63	0.79	0.96	0.78
Romania	0.38	0.38	0.38	0.41	0.45	0.51	0.55	0.45	0.46	0.5	0.48	0.39	0.38	0.49	0.48
Latvia	0.41	0.36	0.4	0.53	0.65	0.55	0.58	0.45	0.61	0.7	0.66	0.61	0.69	0.63	0.44
EU CEE	**0.75**	**0.73**	**0.76**	**0.77**	**0.82**	**0.80**	**0.86**	**0.89**	**0.96**	**1.12**	**1.16**	**1.15**	**1.15**	**1.19**	**1.03**

Source: Eurostat.

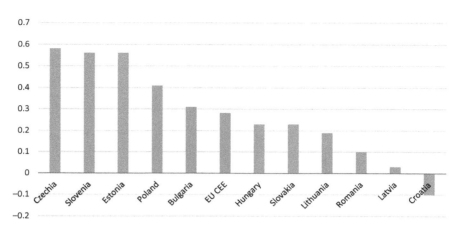

Figure 8.1 Changes in shares of GERD/GDP in percentage points of GDP 2002–16
Source: Calculations based on Table 8.1.

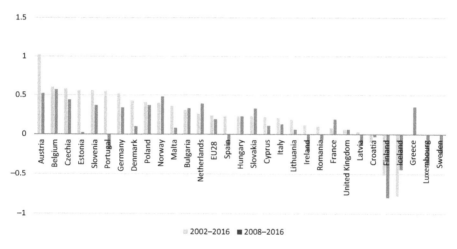

Figure 8.2 Changes in GERD/GDP ratios in percentage points between 2002–16 and 2008–16
Source: Authors' calculations based on Eurostat.

In this respect, in Austria, Belgium, Czechia, Slovenia, Germany, Poland, Norway, Bulgaria, the Netherlands, Hungary, Slovakia and Greece, R&D expenditures were anti-cyclical, while in Portugal, Spain, Ireland, Latvia, Croatia, Finland, Iceland, Luxembourg and Sweden, R&D was pro-cyclical.

This brief analysis suggests that despite the 2008 crisis, investment in R&D in CEE increased until 2012, after which CEE countries, except Poland,

Bulgaria and Croatia, have shown declining investment in R&D. We presume that the increases in CEE after 2008 are largely due to the EU support for R&D and innovation through Structural Funds. Moreover, the increase in R&D investments in all CEE countries in this period (2008–12) outperformed the decrease in the 2012–16 period (except Latvia). In this respect, EU funds play a very important potential counter-cyclical role in preventing the further decline of GDP.

Growth in GNI and GNI per capita in CEE

Growth rates were severely hampered throughout the EU after the 2008 crisis (see Figures 8.3 and 8.4). After 2008 CEE grew at slightly higher rates than the EU North and EU South. However, the considerably high growth rates achieved by the CEE during the 2002–16 period is at odds with the very low level of R&D expenditures in CEE. In particular, the high growth rates attained by Romania and Bulgaria cannot be linked to R&D investments. We need a perspective which is broader than R&D and which can capture the diversity of technology efforts that have been taking place in EU catching-up economies. This simple observation has led us to the construction of alternative framework which capture production capabilities as well as innovative capabilities, structural issues underlying the technology upgrading process and also global knowledge interactions taking place to contribute to further growth.

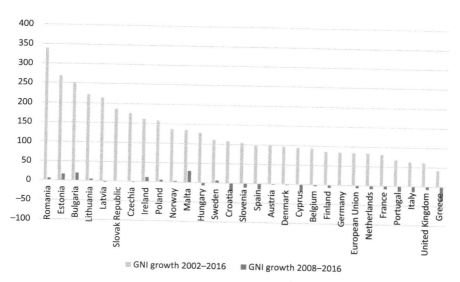

Figure 8.3 GNI growth rate in the EU countries, 2002–16 and 2008–16 (%) (Atlas method, current USD)

Source: World Bank, World Development Indicators.

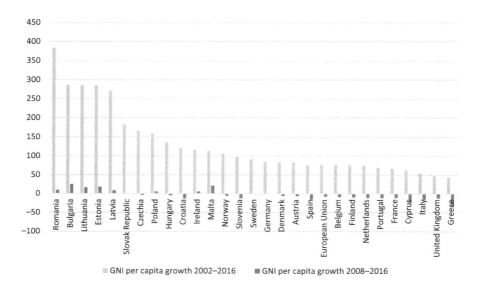

Figure 8.4 GNI per capita growth rate in the EU countries, 2002–16 and 2008–16 (%) (Atlas method, current USD)

Source: World Bank, World Development Indicators.

A comprehensive view on technology and growth in CEE: indexes of technology upgrading

Why do we need an industrial/technological upgrading perspective? The underlying idea behind this approach is that growth is not solely driven by investment in R&D and disembodied knowledge. Capital accumulation is also important, but only if it contains a large learning or assimilation of technological knowledge component. In that context, technology upgrading is the outcome of interactions of 'a set of institutions, incentives and policies that can mobilize huge savings and put them to productive use, while at the same time promoting learning efficiency and a broad domestic knowledge base' (Ernst 1998). However, while being very relevant, this approach is still underdeveloped in terms of economic theory. For the time being, there is no theory of industrial/technological upgrading but only a few vague stylisations. In Radosevic and Yoruk (2015, 2016a), we review the literature on this area and develop a conceptual approach, which is then applied in Radosevic and Yoruk (2016b, 2018).

The underlying idea behind the technology upgrading approach is the importance of structural differences between low-, middle- and high-income countries. In this respect, our approach is in line with the ideas of new structural economics (Lin 2015) and Schumpeterian economics (Lee 2013; Aghion et al. 2013). Our analysis in this chapter should answer an important policy question in the EU context: what is the position of CEE countries in the context of industrial and technology upgrading within the wider Europe?

A theoretical and conceptual basis of the new metrics is developed in Radosevic and Yoruk (2016b). It conceptualizes technology upgrading as a three-dimensional process composed of intensity and different types of technology upgrading through various innovation and technology activities; broadening of technology upgrading through different forms of technology and knowledge diversification; and interaction with the global economy through knowledge import, adoption and exchange. All three dimensions have strong grounding in the respective literatures on firm-level technology upgrading, structural change and growth, and integration in the global economy.

The index of technology upgrading is conceptually based on two dimensions, the intensity of technology upgrading (Index A) and the breadth or structural features of technology upgrading (Index B), which jointly form the index. A third dimension is the index of technology and knowledge exchange (Index C), which is a proxy for interaction with the global economy; it does not form part of the overall index but operates as separate index and helps us to understand how economies go about this third dimension of technology upgrading. Index C interacts with the index of technology upgrading (Indexes A and B) but does not directly contribute to it (see Table 8.2). The reasons for this are related to the varying role – complementary or substitutive – that technology and knowledge exchange can play in relation to domestic technological activities, which are the primary drivers of technology upgrading.

The data are classified into two main categories and six components of the technology upgrading framework to create an index of technology upgrading (ITU). We generate a separate index for the technology and knowledge exchange element (ITKE) (see Table 8.2).

Radosevic and Yoruk (2015) applied a new metrics of technology upgrading to CEE countries on a sample of 42 economies ranging from lower-middle-income to upper-high-income level economies. The index of technology upgrading represents a proxy of potential for technology upgrading., A situation where a country has a low income per capita but a high index of technology upgrading suggests that this country has good potential for growth based on technology upgrading. Meanwhile, a country that currently enjoys high growth rates but performs poorly on the index of technology upgrading is likely to face limits to further long-term growth. Radosevic and Yoruk (2018) have explored this issue in the context of the middle-income trap, with specific focus on different income levels. In this chapter, we use an identical approach and estimation methodology with the aim of exploring the issues of technology catch-up in the EU28. We follow a standard composite indicators methodology for ITU indexes which we summarise in the Appendix.

Table 8.2 Indexes of technology upgrading

Index	Component	Indicators
INDEX A. INTENSITY AND TYPES OF TECHNOLOGY UPGRADING (SCALE)	**Index 1. Production capability**	ISO9001 certificates pmi
		Trademark applications, resident pmi
		Extent of staff training Q.5.08 1–7 (best)
	Index 2. Technology capability	Patent applications, resident (to national office) pmi
		Patent applications to USPTO (total = direct and PCT national phase entries) pmi
		Patent applications to EPO (total = direct and PCT national phase entries) pmi
		Industrial design count, resident (by origin) pmi
	Index 3. R&D and knowledge intensity	Business enterprise sector R&D expenditures as % of GDP
		Company spending on R&D Q.12.03 1–7 (best)
		Research and development expenditure (% of GDP)
		Researchers in R&D (per million people)
		Technicians in R&D (per million people)
		Science publications: Scientific and technical journal articles pmi
		Science citations pmi
		Quality of scientific research institutions Q.12.02 1–7 (best)
		University – industry collaboration Q.12.04 1–7 (best)
INDEX B: BREADTH OF TECHNOLOGY UPGRADING: STRUCTURAL FEATURES (SCOPE)	**Index 4. Infrastructure: human capital, physical and organisational**	Average years of schooling 25+
		Quality of maths and science education Q.5.04 1–7 (best)
		Availability of research and training services Q.5.07 1–7 (best) 2012–13
		Availability of scientists and engineers Q.12.06 1–7 (best)
		Fixed broadband Internet subscribers (per 100 people)
		Gross fixed capital formation as % of GDP
	Index 5. Structural change indicators	Technology diversification (changes in patenting structure) WIPO
		Technology diversification (changes in patenting structure) EPO

INDEX C: INTERACTION WITH GLOBAL ECONOMY	Index 6. Firm level capabilities	Buyer sophistication Q.6.16 1–7 (best)
		Change in demand for innovation (buyer sophistication) 1–7 (best))(% change in Q. 6.16)
		Availability of state-of-the-art technologies Q.9.01 1–7 (best)
		Changes in availability of latest technologies, 1–7 (best)(% change in 9.01)
		Number of firms in Forbes firms pmi
		Firm level technology absorption Q.9.02 1–7 (best)
	Index 7. Technology and knowledge exchange (ITKE)	Technology balance of payments (receipts) in US$
		Technology balance of payments (receipts) as % of GDP
		Share of exports in complex industries in total exports (SITCRev3 5 71–79 87 88)
		Technology balance of payments (payments) in US$
		Technology balance of payments (payments) as % of GDP
		Foreign direct investment, net outflows (% of GDP)
		Foreign direct investment, net inflows (% of GDP)

Source: Radosevic and Yoruk (2015, 2016a, 2016b, 2018).

Indexes of technology upgrading

Table 8.3 illustrates our technology upgrading index measures and the percentage change in the main index ITU from 2006 to 2015, as congregated into five major groups of countries in the EU. The leading group is ten developed economies which we label as the 'North' group (Sweden, Finland, Denmark, Germany, Netherlands, France, UK, Ireland, Belgium and Austria). There is a significant gap between this and the second group, which is somewhat less homogeneous and forms the EU 'periphery', consisting of the EU South (Portugal, Italy, Spain, Greece) and EU East (Baltic states 3 – Estonia, Latvia and Lithuania; Visegrád 5 – Czechia, Slovakia, Poland, Hungary, Slovenia; and South-East 3 – Bulgaria, Romania and Croatia). These two groups remain identical between 2006 and 2015, showing that the technology gap has not been closed by any of the periphery economies. The upper periphery groups remain composed of three South EU economies (Italy, Portugal and Spain) plus Estonia and two Visegrád 5 economies (Slovenia and Czechia).

The ITU, as a framework that tries to capture the broader scale and scope of technology upgrading, shows that there has been a decline in the index in all macro regions except Baltic 3. Moreover, the decline has been the biggest at the EU periphery (−7.97%) compared to the EU North (−2.32%). Within the periphery, the decline has been the greatest in SEE-3 (−21.3%), followed by the Visegrád 5 (−12.9%) and EU South (−6.2%). We can observe an opening of the technological capability gap between the EU North and the periphery, with the exception of the Baltic states. The homogeneity of results based on ITU is quite high, as we can observe identical trends in all periphery countries (except Portugal) and a polarisation of the EU North of those countries which have improved their position based on ITU and those which have declined in relative terms.

Index A and Index B components of ITU, as well as Index C, show changes in varied directions by macro region and by country. Romania, for instance, a country with the highest growth rate, performs well in Index A and Index C. This suggests favourable conditions for production capability and knowledge interactions with foreign partners to compensate structural changes in the country. In the Baltics region, we can observe a positive link between the three upgrading indexes and the growth rates of these countries. In the following sections we explore these factors in detail in the context of macro-regions and CEE countries.

Analysis of technology upgrading in the context of catching up and growth

In this section, we focus on policy-relevant insights that stem from technology upgrading metrics. First, we explore the relative positions of the EU macro-regions on all four indexes of technology upgrading and their components.

Table 8.3 Technology catching up and falling behind based on ITU indexes for EU25 and its macro-regions 2006–15

	2006				2015				2006–15			
	Index A	Index B	Index C	ITU	Index A	Index B	Index C	ITU	% change in Index A	% change in Index B	% change in Index C	% change in ITU
BEL	38.0	61.5	19.0	99.5	45.4	64.9	12.9	110.3	19.7	5.4	−31.8	10.88
NLD	53.9	65.8	83.7	119.7	55.3	66.0	60.0	121.3	2.6	0.4	−28.4	1.41
GBR	46.2	64.6	33.3	110.8	45.1	66.0	22.3	111.1	−2.3	2.2	−33.1	0.31
DEU	70.0	61.1	21.2	131.1	68.6	62.9	22.6	131.5	−2.0	2.9	6.2	0.29
FRA	48.0	61.5	23.4	109.5	47.0	62.6	22.2	109.6	−2.1	1.9	−4.8	0.12
IRL	37.2	65.7	48.9	102.9	36.7	65.4	82.3	102.1	−1.4	−0.5	68.2	−0.81
DNK	60.4	72.8	10.9	133.3	61.9	62.6	11.1	124.6	2.5	−14.0	2.1	−6.55
AUS	55.3	62.5	12.0	117.8	55.1	54.8	10.6	110.0	−0.2	−12.2	−12.0	−6.60
FIN	68.9	80.2	17.7	149.2	63.7	69.0	12.3	132.7	−7.6	−14.0	−30.5	−11.06
SWE	70.1	79.8	20.6	149.9	67.7	65.4	20.9	133.1	−3.4	−18.1	1.1	−11.23
EU North									**0.6**	**−4.6**	**−6.3**	**−2.32**
PRT	24.2	38.0	6.8	62.1	34.4	45.1	6.2	79.4	42.2	18.7	−8.8	27.89
ITA	37.9	39.1	15.8	77.1	35.1	34.2	12.1	69.3	−7.4	−12.6	−23.0	−10.00
ESP	38.2	45.4	14.9	83.6	26.3	42.3	12.4	68.6	−31.1	−7.0	−16.6	−18.01
GRC	16.8	40.6	2.5	57.4	12.4	30.9	2.9	43.3	−26.3	−23.9	17.1	−24.61
EU South									**−5.6**	**−6.2**	**−7.8**	**−6.18**
SVN	35.0	41.4	8.6	76.4	33.7	38.7	11.0	72.4	−3.9	−6.4	27.5	−5.26
POL	12.2	33.4	9.4	45.6	11.8	31.4	9.9	43.2	−2.9	−6.2	5.4	−5.34
CZE	36.4	52.3	11.2	88.7	32.0	44.1	13.1	76.1	−12.0	−15.7	17.1	−14.20
SVK	15.0	44.8	11.2	59.7	15.6	34.7	13.6	50.3	4.3	−22.5	21.0	−15.80
HUN	24.4	39.8	23.5	64.2	13.2	35.7	15.5	48.8	−45.9	−10.4	−34.1	−23.88
VIS-5									**−12.1**	**−12.3**	**7.4**	**−12.90**
LAT	14.7	29.4	3.2	44.1	17.0	32.3	5.8	49.3	16.1	9.8	84.1	11.89
LTU	13.7	39.6	5.0	53.3	19.8	39.7	6.2	59.5	44.1	0.4	24.3	11.65
EST	26.0	47.5	9.1	73.5	31.0	43.9	4.6	74.9	19.1	−7.4	−49.7	1.96
BLT-3									**26.4**	**0.9**	**19.5**	**8.50**
ROU	9.3	33.8	5.2	43.2	10.2	26.5	7.8	36.6	8.9	−21.8	49.2	−15.12
BGR	13.1	29.6	6.7	42.8	11.6	21.8	4.7	33.4	−11.9	−26.4	−29.3	−21.93
HRV	12.7	35.4	6.7	48.1	8.5	26.7	6.1	35.2	−33.2	−24.6	−9.8	−26.88
SEE-3									**−12.1**	**−24.3**	**3.4**	**−21.31**
EU Periphery									**−0.8**	**−10.4**	**5.6**	**−7.97**

As expected, the EU periphery trails behind the EU North on both indexes of technology upgrading. Regarding the intensity of TU (Index A), the periphery is at 40% of the EU North level, and regarding the scope of TU (Index B) it is at 60% of the EU North level (see Figure 8.5). This better performance of scope relative to intensity of technology upgrading is a common feature of all periphery macro-regions and, as we will go on to discuss, this is due to their comparatively better infrastructure as well as structural change. In fact, the poorer the macro-region, the better its performance in terms of scope compared to intensity of technology upgrading. Regarding the index of technology and knowledge exchange, the periphery also trails behind the EU North, with only the Visegrád 5 countries having a much more developed technology and knowledge exchange. This is in tune with other results which show the existence of a Central European manufacturing cluster linking the EU industrial core to the Visegrád 5 economies (IMF 2013).

What lies behind the significant gap between the EU North and periphery in intensity, and behind the lesser gap in the scope of technology upgrading potential? Figure 8.6 shows that the significantly lower intensity of technology upgrading is strongly driven by big differences in technological capabilities (TC). In Index A, these are patenting-related activities which in periphery countries rank particularly low on a world scale. In TC the gap is one-third; in R&D it is slightly above 50%, while in production capability it is less that 30%. The smaller gap in the scope of technology upgrading potential is due to the better position of the periphery in terms of infrastructure and structural change, with a gap to the EU North of around 30%. However, the biggest gap here is with respect to firm capabilities, which are less than 50% those of the EU North (44.9%).

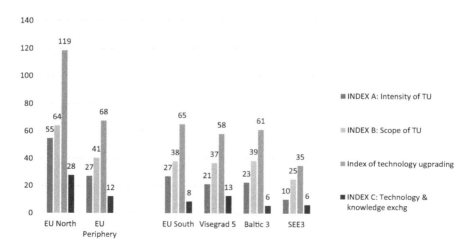

Figure 8.5 EU25 macro-regions in indexes of technology upgrading in 2015

Note: Based on country averages.

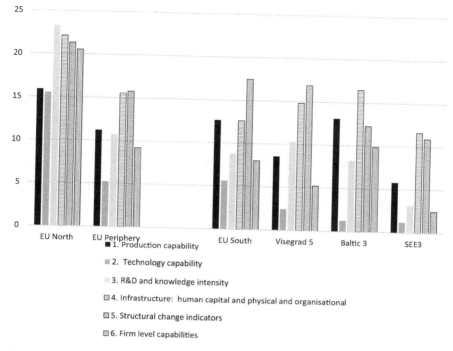

Figure 8.6 Levels of EU25 macro-regions in different components of technology upgrading potential in 2015

This pattern of technological and firm capabilities being by far the lowest components of ITU is present in all EU periphery macro-regions. Also, all macro-regions perform relatively better regarding production capabilities, infrastructure and structural change when compared to the EU North as a reference. This pattern of relative underperformance in technology capabilities and firm capabilities, and overperformance in infrastructure and structural change, holds true in relation to GNI pc gaps when compared to the EU North in all macro-regions. Therefore, we can take this to be a stable structural feature of the EU periphery, with important policy implications.

Infrastructure: human capital, physical and organisational

A crucial question is what has led to the increased technological gap within the EU25? Figure 8.7 shows changes in different components of ITU by macro-region, and Figure 8.8 by country.

Figure 8.7 shows the overall improvement in the EU25 regarding R&D and knowledge intensity in all macro-regions as well as improvements in terms of

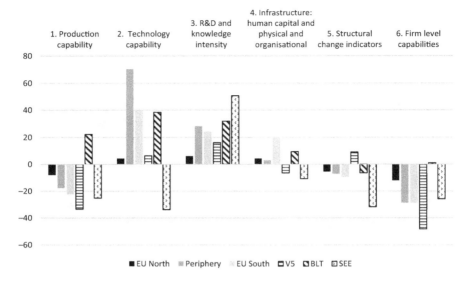

Figure 8.7 Changes in components of ITU 2006–15 in EU25 macro-regions (%)

Note: For the Baltic states, for presentation purposes, we have reduced the change in the technological capability component for Lithuania from 324% to 100% due to the huge increase in the number of patents from a very low base level.

technology capability in all but the SEE-3 region. For instance, R&D and knowledge intensity and technology capability are dimensions of technology-based growth which are well captured by the European Innovation Scoreboard (EIS), and thus there is a high compatibility of changes in this respect between ITU and EIS. Regarding infrastructure, there is no clear trend within macro-regions, where two out of six macro-regions (Visegrád 5 and SEE3) have fallen behind, while in others the infrastructure has improved. However, in all other components, EU macro-regions have fallen behind, with the exception of the Baltics in production capability and to some extent firm capabilities, and the Visegrád 5 regarding structural change. However, the overall trend that emerges from individual components of ITU is improved R&D and technology capability and smaller, varied changes in infrastructure, but a major lag in firm capabilities and production capabilities, as well as lesser deterioration regarding structural change.

These macro-regional trends roughly hold across individual countries. Thus, broad patterns of improved R&D and technological capability accompanied by a relative decline regarding production and firm capabilities can be observed across the majority of the EU25 economies. In production capability and structural change components 17 economies, and in firm capabilities 21 out of 25 economies, have fallen behind; meanwhile in R&D 19 economies, in infrastructure 16 economies and in technology capability 12 out of 25 economies have improved.

Index C, namely, the Index of Technology and Knowledge Exchange (ITKE), is a separate index which does not add cumulatively to the index of technology upgrading. The forms and types of technology transfer are quite varied and statistical indicators can only very poorly capture the accumulated capabilities which cross national borders. This is less of an issue with disembodied knowledge transfer, as depicted through payments and receipts for technological knowledge, except for several countries where transfer pricing plays an important role as a mechanism of tax evasion (e.g. Ireland, the Netherlands and Hungary within the EU25). Capturing accumulated knowledge through export figures is a challenging issue; in future, trade in value-added figures could be a great help in this respect, although their availability is still limited. FDI flows are very remotely related to knowledge flows, and supporting evidence is very inconclusive and context dependent. A simple relationship between levels of productivity and our composite index of technology and knowledge exchange shows a very weak relationship with EU25. This reflects the ambiguity of this index, from which it is difficult to discern whether knowledge inflows operate as a substitute or complement to their own technology activities.

Figure 8.8 excludes Ireland and the Netherlands, whose inclusion would give a very distorted picture. While within indexes of technology upgrading

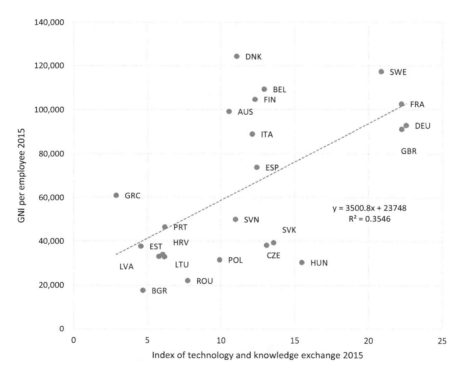

Figure 8.8 Labour productivity (GNI per employee) and Index of Technology and Knowledge Exchange (ITKE) relationship (2015) (without Ireland and the Netherlands)

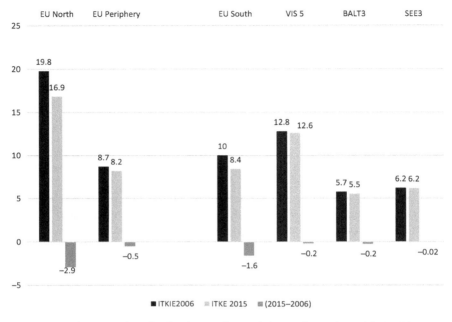

Figure 8.9 Index C – Index of Technology and Knowledge Exchange (ITKE) by EU25 macro region, 2006, 2015 and change 2006–15 (without Ireland and the Netherlands)

we can observe, on average, a strong correlation with productivity levels, in the case of Index C the relationship reflects much more the different strategies of involvement in the global economy. The EU North is no longer as homogeneous as it used to be similar to the EU periphery where the Baltics, SEE and EU South (Portugal and Greece) are mixed at the low end of the index. In the middle of the regression line, we find both the EU North, EU South (Italy and Spain) and all Visegrád 5 economies. The most striking are the very similar index values of the Visegrád 5 and North/South EU group. Given their lower levels of productivity, the Visegrád 5 have an exceptionally high level of technology and knowledge exchange. We would argue that this reflects the Central European Manufacturing cluster, which includes the EU manufacturing core (Germany, Austria, Netherlands, France, Belgium) and the Visegrád 5 economies which have become an integral part of this cluster (see IMF 2013).

It seems that the 2008 crisis did not erode this cluster; instead the cluster has expanded to include a few other periphery economies (Figures 8.9 and 8.10). While overall, EU North and EU South links with the global economy have declined, this has not been the case to such an extent with the CEE countries, where the decline in links for all three CEE regions has been minimal.

However, the picture of individual countries shows that there have been some interesting changes in this period (see Figure 8.10). The Visegrád 5 intensity of links has actually declined due entirely to Hungary. Although all the Visegrád countries (except for Slovenia) experienced a decrease in FDI flows, Hungary experienced a dramatic fall in both FDI inflows and outflows over the period 2006–2015. Slovenia, on the other hand, not only continued to attract FDI inflows, but also considerably increased its royalty receipts. The intensity of links of Romania and Latvia (not shown on graph due to the huge increase but from a very low base) considerably improved over the period. This is due to an increase in the share of complex industries (further high tech exports) high-tech exports in their total exports compared to other countries in their respective regions, and to

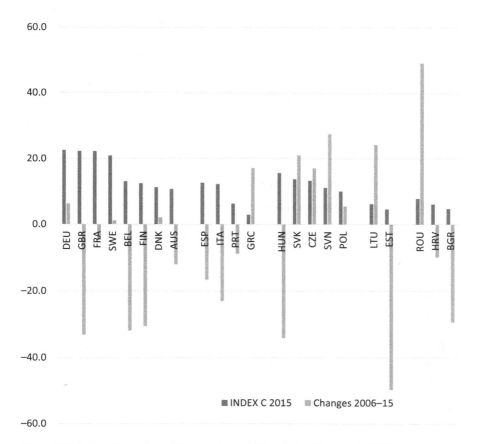

Figure 8.10 Index C – Index of Technology and Knowledge Exchange (ITKE) by country in 2015 and changes in the index between 2006 and 2015 (%)

Note: The figure does not include Ireland, the Netherlands and Latvia, whose index in 2015 was 82.3, 60.0 and 5.8, respectively, and whose changes between 2006 and 20015 were +68%, −28% and +84%, respectively.

transfer pricing in their technology balance of payments. The decrease in Estonia's intensity of links is due to a decrease in FDI inflows and outflows, the sharpest among the three Baltic states.

Within the EU North, German links have increased mainly due to the increase in royalty receipts, while links for all other EU North economies have declined. The main factor that offsets Belgium, Austria and UK's position in terms of intensity of links is the significant decrease in FDI inflows and outflows, compared to Germany. Finland suffered from the steepest decline in the share of high-tech exports in total exports. The only exception in this respect is Ireland (not shown on the graph due to the huge increase) whose links increased by 68% at a level of 82.3 on Index C due to continuing FDI flows, the important role of technology balance of payments and transfer pricing, and the increasing share of high-tech exports in total exports. Links for the Netherlands declined by 28% but, given the important role of technology balance of payments and transfer pricing, it is difficult to discern financial from technological (knowledge) components. Links for the EU South declined overall despite significant increases in Greece, though from a very low base.

Overall, with respect to the technology and knowledge exchanges of EU 25, we can observe a polarisation between, on the one hand, Germany and the Visegrád economies, which increasingly includes Romania, and on the other hand, the rest of the EU, which shows a decline in intensity as well as technology and knowledge exchanges.

Conclusions and policy issues

In this chapter, we have measured the innovation and technology activities of the EU25 within the technological upgrading framework. The analytical value of this framework is relevant as it focuses metrics on the dimensions of technology upgrading that matter for the growth of the broadly defined EU catching-up economies.

We have argued that the research, technology, development and innovation (RTDI) issues of relevance for catching up cannot be understood or conceptualised only within the R&D-based growth model. The CEE countries are predominantly technology users; the pattern of their technology upgrading is different. With this motivation in mind, we have created a composite indicator of innovation capacity and performance of the CEE countries, as well as of the EU25, which is meaningful from the perspective of countries lagging behind the world technology frontier. This is an important modification given the strong need to refocus the innovation policies of the CEE countries on issues of greater relevance for their current technology and industry upgrading.

We have conceptualised technology upgrading as a three-dimensional process, consisting of dimension 1 (the vertical axis), reflecting the intensity of technology upgrading as depicted by different types of innovation activities; dimension 2 (the horizontal axis), depicting the spread or breadth of technology such as the diversity of technological knowledge, types of supporting infrastructure and structure of firms which carry out technology upgrading; and dimension 3 (the diagonal axis), describing knowledge inflows into the economy through a variety of forms such as trade, FDI and knowledge exchange.

Three conclusions stem from the Index of Technology Upgrading components which seem to have major relevance for policy making.

First, we can observe a decline in most of the EU25 economies of their production capabilities despite, on average, significant improvements in R&D and technology capability. This is important, as production capability is much more closely related to export and trade than R&D and technology capability, particularly in countries lagging behind the technology frontier. This suggests that the EU has serious weaknesses in converting its R&D and technological knowledge into production capabilities. The Index of Technology Knowledge Exchange confirms this by showing a decline in the majority of the EU25, except in economies that belong to the Central European manufacturing cluster.

Second, the ITU components show improvements in infrastructure and structural changes in most of the EU economies, but an overall relative decline in firm capabilities. This is probably a reflection of the declining role of large EU firms in the global economy and the very weak firm capabilities in the EU periphery. Again, this shows the limitations of current EU supply oriented RDI policies which continue to reinforce the so-called European paradox.

Third, increased knowledge interaction between 2006 and 2015 has been confined to the German-led Central European manufacturing cluster (Slovenia, Slovakia, Czechia, Poland, Hungary and recently, it seems, Romania). This fits well with evidence on trade within the EU showing that this area is the one which has increased its relative share in intra-EU trade (see WIIW 2016). Overall, stagnant technology and knowledge exchange for the majority of the EU25, especially the EU South and parts of SEE, suggest that foreign direct investment (FDI), subcontracting and global value chain (GVC) policy is not a factor of regional advantage. It seems that the EU RDI policy operates as a substitute for technology and knowledge exchange rather than as a complement to it.

Within this context, we can observe a polarisation of the CEE into countries which are members of the German-led central European cluster and other countries which do not benefit from access to European and global value chains. Given their peripheral and semi-peripheral positions, future growth prospects of the CEE countries are strongly dependent not only on their trade, FDI, GVC and other knowledge flows with the EU core, but also on their accumulation of production, technology and R&D capabilities. EU membership has improved their standing regarding technology and R&D capabilities, as well as regarding technology infrastructure. However, their key weakness are weak firm-level capabilities which are a key ingredient for converting R&D and technological knowledge into production capabilities. Improvement in R&D and technology capabilities has been unrelated to their production and firm capabilities which has de facto opened up new structural gaps in their innovation systems. EU structural funds represent a unique 'window of opportunity' to close these gaps by promoting the coupling of investments in enterprise R&D and labour skills with technology upgrading in design, engineering, management and production capabilities. However, there is emerging evidence that this challenge is not yet well understood, as demonstrated in inconsistent and 'zigzag' policies (Breznitz and Ornston 2017).

All in all, our analysis depicts a much more worrying picture regarding the prospects of the EU as a convergence machine. From the ITU perspective, we can observe an increased technology gap rather than technology convergence. It seems that this increasing technology gap is not driven by R&D policies, but by the disconnection between EU R&D and other policies such as FDI and GVC policies, between technology and production capability–related policies and improvements, and ultimately by weak firm organisational capabilities. In other words, the EU has reached limits where only R&D based policy can operate as a driver of technology convergence It is necessary to re-examine other policy areas relating to industrial policy, financial systems and corporate governance. It seems that the ultimate weakness for the technology gap lies in non-technological factors such as poor corporate governance and weak capital markets which do not favour growth and the emergence of large technology-based firms which could commercialize and implement acquired R&D and technological knowledge, and function as network organisers. At the EU level, current policies that promote the expansion of R&D via structural funds only serve to deepen the R&D-implementation gap. In order to close this gap, these policies should be re-examined to favour the implementation of innovations at the regional level.

Notes

1 For evidence see Dobrinsky et al. (2006) and Alam et al. (2008).
2 Our analysis is confined to EU economies with the exception of Malta, Cyprus and Luxembourg, which are economies with either quite specific economic structure or size which would not add qualitatively new insights to our analysis.
3 For example, the OECD Growth Study (OECD 2003) has identified a clear positive linkage between private sector R&D intensity and growth in per capita GDP for OECD economies. The analysis could find no clear-cut relationship between public R&D activities and growth, at least in the short term.

References

Aghion, P., Harmgart, H., & Weisshaar, N. (2010). Fostering Growth in CEE Countries: A Country-tailored Approach to Growth Policy, *EBRD Working Paper* No.118, Available at: www.ebrd.com/downloads/research/economics/workingpapers/wp0118.pdf

Aghion, P., Akcigit, U., & Howitt, P. (2013). What Do We Learn from Schumpeterian Growth Theory? *NBER Working Paper Series* No 18824, February.

Alam, A., Casero, P.A., Khan, F., & Udomsaph, C. (2008). *Unleashing Prosperity: Productivity Growth in Eastern Europe and the Former Soviet Union.* World Bank, Washington, DC.

Breznitz, D., & Ornston, D. (2017). EU Financing and Innovation in Poland, *EBRD Working Paper* No. 198, January.

Dobrinsky, R., Hesse, D., & Traeger, R. (2006). Understanding the Long-term Growth Performance of the East European and CIS Economies. *Discussion Paper series*, No 2006–1, United Nations.

Ernst, D. (1998). Catching-up crisis and industrial upgrading: Evolutionary aspects of technological learning in Korea's electronics industry. *Asia Pacific Journal of Management*, 15(2), 247–283.

Freudenberg, M. (2003). Composite Indicators of Country Performance: A Critical Assessment. *STI Working Paper* 2003/16, OECD.

Gereffi, G. (1999). International trade and industrial upgrading in the apparel commodity chain. *Journal of International Economics*, 48(1), 37–70.

IMF (2013). German-Central European Supply Chain-Cluster Report: Staff Report, First Background Note, Second Background Note, Third Background Note, *International Monetary Fund European Dept., Country Report* No. 13/263, August 2013.

Labaye, L., Sjatil, P.E., Bogdan, W., Novak, J., Mischke, J., Fruk, M., & Ionut, U. (2013). A new dawn: Reigniting growth in Central and Eastern Europe', McKinsey Global Institute, December 2013, Available at: www.mckinsey.com/featured-insights/europe/a-new-dawn-reigniting-growth-in-central-and-eastern-europe

Lee, K. (2013). *Schumpeterian Analysis of Economic Catch-up, Knowledge, Path-creation and the Middle-Income Trap*. Cambridge: Cambridge University Press.

Lin, J.Y. (2015). The Washington consensus revisited: A new structural economics perspective. *Journal of Economic Policy Reform*, 18(2), 96–113.

Lucas, R.E. (1988). On the mechanics of economic development. *Journal of Monetary Economics*, 22, 3–42.

OECD (2003). *The Sources of Economic Growth in OECD Countries*. Paris: OECD.

Radosevic, S., & Yoruk, E. (2015). A New Metrics of Technology Upgrading: The Central and East European Countries in a Comparative Perspective, *GRINCOH Working Paper* No. 3.04, Available at: www.grincoh.eu/media/serie_3_knowledge__innovation__tech nolog/grincoh_wp_3.04_radosevic_yoruk.pdf

Radosevic, S., & Yoruk, E. (2016a). A New Metrics of Technology Upgrading: The Central and Eastern European Countries in a Comparative Perspective. *UCL Centre for Comparative Studies of Emerging Economies (CCSEE) Working Paper* No. 2016/2. Available at: www.ucl.ac.uk/ssees/comparative-studies-emerging-economies/working-papers

Radosevic, S., & Yoruk, E. (2016b). Why do we need theory and metrics of technology upgrading? *Asian Journal of Technology Innovation*, 24(Sup 1), 8–32. https://doi.org/10.1080/19761597. 2016.1207415

Radosevic, S., & Yoruk, E. (2018). Technology upgrading of middle income economies: A new approach and result'. *Technological Forecasting and Social Change*, 129, 56–75.

Romer, P.M. (1990). Endogenous technological change. *Journal of Political Economy*, 98(5), 71–102.

WIIW (2016). The Evolving Composition of Intra-EU Trade, *WIIW Research Reports* No. 414, November 2016.

Appendix

Methodology for index construction

The individual indicators in Table 8.2 are used to construct the three technology upgrading indexes Index A, Index B and Index C by using composite index methodology.

A typical composite indicator will take the form (Freudenberg 2003: 7):

$$(1) \quad I = \sum_{i=1}^{n} w_i X_i$$

where

I: Composite index,
X_i: Normalised variable,
w_i: Weight of the X_i, $\sum_{i=1}^{n} w_i = °1$ and $0 \leq w \leq 1$
i: 1, ..., n.

Equation (2) shows explicitly the normalisation method (Min–Max) used:

$$(2) \quad I_c = \sum_{j=1}^{J} \sum_{m=1}^{M} w_{jm} \left\{ (X_{jmc} - X_{jm}^{min}) \,|\, (X_{jm}^{max} - X_{jm}^{min}) \right\}$$

where c indicates country, j and m are indicator and component subscripts and min and max denote the minimum and maximum values of each indicator across countries.

Explanations for composite index measures

Technology upgrading intensity index (Index A)

The type and intensity of technology upgrading depends on the production and technology capabilities as well as the skills of enterprises and the population, investments and outputs in new knowledge creation and generation, and the extent of R&D activities. These are essential to technology upgrading, as without them product and process innovations cannot be developed.

Index A is composed of three components: production capability (Index 1), technology capability (Index 2) and R&D and knowledge intensity (Index 3). Accordingly:

Index A = Index 1 + Index 2 + Index 3

Production capability (Index 1) aims to capture the rate of activities and output in relation to production activity. It is composed of three indicators:

1 ISO 9001 certificates (per million inhabitants), taken from the International Organization for Standardization (ISO); values between 2006 and 2015 are used in the analysis.
2 Trademark applications, resident (per million inhabitants), taken from World Intellectual Property Organization (WIPO); values between 2006 and 2015 are used in the analysis.
3 The extent of staff training, taken from World Economic Forum Global Competitiveness Report (WEF GCR) Question Q.5.08; values between 2006 and 2015 are used in the analysis. It is based on the question 'In your country, to what extent do companies invest in training and employee development?' (1 = not at all; 7 = to a great extent.)

Technology capability (Index 2) is built on measuring technology generation capabilities, mainly in terms of patents. It is composed of four indicators drawn from the World Intellectual Property Organization (WIPO), and values between 2006 and 2015 are used in the analysis:

4 Patent applications, resident, to the national office (per million inhabitants).
5 Patent applications to USPTO (per million inhabitants).
6 Patent applications to EPO (per million inhabitants).
7 Industrial design count, residents (per million inhabitants).

R&D and knowledge and intensity (Index 3) aims to capture the knowledge developed by investments in R&D as well as the influence of capabilities embodied in people (i.e. R&D personnel, scientists and their publication outputs). It draws on eight indicators. For each one, values between 2006 and 2015 are used in the analysis.

8 Business enterprise sector R&D expenditures (% of GDP), taken from Eurostat.
9 Research and development expenditure (% of GDP), taken from the World Bank.
10 Researchers in R&D (per million inhabitants), taken from the World Bank.
11 Technicians in R&D (per million inhabitants), taken from the World Bank.
12 Scientific and technical journal articles (per million inhabitants), taken from the World Bank.

13   Science citations (per million inhabitants), taken from SJR – Scimago Journal and Country Rank (www.scimagojr.com/).
14   The quality of scientific research institutions, taken from the WEFGCR Question 12.02. It is based on the question: How would you assess the quality of scientific research institutions in your country? (1 = very poor; 7 = the best in their field internationally.)
15   University-industry collaboration in R&D is taken from WEFGCR Question 12.04. It is based on the question: To what extent do business and universities collaborate on research and development (R&D) in your country? (1 = do not collaborate at all; 7 = collaborate extensively.)

Technology upgrading breadth index (INDEX B)

The breadth of technology upgrading lies in structural features and changes in these structural features. Structural features are based on human capital, physical capital and organisational issues.

Index B is composed of three components: human capital, physical and organizational infrastructure (Index 4); structural change (Index 5); and firm-level capabilities (Index 6). Accordingly:

Index B = Index 4 + Index 5 + Index 6

Human capital, physical and organizational infrastructure (Index 4) is built by measuring the influence of capabilities embodied in people throughout the wider population in terms of education, the response to skills demand, the extent people exploit available infrastructural technologies and the level of fixed investment. Accordingly, it is composed of six manifest indicators:

1   Average years of schooling for ages 25+, taken from the Barro–Lee database. The values for each year between 2006 and 2015 are extrapolated using the data from 1950 to 2010.
2   The quality of maths and science educational institutions, taken from WEFGCR Question 5.04 for the years 2006–15. It is based on the question: How would you assess the quality of maths and science education in your country's schools? (1 = poor; 7 = excellent – among the best in the world.)
3   The availability of specialized research and training services, taken from WEFGCR Question 5.07 for the years 2006–15. It is based on the question: In your country, to what extent are high-quality, specialized training services available? (1 = not available; 7 = widely available.)
4   The availability of scientists and engineers, taken from WEFGCR Question 12.06 for the year 2006–15. It is based on the question: To what extent are scientists and engineers available in your country? (1 = not at all; 7 = widely available.)

5   Fixed broadband Internet subscribers (per 100 people), taken from the World Bank for the years 2006–15.
6   Gross Fixed Capital Formation as % of GDP, taken from the World Bank for the years 2006–15.

Structural change (Index 5) aims to capture, over time, changes in technology capability, demand structure and level of available technologies. It comprises six indicators. The first two indicators use patent data from WIPO to calculate the Herfindahl-Hirschman Index. By this, we aim to assess the level of diversification by technology field/class in the patenting structure of countries. The formula for the Herfindahl-Hirschman index calculation is given below:

$$H = \sum\nolimits_{i=1}^{n} s_i^2$$

Where s_i is the share of patents of a country in a specific technology field. The index is calculated for each of the countries based on the WIPO technology classification. The same method is applied to calculate the Herfindahl-Hirschman index for national patent applications (Indicator 22), applications to EPO (Indicator 23) and applications to USPTO (Indicator 24).

7   Herfindahl-Hirschman Index for total national patent applications.
8   Herfindahl-Hirschman Index for patent applications to EPO.
9   Buyer sophistication, taken from WEFGCR Question 6.16 for the years 2006–15. It is based on the question: In your country, how do buyers make purchasing decisions? (1 = based solely on the lowest price; 7 = based on a sophisticated analysis of performance attributes.)
10 Change in buyer sophistication (annual % change in Q. 6.16 between 2006–15).
11 Availability of state-of-the-art technologies, taken from WEFGCR Question 9.01 for the years 2006–15. It is based on the question: To what extent are the latest technologies available in your country? (1 = not available; 7 = widely available.)
12 Change in the availability of the latest technologies (annual % change in Q.9.01 between 2006–15).

Firm-level capabilities (Index 6) has two manifest indicators:

13 Number of firms in Forbes 2000 (per million inhabitants) for the years 2006–15.
14 Firm-level technology absorption, taken from WEFGCR Question 9.02 for the years 2006–15. It is based on the question: To what extent do businesses in your country absorb new technology? (1 = not at all; 7 = aggressively absorb.)

Index of Technology and Knowledge Exchange (ITKE)

This index aims to capture the influence of the global interactions of countries by which knowledge flows take place. We assess the impact of such interactions as complementary to technology upgrading. The index comprises seven manifest indicators:

1   Technology balance of payments (receipts) in USD, taken from the World Bank for the years 2006–15.
2   Licencing receipts as % of GDP, taken from the World Bank for the years 2006–15.
3   Technology balance of payments (payments) in USD, taken from the World Bank for the years 2006–15.
4   Licencing payments as % of GDP, taken from the World Bank for the years 2006–15.
5   The share of exports of complex industries in total exports (SIT-CRev3 5 71–79 87 88). Data for this indicator have been extracted from UNComtrade for the years 2006–15. We calculated the share of exports in the total exports of each country, particularly in SITC Rev.3 sectors: 5 – Chemicals and related products, n.e.s.; 71 to 75 Machinery (Power generating machines, special industrial machinery, metalworking machinery, general industrial machinery, n.e.s, office machines); 76 – telecommunications equipment; 78–79 transport equipment (road vehicles, other transport equipment); 87–88 electrical and optical (scientific equipment, n.e.s., photo apparatus n.e.s., clocks).
6   Foreign direct investment, net outflows (% of GDP), taken from the World Bank for the years 2006–15.
7   Foreign direct investment, net inflows (% of GDP), taken from the World Bank for the years 2006–15.

Part III

Regions, space, territory

9 Regional dynamics and structural changes in Central and Eastern European countries

Grzegorz Gorzelak and Maciej Smętkowski

Introduction

The aim of this chapter is to analyse the regional dynamics of the Central and Eastern European (CEE) countries – EU(10).[1] The chapter seeks answers to the following research questions: (a) Has the regional development of CEE countries been in line with J. Williamson's hypothesis, which suggests that the relationship between the level of national development and the magnitude of regional differences[2] resembles an inverted letter U? (b) What have been the main factors responsible for the changes in their spatial pattern? (c) How has the economic crisis affected the growth dynamics of these regions? Empirical studies focused on regional development patterns versus national income level change. The present growth processes were analysed in relation to long-lasting spatial patterns, created over centuries and referred to by the Braudelian term 'longue durée'.

Owing to their robust economic development during the decade preceding the financial crisis of 2008–09 (out of which only Poland emerged without an open recession; see the chapters by Orłowski and Capello in this volume), the CEEs have significantly closed the gap to the 'old' Member States (EU15). On the one hand, this was a result of a good global economic climate until the financial crisis of 2008, and on the other, a direct and indirect consequence of their accession to the EU. This trend was halted by the global economic crisis of 2008, which invites questions concerning the reactions of the regional structures of the analysed countries and the spatial effects of economic growth during the time of economic prosperity preceding the crisis.

Earlier studies on regional development in the CEE countries clearly showed that these countries saw a marked increase in regional differences, mainly due to the fast development of their capital city regions (e.g. Gorzelak 1996; Petrakos 2001; Römich 2003; Ezcurra et al. 2007; Smętkowski and Wójcik 2013), along with the phenomenon of metropolisation that has shaped a great part of structural change in the post-socialist countries. This divergence corroborated Williamson's (1965) hypothesis, stating that the small regional differences typical for countries with low levels of development tend to increase rapidly in the first stage of their economic growth. As the next step, however, according to this theory, the divergence should be halted and, in the long term, the magnitude of regional differences should fall to its original levels. It should be noted that some researchers question the validity of the last stretch of this curve, and indicate new factors of development related to the role of innovation. Capello (2007: 94) observed that Willamson's hypothesis may be difficult to prove regarding the third phase of the process (convergence), as it could be caused by the overlapping of different stages of economic growth associated with subsequent waves of innovation. In consequence, the differences generated during the first phase may be reinforced or even widened (Figure 9.1). It seems that such processes can be curbed, not when poorer regions become attractive for the products and services typical of mature markets, but when they themselves become places where innovative products in the first phase of their lifecycle are manufactured, or when the innovation potential of the core regions wanes or weakens. On the other hand, some authors (e.g. Szörfi 2007; Barrios and Strobl 2009) claim that the convergence assumed by the Williamson curve can be observed in the European Union, although this can be better explained by other factors, such as the systemic transformation in post-communist countries, monetary union, access to Structural Funds or improvement in institutional capacity rather than by the mere level of development.

The issue of how regional differences affect economic performance is considerably less frequently discussed in the literature. Consequently, there is little evidence to prove that the magnitude of such differences significantly affects the process of development in the short term. At the same time, it is often assumed that strong (and sometimes regarded as excessive) regional divergence is a negative phenomenon, as it precludes full utilisation of the development potential (mostly existing labour) of peripheral regions, and because it can exacerbate

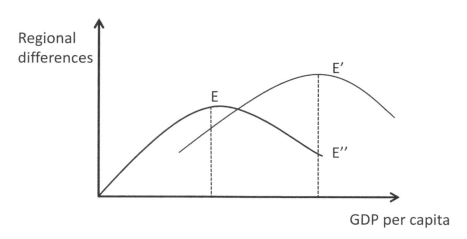

Figure 9.1 Regional differences and income levels

Note: E' - polarisation as result of new wave of innovation
E" - equalisation as result of diffusion of innovation

Source: Based on Capello (2007, p. 94).

social problems in poorer regions. As a result, the regional policies of many countries aim to reduce regional differences, primarily those measured by gross regional product per capita (Boldrin and Canova 2001). More often than not, such policies fail to achieve the anticipated results, which calls for reformulating the traditional model and for a policy supporting competitiveness. In parallel, internal differences are highlighted as well as the leading role of urban areas (OECD 2010). This is even more pertinent in view of the fact that, as indicated by the report published by the World Bank (2009), the spatial concentration of economic activity produces a number of benefits, notably increased productivity and innovativeness, as well as enhanced adaptability to changing external conditions. However, such concentrations should present diversified economic structures, should be well connected with other poles of economic activity and should be easily accessible by modern means of mass transportation. In short, they are the centres nowadays labelled as metropolises.

This chapter intends to show to what extent the development of CEE regions has followed the Williamson curve, and to indicate spatial patterns characterising regional differences in the period of rapid economic growth and recession, induced in most countries by the economic crisis of 2008–09. The analyses are conducted on the level of the NUTS3 sub-regions, as they more closely correspond to functional urban regions than the NUTS2 regions, which are strongly diversified internally, especially in those containing large cities (Smętkowski et al. 2011). However, other analyses of regional development in CEE countries (Dyba et al. 2018) to some extent support the results of our studies, though the larger territorial scale does not allow for a full comparison of results.

The national context underpinning the development of CEE regions in terms of the dynamics of economic growth is discussed in the chapters by Orłowski and Capello in this volume. The regional differences and dynamics are shown against this background, using the coefficient of variation and its dependence on both the level and the dynamics of economic development.

The longue durée

The transformation of the post-socialist countries, begun in the years 1989–92, was perhaps one of the most important (and successful) socio-economic and political experiments in modern history. A group of countries managed to restructure their political systems, social attitudes and systems of values, and – by joining the European Union in 2004–07 – were able to advance from 'second' to 'first' periphery – or to use Immanuel Wallerstein's terminology, from periphery to semi-periphery (Wallerstein 1974).

However, space is slow to change. Fernand Braudel's 'long duration' (Braudel 1982) is an inherent feature of territorial and institutional systems. Naturally, the slow pace of spatial change does not imply an absolute prettification of social and economic territorial structures. On the contrary, over the span of long historical periods, we have witnessed many significant transformations, both positive and negative in impact. Some countries and regions prove able to achieve a fast and lasting advancement in the economic hierarchy of the world, while others plunge into relative (and sometimes complete) backwardness.

We should therefore not try to understand the present processes or make an outlook on the future without reflecting on the long history of Central and Eastern Europe. Most of this part of the continent, with a few exceptions, has been located 'east of the West, and west of the East' throughout the last millennium, and the most eastern part has been in the second periphery for their entire history.

Most CEE countries, for centuries (if not millennia) have been a part of the eastern periphery of Europe. With some exceptions (Thrace, Dacia and later Panonia), all CEE regions – being located north of the Danube river and east of the Rhine river – were beyond the limits (*limes*) of the Roman Empire. These territories were not included in none of the great kingdoms that emerged after the collapse of ancient Rome: neither the state of Charlemagne, nor – with the exception of Bulgaria – the Byzantine Empire. At the beginning of the second millennium, only the Czech and Moravian lands had closer contacts with the empire of Otto I the Great, the founder and the first Caesar of the Holy Roman Empire – the rest of CEE was beyond most of European processes.

The borders of the Byzantine Empire reflected the spread of western Christianity in CEE Europe, which did not transgress them (Central and Eastern Europe was divided into two parts: one, with Poland, the Baltic countries, the former Czechoslovakia, Hungary, Slovenia and Croatia, which were influenced by the Catholic denomination; and the second, with Russia, Belarus, Ukraine, Bulgaria, Serbia, Macedonia and partly Romania and Bosnia, which were embraced by the Orthodox Church). Thus, the first important dividing line (in fact a fuzzy 'zone') was established by the split into Eastern and Western Christianity, ultimately confirmed by the Great Schism of 1054. What is now the Baltic Republics, Poland, Slovakia, Czechia, Hungary and Slovenia remained on the western side of this cultural, religious and later political frontier – and the lands on the eastern side adopted Orthodox Christianity, with all later consequences of this fact. The different economic systems adopted on the two sides of this line had their political bearing: as Pipes (1999) indicates, lack of full property rights in the East led to limited political freedom. As a result, autocratic relations between the population (which could hardly be called a 'society') and the ruling elite have been a dominant pattern in the Russian empire, and to a great extent shape the current political model of Russia. Moreover, political attitudes and economic values do still differ on the two sides of this millennial border, as can be seen in the two post-Soviet republics – Ukraine and Belarus[3] – which combine territories on both sides of the line.

The second important boundary, so relevant to Central and Eastern Europe, was established in the 13th century. In between these two major processes, an internal division took place within CEE: it was divided along the line of Stockholm-Gdansk-Warsaw-Budapest-Zadar. Medieval modernization – of which urbanization was the most important element – was weak to the east of this line. The Romanesque style did not transgress the line (Karłowska-Kamzowa

1997), nor did the Catholic cloisters (they were an important means of institutional and cultural modernisation). Today, in the Central European countries (in Poland, Hungary and Slovakia), regions located west of the line present better potential for development in the open, competitive economy of post-socialist times than those located on the eastern side. This is another proof of the validity of the concept of 'long duration', which attributes the present features of territorial socio-economic entities to their long historical trajectories and development paths.

The Great Discoveries of the 15th century triggered another important division of Europe. To make a long story short, it is enough to indicate that the inflow of silver and gold (at that time an international currency) from the New World triggered inflation that slowly moved from the west eastwards. In the course of the 16th century, the prices of grain in France grew seven times (Davies 1996; Kaczyńska and Piesowicz 1977). The increased profitability of grain production and exports to Western Europe pushed the eastern part of the continent back into feudalism (so-called second serfdom) and dependence on technologically backward agriculture, underdeveloped towns and manufacturing, low productivity of agriculture, lower levels of education, and ostentatious consumption by wealthy noblemen, which delayed industrialisation and the creation of a capitalist system by more than two centuries. This was the process pushing most of the lands east of the line to Wallerstein's periphery.

Thus, most of Central and Eastern Europe has been located between the two major boundaries dividing the continent: the cultural-religious boundary and the economic frontier. The northern part of CEE found themselves on the more progressive side of the former and the unfavourable side of the latter. The southern part was additionally hit by the Ottoman dominance that lasted for several (up to four, depending on the territory) centuries.

It is a strange paradox of history that the two recent divisions of Europe have repeated and strengthened the old ones. First, the Iron Curtain was placed almost exactly along the border of second serfdom, with the exception of eastern Austria. As a result, the countries that had been deprived by history of developmental chances and were delayed not only in quantitative, but also in qualitative (structural, cultural and institutional terms), were further deprived of the chances of economic prosperity and technological progress. Second, the 'golden curtain' (the external border of the European Union) in its northern part almost exactly repeats the cultural-religious division that is now over 1,000 years old. History matters, and this can be seen nowadays equally in the regional differences of Central and Eastern Europe.

The regional patterns of the CEE countries

In the CEE countries, the period of transition largely came to an end in the 1990s (Gorzelak and Smętkowski 2010). The next decade was epitomised by new challenges accompanying the accession of these countries to the European Union. At the same time, this was a period of a global economic upswing.

The differences in GDP per capita within the CEE countries are even more pronounced than between these countries. In 2000, there were three distinct groups of regions, based mostly on the differences in income level between individual countries (Figure 9.2). The first group was composed of the Slovenian regions (except the Pomurska region) with GDP per capita over EUR 8,000 (exchange rates), and Czech regions with GDP per capita over EUR 4,000. The second included the regions of the remaining Visegrád and Baltic states (most of them above EUR 3,000), and the third – the Bulgarian and Romanian regions (only a few of them had per capita incomes in excess of EUR 2,000). During the past 15 years, considerable changes have been observed in this respect, mainly due to the improvement in most regions of Slovakia and Estonia, as well as the catching-up of some Romanian regions located in the main transport corridors on and near the Hungarian border. The division along the east–west axis has also become clearer, visible primarily in Poland and Hungary, as a consequence of the low development level of regions situated along the eastern borders of these countries.

The regional differences can be measured using a number of indicators such as the weighted or unweighted coefficients of variation, the Gini coefficient or the Theil index (e.g. Smętkowski and Wójcik 2012). These are all characterised by varying degrees of susceptibility to the number of units being measured. Regardless of the above, the factors which have a comparable if not stronger impact on the results are the differences in the administrative divisions of these countries. Therefore, the magnitude of regional differences between countries should be treated with caution. However, this reservation does not apply to the dynamics of regional convergence or divergence, which are much less dependent on a given administrative division or selected indicator (cf. Smętkowski 2013). For this reason, in our analysis, we

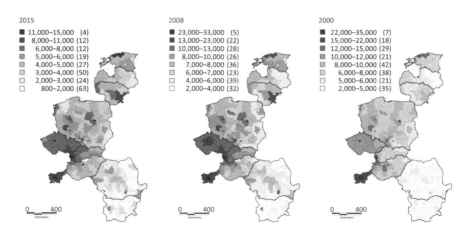

Figure 9.2 GDP per capita in CEE NUTS3 regions (EUR)

used the coefficient of variation in a dynamic approach, calculated for the NUTS3 regions in which large cities are combined with their urban regions, in order to minimise the impact of the statistical divisions on the results of the analysis.

In terms of the entire CEE macro-region, regional convergence at the NUTS3 level was observed in the analysed period for GDP per capita measured in EUR (Figure 9.3). During the past 15 years, the value of the coefficient of variation fell by about 15 percentage points. Convergence was visible mainly after the first stage of transition was over, that is, in the post-2000 period, and particularly in the years 2004–07, which were characterised by the pre-crisis economic boom. This trend, however, came to an abrupt end during the financial crisis, which began in 2008 (Gorzelak, 2011). The convergence was even greater after the 10 capital city-regions were excluded from the analyses (resulting in a roughly 20 percentage point drop in the coefficient of variation). This means that the differences between the non-capital regions were narrowing quickly, which could suggest club convergence, a process whereby the income levels of regions with similar structural characteristics tend to equalise.

In the national dimension, an opposite tendency could be observed until 2008–10, that is, a clear divergence of regional GDP per capita (Figure 9.4). After the crisis of 2008–09, only in Romania and Estonia did regional differences increase, while in all other countries they stagnated or even decreased a

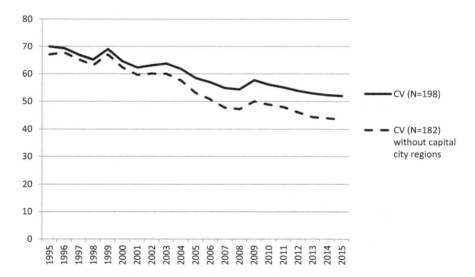

Figure 9.3 Macro-regional convergence measured in EUR, 1995–2015★

★ CV – coefficient of variation: GDP per capita EUR at NUTS3 level

Source: Prepared by the authors based on Eurostat data.

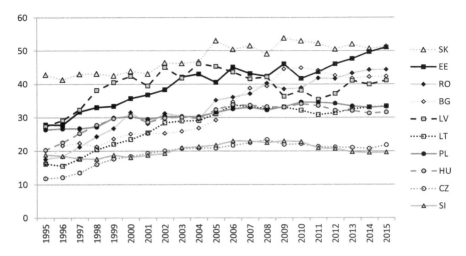

Figure 9.4 Regional differences (NUTS3) in CEE countries, 1995–2015*

* Coefficients of variation: GDP per capita; large cities were combined with surrounding NUTS3 regions.

Source: Prepared by the author based on Eurostat data.

little (although in the last years of the study an increase occurred in Latvia). An analysis of the differences in regional incomes within the CEE countries leads to the following conclusions:

*   The best developed countries, Czechia and Slovenia, were also the most cohesive in terms of differences in regional GDP per capita, a feature that quite distinctly distinguished them from the remaining countries.
*   Poland and Hungary were both countries with an average level of regional differences, and relatively stable values of the coefficient of variation in the analysed period.
*   The Baltic states saw a rapid increase in regional GDP differences until 2006; the trend continued in Estonia, slowed down considerably in subsequent years in Lithuania, while regional convergence occurred in the case of Latvia until 2012, but reverted again in recent years.
*   In Romania and Bulgaria, there was a rapid polarisation of regional incomes; both these countries are among those with the widest differences, but the trend has slowed down in Bulgaria, while in Romania it is still thriving.
*   Slovakia was the country with the widest regional differences in terms of GDP, and at the same time one of leaders in regional polarisation (along with Estonia and Bulgaria), which was mainly due to the rapid development of the Bratislava city-region.

Exclusion of capital city-regions from the analysis produces different results (Figure 9.5). The following observations can be made:

- Poland and Romania – countries with the greatest polycentricity of their settlement systems within the analysed group (ESPON 2004) – were characterised by the largest, and growing, regional polarisation, which could indicate the metropolisation processes taking place in selected large urban centres; however, in Poland, trickle-down effects also positively affected other secondary cities, as regional convergence has been observed since 2012.
- Polarisation processes (visible on a greater magnitude post-2000) were also taking place in Lithuania, Bulgaria and Slovenia until the 2008–09 crisis, which – especially in the former two countries – could suggest that diffusion was occurring within a bipolar settlement system, but then petrified in Lithuania and continued to grow in Bulgaria, while declining in Slovenia.
- Starting from 2000, Latvia, and to some extent Hungary, were the scenes of convergence until 2009, which could be viewed as proof of diffusion of growth from the capital city region to the most lagging regions; however, the crisis halted this process.
- Regional differences in Slovakia were the most volatile: following rapid polarisation in the period 2002–06, the subsequent years saw considerable convergence, which could be a result of the relatively low economic diversification of some regions that made them vulnerable to external shocks.

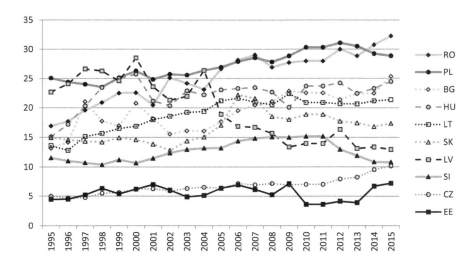

Figure 9.5 Regional differences (NUTS3) in CEE countries with the capital city regions excluded, 1995–2015★

★ Coefficients of variation GDP per capita.

Source: Prepared by the authors based on Eurostat data.

- In Estonia and Czechia, the GDP per capita differences between non-capital regions were the smallest and quite stable until 2012, which may indicate structural similarities between regions. However, polarisation processes have already begun, either as result of the better performance of large cities like Tartu and Brno, or the relative decline of GDP per capita in problem regions.

Another interesting question is whether the changes of regional differences were correlated with the GDP dynamics of the national economies. The panel data analysis for the years 1995–2015 did not confirm such a relationship (Figure 9.6). This could be explained by the existence of two situations: the

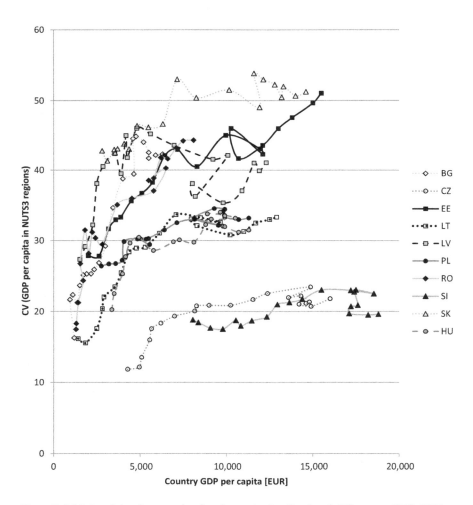

Figure 9.6 National development level and magnitude of regional differences, 1995–2015

Source: Prepared by the authors based on Eurostat data.

first comprised examples of real GDP decrease (i.e. crisis), accompanied by an increase in regional differences. The second involved cases of high GDP growth rates (over 5% annually) accompanied by regional convergence; however, this situation was encountered less frequently than the opposite (i.e. regional polarisation). Nonetheless, even the exclusion of the preceding marginal cases from the analysis did not lead to a statistically significant correlation. To sum up, we can formulate the hypothesis that the lack of such a relationship could result, first, from the specific features of particular countries related to their spatial growth patterns and, second, from a certain volatility of GDP growth rates in particular less developed regions. Such regions, where a leading cluster or enterprise accounts for a high share in the regional income, are highly exposed to external shocks that may lead, in turn, to significant fluctuations of regional GDP.

An analysis of the relationship between national development levels measured in EUR and regional differences allows us to verify Williamson's hypothesis directly (Figure 9.6). In the period when their GDP was growing but did not exceed EUR 6,000–7,000 per capita (the first phase), a rapid increase in regional differences could be observed. After this level had been reached, the growth of regional differences became considerably slower or even stopped in some countries (the second phase). However, no significant decrease in the values of variation coefficients (the third phase) – as anticipated by this hypothesis – could be observed, even though the years following the 2008 economic crisis were quite volatile in that regard, both in terms of GDP per capita and changes in regional income differences. Therefore, the CEE countries can serve – in general – as an example corroborating Williamson's hypothesis in the first two stages. The major exception was Estonia, in which the tendency for divergence was revealed again after exceeding the level of about EUR 12,000 per capita. This may be fostered mainly by the innovation-driven development in Tallinn (e.g. Kalvet 2007). However, we should take into account the small size of the country and limited number of NUTS3 regions, which may also affect the results.

Internal regional dynamics in the CEE countries

It is interesting to explore the relations between national and regional levels of development in a more detailed way on the maps (Figure 9.7). It is striking that, during the last 15 years, the existing economic structures have tended to be petrified spatially,[4] no matter if the national economies grew fast or were in the phase of stagnation or even decline. Moreover, the accession to the EU has not influenced the regional patterns of these countries. The general east-west divisions have not been challenged, nor has the metropolitan/non-metropolitan divide changed much.

The major changes included a relative deterioration of the economic situation in the eastern areas of some of countries (thus strengthening the historical spatial patterns), a process which was best visible in Romania, in its Moldovan part, although the position of some of the Danubian regions in the east also weakened.

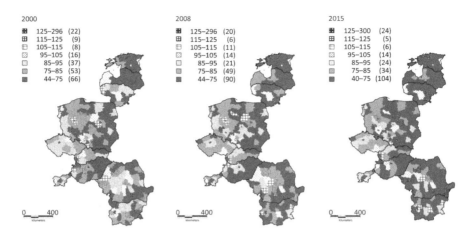

Figure 9.7 Regional GDP per capita (country average = 100)

A similar situation could be observed in Hungary. In Poland, this process could be witnessed in some regions directly neighbouring Ukraine, and in Bulgaria – in the regions forming a belt adjoining the coastal areas. This leads to a general conclusion that the proximity of the external border of the European Union and of other impermeable borders could pose a barrier to development. Meanwhile, the situation of the best-developed regions in relation to the national average was basically stable. This group included, above all, the capital city regions and regions of other big cities, mainly in countries with a polycentric settlement structure, such as Poland or Romania. The few exceptions were the regions whose economies are based on extraction and/or processing raw materials in Poland (Legnica and Płock), harbour regions (Bulgaria, Lithuania, Slovenia), and regions situated within the key transport corridors (e.g. Vienna-Budapest). In addition, the non-metropolitan regions where large-magnitude foreign investments were made performed relatively better (e.g. Žilinský kraj in Slovakia).

Furthermore, a particularly fast divergence of the growth rate could be observed in Bulgaria, with its rapidly developing capital city region, including Sofia and Varna and the south-west of the country stretching from Sofia to the Greek border, whereas the growth dynamics of the majority of the remaining regions were relatively weak. Large spatial differences could also be observed in Hungary, but here they were not as strongly translated into increased coefficient of variation values, since rapid development was recorded primarily in the better developed western regions. In Poland, weaker development dynamics could be observed along the country's western border with Germany, similarly to the case of Czechia, where the regions situated in the western parts of the country developed at a slower rate (in this latter case, regional differences were stable, largely due to unchanged patterns of FDI flows; De Castro, Hnát 2017).

The accelerated growth of the capital city region and other large cities is of special interest. The CEE countries have gone through delayed and accelerated restructuring, most pronounced in highly developed, urbanised and industrialised regions. This restructuring has been performed mainly though deindustrialisation. However, only in metropolitan areas could the loss of industrial structures be coupled by the fast development of a high-quality, internationally linked, diversified service sector. This sector could not have developed in other places, since they were not attractive for foreign and domestic investors who specialised in advanced producer services or modern and creative industries, or who constructed malls, hotels and entertainment centres. A recent study (Smętkowski 2018) provides a deeper insight into the nature of the metropolitan/non-metropolitan divide. It indicates first that the role of FDI was especially pronounced in metropolitan regions, and much less evident elsewhere, which increased the processes of regional divergence, mostly in the first phase of transition. Second, the development of large cities depended on vast resources of human capital, as such cities attracted students and qualified specialists from other regions.

In contrast, many non-metropolitan regions, which in 2000 had a GDP per capita above 105% of the national average, developed slower than the national rate in 2000–2008. These were predominantly regions with well-developed industrial specialisations (e.g. the western regions in Hungary; Bielsko-Biała, Toruń and Bydgoszcz in Poland; Gorj, Arad, Braşov and Covasna in Romania; and Stara Zagora in Bulgaria), and regions with harbour functions (Klaipėda in Lithuania, Burgas in Bulgaria, Constanţa in Romania). Only a few of these regions developed faster, alongside Poland's Legnica-Głogów Basin (copper and silver mining). Less developed regions grew, as a rule, much more slowly than the country averages. Only 16 of them recorded a higher rate of growth, mainly those regions in the vicinity of large cities in Poland, Latvia and Hungary, while in Romania, those situated in the transport corridor of National Road 1. This group also includes two regions with a well-developed automobile industry, which have attracted considerable investments from abroad (KIA – Žilinský kraj in Slovakia, and Renault – the Argeş region in Romania).

In the period after the crisis, some interesting changes in the regional patterns occurred (Figure 9.8). The metropolitan cores lost their primacy in GDP dynamics, since some diffusion to their immediate surroundings took place. This could be observed mainly in Poland, but also in Bulgaria, and to some extent in Czechia, Romania and Hungary. Bratislava and Tallinn maintained their positions of national champions. Moreover, some regions that had undergone successful industrial restructuring (based on attracting technologically advanced foreign investments) were able to display high dynamics (Podkarpackie in south-eastern Poland; some Transylvanian regions in Romania; the Debrecen region and strategically located region of Győr in north-eastern Hungary). In Czechia, the western region Plzeň rebounded quickly from the crisis. The transport corridor connecting Bulgaria with Istanbul also developed relatively fast.

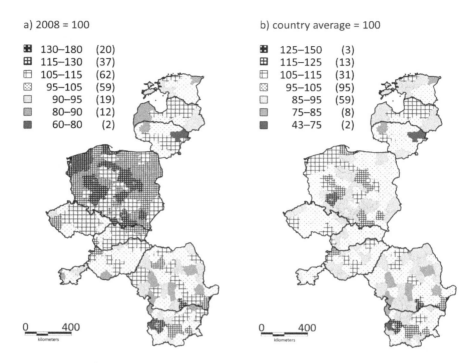

a) 2008 = 100

	130–180	(20)
	115–130	(37)
	105–115	(62)
	95–105	(59)
	90–95	(19)
	80–90	(12)
	60–80	(2)

b) country average = 100

	125–150	(3)
	115–125	(13)
	105–115	(31)
	95–105	(95)
	85–95	(59)
	75–85	(8)
	43–75	(2)

0 ___ 400
kilometers

0 ___ 400
kilometers

Figure 9.8 Real GDP change, 2008–15

Conclusions

During the initial stage of transformation, regional polarisation processes were on the increase in all the countries and did not stop till the end of the analysed period (2015) in Romania, Bulgaria and Estonia. The former two countries were still below the national GDP per capita level of EUR 6,000–7,000, at which regional divergence was halted in the majority of the analysed countries. The latter country may serve as a potential example of a second wave of regional divergence, revealed after exceeding the level of about EUR 12,000 per capita. This could be the result of innovation-driven development in Tallinn. However, another possible explanation, related to the cross-border diffusion of economic growth from the neighbouring Helsinki city-region, might also be valid.

Regardless of this specific case of Estonia, the CEE countries can serve as an example corroborating the Williamson hypothesis in the first two stages (i.e. polarisation and stabilisation). However, the panel analysis did not find any correlations between the rate of economic growth and changes in the coefficient of variation of the regional GDP in the short term. In other words, regional convergence or divergence did not depend on the national economic performance in the CEE countries in a given year and vice versa.

Furthermore, the change in regional differences is not correlated to the magnitude of these differences, as the coefficient of regional GDP per capita variation differs significantly from country to country. The greatest cohesiveness of regional GDP per capita could be observed in the best-developed countries of Slovenia and Czechia. However, Slovakia and Estonia, which came next on the scale of GDP per capita, encountered the widest regional differences (partly as a result of the small number of NUTS3 regions, but the impact of Bratislava and Tallinn city-regions was also significant).

One of the likely explanations for the stabilisation of regional differences in the majority of countries is the reduced investment risk following EU accession and the greater interest of foreign investors in some less-developed regions – those which offered relatively favourable conditions (i.e. have former industrial experience, like Rzeszów in south-eastern Poland or Miskolc in north-eastern Hungary). The increased availability of EU funds under the Cohesion and Common Agricultural policies could also have played a role, as such funds were concentrated in less developed regions in the majority of the analysed countries (see the chapter by Bachtler and Ferry in this volume); however, their direct impact on national and regional development have until now – at least in Poland – been rather mediocre and have relied mostly on demand-side effects (Gorzelak 2017). Other studies provide a rather inconclusive picture in this respect, stating that the effects of the Cohesion Policy on regional development in CEE countries 'vary' (Dyba et al. 2018: 90).

The significance of metropolisation processes is still clearly visible in the CEE countries, and most easily observable in the capital city regions and regions with other large urban centres (especially in Poland and Romania, which have the most polycentric urban structures), driving their fast development. With capital city regions excluded from the analysis we can observe a strong petrification of the spatial structures, that is, a rather uniform development of the remaining regions. What, therefore, can be said about the general territorial outcomes of the post-socialist transformation in Central and Eastern European countries? Two general processes can be observed:

- The growing role of large cities, and especially capital cities, which concentrate foreign investment, in both advanced producer services and modern manufacturing, in their surroundings, producing high value added per employee. Only in the largest cities, well connected by modern transportation links (international airport, motorway, rail) were such services able to replace the manufacturing sector. Smaller industrial centres experienced a period of decline from which only a few have been able to re-emerge. After initial concentration in the core cities, growth gradually spread to adjacent areas, and in the last stage, these areas have noted faster growth than the cities themselves. Suburbanisation was one of the leading factors behind this deconcentration.
- The stagnation of most peripheral regions deprived of big cities, which suffer the syndrome of underdevelopment (poor connectivity, low-skilled labour force, outmigration, poor infrastructure, domination of traditional

sectors – agriculture and forestry – poor attractiveness for external investment; Pavlinek 2004) and insufficient internal investment potential. Only a
few such regions have had an external chance to accelerate their development – location along a main international transportation corridor is one
such case – as well as tourist potential (this last factor operates on a much
smaller territorial scale). Location at the border – especially the external
border of the EU – constitutes an unfavourable condition for growth. It
should be stressed that the traditional east-west divide is – in general –
equally valid in modern times.

However, some manifestations of growth diffusion can be noticed:

• The deconcentration of major urban centres stemming from suburbanisation on the one hand and location of FDI on the other hand.
• Accelerated growth along major transportation corridors of international
  importance.
• The successful industrial restructuring of some peripherally located industrial districts – especially those which posed attractive potential for technologically advanced foreign investments.

This typology resembles that proposed by Lux (2018b), in which he distinguished similar types of regions – metropolitan, intermediate (enjoying successful industrial restructuring) and non-metropolitan (with relatively limited
potential for growth). However, contrary to Lux, the authors of this chapter
have doubts as to whether the strategies and policies aiming at promoting the
'endogenous' development of regions in the last category will be successful in
the globalised economy. Instead, policies supporting diffusion of growth from
the centres of development seem to be a more promising idea; however, this
would inevitably deepen the relative underdevelopment of lagging regions
deprived of the possibility of acquiring positive impulses for service-oriented
metropolitan, regional and/or industrial districts. This is especially true, as the
crisis strengthened the role of exogenous growth factors, particularly the role of
FDI inflow (Smętkowski 2018).

We may assume that these tendencies will continue to manifest themselves
in the future, as even the recent crisis has not disrupted existing territorial patterns significantly. Perhaps with the exception of Budapest, the largest cities of
Central and Eastern Europe are well ahead of massive diseconomies of scale
and some of them are rather facing depopulation due to suburbanisation than
overcrowding. However, they are likely to maintain their dominance in knowledge services and modern industries. Due to the rapid development of modern
transportation links (see the chapter by Komornicki in this volume), these hubs
will also increase their attractiveness for FDI. Metropolisation will therefore
proceed, but most likely at a slower pace, and will spread to adjacent regions,
resembling the processes observed in Western Europe.

The non-metropolitan regions will undergo further differentiation. Those
that are able to take advantage of favourable location conditions (major

international transport corridors, tourist potential, successful trans-border cooperation, successful industrial development) will be able to accelerate their growth. The remaining peripheries will have great difficulties in assuming faster growth and positive restructuring, and their problems will be aggravated by migrations outflows (see the chapter by Fihel and Okólski in this volume). The east-west divide will likely not be overcome, and the (decreasing) inflow of funds for the EU will prevent any change to this pattern. This confirms the hypothesis of 'historically embedded' growth processes (Lux 2018a).

Notes

1 This study does not include Croatia, an EU member since 2014.
2 We deliberately do not use the term 'disparities', which has inherent value judgments. Not all regional differences can be labeled as negative – some are 'natural', stemming from structural differences, in most cases rooted in the distant past and therefore difficult to overcome. 'Discrepancies' would have been justified if 'proper' or 'acceptable' differences were specified and only those that were greater could be called 'discrepancies'.
3 It has been demonstrated (Slonimski and Slonimska 2005) that in western regions of Belarus (west of the mid-war Polish border), entrepreneurs demand more economic freedom, while eastward of this border, they demand more state support. Moreover, the voting patterns in Ukraine have been clearly influenced by the mid-war state border between Poland and the USSR.
4 This observation does not contradict the national divergence discussed above, as it only points to the low mobility of regions between various categories of development.

References

Barrios, S., & Strobl, E. (2009). The dynamics of regional inequalities. *Regional Science and Urban Economics*, 39, 575–591.
Braudel, F. (1982). *L'Europe*. Paris.
Boldrin, M., & Canova, F. (2001). Inequality and convergence in Europe's regions: Reconsidering European regional policies. *Economic Policy*, 16(32), 205–253.
Capello, R. (2007). *Regional Economics*. London and New York: Routledge.
Davies, N. (1996). *Europe: A History*. Oxford: Oxford University Press.
De Castro, T., & Hnát, P. (2017). Czech FDI performance: Between global value chains and domestic reforms. In: B. Szent-Iványi (ed.), *Foreign Direct Investment in Central and Eastern Europe. Post-crisis Perspectives*. Cham, Switzerland: Palgrave Macmillan.
Dyba, W., Loewen, B., Looga, J., & Zdražil, P. (2018). Regional development in Central-Eastern European Countries at the beginning of the 21st century: Path dependence and effects of EU Cohesion Policy. *Quaestiones Geographicae*, 37(2), 77–92.
ESPON. (2004). *Project 1.1.1. Potentials for Polycentric Development*. Stockholm: NORDREGIO.
Ezcurra, R., Pascual, P., & Rapu, M. (2007). The dynamics of regional differences in Central and Eastern Europe during transition. *European Planning Studies*, 15(10), 1397–1421.
Gorzelak, G. (1996). *The Regional Dimension of Transformation in Central and Eastern Europe*. London: Jessica Kingsley Publishers.
Gorzelak, G. (2011). The financial crisis in Central and Eastern Europe. In: G. Gorzelak (ed.), *Financial Crisis in Central and Eastern Europe: From Similarity to Diversity*. Warszawa: Scholar.
Gorzelak, G. (2017). Cohesion policy and regional development. In: S. Hardy, J. Bachtler, P. Berkowitz & T. Muravska (eds.), *EU Cohesion Policy. Reassessing Performance and Direction*. London and New York: Routledge, pp. 33–54.

Gorzelak, G., & Smętkowski, M. (2010). Regional development dynamics in Central and Eastern European countries. In: G. Gorzelak, J. Bachtler & M. Smętkowski (eds.), *Regional Development in Central and Eastern Europe Development Processes and Policy Challenges*. London and New York: Routledge.

Kaczyńska, E., & Piesowicz, K. (1977). *Wykłady z powszechnej historii gospodarczej* (*Lectures in Economic History of the World*). Warszawa: PWN.

Kalvet, T. (2007). The Estonian Information Society Development Since the 1990s, *Praxis Working Paper* No 29.

Karłowska-Kamzowa, A. (1997). Europejski kontekst polskiej przestrzeni historyczno-kulturowej (European context of Polish historic-cultural space). In: A. Kuklinski (ed.), *Problematyka przestrzeni europejskiej* (*Problematique of the European Space*). Warszawa: EUROREG.

Lux, G. (2018a). Regional development paths in Central and Eastern Europe and the driving forces of restructuring. In: G. Lux & G. Horvath (eds.), *The Routledge Handbook to Regional Development in Eastern and Central Europe*. London and New York: Routledge.

Lux, G. (2018b). Reintegrating economic space. The metropolitan – Provincial divide. In: G. Lux & G. Horvath (eds.), *The Routledge Handbook to Regional Development in Eastern and Central Europe*. London and New York: Routledge.

OECD (2010). *Regional Development Policies in OECD Countries*. Paris: OECD Publishing.

Pavlínek, P. (2004). Regional development implications of foreign direct investment in Central Europe. *European Urban and Regional Studies*, 11(1), 47–70.

Petrakos, G. (2001). Patterns of regional inequality in transition economies. *European Planning Studies*, 9(3), 359–383.

Pipes, R. (1999). *Property and Freedom*. New York: Alfred A. Knopf.

Römich, R. (2003). Regional differences within accession counties. In: G. Tumpel-Gugerell & P. Mooslechner (eds.), *Economic Convergence and Divergence in Europe: Growth and Regional Development in an Enlarged European Union*. Cheltenham: Edward Elgar.

Slonimski, A., & Slonimska, M. (2005). Specyfika przedsiębiorczości mieszkańców zachodnich i wschodnich regionów Białorusi (Entrepreneurship in Western and Eastern regions of Belarus). *Studia Regionalne i Lokalne*, 1(19), 35–44.

Smętkowski, M. (2013). *Rozwój regionów i polityka regionalna w krajach Europy Środkowo-Wschodniej w okresie transformacji i globalizacji* (*Regional Development and Regional Policy in Central and Eastern European Countries in the Period of Transformation and Globalisation*). Warsaw: Scholar.

Smętkowski, M. (2018). The role of exogenous and endogenous factors in the growth of regions in Central and Eastern Europe: The metropolitan/non-metropolitan divide in the pre- and post-crisis era. *European Planning Studies*, 26(2), 256–278.

Smętkowski, M., Gorzelak, G., Kozak, M., Olechnicka, A., Płoszaj, A., & Wojnar, K. (2011). *The European Metropolises and Their Regions: From Economic Landscape to Metropolitan Networks*. Warszawa: Wydawnictwo Naukowe Scholar.

Smętkowski, M., & Wójcik, P. (2012). Regional convergence in Central and Eastern European countries – A multidimensional approach. *European Planning Studies*, 20(6), 923–939.

Szörfi, B. (2007). Development and regional differences – Testing the Williamson curve hypothesis in the European Union. *Focus on European Economic Integration*, 2, 100–121.

Wallerstein, I. (1974). *The Modern World System: Capitalist Agriculture and the Origins of the European World Economy in the Sixteenth Century*. New York: Academic Press.

Williamson, J.G. (1965). Regional inequalities and the process of national development. *Economic Development and Cultural Change*, 13, 3–45.

World Bank (2009). Reshaping Economic Geography, *World Development Report 2009*, Washington DC.

10 Land-use and ownership changes of agriculture

Jerzy Bański

Introduction

The socioeconomic and political transformation in the Central and Eastern European countries (CEECs), induced by the fall of the communist system, was characterised by far-reaching change in agricultural management. The transformation entailed, first and foremost, the closedown of the so-called socialised (i.e. state-owned and cooperative) sector and the return of its assets into private hands. Generally speaking, the process of privatisation in farming restored ownership to what it had been in the period prior to the installation of the communist-controlled economy, albeit with the need for efficient, modern agriculture ensuring the introduction of new forms and methods of production. The main component of the changes being ushered in was land, and this fact offers a good indication of the direction being taken by agricultural policy in the countries of the region.

Up to the end of the 1980s, the food economy of Central Europe was based upon a socialised sector represented by the Production Cooperatives and State Farms. This reflected the adoption of communist-era economic tenets which saw ownership as almost universally a matter for the state – either directly, or via Cooperatives. Ideas about collective management, in line with the model of the Soviet *Kolkhoz* and *Sovkhoz*, were ushered in following the Second World War as a cohesive Eastern Bloc took shape. Individually owned farms were then eliminated en masse, their assets taken over on various bases and different types of communist-era farms were established. Ownership of large farms was transferred to the state by way of nationalisation, while owners of small farms were forced into a collectivised approach, through inclusion within the aforesaid Production Cooperatives. Collectivisation of the farming sector was far-reaching in almost all of the CEECs (Swain 1985; Turnock 1989). However, the exceptions were Poland and the former Yugoslavia, where private agriculture remained dominant (Bański 2011; Hartvigsen 2013; Brouwer et al. 1991).

The systemic transformation in the farming sector was largely achieved in the last decade of the 20th century. This can be seen as a period in which agricultural reform was pursued across the entire region. However, the results – alongside those arising out of CEECs' accession to the EU – are still being shaped, and land managed to meet the needs of agriculture may serve as the proverbial 'litmus paper' for the transformations being achieved. For example, changes of ownership initiated a process by which land became fragmented (Giovarelli and Bledsoe 2001; Lerman et al. 2004). This was most marked in Romania, where – thanks to new land restitution measures – several million new users of land made their appearance (Balteanu and Popovici 2010). However, farmland is also subject to strong pressure exerted by other forms of land use, mainly associated with the development of settlement and technical infrastructure. Furthermore, the need to raise the level of efficiency of food production has forced certain changes in farm management structure, and has led to a cessation of use of land with the weakest agroecological potential (this mostly being reassigned for afforestation).

All the phenomena referred to above have contributed to reductions in the total areas of farmland noted in every country under study here (Bański 2017; Bicik and Jelecek 2009; Balteanu and Popovici 2010; Janku et al. 2016; Toth-Naar et al. 2014).

Specifically, the work detailed here seeks to discuss the structural and ownership-related changes that have affected agricultural land-use since communism collapsed. To this end, the analysis includes the given region's five largest CEECs: Poland, Czechia, Slovakia, Hungary and Romania. These create a contiguous and basically compact area, with the countries resembling one another in terms of physical geography, and conditions for farming being basically similar (given that they represent the temperate-zone climate).

The notion of farmland is understood to include that land which participates directly in agricultural production. This definition would therefore embrace arable land, land under permanent cultivation and various kinds of agricultural grassland (*Glossary* . . . 2003; FAOSTAT 2013). However, forestry has been excluded from the analysis, even though some countries do regard it as an integral part of their agricultural sector. It should also be emphasised that statistical offices in the countries studied have adopted various definitions of what constitutes farmland, as well as various means of gathering data. This inevitably means some of the statistical material under analysis is actually non-comparable in certain cases.

The statistical material comes mostly from Eurostat, and the scale on which comparisons are made is general enough to support the contention that differences should not distort the analytical results excessively.

Farming-sector land use and ownership in the pre-transformation period

As already stated, in the period prior to the systemic transformation, a clear majority of all farmland in the CEECs belonged to the state, either directly, or via Production Cooperatives. Only in Poland and the former Yugoslavia did most farmland remain in private hands throughout the communist era (Bański 2011; Brouwer et al. 1991).

In the case of the Yugoslavia ruled by Marshal Josip Broz Tito, who stood up to the hegemony of the USSR, the different model adopted allowed for the continued existence of individually owned farms and private ownership. In contrast, in Poland, the nationalisation and collectivisation of agriculture encountered fierce resistance on the part of individual farmers who had only assumed ownership of land a few decades previously, following belated reforms in the wake of a protracted period of feudalism.

Thus, in the former Yugoslavia, the peak period of communism still saw private farms accounting for around 85% of agricultural land, while in Poland the corresponding figure was around 76% (Bański et al. 1999). By comparison, in Hungary, private agriculture had at its disposal just 15% of all the land managed by the sector at that time, with figures as low as 10% and 6% characterising Romania and the former Czechoslovakia, respectively (*Historia . . . 1991*).

The situation as regards ownership and the management of farmland in the different countries of the region was very much dependent on the model of communist-era agriculture adopted, as well as the methods by which ownership was nationalised and collectivised. Within the agrarian structure, the largest area of farmland was under the management of large cooperatives or state enterprises characterised by favourable land layouts. An exception was agriculture in Poland, where there was a prevalence of small farms afflicted by excessive fragmentation. The latter should typically be regarded as an unfavourable process, given the additional costs its generates, and the time farmers may have to take to commute from one area of their land to another. The use of large machines is also obviously hindered (or prevented altogether), while borders between plots are extended maximally, and the setting aside of boundary strips is rendered impossible. All these aspects make it essential that a dense network of roads leading to plots is put in place, complicating matters when it comes to land registration, and sometimes even provoking conflicts between owners.

In Hungary, post-war agricultural reform first led to an increase in the numbers of private farms, only for the subsequent process of collectivisation (in the 1950s) to ensure the takeover of their land by State Farms and communist-style Production Cooperatives. The former took on the larger farms, while the latter were founded upon small farms, whose owners were forced to join the Collectives. In the heyday of communism, Hungary had 1,500 Cooperatives in operation, with these accounting for around 75% of all the country's farmland, alongside State Farms that were 124 in number (Kovacs 2005).

In Poland, as in Hungary, the first post-war years also brought an increase in the numbers of private farms. Overall, the period 1945–49 saw more than 6.1 million hectares of land put into the hands of peasants, with 5.6 million hectares of this assigned to the establishment of around 814,000 new farms, while the rest helped enlarge the very small farms existing previously. However, two years after the war ended, a change of state agricultural policy took hold, with an ever-greater role being assigned to collectivisation. This worked towards the establishment of modern agricultural enterprises, as well as the prevention of land fragmentation. However, it also reflected the political dogma, and not least the desire to ensure a weakened role for private agriculture. And so it was that intensive collectivisation, in general against the will of peasants, continued until 1956, and led to the emergence of over 10,000 Cooperatives. Various repressive measures were applied against those opposing the collectivisation, inter alia associated with the compulsory supply of farm products. Cooperatives enjoyed the authorities' support, thanks to which they obtained economic privileges and were adequately supplied with the means of production.

However, the greatest role of all was played by the State Farms founded in 1949. These arose, first and foremost, in the place of the largest, formerly German, estates in the north-west and west of the country that were gained by Poland after the war. They were also founded in south-eastern Poland, in areas from which people of Ukrainian ethnicity had been newly expelled. The State Farms reached their zenith in terms of area of farmland (i.e. around 3.5 million hectares) at the end of the 1970s.

For their part, the authorities in communist Romania set about their work on nationalisation in 1948, by taking over land formerly in the ownership of the Royal Family and the Church, as well as large farms, where 'large' denoted anything over 50 hectares in area. At the same time, smaller-scale properties were collectivised, in a process that only came to an end in 1962. The culmination of the twin nationalisation and collectivisation effort was reached with the passing of a 1974 act that confined the handing-on of land ownership rights to inheritance. As a result of these processes, just around 10% of farmland remained in private hands, and this was mostly characterised by low quality terrain, predominantly located in mountainous areas. As of 1989, the principal form of land ownership was the Production Cooperative, with units of this type running 59% of all farmland. The State Farms amounted to almost 30% of all farmland (Balteanu and Popovici 2010).

In the same way, in the former Czechoslovakia, the communist era saw land taken almost entirely into public hands. The collectivisation of agriculture brought about an enlargement in the sizes of cultivated fields (i.e. land defragmentation), and this made it possible for crops to be grown over more sizable areas on which larger farm machinery could be used. In consequence, farmland structure as such underwent change, but there was also a transformation of the rural landscape, with monocultures of limited biodiversity coming to dominate (Janku et al. 2016). The most important role was that played by the Production Cooperatives, which managed more than 60% of all agricultural land. In turn, Czechoslovakia's State Farms had about 30% land at their disposal. Nevertheless, the situation as regards ownership was a quite complex one, as land remained in the hands of private individuals, even though they were not actually able to utilise it. This reflected the way in which the actual managers of farmland were the aforementioned Cooperatives or State Farms, with the true owners therefore being in possession 'on paper' only. This was of course an ideal way of ensuring that the persons in question neither received compensation nor had an actual stake in the activity being engaged in (Bandlerova and Marisova 2003).

The contemporary management of agricultural land

Changes of land ownership and their most important results

In the early 1990s, in all the countries in Central and Eastern Europe, a process of the restitution and privatisation of farm assets began. The reprivatisation reform slated for Hungary was pursued in the 1992–96 period, with 2.5 million hectares of farmland from the Cooperatives and 200,000 hectares from the state farms being earmarked for this purpose. The reform entailed compensation for the value of lost assets (in fact it was coupons capable of being traded on the market that were introduced), as well as the dividing-up and handing-out of land between members of former Cooperatives, as these organisations underwent restructuring. In the case of the State Farms, some land was sold off to private investors. However, it was quite typical for those involved to be the former managers of the said Farms, or else those who had been on their teams of workers. It is estimated that some 1.5 million people obtained land that had previously been under joint ownership (in both forms Cooperatives and State Farms). In turn, 500,000 received their own land back, while a further 500,000 received so-called golden crown land[1] (Kovacs 2005).

Through the privatisation and restitution work engaged in, the ownership structure changed almost totally. As of 2011, around 80% of all farmland was back in private hands (Toth-Naar et al. 2014). The result was the shaping of two main types of farm: the agricultural enterprise (Cooperative or production company) and the larger-scale farm. 2013 data from the Hungarian Central Statistical Office make it clear that there were 8,800 entities of the first kind, making use of some 2,122,000 hectares of land, as well as 482,500 farms of the second type on around 2,468,000 hectares. The principal type of private ownership involved a group of small farms covering just a few hectares each, while the agricultural enterprises were predominantly those with holdings of several hundred hectares at minimum.

The processes in question also led to the fragmentation of land. Large, uniform areas of cultivated fields were divided up into smaller plots, to meet the needs of farmers usually farming areas covering less than 10 hectares. These were then unfavourable changes, given that the land passed over to entities not achieving very high levels of efficiency, and often in fact satisfied with meeting their family's own immediate needs. The owners here had frequently taken up work in other branches of the economy (Sadowski and Takacs-György 2005). Some of the urban-based beneficiaries of privatisation left land fallow, abandoned it altogether or offered it for sale. Furthermore, a process of demographic ageing was taking place in rural areas, with the result that the period from the onset of the privatisation process through to the year 2000 brought a roughly 30% decline in the number of private farms. The years 2000–2010 witnessed a further 50% decline.

The Romanian model for the privatisation of farmland was grounded in the 1991 Land Fund Act, which provided for the return of up to 10 hectares of farmland to each former owner that had been required to hand land over to the Cooperatives of the communist era. The process of restoring rights of ownership was run by a Commission set up especially for this purpose. The Act prohibited transfers of ownership of the land in question for a ten-year period, while also stipulating that the maximum permissible size of a farm was 100 hectares (later increased to 200 hectares). Subsequent years brought the adoption of new acts that ushered in liberalisation. As a result of the activity in ownership transformation, nearly 9 million hectares of land were returned to their former owners. With a view to agriculture being privatised, Romania set up a State Property Agency enjoying the right to sell or lease the land of the commercial-law companies that had been established.

The number of farms in Romania increased dramatically to around 4 million (Benedek 2000), with the subsequent decline proceeding only quite slowly, such that there remained around 3.5 million farms as of 2013. As in the case of Hungary, a negative impact of restitution of ownership was the dividing-up of former Cooperative land into small parcels. At the beginning of the new century, the mean size of a private farm was just 1.9 hectares. Furthermore, it is estimated that over 60% of the farmers who had land returned to them were elderly people whose decisions to pass farms on to the heirs resulted in yet further fragmentation of the land.

In the cases of Czechia and Slovakia, it was accepted that private ownership of land had been suspended through the 1948–89 period, making restitution post-1990 a real possibility in consequence. A return of (up to 150 hectares of) farmland could be applied for by people who were permanent residents of the then Czechoslovakia and had either been owners of land in 1948, or were the direct heirs of such people. Where there was no possibility of a direct return of land, substitute real estate could be made available, or compensation given in the form of Treasury Bonds. The effect of these privatisation processes was that around 3.4 million hectares of farmland passed into private hands, with just 400,000 hectares remaining under the administration of the state (Bicik and Jelecek 2009). That land was placed in a State Land Fund that could be utilised by private farmers, companies and Production Cooperatives alike, while from 1999 onwards land could be sold to persons permanently resident in Czechia.

In Slovakia, land restitution was in a sense hindered by the fact that fields still enjoyed a contiguous distribution next to one another. In this situation, the separating-off of parcels of land from units of large size already in existence made no economic sense. In the 1990s, rights of ownership were either conferred upon or restored to around half of all farmland. Other land remained under the administration of the Slovakian Land Fund, with land under no ownership being nationalised and handed over for use by cooperatives at local-government level. In contrast, land previously in the hands of the communist-era Cooperatives and distributed in larger contiguous blocks remained so, thanks to a process of transformation into commercial-law companies.

The changes of ownership taking place in Polish agriculture differed from region to region. As was noted earlier, throughout the communist era there was a prevalence here of land ownership within individually owned family farms. These were typically units of very limited area, among which a great many were basically self-supplying, serving only as supplements to a more typical job, offering extra income, or simply food, for the owner. Production Cooperatives developed in Poland's Western Lands, in which a tradition of joint management had long before taken hold. In contrast, what emerged in the north-west and north were very large State Farms, this transformation being achieved more readily over the large areas of land which were no longer managed by anyone. As of 1989, the country had 1,666 State Farms, most of them loss-making (Zgliński 2003). Privatisation of land was mainly concentrated in areas that had previously hosted these State Farms.

However, in Poland, returns of land did not proceed in the manner observed in other countries of Central Europe, only in fact being engaged in occasionally.

In Poland, the idea that won through entailed the total, abrupt closedown of the State Farms – a decision that has not been appraised uniformly. While proponents regarded the communist-era Farms as entirely unsuitable for adjustment to free-market conditions (Bański 2011; Zgliński 2003), opponents criticised the policy for its drastic handling. This was all the more so given that at least some of the State Farms were in a better economic condition and might, following reform, have adapted (or been adapted) to the new economic reality. A further key argument against the rapid abolition process, of course, entailed the human factor, since thousands of people were deprived of work in circumstances where alternative sources of upkeep were lacking. An effect arising from the closure of the State Farms was dramatically increased unemployment in pockets associated with those specific areas, as well as poverty, social exclusion, and the decapitalisation and devastation of what were, in essence, public assets. The last of the so-called Państwowe Gospodarstwa Rolne (State Agricultural Farms, PGR) closed in 1994, while the land from these had first and foremost passed into the hands of legal entities (mainly capital companies). Only to a more limited extent were natural persons involved in this process. In general, the legal entities bought up large (100+ hectare) areas of land, while natural persons (mainly small farmers) acquired smaller parcels where they were involved.

The transformation of ownership in the CEE countries gave rise to the fragmentation of land in terms of both utilisation and ownership (Hartvigsen 2014). In Romania and Hungary in particular, the large farms previously in state hands gave way to small, non-competitive entities. A large number of owners and users of farmland thus came into existence, only for this number to decline steadily year by year thereafter. This may attest to a concentration of land in larger units, but changes of this kind are, in fact, still taking place slowly. In Hungary, a clearly 'bipolar' situation has arisen where farms are concerned, with many small examples of a couple of hectares at the one extreme, and large production holdings at the other. Farms in the first category have only a limited amount of land at their disposal, and tend to play only a limited role where output is concerned. However, they have had an important social role to play in rural areas, due to their stabilisation of the labour market and securing of at least a minimum income. A similar role is played by the small 'social' farms in Poland or Romania (Figure 10.1).

Farms of the second (production holding) category are not numerous when set against the family farm holdings, which still have over 70% of all farmland at their disposal. However, the significance of these kinds of farms ought in fact to increase, given their access to their own resources for investment, and their capacity to make use of modern methods in both production and management. In Czechia and Slovakia what has mainly happened is a fragmentation of land ownership, not in fact leading to greater fragmentation of land use. Through the transformation of what had hitherto been Cooperatives, there emerged agricultural companies or other kinds of legal entity covering large areas and having considerable productive potential at their disposal. Farms covering more than 500 hectares in fact account for just 3.8% of the total number, while still making use of more than 72% of all land utilised in agriculture (Basek and Divila 2008).

It is worth nothing that, besides Poland, where the system has long been based around family farms, the countries under study have failed in their attempts to increase the role of farmer-managed farms. Indeed, the attempts to reactivate small individually owned farms ended in failure from the economic point of view. Thus, food production in most of these countries is dominated by producers of various organisational forms, be they holdings, Cooperatives, companies and so on, all with large areas of farmland at their disposal.

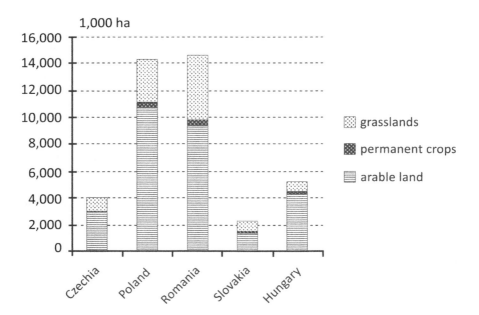

Figure 10.1 Share of agricultural land and average farm size in Central Europe

The market for land

In the first years of the systemic transformation there was only limited movement on the market for agricultural land. This was conditioned by the general socioeconomic situation in the region, compounded by uncertainty regarding the future. There was also a lack of experience from the past in this field. Furthermore, a brake was applied by legal regulations that ushered in transitional limits on the sale of land. Where trade did take place, it involved small areas of farmland located in areas attractive from the tourist point of view or in the vicinity of large urban centres, and hence redesignated for other economic functions, mainly for residential purposes. For example, in Czechia in the years 1992–2002, just 174,000 hectares of farmland changed hands (Zadura 2005).

In Poland, the limited 'flow' of land reflected limited demand, as well as prohibitions on foreign acquisitions put in place. Most activity on the market for land thus revolved around former State Farm–managed areas. In the years 1996–2004, between 100,000 and 190,000 hectares of land were bought and sold annually.

Up until 2003, the purchaser of a piece of farmland in Poland might be any natural person of Polish citizenship. However, 2003 ushered in a new act that confined purchases of farmland to those who had at least basic agricultural training at secondary or tertiary level, or else people who could document experience working in farming. On the other hand, Poland's accession to the EU in 2004 brought a theoretical lifting of the ban on land purchases by citizens of other EU Member States, albeit with a 12-year transition period introduced in the cases of farmland and forest land. However, in 2016, a new act on shaping the agricultural system was introduced, which resulted in significant restrictions on the flow of agricultural land even for Polish citizens. In other CEE countries (Czechia, Lithuania, Latvia, Estonia and Slovakia) the period of this kind was of shorter duration, lasting for just seven years (Burger 2006).

Farmland usually attracts lower prices than land of other categories, though there are variations relating first and foremost to location vis-à-vis large urban centres, on soil quality and on land-use category. For example, in 2011, prices of farmland ranged from EUR 260 to 5,500 per hectare (Strelecek et al. 2011). As of 2007, the value of small plots (of up to 1 hectare) with non-agricultural designations was EUR 59,000 on average. In turn, the land prices achieved by plots exceeding 5 hectare, with an agricultural designation, were EUR 1,324 per hectare on average.

Once communism had fallen, all of the countries under analysis experienced a permanent increase in the prices of agricultural land. Indeed, the trend intensified immediately prior to countries' accession to the European Union. In Hungary, an increase in land prices reflected the expectation that land would be acquired by foreigners, and that advantage might be taken of farm subsidies (Popp and Stauder 2003). According to Eurostat data, the average price of farmland in Czechia increased over the 2000–2009 period from EUR 1,555 to 2,249 per hectare. The equivalent increase in Slovakia was from EUR 895 to 1,256, while the increase characterising Romania in the 2000–2005 period was from EUR 351 to 879 per hectare. In fact, Romania, Hungary and Poland recorded some of the greatest increases in prices of agricultural land, even in global terms. In the case of Poland, the mean price for a hectare of land sold privately in 1992 was EUR 298, but by 2016 this had risen all the way to EUR 9,169. Land here nevertheless remains far cheaper than its equivalent in Western Europe. For comparison, the average price per hectare of agricultural land in 2016 in the Netherlands was EUR 57,900, in Belgium EUR 34,700, in Germany EUR 22,300 and in Italy EUR 19,800.

It is worth giving separate attention to the matter of land leasing, especially in Czechia, Slovakia and Hungary – given the very important role it played in shaping the land-use structure. As of the early 2000s, it is estimated that as much as 95% of all farmland in the country has been leased out. From among 3.5 million owners of farmland, with holdings of just 0.44 hectares on average, less than 1% have taken up actual farming activity (Bicik and Jelecek 2009). The remaining owners of the land are not involved in farming, with their land then being rented out to agricultural production firms or small groups of farmers. The costs of hire depend on the location and soil quality, but are at levels not less than 1% of the actual value. Thanks to the widespread nature of the phenomenon of leasing, a favourable agrarian structure with rational distribution of land parcels has remained in place. A similar situation applies in Hungary, where leasing accounts for around 70% of all farmland, including as much as 93% of that under the management of production companies (Toth-Naar 2014).

In Poland, every fifth hectare of agricultural land is leased out, but there remain no reliable data, given the typically informal nature of such arrangements where small, one-person farms are concerned. Deals are commonly struck by spoken agreements only. According to *Statistics Poland* (GUS), the average cost of leasing is around EUR 200 per hectare. In the case of land leased from the Polish Treasury, payments are usually determined on a market basis, by way of tendering. Price levels are expressed in relation to current and averaged prices of wheat, as announced each time by GUS.

A diagnosis of the state of agricultural land use

Favourable agroecological conditions in countries of the studied region combine with levels of urbanisation and industrialisation lower than in Western Europe to favour the development of the agricultural sector. The dominance of the agricultural function in rural areas is confirmed by high shares of the overall areas accounted for by farmland – in the range 50%–70%, depending on the country. The greatest potentials where farmland is concerned are in Poland and Romania.

The dominating component of farmland structure everywhere is arable land, on which the prevalent cultivation is of cereals and industrial crops (Figure 10.2). There is far less grassland, which is often concentrated in

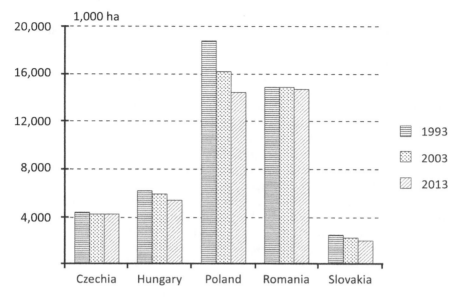

Figure 10.2 Structure of agricultural land in 2015
Source: Eurostat.

upland or wetland areas with lower soil quality. A still less important category in terms of area comprises permanent crops, e.g. fruit trees and vines, which are now very much concentrated in areas enjoying a long tradition of this kind of growing.

All the countries studied display a long-term trend of decline in farmland areas, though the intensity of this phenomenon does vary from one to another. This process in fact began at the beginning of the 20th century, and reflects socio-economic development, including steady urbanisation and industrialisation. Following the fall of the Eastern Bloc, the largest absolute areas of land to be taken out of agriculture were noted in Poland and Romania, mainly as a reflection of the sheer size of these countries. Over the 1993–2013 period, the loss of farmland areas in these two countries alone exceeded 6.5 million hectares, or twice as much as the entire land area of this kind in both Czechia and Slovakia.

In the 1990s, changes relating to areas of farmland and sizes of farms remained limited in scope – a fact that can be linked with the economic crisis which ensued once the Eastern Bloc had fallen, as well as the rather slow pace at which the economy could be built up under the new market system. Only at the end of the millennium did the above period give way to an era of very dynamic change reflecting socioeconomic development, the freeing-up of the market for land following a period of privatisation, and the increasing access to the world market gained by the CEE countries. The need to raise levels of efficiency more or less forced the cessation of agricultural management of land of the poorest quality, which was most often turned back into forest; areas of wasteland also grew. Furthermore, agricultural land was taken over to serve other economic functions.

The most marked reduction in the area of farmland took place in Poland (Figure 10.3). One of the causes of this was the urban expansion taking place in many cities, particularly in the form of ongoing development of residential areas in the suburbs immediately adjacent to large urban centres. This phenomenon intensified greatly in the 2000–2001 period. Farmland was also taken up in the development of new transport infrastructure, especially the construction of expressways and the modernisation of metropolitan transport networks. In contrast, the pursuit of environmental programmes ensured that unprofitable farmland of low quality could be reforested or turned into wasteland. Decline in the area of farmland may also be linked with unfavourable demographic processes, including the ageing of country-dwellers and migratory outflows from peripheral areas. In areas hit by these processes, some of the farms simply went into liquidation. Similar processes could be identified on marginal land in Czechia and Romania (Gajdos 2005; Balteanu and Popovici 2010). However, in the case of the former country, the land-use structure did not undergo any

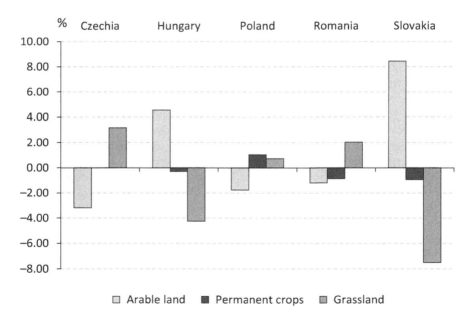

Figure 10.3 Changes in the structure of agricultural land use in the 1989–2013 period
Czechia and Slovakia: 1993–2013
Source: Eurostat.

further major change. This is a result of the rather high level of urbanisation and development of technical infrastructure, as well as the stabilisation of the farming sector within the country's economic system as a whole. The greatest loss of farmland was noted in the zone most influenced by Prague, where housing construction flourished during the period.

Loss of farmland was associated with structural changes, albeit in various different directions (Map 10.1). In Slovakia and Hungary, there was an increase in the share of arable land – at the expense of areas with more permanent crops, as well as meadows and pastures. In Romania, in turn, it was at the expense of permanent crops and arable land that the share of different kinds of agricultural grassland increased, with this reflecting the difficulties the farming sector experienced there. Also worthy of note is the reduced significance of areas with more permanent crops (vineyards and orchards) in Romania, Slovakia and Hungary, with this attesting to an extensification of production, as well as a withdrawal from more highly specialised forms of cultivation (Takacs 2008). This process was almost certainly underpinned by changes of ownership, and the attendant resignation of small farmers from labour-intensive forms of crop-growing, or from those requiring large amounts of own investment and/or modern technologies. Such conclusions gain support in detailed research carried out on the use of land in Romania (Popovici et al. 2013). The result was resignation from intensive forms of cultivation in the years 1990–2000, with certain regions even seeing the total abandonment of cultivation among new owners of land, due to their lack of capacity (in terms of money to invest and professional readiness).

The transformation of the agricultural sector in Czechia also had an influence on structure as regards the types of agricultural land. What mainly increased there was the share accounted for by grasslands, this inter alia reflecting the closure of State Farms in mountain and piedmont areas in which production difficulties arise due to the low-quality agroecological conditions. Lack of support for the agricultural sector on the part of the state provoked a resignation from the low profitability of crop cultivation on arable land, which therefore made way for meadows and pastures, or was reforested. In addition, a decline in the consumption of beef, milk and cheese throughout the nation gave rise to a change in methods of cattle raising. The system of rearing in a closed system requiring fodder produced on arable land gave way to a system based around grazing on grasslands (Bicik and Jelecek 2009).

In Poland, the structure as regards agricultural land use experienced the opposite process, though it is hard to link this with changes of ownership. An increase in the area under permanent cultivation points to an intensification of output. Indeed, fruit and processed products made from it became important export items associated with Poland. Moreover, following accession to the EU, farmers obtained high levels of direct payment for certain species of fruit tree, with this serving as an incentive for new planting. There was also a slight increase in the share accounted for by grasslands – a result that should be linked with more rational use being made of agricultural land.

Farm size structure

According to Eurostat data, as of 2013, the five countries analysed have over 5.7 million farms making use of agricultural land. However, the number varies greatly from country to country (Map 10.1). In Czechia and Slovakia, the overall number of farms is small, as there are just over 20,000 entities. As has already

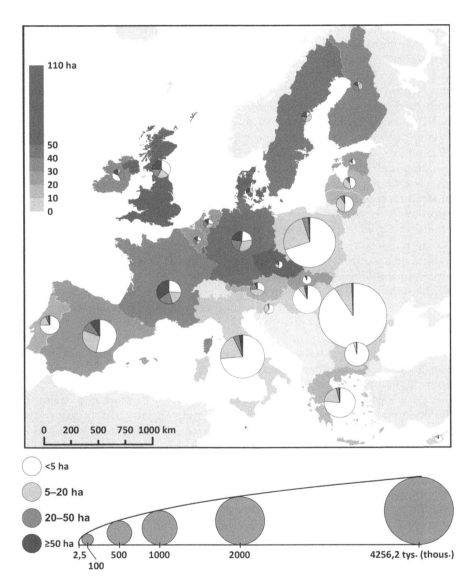

Map 10.1 Numbers, size breakdowns and average sizes of farms in the EU Member States in 2005 (Bański 2010)

been discussed, the processes of the restitution and privatisation of land did not do much to ensure fragmentation in terms of use. In fact, to a great extent land is still being utilised by large or very large businesses.

In contrast, in Hungary, and particularly in Romania and Poland, figures for the numbers of farms achieve very high values. The total number of farms in Romania, Hungary and Poland taken together (at around 5.7 million) surpasses the total number in all the remaining Member States of the EU (5.1 million). In the case of the first two aforementioned countries, such a large number of farms is the effect of the transformation process over the last quarter century. In Poland, this phenomenon took shape via a long historical process. The most severe fragmentation of farms is present in the south and south-east of Poland, where overpopulation in rural areas was long a feature, resulting in a surfeit of labour, while land was traditionally divided up between heirs and successors. In the last several decades it has been possible to observe a decline in the numbers of farms, and an attendant increase in their average size. However, this process only involves the most-fragmented areas to a limited extent.

The decline in numbers of farms is largely the result of increased competition on the global market for food. In Central and Eastern Europe, where there are excessive numbers of small, unprofitable farms, the process in question will intensify still further; and the farms going to the wall will be the weakest ones. For example, in Hungary, just the first years of EU membership saw around 90% of all direct payments to farmers heading for just 100 of the largest entities (*Land* . . . 2013). Small farmers lacking means of their own did not (could not) avail themselves of EU subsidies. Indeed, an estimated 93% of all farmers were excluded from subsidisation. Farms owned by these people frequently went bankrupt. As of 2009, 8.6% of all farms were still in receipt of almost 72% of the total amount of direct payments.

A further consequence of differences in the number of farms relates to the clear size disparities between farms and the areas of farmland they manage. In Czechia, an average farm has over 130 hectares of farmland at its disposal, with land made use of almost exclusively by entities operating on the larger scale. A similar situation applies in Slovakia. In contrast, in Poland, the breakdown of data for areas of farmland in farms of different size groups is more balanced, though this is not in fact a favourable circumstance. The large overall area

Table 10.1 Numbers of entities utilising agricultural land

Country/Year	2005	2007	2010	2013
Czechia	41,180	38,490	22,580	25,950
Hungary	662,370	565,950	534,020	453,090
Poland	2,465,830	2,380,120	1,498,660	1,421,560
Romania	4,121,250	3,851,790	3,724,330	3,563,770
Slovakia	66,360	66,520	23,720	22,050

Source: Eurostat.

Table 10.2 Areas of farmland managed, by farm-size category

Country/ size	less than 2 ha	2–5 ha	5–10 ha	10–20 ha	20–50 ha	50–100 ha	100 ha or over
Czechia	1,820	3,990	29,390	55,590	138,180	169,360	3,085,160
Hungary	138,000	142,670	183,910	268,840	472,980	445,860	3,034,080
Poland	474,910	1,529,270	2,387,340	3,010,790	2,779,080	1,145,010	3,120,900
Romania	1,718,360	2,229,930	1,210,510	571,390	549,250	518,300	6,508,390
Slovakia	9,270	19,120	18,150	22,860	44,190	55,430	1,726,490

Source: Eurostat.

managed by farms in the small size category (covering less than 5 hectares) is for the most part used with only limited efficiency. In Romania, in turn, changes of ownership have given rise to a situation in which mean farm size is of less than 4 hectares, while at the same time around half of all land is utilised by large farms in the size category above 100 hectares. In this case, the value for average farm size is purely theoretical, as the breakdown of farms by size is highly polarised into the two groups of below 2 hectares or 2–5 hectares on the one hand, and in excess of 100 hectares on the other.

Summary

Through to the early 1990s, the farm economy of Central European countries other than Poland and Yugoslavia was entirely dominated by the socialised sector. Agriculture at the level of individual ownership was only of marginal importance. However, in the last decade of the 20th century, the sectors in countries other than Poland underwent total change. Enterprises remaining from the communist era disappeared, while a large number of private owners came back into existence. The most visible effect of this was for the fragmentation of land to proceed far further, albeit with this involving ownership or use, depending on the country.

It is reasonable to consider that, while the countries under analysis took up similar concepts when it came to the privatisation and restitution of land assets, the results proved very different. Adoption of a family-farm model of organisation of the kind known from Western countries could not be regarded as much of a success, while it was large agricultural enterprises that eventually proved most efficient, successfully transitioning from the communist system to the market one.

In the cases of Czechia, Slovakia and in part Hungary, it is possible to speak of major differences between those who actually own land and those who use it. Most farmland is managed by large businesses, while at the same time being under the ownership of a large group of small-scale owners. In Czechia and Slovakia, changes in the agricultural sector did not denote major change in the agrarian structure – a circumstance that may be seen as positive. In contrast, in

Hungary, there was an increase in the number of small farms associated with dispersed cultivated fields. A situation involving two extreme circumstances then began to take hold, with small farms of just a few hectares on the one hand and large production holdings on the other. Farms of the first category have small areas of land at their disposal and tend to play only a minor role where output is concerned. They are nevertheless of considerable social importance to rural areas, given the way they stabilise the labour market and safeguard at least minimal incomes. Farms of the second category are, of course, limited in number compared to the family-owned holdings, but they nevertheless account for a majority share of all the farmland and of agricultural production. The transformation in Romania was, in turn, characterised by far-reaching fragmentation of both ownership and land use, with the result that the situation in the agricultural sector became critical. In Poland, the privatisation process was more regional in nature, with limited changes in central and southern parts, as well as the generation of large individually run farms in the north, in the areas where State Farms had previously operated.

The polarisation of the agrarian structure and strong pressure for some land to be given over to other economic functions encouraged a decline in the area under agriculture, as well as a change in the proportions of arable farmland, with more land used for permanent crops or grasslands). A decline in the proportion of all land given over to farming was noted in all of the countries studied. The changes in farmland structure observed headed in various directions, but attested overall to an extensification of cultivation.

Acknowledgement

Publication prepared under the research projects of the National Science Centre, nb. UMO-2016/23/B/HS4/00421, *Models of Agriculture Transformation in the Countries of Central and Eastern Europe after the Fall of the Eastern Bloc – Review of Achievements, Determinants and Development Scenarios.*

Note

1 The unit used traditionally in Hungary to assess the quality of farmland.

References

Balteanu, D., & Popovici, E. (2010). Land use changes and land degradation in post-socialist Romania. *Romanian Journal of Geography*, 54(2), 95–105.

Bandlerova, A., & Marisova, E. (2003). Importance of ownership and lease of agricultural land in Slovakia in the pre-accession period. *Agricultural Economics*, 49(5), 213–216.

Bański, J. (ed.) (2010). *Atlas of Polish Agriculture*. Warszawa: Institute of Geography and Spatial Organization PAS.

Bański, J. (2011). Changes in agricultural land ownership in Poland in the period of the market economy. *Agricultural Economics*, 57(2), 93–101.

Bański, J., Ilieva, M., & Iliev, I. (1999). Agricultural Land Use in Bulgaria and Poland – An Attempt at a Comparison. *Problems of Geography*, 1–2, s.69–76, Sofia.

Bański, J. (2017). The consequences of changes of ownership for agricultural land use in Central European countries following the collapse of the Eastern Bloc. *Land Use Policy*, 66, 120–130.

Basek, V., & Divila, E. (2008). Struktura czeskich gospodarstw rolnych – dziś i jutro, [in:] *Dziś i jutro gospodarstw rolnych w krajach Centralnej i Wschodniej Europy*, Prace IERiGŻ, 98, 53–66, Warszawa.

Benedek, J. (2000). Land reform in Romania after 1989: Towards market oriented agriculture? In: P. Tillack & E. Schulze (eds.), *Land Ownership, Land Markets and their Influence on the Efficiency of Agricultural Production in Central and Eastern Europe*. Halle/Saale: IAMO.

Bicik, I., & Jelecek, L. (2009). Land use and landscape changes in Chechia during the period of transition 1990–2007. *Geografie*, 114(4), 263–281.

Brouwer, F., Thomas, J., & Chadwick, M. (1991). *Land Use Change in Europe: Processes of Change, Environmental Transformations and Future Patterns*. Springer Sciences + Business Media.

Burger, A. (2006). Why is the issue of land ownership still of major concern in East Central European (ECE) transitional countries and particularly in Hungary? *Land Use Policy*, 23, 571–579.

FAOSTAT glossary (2013). Glossary of Environment Statistics, *Studies in Methods, Series F*, No. 67, United Nations, New York, 1997.

Gajdos, P. (2005). Marginal regions in Slovakia and their developmental disposabilities. *Agricultural Economics*, 51(12), 555–563.

Giovarelli, R., & Bledsoe, D. (2001). Land Reform in Eastern Europe, FAO.

Glossary of Statistical Terms (2003). OECD, https://stats.oecd.org/glossary.

Hartvigsen, M. (2013). Land reform in Central and Eastern Europe after 1989 and Its Outcome in the Form of Farm Structures and Land Fragmentation, *Land Tenure Working Paper* No. 24, FAO.

Hartvigsen, M. (2014). Land mobility in a Central and Eastern European land consolidation context. *Nordic Journal of Surveying and Real Estate Research*, 10(1), 23–46.

Historia Polski w liczbach. Rolnictwo. Leśnictwo (1991). Warszawa.

Janku, J., Sekac, P., Barakova, J., & Kozak, J. (2016). Land use analysis in terms of farmland protection in the Czech Republic. *Soil and Water Resources*, 11(1), 20–28.

Land concentration, land grabbing and people's struggles in Europe (2013). Transnational Institute (TNI) for European Coordination Via Campesina and Hands off the Land network, FIAN.

Kovacs, T. (2005). Restructuring agriculture. In: G. Barta, E. Fekete, I. Szorenyine & J. Timar (eds.), *Hungarian Space and Places: Patterns of Transition*. Pecs: Centre for Regional Studies, pp. 259–271.

Lerman, Z., et al. (2004). *Agriculture in Transition – Land Policies and Evolving Farm Structures in Post-Soviet Countries*. Lexington Books.

Popovici, E., Balteanu, D., & Kucsicsa, G. (2013). Assessment of changes in land-use and land-cover pattern in Romania using Corine land cover database. *Carpathian Journal of Earth and Environmental Sciences*, 8(4), 195–208.

Popp, J., & Stauder, M. (2003). Land market in Hungary. *Agricultural Economics*, 49(4), 173–178.

Sadowski, A., & Takacs-György, K. (2005). Results of agricultural reform: Land use and land reform in Poland and Hungary. *Studies in Agricultural Economics*, 103, 53–70, Budapest.

Strelecek, F., Jelinek, L., Lososova, J., & Zdenek, R. (2011). Relationship between the land rent and agricultural land prices in the Czech Republic. *Statistica*, 48(2), 49–59.

Swain, N. (1985). *Collective Farms Which Work*. Cambridge: Cambridge University Press.

Takacs, I. (2008). Longitudinal analysis of changing partial efficiency of assets in the EU agriculture at the beginning of the new 21st century. *Annals of the Polish Association of Agricultural and Agribusiness Economists*, 10(5), 149–154.

Toth-Naar, Z., Molnar, M., & Vinogradov, S. (2014). Impact of land use changes on land value in Hungary. *Roczniki Naukowe, Stowarzyszenie Ekonomistów Rolnictwa i Agrobiznesu*, 16(6), 500–504.

Turnock, D. (1989). *Eastern Europe: An Economic and Political Geography*. London: Routledge.

Zadura, A. (2005). Zarządzanie gruntami rolnymi w krajach Europy Środkowo-Wschodniej, Ekonomiczne i społeczne uwarunkowania rozwoju polskiej gospodarki żywnościowej po wstąpieniu Polski do Unii Europejskiej, 6, Program wieloletni 2005–2009, IERiGŻ PIB, Warszawa.

Zgliński, W. (2003). Skutki transformacji Państwowych Gospodarstw Rolnych w ujęciu przestrzennym. In: A. Stasiak (ed.), *Przemiany zagospodarowania terenów wiejskich w Polsce*. Biuletyn KPZ.

11 Transport infrastructure and accessibility

Tomasz Komornicki

Introduction: methods and data

This chapter presents the conditions and state of development of transport networks that existed at the very beginning of the transition period in Central and Eastern Europe, and the changes that took place during 1990–2015, as well as their multifold consequences. The analysis is focused on road and railway networks. A description of investment measures co-financed by the European Union structural funds is provided. The effects of new investment projects are evaluated with the use of accessibility indicators. The chapter is based on the results of international projects (inter alia ESPON TRACC, GRINCOCH; Komornicki 2013a) and projects financed from national sources (EURODAC).[1]

One of the aims of the debate that has been launched is to answer the question: to what extent has the state and pace of development of transport infrastructure constituted a barrier hampering transformation processes – or, on the contrary, a factor accelerating it.

The analysis is conducted for two periods: (a) the pre-accession transformation (until the year 2004) and (b) the years after the major EU enlargement. In the first case, analysis was based primarily on the literature on the subject, while in the second case, comparable statistical data and the results of empirical studies – especially those related to changes in spatial accessibility – were used. The spatial scope of this study encompasses the new member countries of the EU, whose entry to the European Union took place in 2004 and 2007. Croatia is also partly accounted for (accession in 2012), but this was not always possible due to the unavailability of comparable data.

Methodology and data sources

The study is based on a variety of research methods which were applied earlier in the studies and projects quoted. The method of potential accessibility, considered as an objective measure of the state of development of infrastructure in the region of Central Europe, is among the most important of these. Potential accessibility is based on the negative exponential distance-decay function which produces the well-known potential accessibility indicator. The closer the opportunity (mass of each other region), the more it contributes to accessibility. The larger the opportunity, the more it influences accessibility. The travel time between any pair of transport zones was calculated by applying the method of identifying the shortest travel routes according to Dijkstra's algorithm (Hansen 1959; Geurs and Eck 2001).

The basic feature of potential accessibility is the fact that the attractiveness of a destination increases along with its size and decreases with the elongation of physical, time and economic distance:

where:

$$A_i = \sum_j f_1(M_j) f_2(c_{i_j})$$

A_i – transport accessibility of a unit (transport district) i,
M_j – masses available in unit (transport district) j,
c_{ij} – total time distance linked with travel/transportation services from transport district i to transport district j (Stępniak and Rosik 2013; Rosik et al. 2015)

The potential accessibility was calculated for various sets of units. Most frequently these were the NUTS3 units, as in the study for the European Union (Spiekermann et al. 2013), or the entire continent of Europe (Rosik et al. 2018).

In the GRINCOH project, the simple measure of timewise accessibility was used. Analysis concerned the shortening of travel time due to the realisation of transportation projects between the main metropolises of the region. In other studies (ESPON FOCI), the measure of so-called daily accessibility was applied, defining (in a binary manner) the possibility of a single-day round trip using public transport between the pairs of towns for a definite set of towns.

The chapter refers to commonly available data from EUROSTAT, and to the databases developed within the framework of GRINCOH and ESPON TRACC projects, as well as the databases owned by the Institute of Geography and Spatial Organization of the Polish Academy of Sciences.

Pre-accession period (1990–2004)

During the period of the centrally planned socialist economy, the transport infrastructure of the countries of Central and Eastern Europe functioned in quite specific demand conditions. The main prerequisite for making new investments was satisfying the needs of heavy industries, and partly also of the military. A strongly pronounced concentration of cargo, as well as passenger transport could be observed, resulting, in particular, from the existence of large state enterprises. The directions of international transport were determined by the existence of the Iron Curtain, which resulted in high numbers of transhipments between both Baltic and Black Sea ports. The existing overland transport infrastructure, based largely on railways, satisfied the demand at the time. Railroads were systematically electrified. Efforts were also made to avoid undue wear of assets. Until the very point of collapse of the socialist system, new railway lines were also being built (such as the Polish Central Railway Route, connecting the industrial concentration in the south with the Baltic ports of Gdańsk and Gdynia; however, this route has not yet been completed). Concerning road transport, local roads were given hard surfaces on a large scale (e.g. in eastern Poland, in Romania and in Bulgaria). Eastern Germany and partly also western Poland were still using the heavily worn down pre-war German motorway network. During the 1970s, some countries of the region started to modernise their road networks. The first new motorways were built in then Czechoslovakia (between Prague and Bratislava) and in Hungary (between Budapest and the Balaton Lake). In other countries, dual carriageways were built, although did not meet the standards of true motorways (in Poland, between Warsaw and Upper Silesia; in the Soviet Union, in the Belarus SSR). The investment projects slowed down with the economic crisis, which appeared in the majority of these countries during the 1980s. In Poland, these projects came to a complete halt.

The systemic transformation, which started in 1989, caused an abrupt change in the conditions in which the transport systems of the Central and Eastern European countries functioned. This change was expressed, first of all, through:

- A shift in the directions of foreign trade from the countries of the region towards Western Europe (indirectly also due to transit across some of these countries, such as Poland);
- A return to the natural patterns of the seaport catchments (e.g. transfer of Czech cargoes to Hamburg), which initially weakened the position of the Baltic ports located in the new Member States;
- The appearance of new geopolitical barriers due to war in the former Yugoslavia, which influenced the directions of transit not only from Bulgaria, but also from Greece and Turkey;
- De-concentration of production due to structural changes (the frequent collapse of large state-owned enterprises, technological changes), as well to institutional changes (the emergence of many small private firms), which ultimately led to the dispersion of both cargo and passenger traffic (in this last case also because of the spatial dispersion of jobs);
- A massive increase in private car ownership as a reaction to the earlier constraints in this domain (Komornicki 2003), but also as a natural consequence of the dispersion of travel directions and generally increased mobility;
- Deterioration in the economic situation of some public transport operators (lifted subventions, increased competition).

The existing transport infrastructure could not cope with the new challenges mentioned above. The transport system proved to be too inflexible with respect to the systemic transformations. The scale of problems involved was, however, different in the particular countries of the region. Problems were relatively bigger in Poland (mainly because of the deeper and faster de-concentration of the economy) and in the countries of the former USSR (especially in the Baltic republics, where the shift in trade directions was even more drastic). Meanwhile, in Czechia, Slovakia, Hungary and Slovenia railway transport, and mass passenger transport in general, retained a stronger position. In the very same countries, the investment process in transport was not interrupted. During the 1990s, especially in Slovenia and Hungary, new elements of road infrastructure were still being constructed (already partly in cooperation with private concessionaries). Other countries, including Poland, Romania and the Baltic states, which faced budgetary problems, had difficulties disbursing even small amounts for new investment projects. With time, as the perspective of EU membership became clearer, these countries adopted the tacit strategy of waiting for means from the European Union.

The change in the directions of economic relations, mentioned several times before, did not result in the immediate modifications of the investment plans. There was definite inertia as regards spatial planning in the transport domain (Komornicki 2005). The so-called Pan-European Corridors, determined at the beginning of the 1990s (the basis for the future pattern of the TEN-T network in Central and Eastern Europe) were largely a repetition of earlier plans, elaborated well before 1990. The role of transit as a growth factor for the regions was overestimated. It was not recognised that, after the expansion of the European Union, its outer boundary would become a strongly formalised spatial barrier (Rykiel 1990; Komornicki 1999). Essential modifications with respect to the earlier designs concerned the Via Baltica route (the need to connect the Baltic states with the EU) and transport links in the Balkans (the establishment of alternatives for the traditional corridor of Zagreb-Belgrade-Thessaloniki).

On the eve of accession to the European Union, the network of motorways and expressways was very unevenly developed in the countries of Central and Eastern Europe. It was definitely the best in Slovenia, followed by Czechia and Hungary. These three countries had already started the construction of motorways before 1989 and continued their construction during the pre-accession transformation period, which was not the case in the remaining countries of the region. Owing to this fact, the road networks of the three countries became connected with the networks of western European countries (the routes: Ljubljana-Vienna, Ljubljana-Venice, Budapest-Vienna and Prague-Nuremberg). The Czech and Hungarian networks assumed a classic radial pattern, with the centres in the capital cities. In Poland, Slovakia, Romania and Bulgaria, only the beginnings of the respective motorway/expressway networks functioned, while in Latvia and Estonia there were practically no such networks at all.

Road transport after 2004

In all the countries of the region, road transport strengthened its position after the transformation as the most important branch of transport. Its domination was usually greater in passenger traffic than in cargo (where railways retained a more pronounced position). Besides this, there was a gradual increase in the role of air transport regarding passenger travel and a decrease in seaborne transport of cargo. The dynamic growth of private car ownership was one of the major causes of this modal shift.

The increase in car ownership in some Central European countries was far ahead of the rate of economic growth (compare with the chapter by Swianiewicz in this book). The increases in car ownership indices in some countries (especially in Poland, but also in Bulgaria and Romania) took place 'beyond capacities' (Komornicki 2011). With time, however, it became an expression of increasing mobility (job commuting, facultative mobility). After 2004, increments in car numbers generally slowed down (see Figure 11.1 and Table 11.1). In countries such as Hungary and Slovenia, the increase did not exceed 20% in the entire period 2005–16. Yet, a fast and virtually linear increase in the numbers of passenger cars could still be observed in Poland, Romania and Slovakia. One of the reasons for this was the uncontrolled inflow of used cars from Western Europe which followed after the accession to the EU. The automobile stock in some countries got older at that time. The fast increase in the numbers of passenger cars, however, was not followed by a parallel increase of road traffic: for instance, in 2005–10 in Poland, the overall traffic of motor vehicles on national roads increased by 22%, while during the next five-year period (2010–15) by only 16%. In 2016, the highest level of motorization was recorded in Poland, Slovenia and Estonia; definitely the lowest was in Hungary and Latvia (Table 11.1).

For the majority of countries in the region, the period after the accession did not bring any further shift of cargo movement towards road transport. The share of this means of transport dynamically increased during the first years of membership, but later on, due to the economic crisis, it fell to a level even lower than in 2005 (Figure 11.2 and Table 11.1). After 2010, a slow increase of road

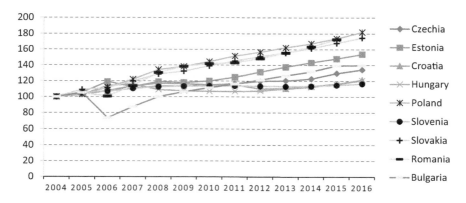

Figure 11.1 Private car ownership in the countries of Central Europe (2004–16)

Source: Eurostat.

Table 11.1 Transport flows and car ownership in Central Europe (2006–16)

Countries	Road cargo transport		Rail cargo transport		Car ownership		Air traffic	
	2016 (thous. tons)	increase 2006–16 (2006=100)	2016 (thous. tons)	increase 2006–16 (2006=100)	2016 (cars / 1,000 inhab.)	increase 2004–16 (2004=100)	2016 (passengers)	increase 2006–16 (2006=100)
Bulgaria	146,636	97	14,226	65	443	140	:	:
Czechia	431,889	97	98,034	101	502	134	13,672,362	112
Estonia	34,581	102	25,364	41	534	154	2,214,989	144
Hungary	197,759	79	50,047	91	338	121	11,668,151	142
Latvia	63,389	116	47,819	98	341	112	5,384,160	216
Lithuania	63,571	113	47,651	95	456	116	4,787,561	266
Poland	1,313,657	146	222,523	76	571	182	32,266,742	235
Romania	216,107	64	52,618	77	:	:	15,153,719	309
Slovakia	156,179	86	47,548	91	390	175	2,158,261	102
Slovenia	75,033	86	18,595	109	531	116	1,404,152	106

Source: Eurostat.

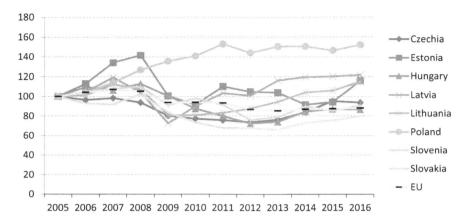

Figure 11.2 The dynamics of road cargo transport in the countries of Central Europe (2005–16)

Source: Eurostat.

cargo traffic could be observed. The level from 2005 was very clearly exceeded only in the Baltic states, which (especially Lithuania) developed a concentration of road transport operators on a European scale (Brach 2013). The strong position of Lithuanian carriers was originally built on knowledge of the former Soviet Union markets. After accession to the European Union, the car park was quickly modernized there. As a result, with simultaneous problems on the Russian market (the embargo on food), the operators successfully transferred part of their activities to Western Europe, where they carry out cabotage services. Moreover, due to tax regulations, some Polish transport companies registered their businesses in Lithuania.

A totally different situation was witnessed solely in Poland. Here, the financial crisis of 2008 did not result in a breakdown in road cargo transport (one has to remember that Poland avoided recession in this period). The traffic increased rapidly until 2011, when it stabilised at around 50% above the level just after accession. Polish road transport operators joined the group of leading operators in Europe, accounting in 2016 for 9.2% of the entire transport activity in the EU.

The previously described differentiation of the initial state (before 2004) determined the strategy of using EU funds in the successive financing periods. Countries like Hungary, Czechia and Slovenia aimed at completing their base networks, which often meant investing in the segments linking their networks with those of neighbouring countries. They also tried to eliminate the bottlenecks in their road systems. In this sense, the objectives of their road development policies were subordinated to the aims of EU transport policies (specified, for instance, in the White Paper 2001 and in the documents which set down the basis for the development of the TEN-T network). The situation of other countries was quite different. Delays in the realisation of investments were so severe that these countries tended to make maximum use of European funds for the realisation of basic segments, linking main urban centres or accommodating mass transit. In view of the bigger spatial scale of some countries (especially Poland and Romania), this also implied a dispersion of investment outlays.

In consequence, increases in the length of motorway networks were strongly differentiated in the years 2005–16 (see Figure 11.3 and Table 11.2). During the first years of membership, Hungary extended its network the most. In successive years (after 2008) the greatest increases took place in Poland, Romania (more than 300% increase) and to a lesser degree, Bulgaria. The increase observed in Czechia was associated with a change in status of the existing expressways to motorways. If we take Polish expressways into account, it would appear that the development of the network was the most spectacular in Poland (exceeding 500%).

When evaluating the geographical distribution of road projects co-financed by the EU (Map 11.1), it should be noted that they were more concentrated in the western part of the Central and Eastern Europe (Slovenia, Czechia, western Poland and western Slovakia). Owing to the implementation of these projects, an improvement took place in the integration of the fast road traffic networks of these countries with the networks of the 'old' Member States (new connections were built between Poland and Germany, and between Czechia and Germany, and the construction of the Czech-Austrian and Bulgarian-Greek connections is well advanced). There was also an improvement in the mutual

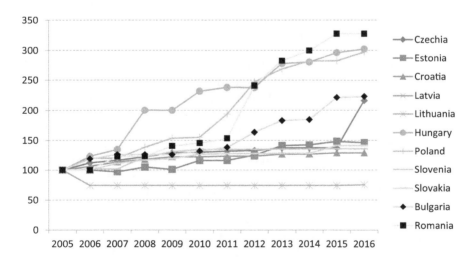

Figure 11.3 Length of the motorway networks in the countries of Central Europe (2005 = 100)

Source: Eurostat.

Table 11.2 Transport infrastructure in Central Europe (2006–16)

Countries	Motorways		Railways	
	2016 (km)	increase 2006–16 (2006 = 100)	2016 (km)	increase 2006–16 (2006 = 100)
Bulgaria	740	188	4,029	97
Croatia	1,310	121	2,604	96
Czechia	1,223	193	9,564	100
Estonia	145	146	1,161	97
Hungary	1,924	245	7,811	96
Latvia	:	:	1,860	82
Lithuania	314	102	1,911	108
Poland	1,640	247	19,132	95
Romania	747	328	10,774	100
Slovakia	463	141	3,206	88
Slovenia	773	134	1,209	98

Source: Eurostat.

integration of the networks of some of the accession countries (first of all between Poland and Czechia, Hungary and Slovenia, as well as Hungary and Romania), also including connections with Croatia.

Altogether, considering the support from European funds for the development of the motorway/expressway network in CEE countries (2004–15), it could be said that from the point of view of internal cohesion of primary centres in individual countries, this support was most effective in Poland, Czechia and Bulgaria. At the same time, as far as connections with the 'old' Member States are concerned, the greatest progress was observed in all the countries analysed, except for the Baltic states. Owing to their own as well as Hungarian investment projects, the peripherally located Romania became an undoubted beneficiary in these terms. Visible progress must also be acknowledged regarding Polish-German connections. Investments in the road infrastructure, made during the period 2004–15, were also beneficial for Croatia which was then preparing for EU membership. Among the countries not belonging to the Community, but taking advantage from the developments analysed here, we should mention Ukraine and Turkey. In absolute terms, in 2016 Hungary, Poland, the Czechia and Croatia had the longest network of motorways (Table 11.2). In the case of Poland, however, the statistics do not include expressways, the standard of which is close to motorways.

In the current financial perspective (2014–20) the largest means for developing transport infrastructure have again been assigned to Poland. It is now expected, in particular, that the expressway be completed on the basic TEN-T corridor North Sea – Baltic Sea (Via Baltica). A further useful financial instrument, supporting international connections, has been the CEF (Connecting Europe Facility) mechanism.

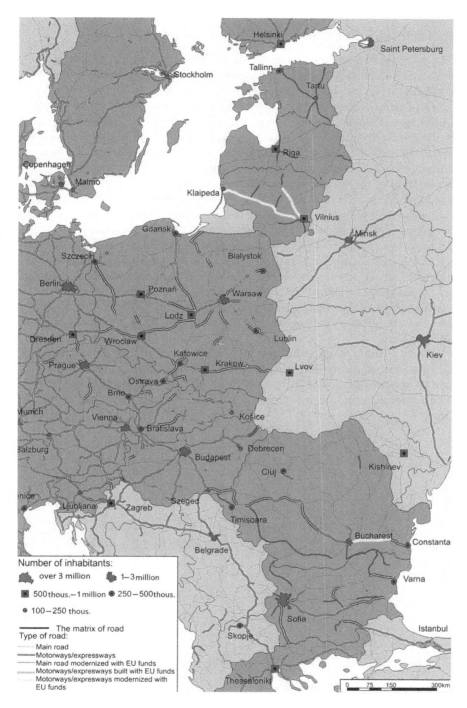

Number of inhabitants:

- over 3 million
- 1–3 million
- 500 thous.–1 million
- 250–500 thous.
- 100–250 thous.

The matrix of road
Type of road:
- Main road
- Motorways/expressways
- Main road modernized with EU funds
- Motorways/expressways built with EU funds
- Motorways/expressways modernized with EU funds

Map 11.1 Investments in motorways and expressways co-financed by the European Union in the years 2004–15

Rail transport after 2004

The role of railways in cargo transport increased in the majority of the analysed countries immediately after their accession to the European Union (Figure 11.4 and Table 11.1). Exceptions were Latvia and Estonia, where the general significance of railways remained low. The biggest increase was observed in Czechia. In the case of Poland, despite the overall rapid increase in transport flows, rail traffic grew only marginally. In subsequent years there was a slowdown in the entire region, associated with the economic crisis. Thus, in 2009 in all countries, rail cargo transport was smaller than in 2005. The following years brought a differentiation of the situations across the region. In 2016 it was only in Czechia and Slovenia that the intensity of transport was noticeably higher than 11 years earlier (by approximately 15%). In the majority of countries stagnation reigned, meaning, in fact, a decrease in the relative role of railways. A slow, systematic decrease of rail transport flows was observed in Poland, Romania and Croatia, and a total collapse in Estonia. Reasons for the weakening position of rail freight transport include (1) less flexibility of this mode of transport, combined with a differentiated structure; (2) faster development of road infrastructure in the first years after accession to the EU; (3) the strong position of road carriers in some countries of the region; and (4) a decrease in the transport of some bulk goods.

The described changes did not alter the fact that in 2016, the largest rail cargo transport was recorded in Poland (22 million tons; Table 11.1). Relative to the size of the country, they were also very significant in Czechia. The importance of rail in the transport of goods in Bulgaria was by far the smallest.

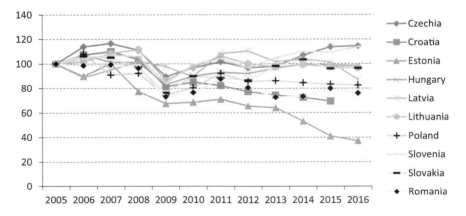

Figure 11.4 Dynamics of cargo transport by railways in Central and Eastern Europe (2005 = 100)

Source: Eurostat.

The financial scale of railway investment projects was smaller than in the case of the road projects. At the same time, many of the rail projects were very costly. It is hard to identify the exact nature of the necessary investments. The majority of projects were devoted to the modernisation of existing networks, mainly aimed at adapting them to higher train speeds. Virtually no new lines were built (the sole exception, in practical terms, being the Latvian projects: the connection to the new seaport and construction of second tracks). In the majority of countries modernisation encompassed one or several longer railway routes, most frequently along the directions of the TEN-T corridors (see Map 11.2). A large proportion of the modernised lines served the domestic connections within particular CEE countries. This was the case of all projects in Lithuania, Estonia and Slovakia, as well as the majority of Polish projects. Regarding connections to the old member countries of the EU, a significant role was played by reconstructions of routes from Poland and Czechia to Germany, and from Hungary towards Austria. The longest railway routes (corridors), whose important sections were subject to modernisation were: the corridor crossing southern Poland (from the border with Germany, through Cracow, to the border with Ukraine), and the route from Vienna through Budapest towards Bucharest. There were also long lines inside Bulgaria (from Sofia to the Black Sea coast and towards the Turkish border) and within Poland (from Warsaw to Gdańsk).

In 2016, Poland, Romania and Czechia had the longest railway networks (Table 11.2). In the period 2006–16, the length of the lines only increased in Lithuania, and did not change in Czechia and Romania. In the remaining countries of Central Europe, the network was still slowly shrinking.

In the current financial perspective (2014–20), the European Union has assigned higher financial resources to the construction and modernisation of railroad infrastructure as compared to road infrastructure. Modernisation is supposed to be performed first of all on the main routes along the primary TEN-T corridors.

In summing up the spatial distribution of the investment projects in railroads supported by the European Union and their effectiveness, it should be noted that the projects undertaken were almost exclusively aimed at modernisations; none of the CEE countries decided to use EU resources to finance an important new railway line (including high speed lines). The scale of the modernisation was very differentiated, as was the initial technical state of particular railway routes, and this bore an influence on the ultimate effect in terms of improved accessibility in certain directions. Projects of domestic importance dominated, but many of them contributed, at the same time, to a significant shortening of travel times between the metropolises in neighbouring countries. There was an improvement in the mutual railway accessibility between the cities of the Visegrád Group countries (southern Poland, Czechia, Slovakia, Hungary) and Slovenia, while at the same time the railroad systems of the Baltic states and of Bulgaria and Romania remained isolated from the remaining parts of the region, and hence also from the entire European Union.

Number of inhabitants:

🐛 over 3 million   🐛 1–3 million

■ 500 thous.–1 million   ● 250–500 thous.

● 100–250 thous.

⸺ Railway lines

⸺ Rail projects

0   75   150   300km

Map 11.2 Railway-related investments, co-financed by the European Union in the years 2004–13

Air transport after 2004

Accession of the CEE countries to the European Union meant a very pronounced intensification of traffic in airports (Figure 11.5). This was first associated with the deregulation of the respective market and the appearance of the low-cost airlines. The increase in demand related to migration (the opening of labour markets in Western Europe) and tourism was also of great importance. The increases in air traffic were not evenly spread throughout the region. Unquestionably the largest occurred in Poland, Hungary, Lithuania and Latvia. In Poland and in the Baltic states, this can be explained by the scale of emigration (generating secondary journeys). In Hungary, an essential factor was the appearance and growth of its own low-cost operator (WizzAir). In addition, the increases in Lithuania and Latvia were also partly due to their peripheral location, while in Poland to the existence of a network of domestic airports and connections between them. In 2016, the largest air passenger traffic was noted in Poland (32 million; Table 11.1). However, in relation to the number of inhabitants, the number of air transport users was higher in Czechia and Hungary.

Consequently, in both successive financing periods, emphasis was placed on the development of airport infrastructure (both in terms of modernisation of runways and of passenger terminals). The only new airports which appeared with support from European Union funds in the CEE countries were the Polish airports of Lublin and Modlin (in both cases a part of the previously existing airfield infrastructure was used, having served different purposes before). In addition, numerous modernisations and the construction of new terminals were carried out. These concerned almost all the airports in Poland, the facilities located in the Baltic states (capital city airports and the airport in Kaunas) and Ljubljana, Budapest and Sofia.

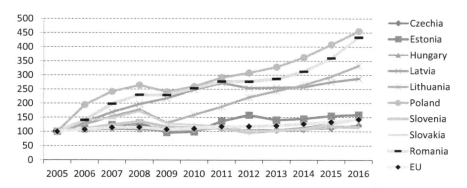

Figure 11.5 Passenger air traffic in the countries of Central Europe (2005–16)

Source: Eurostat.

The investments into air transport infrastructure increased the network of connections of several airports. In the larger ones (Warsaw, Budapest, Sofia), the outlays increased the throughput of runways and terminals, allowing for the opening of new connections and improvement of service quality. In the facilities of regional character (mainly in Poland), these investments primarily benefited the low-cost carriers, catering to the traffic towards the countries that became the main destinations for migrants seeking work (the United Kingdom, Norway, Ireland), and also the traditional airlines, transporting passengers to the hubs in Western Europe. The increase of tourist passenger traffic was also one of factors which influenced air transport in the CEE. However, several projects did not contribute to a significant intensification of traffic, and the economic profitability of these projects and of their respective facilities remains questionable.

Accessibility changes

The best measure which illustrates the changes in the transport connections between territorial units is provided by the potential accessibility indicator (described in the methodology sub-chapter). Studies of this kind of accessibility on the European scale have been conducted for several years already, mainly by German teams (Spiekermann, Schurmann 2007), and also for the purposes of the ESPON projects (1.2.1., 1.1.3, ESPON, SeGI, FOCCI). In addition, some countries (e.g. Poland and Czechia) carry out this kind of analyses for their territories.

In 2001, almost the entire area of the CEE countries was characterised by relatively low values of the multimodal potential accessibility.[2] Higher values of the accessibility index (over 120% of the average for the ESPON space) were noted mainly in some capital cities, owing to the larger airports located there (Prague, Warsaw, Budapest), and in Bratislava (in the neighbourhood of Vienna). In northern Romania, central Bulgaria, and in part of territory of the Baltic states, the values of the index fell below 40% of the average for the ESPON space. It is important to note that, on the cartographic image, the infrastructural routes inside the CEE countries are almost invisible. The image is, therefore, strongly shaped by the very geographical distance from the European Core Area (the so-called Pentagon). The sole significant disturbance to this pattern arises from the presence of airports. This is understandable insofar as the quality of the surface transport over the entire area considered – with the exception of fragments of territories in Czechia and Hungary – was uniformly low.

The spatial pattern of the index values for the year 2012 is distinctly different (Map 11.3), this being partly due to the effects of investment supported by EU funds. However, interpretation of these results ought to allow for the impact of

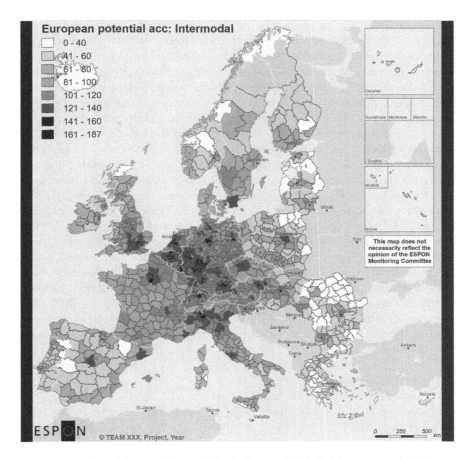

Map 11.3 Multimodal potential accessibility in Europe (2012) (Spiekermann at al. 2012)

other factors on changes in the spatial distribution of values in the multimodal potential accessibility index. These other factors include, in particular:

- Changes in the distribution of masses (migration of people to a greater extent heading to the larger cities in each country);
- Deregulation, decentralisation and, consequently, development of air transport, strengthening the centres equipped with airports (also those of regional character);
- Improvement of accessibility in other regions of Europe, influencing the average value of the index to which the results relate.

Despite these reservations, it is possible to identify certain effects of the development of a linear infrastructure in the inter-metropolitan setting within the CEE area. The image obtained indicates a distinctly greater polarisation in terms of potential accessibility within CEE, as well as in particular countries. The boundaries between the old and new Member States are clearly less visible. In the case of western Czechia, western Slovakia, northern Hungary and north-western Poland, connectivity to the zones of good accessibility in Germany and Austria improved. The spatial distribution of the values in the accessibility index for the remaining countries is still characterised by the existence of 'islands' of better accessibility. Side by side with Warsaw, such islands are also manifested – to an even higher degree than before – in Bucharest and Sofia, and also in the capitals of the Baltic states, as well as some Polish centres (especially the region of Cracow and Upper Silesia), as well as Romanian centres. Some NUTS3 units, including cities such as Timisoara, Klaipeda, Wroclaw and Gdansk, distinguish themselves against the background of the surroundings. Some of the transport corridors into which significant funds from the European Union were invested are also clearly visible. This applies, in particular, to two parallel corridors in Poland (Warsaw-Berlin and Dresden-Cracow-Ukraine border, with investments, in both cases, into railway and road infrastructure). Altogether, an improvement in the relative level of multimodal accessibility on the European level – which could be brought about, in particular, through investments supported by EU funds – took place in the following areas of the CEE countries (Komornicki 2013a):

• Western Lithuania
• Northern Poland (Gdansk region)
• Southern Poland (the belt from Wroclaw up to the Ukrainian border)
• Western Czechia
• North-eastern Czechia (Ostrava region)
• Western Hungary
• Western Romania
• Western Bulgaria (the capital region).

At the same time, more distinctly than at the beginning of the preceding decade, there are the least accessible zones for which the relative level of multimodal accessibility even decreased. These are:

• Northern Romania (where there were no EU supported investment projects)
• South-western Bulgaria (despite the investment projects undertaken)
• North-eastern Poland (despite the investment projects undertaken).

A different measure of accessibility is constituted by so-called daily accessibility, which corresponds to the possibility of a daily return journey in metropolitan settings (Komornicki 2013b, ESPON FOCI Final Report) using public transportation. The CEE area is handicapped in this respect. In particular, there are very few pairs of cities mutually accessible within one day using railway transport. This number includes a couple of Polish cities (with connections to Berlin), Czech cities (with connection to Dresden), as well as Bratislava and Budapest (with connections to Vienna). Besides these, daily accessibility exists between Ljubljana and Zagreb. In Romania and Bulgaria, as well as in the Baltic states, no pair of metropolises is mutually accessible on a daily basis by rail (regarding the two first countries, the same applies to air transport).

The changes in daily accessibility that can be attributed to the intervention of the European Union can hardly be assessed unambiguously. It can be assumed that, due to investments made into railways, conditions for such changes have been provided (their actual realisation also ultimately depending upon the organisational factor), thereby securing overland, public daily connections between

- Warsaw and Gdansk
- Prague and Munich
- Budapest and Ljubljana.

Investments into airports might contribute to improved daily accessibility for the smaller capital city centres (the capitals of the Baltic states, Ljubljana and Sofia). In the cases of the remaining regional airports (especially in Poland) such an improvement can hardly be expected, in view of the structure of airborne traffic at these airports.

The most recent analysis of road accessibility (for the year 2015; Rosik et al. 2017) shows the effects of changes, both for the of the pre-accession period and for the later period, carried out with the use of European Union funds (Map 11.4). This analysis demonstrates that the zone of good accessibility (surrounding the 'Pentagon' of the European Union) already encompasses entire Slovenia and Czechia as well as western Slovakia, western Hungary and southwestern Poland. At the same time, this study confirms the existence of strong territorial polarisation (more pronounced than before) in the domain of accessibility. This polarisation exists both at the level of the entire macro region and inside particular countries. This is a natural consequence of undertaking large transport-related investment projects, and, simultaneously, evidence that the respective activities have not yet been finalised.

The results of the analysis confirm the fact that, for Central Europe, the main determinant of the level of accessibility is constituted by the location (and infrastructural connection) with respect to the core of the European Union. Other poles that might potentially exert influence on this area are the Russian agglomerations (Moscow and Saint Petersburg), as well as Istanbul. It is only in the latter case, however, that a true influence can be identified on the territory of Bulgaria by connections with Turkey. The influence of the Russian agglomerations (also those in Belarus and Ukraine) is completely marginal in view of their magnitude, the geographical distance, and the poorly permeable outer boundary of the European Union.

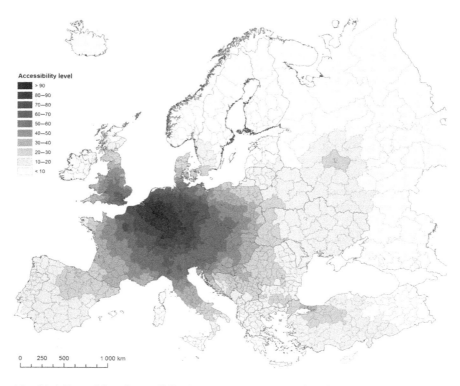

Map 11.4 Potential road accessibility in Europe in 2015 (Rosik at al. 2018)

Conclusions

The transport system of the countries of Central and Eastern Europe was extensively developed during the period of the centrally planned socialist economy, and it was not prepared for the systemic transformation of the year 1989. The situation was somewhat better only in Czechia, Hungary and Slovenia (partly owing to their geographical location). The dynamic economic development which began in the majority of these countries in the 1990s was to some degree slowed down by the state and the inadequacy of their transport infrastructure. The role of this factor was, however, moderate, given the scale of the unused reserves and resources, as well as other factors regarding the location of FDI and other investments (supply from privatised enterprises, cheap labour force). It was only in later years, as the simple factors of growth became exhausted, that the infrastructural issues (and hence also transport accessibility) started to gain in significance. Undertaking significant investment effort (especially after accession to the European Union) brought differentiation in the levels of accessibility, with a clear distinction between the 'winners' and the 'losers'.

In this sense, despite the significant improvement observed in all countries, accessibility became a factor contributing to economic polarisation. Hence, it can be stated that in the initial period (immediately after the transformation), the negative role of the inappropriate transport infrastructure was smaller that might have been expected. The condition of the infrastructure slowed down economic development, but to a lesser extent than it would have done without parallel rapid transformation processes. In the second phase of transformation (after the year 2004), this negative role of inappropriate infrastructure increased relatively with respect to the peripheral areas, where the scale of the new transport investment projects was more limited.

The inadequacy of infrastructure to the systemic transformations also exerted influence on the situation of societies in the countries under study. In conjunction with mass car ownership, it caused an increase in distance and travel time to work and to several services. At the same time, the worsening of the public transport service (in areas where low demand did not ensure profitability for carriers) brought local transport-related social exclusion, which made coping with social problems in marginalised areas even more difficult.

The situation described was obviously differentiated between particular countries. We can group these countries, roughly, into the following types.

Type A: Czechia, Slovakia, Slovenia. Countries with a well-developed infrastructure as of 1989 and with a relatively slow rate of change in the transformation period (moderate increases in traffic, preservation of the role of railways and of the technical state of the earlier infrastructure, the relatively smaller scope of transport-related projects supported with funds from the European Union). Transport accessibility has not significantly limited their economic development, nor has it led to transport-related exclusion on any major scale.

Type B: Hungary. A country with a well-developed infrastructure as of 1989, dynamically developing its road infrastructure during the period of transformation (in the concessionary system and with the use of EU funds), characterised, simultaneously, by moderate increases in traffic and by fast growth of car ownership and very pronounced dynamics in the air transport market. Transport accessibility has not significantly limited the possibilities of economic development, nor has it brought transport-related exclusion on a major scale.

Type C: Poland. A country with a less developed infrastructure as of 1989, in which there occurred a spectacular increase in road and air transport, an extreme load of heavy road transit, an unprecedented explosion of car ownership, significant wear and shortening of the railway network, and very fast development of infrastructure after the year 2004 (beginning with new road infrastructure). Transport accessibility underwent a significant polarisation and started to play the role of a development barrier in some regions, with the local appearance of transport-related social exclusion.

Type D: Lithuania, Latvia and Estonia. Countries with a less developed and spatially inadequate infrastructure as of 1989, in which there was a rapid increase in road and air traffic, with heavy loads of road transit, and a moderate scale of new investment projects.

Type E: Romania and Bulgaria. Countries with the least developed infrastructure in the year 1989, in which no big increase in traffic was observed, but where there was (although with a delay) a fast increase in car ownership and quite important new infrastructural investment projects were realised.

The investment projects, undertaken in the analysed countries (after 1989) increased the internal polarisation regarding accessibility and the broadly conceived transport situation. This increase of spatial polarisation took place both on the scale of the entire CEE macro region and inside the particular countries (especially the bigger ones, like Poland and Romania). This appears to be an unavoidable consequence of the wide program of investment undertakings (Komornicki 2013a).

In general, the projects carried out in railway transport were almost exclusively modernisations. Construction of longer new routes was not undertaken. The existing lines were modernised, as a rule, to accommodate speeds not exceeding 160 km/h (only in some cases on particular lines, 200 km/h). The CEE countries did not opt for constructing high speed railways. Meanwhile, the majority of the larger road projects were new developments (construction of motorways and expressways). In air transport, airport extensions dominated (most often new or improved objects within existing facilities).

The countries featuring an advanced level of transport network development concentrated on completing their road systems (Czechia, Hungary), or even moved the emphasis over to railway investments (Slovenia). The countries in which the transport infrastructure development delays were more serious conducted the policy of more dispersed investment in the spatial sense, and often also in the modal sense (Poland). Efforts were made to eliminate bottlenecks in both road and rail transport. As a result, despite the expending of significant funds, the network effect of new routes was not always generated.

Investment projects were mostly concentrated in the western part of the CEE area (Slovenia, Czechia, western Poland and western Slovakia) and, within the particular countries, also more frequently in their western parts. In this context, the investment process might be perceived in categories of diffusion of innovation (diffusion of modern transport systems) from Western Europe towards the new member States. This means, at the same time, that investment projects appeared to be more a response to the already existing demand (from cargo and passenger traffic) than they were used as an instrument of regional and/or spatial policy (support for peripheral areas which, in the majority of CEE countries, are concentrated in their eastern parts; Komornicki 2013a).

The investments realised contributed to better integration of the transport systems in CEE countries with the old member countries (mainly with Germany and Austria) and, to a somewhat lesser degree, to mutual integration between the accession countries (first of all regarding the connections of Hungary with its neighbours). Links across the external boundary of the European Union improved only in a couple of locations. The eastern boundary of the Union remained a barrier to the development of network connections between the metropolises of CEE countries.

Notes

1 The chapter is partly the result of research carried out under a grant financed by the Polish National Science Centre No. 2014/13/B/HS4/03397.
2 The analysis, here reported, made use of two studies, carried out according to a similar methodology in the framework of the ESPON 1.2.1 project (state as of 2001) and in the framework of the ESPON TRACC project (state as of 2012). In both cases, multimodal potential accessibility was analysed. The spatial reference unit was NUTS3, with the results being presented in the form of the indicator related to the European average (equivalent to the ESPON space). Complete comparability of the two time instants is not possible, for reasons, in particular, associated with the changes in the setting of NUTS units. Besides, the results of the ESPON TRACC project (in the form of the values of the indicator) were not fully known at the time of writing. For these two reasons it was only possible to compare the cartographic images originating from the two analyses.

References

Brach, J. (2013). Pozycja polskich międzynarodowych drogowych przewoźników ładunków na europejskim rynku drogowego międzynarodowego transportu towarowego – przyczyny sukcesu, (The position of Polish international road freight carriers on the European market of international road freight hauling – reasons behind he success). In: J. Rymarczyk, M. Domiter & W. Michalczyk (eds.), *Integracja i kryzysy na lokalnych i globalnych rynkach we współczesnym świecie*. Wrocław: Wydawnictwo Uniwersytetu Ekonomicznego we Wrocławiu, pp. 85–104.
ESPON 1.1.3. Final Report, 2006, www.espon.eu
ESPON 1.2.1. Final Report, 2004, www.espon.eu
ESPON FOCI Final Report, 2010, www.espon.eu
ESPON SeGI Interim Report, 2012, www.espon.eu
ESPON TRACC Interim Report, 2012, www.espon.eu
Geurs, K.T., & Eck, R. van (2001). Accessibility Measures: Review and Applications. RIVM report 408505 006. National Institute of Public Health and the Environment, Bilthoven.
Hansen, W.G. (1959). How accessibility shapes land-use. *Journal of the American Institute of Planners*, 25, 73–76.
Komornicki, T. (1999). Granice Polski. Analiza zmian przenikalności w latach 1990–1996. *Geopolitical Studies*, 5, 348, IGiPZ PAN, Warszawa.
Komornicki, T. (2003). Factors of development of car ownership in Poland. *Transport Reviews*, 23(4), 413–432.
Komornicki, T. (2005). Specific institutional barriers in transport development in the case of Poland and other Central European transition countries. *IATSS Research*, 29(2), 50–58.
Komornicki, T. (2011). Przemiany mobilności codziennej Polaków na tle rozwoju motoryzacji. *Prace Geograficzne*, 227, IGiPZ PAN.
Komornicki, T., 2013a, Task 4 Assessment of Infrastructure Construction, Its Role in Regional Development, report in: GRINCOH Project WP6 Territorial dimension of EU integration as challenges for cohesion policy.
Komornicki, T., 2013b, *Infrastruktura Transportowa*, w: Terytorialny wymiar rozwoju. Polska z perspektywy badań ESPON (red. A. Olechnicka & K. Wojnar). Warszawa: ESPON, str. pp. 104–117.

Rosik, P., Stępniak, M., & Komornicki, T. (2015). The decade of the big push to roads in Poland: Impact on improvement in accessibility and territorial cohesion from a policy perspective. *Transport Policy*, 37–134–14.

Rosik, P., Pomianowski, W., Goliszek, S., Stępniak, M., Kowalczyk, K., Guzik, R., Kołoś, A., & Komornicki, T. (2017). Multimodalna dostępność transportem publicznym w Polsce (Multimodal public transport accessibility of Polish Gminas/Municipalities). *Prace Geograficzne*, 258.

Rosik, P., Komornicki, T., Goliszek, S., & Duma, P. (2018). Improvement of accessibiliy in Eastern Europe due to implementation of road projects in the Via Carpatia corridor. *Mitteilungen der Österreichischen Geographischen Gesellschaft*, 160, 177–196.

Rykiel, Z. (1990). Koncepcje granic w badaniach geograficznych. *Przegląd Geograficzny*, 62, 263–273.

Spiekermann, K., & Schürmann, C. (2007). Update of Selected Potential Accessibility Indicators. Final Report. Spiekermann & Wegener, Urban and Regional Research (S&W), RRG Spatial Planning and Geoinformation.

Spiekermann, K., Wegener, M., Květoň, V., Marada, M., Schürmann, C., Biosca, O., Ulied Segui, A., Antikainen, H., Kotavaara, O., Rusanen, J., Bielańska, D., Fiorello, D., Komornicki, T., Rosik, P., & Stepniak, M. (2012). TRACC Transport Accessibility at Regional/Local Scale and Patterns in Europe. Draft Final Report. ESPON Applied Research.

Stępniak, M., & Rosik, P. (2013). Accessibility improvement, territorial cohesion and spillovers: A multidimensional evaluation of two motorway sections in Poland. *Journal of Transport Geography*, 31, 154–163.

White paper – 'European transport policy for 2010: Time to decide' Brussels, 12.9.2001, COM (2001) 370 final.

12 Environmental transformation in CEE countries

Zbigniew M. Karaczun and Andrzej Kassenberg

The driving forces

The process of transformation in the area of environmental protection in Central and Eastern Europe (CEE)[1] after 1989 took place with different intensity and at a different pace in each of the countries concerned. Various objectives were also set. This was a result of the internal conditions and level of environmental awareness of individual countries, as well as openness to changes in their political and economic elites and societies. It seems, however, that these changes can be linked to a broader, global and more long-term process, the origins of which date back to the 1960s. It was then that two publications appeared, which marked the beginning of a modern approach to environmental policy and started the process of globalisation in environmental protection.

The first one was Rachel Carson's book *Silent Spring*, published in 1962 (Carson 1962). This book attracted a broad response in the United States and gave rise to a nationwide discussion about the need to integrate environmental protection into economic development strategies. As a direct result of Carson's book, pesticides used in agriculture were placed under stricter supervision by public services and, indirectly, this led to setting up the US Environmental Protection Agency and establishing the first professional environmental organisations to fight for improvement in the quality of the environment.

The second important publication in the 1960s was the report by UN Secretary-General Sithu U'Thant, presented during the 23rd Session of the UN General Assembly in August 1969 (U Thant 1969). For the first time at such a high level, a statement about the limited nature of natural resources, resulting from the finite physical size of the globe, was formulated, and it was pointed out that environmental problems were no longer purely local in nature but had an impact on the entire world.

An indirect consequence of the Report by U Thant was the organisation in 1972, in Stockholm, under the aegis of the United Nations, of a conference titled 'We Have Only One World'. It adopted a 26-point declaration setting the direction of necessary actions for environmental protection. Its first point clearly indicated that the right to live in a clean and non-degraded natural environment is one of the fundamental human rights, and point 13 called on public authorities and national governments to take decisive action to improve the quality of the environment.[2] One of the outcomes of the Stockholm Conference was the adoption by the European Economic Community (EEC) of the first Environmental Action Programme and the understanding that, without broad cooperation, it would not be possible to halt the negative trends of devastation of the natural environment.

Environmental policy developed equally dynamically in the 1980s and 1990s. The first of these decades saw the entry into force of the first global environmental convention, the Vienna Convention, which aimed to protect the ozone layer. At that time, the World Commission on Environment and Development, named after its chairperson the 'Brundtland Commission', began its work. The result of this work was the report 'Our Common Future', in which for the first time the term 'sustainable development' was defined as development that, while striving to achieve the goals of the present, does not compromise the ability of future generations to achieve their own goals. Almost at the same time, the European Community decided that environmental policy should be one of its responsibilities. The Single European Act of 1987 introduced the new title 'Environment', which provided the first legal basis for a common environmental policy aimed at maintaining the quality of the environment, protecting human health and ensuring the rational use of natural resources.[3] The rationale behind the adoption of such legislation was that individual measures to protect the environment – whether taken by households, businesses, individual municipalities or countries – were insufficient, and that international cooperation was necessary. In 1993, the Maastricht Treaty adopted legislation establishing environmental policy as one of the integral areas of EU activity.[4]

Therefore, it can be assumed that the development of environmental policy that took place in Western European countries after 1972, and the growing awareness that environmental problems require extensive international cooperation, contributed to the fact that after 1989, when the process of systemic transformation began in CEE countries, one of the areas in which support was offered to these countries was environmental protection.

This was important, as until the end of the 1980s, CEE countries had not actively participated in the global process of environmental policy development. This was due to several reasons, both ideological – it was assumed that in socialist countries development could not have negative consequences for society, including those in the form of degradation of the natural environment, and economic reasons – the precedence of economic plans over social and environmental objectives, which in effect led to an environmental crisis in many countries of the region (Hill 1992). Another important reason was the fact that the countries of the region did not participate in the Stockholm Conference. Initially, they had not intended to boycott it, but since the German Democratic Republic (which was not a member of the UN at the time) was not invited to the conference, both the Soviet Union and most of the other CEE countries refused to participate in the meeting. Only delegations from Romania and Yugoslavia attended the conference (Lang 2003). The absence of politicians and specialists from CEE countries at the conference deprived them for a long time of an opportunity to be part of the changes in environmental awareness and formulation of the foundations of modern environmental protection.

Nevertheless, as early as the 1970s, pro-environmental ideas began to permeate this region as well. The first informal social initiatives aimed at stopping the degradation of the environment emerged and the authorities also reacted by establishing the first public institutions whose aim was to coordinate environmental protection actions. On 29 March 1972, the Ministry of Local Economy and Environmental Protection was established in Poland, and in Hungary the Office for Environmental Protection and Nature Conservation was established, which, after its merger with the National Office for Water Management (in 1987) adopted the name of the Ministry for Environmental Protection and Water Management. In Czechoslovakia, the Federal Committee for the Environment was created and environmental regulations were introduced. By the late 1970s, Czechoslovakia had passed four major environmental laws and over 350 environmental regulations. The four major laws regulated air, water, agricultural land and forestry. There was no law regulating waste until 1991. However, due to the lack of effective enforcement, and because fines and fees had no deterrent effect in the centralised planned economy, these laws garnered little respect and were largely ignored (Bowman and Hunter 1992). Moreover, in Poland, many environmental laws were enacted and implemented, the provisions of which, like in Czechoslovakia, were not enforced in practice. The situation changed dramatically only after the emergence of the Solidarity movement in September 1980. Already in October that year, the first Polish independent non-governmental environmental organisation, the Polish Ecological Club, was established in Cracow. Even the introduction of martial law in 1981 did not end the development of social activity, and environmental protection problems continued to be treated as politically significant.

In the 1980s, independent environmental organisations were formed in most of the CEE countries (although in Czechoslovakia, Brontosaurus had been active since the mid-1970s); in Hungary the Duna Kör (Danube Circle) was established in 1984, in Eastern Germany the Grüne Liga was created in 1989. In their goals, mission, methods of operation and programme, they referred to the experience of the organisations operating in democratic countries. Their activity attracted support, both because of the slogans advocating the democratisation of social life (most of the environmental organisations operating in CEE countries at that time were more or less openly in opposition to the communist authorities), but also because of the deteriorating quality of the environment in those countries. At the end of the 1980s, the activity of environmental groups in Poland was so strong that environmental protection issues became one of the areas of the Round Table negotiations – talks between the communist authorities and the opposition in Poland, which became the turning point in the process of transformation in the entire CEE. In other countries, too, environmental organisations were active participants in the systemic transformation processes, and in consequence, the newly formed governments devoted more attention to environmental protection (Lang 2003). The formation of democratic govern-ments and the opening of CEE countries to the West allowed these countries to join the international efforts to protect the environment, which resulted in the participation of representatives of all countries in the region at the Earth Summit conference in Rio de Janeiro in 1992.

Pressure on the environment

The starting point for the assessment of the situation with regard to the qual-ity of the natural environment, the effectiveness of its protection and inclusion of the environmental aspects of sustainable development in the development strategy is to identify the pressure on the environment caused by particular economies and societies in the countries covered by the analysis. Generally, the level of this pressure has been influenced by two opposing processes. The changes initiated in Poland in 1989 and then in other countries, although pain-ful, resulted in a significant reduction of the pressure on the environment, pri-marily thanks to the reduction of wastage characteristic of the period before the economic transformation (Jancar-Webster 1991). At the same time, how-ever, mass consumption developed in the CEE countries, causing an increase in environmental pressure. Therefore, it can be assumed that the current amount of pressure exerted on the environment is shaped by these two processes. Their effects can be shown on the example of the energy sector and changes in the efficiency of the use of raw materials and transport.

Energy and resources productivity

During the communist period, the power sector based on the use of fossil fuels and inefficient use of raw materials by industry had a major impact on the huge emissions of pollutants discharged by CEE countries to the environment (into the air and on the land surface (waste) as well as into water (heated cooling water)) and were responsible for a very severe degradation of the region's natu-ral resources. Although it was not possible to solve all those problems between 1989 and 2018 (e.g. in Poland about 80% of electricity production is still based on coal combustion), many programmes were implemented which helped to reduce the pressure exerted by this sector on the natural environment.

The improvement of energy and resource efficiency in CEE countries after 1990 is an indicator that clearly shows the positive effects of reducing the wastefulness of the centrally planned economy. In the period 1990–2016 in all analysed countries of the region, with the exception of Slovenia, there was a significant decrease in energy consumption (significantly higher than the EU28 average), led by Lithuania, Latvia and Romania, where the decrease was over 40% (Figure 12.1). The biggest drop (except for Croatia, Hungary and Slovenia) occurred in the period 1990–2005 and it seems to have been caused mainly by the modernisation of existing industrial plants or by their collapse.[5]

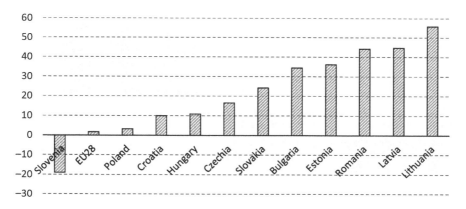

Figure 12.1 Decrease of energy consumption in CEE countries 1990–2016 (in %)

Source: http://appsso.eurostat.ec.europa.eu/nui/show.do?dataset=nrg_100a&lang=en, accessed on 3 August 2018.

Nevertheless, in the period 2000–2016, all these countries also experienced a considerable increase in energy productivity (except Croatia), which was higher than the average in the EU as a whole. This is particularly true for Romania, Slovakia and Bulgaria, as well as Poland, Latvia and Czechia. Despite these positive developments, there is still a significant distance between the average energy productivity in the EU (EUR 8.4/kgoe) and the countries analysed (ranging from EUR 6.0 to EUR 2.8/kgoe in 2016). Further increases in energy productivity, in spite of the existing possibilities – especially in the construction sector (new buildings) and from the improvement in the energy efficiency of existing buildings – will be difficult to achieve as the basic reserves have already been exhausted.

Improvements in resource productivity were much slower between 2000 and 2016. Only five countries scored better than the EU-28 average (Slovenia, Czechia, Latvia, Slovakia and Poland). In Romania, there was a decrease in resource productivity of almost 40% (Table 12.1). The leaders in improving energy and resource productivity are Slovakia, Bulgaria and Lithuania, but all analysed countries still have a lot to do to reach the average EU28 levels.[6]

The amount of the environmental pressure exerted by the energy sector and the resource efficiency of the economy depends to a great extent on the way energy is produced. Energy generation based on the use of coal and other fossil fuels exerts the greatest pressure, while production based on renewable resources (sun, wind, water) exerts the least pressure.

After 1989, all the countries of the region developed energy production based on renewable sources (RES), but the pace varied from country to country. The Baltic states developed this form of energy to become independent from the

Table 12.1 Energy and resource productivity 2000–2016 in CEE countries (changes in %)

Energy productivity	Above 100	RO			SO		
	80–100			BG; LT			
	60–80						
	40–60			PL	LV	CZ	
	20–40		EST; HR	EU28; H		SLO	
	Below 0	0–20	20–40	40–60	60–80
	Resources productivity				

Source: Own assessment based on EUROSTAT data.

http://ec.europa.eu/eurostat/tgm/table.do?tab=table&plugin=1&language=en&pcode=sdg_07_30
http://ec.europa.eu/eurostat/tgm/table.do?tab=table&init=1&language=en&pcode=sdg_12_20&plugin=1, accessed on 25 July 2018.

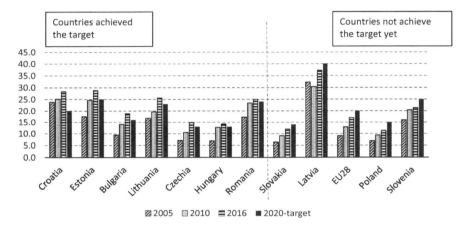

Figure 12.2 Share of renewable energy in gross final energy consumption in CEE countries 2005–15

Source: https://ec.europa.eu/eurostat/tgm/table.do?tab=table&init=1&language=en&pcode=t2020_31&plugin=1, accessed on 3 August 2018.

supply of energy resources and energy from Russia. The situation was different in Poland, where the development of RES was inhibited, as it was considered to be in competition with the country's own coal resources and power generation based on coal combustion. Nevertheless, in all analysed CEE countries in the years 1990–2016, the share of renewable energy in the energy mix increased, in 2016 reaching shares ranging from about 11% in Poland to over 37% in Latvia (the average in the EU-28 was 17%). In 2016, the largest share of RES in the mix was in Sweden, with 53.8%, and Finland with 38.7%. Latvia was ranked third in the EU. It is worth emphasising that seven CEE countries have already achieved their RES development EU targets for 2020, and the remaining countries have a good chance of achieving them, as they need an increase of only 2.0–3.7 percentage points to be on target (Figure 12.2).[7]

Transport

In addition to the positive processes leading to the reduction of pressure on the environment in the countries of the region, there are also phenomena that bring adverse effects from the point of view of sustainable development. One such phenomenon in CEE is the increased importance of road transport leading to the associated development of road infrastructure and a considerable growth in the number of vehicles. In 1990–2016, many of the analysed countries saw a big increase in the total length of motorways and expressways. In practically all of them, this was largely an effect of access to EU funds, especially in Slovakia, Slovenia and Romania (Figure 12.3).[8]

The vehicle saturation rate in the countries in question is approaching (and sometimes even exceeds) the values for the most motorised countries in Western Europe (Figure 12.4). A characteristic feature of this increase is that a significant part consists of second-hand cars imported from Western Europe. In Poland, after the country's accession to the EU, these figures reached as many as one million vehicles a year, half of which were more than 11 years old, and as a result, in 2015, the average age of vehicles in that country was 17 years (to compare, the average age of a car in Germany is 8.9 years, in France 9 years and the EU 10.7 years).[9]

This increase contributed to a significant decline in the role of the railways. In 2000, apart from Lithuania, none of the CEE countries had a higher share of passenger cars in transport than the EU28 average, while in 2016, in as many as seven countries (Croatia, Latvia, Bulgaria, Estonia, Lithuania, Romania and Slovenia) this ratio (> 80%) was similar to the EU28 average (82.9%). There was also a significant increase in the share of road freight transport, bringing

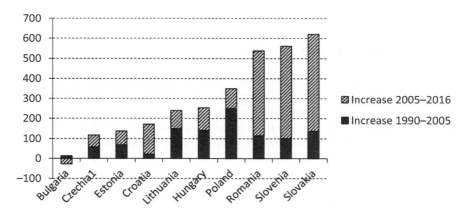

Figure 12.3 Increase in the length of motorways in CEE countries in the years 1990–2016 (in %)

Source: http://appsso.eurostat.ec.europa.eu/nui/show.do?dataset=road_if_motorwa&lang=en, accessed 3 August 2018.

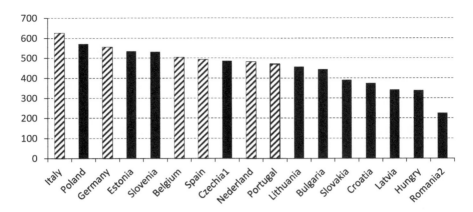

Figure 12.4 Passenger cars per 1,000 inhabitants in 2016 in selected EU countries

Source: http://appsso.eurostat.ec.europa.eu/nui/show.do?dataset=road_eqs_carhab&lang=en, accessed 5 August 2018.

Table 12.2 Modal split road freight transport and passenger cars in 2016 in CEE countries (in %)

Modal split freight road transport	Above 70		PL	EU28; HR
	50–70	CZ; H; SLO	EST	BL; SO
	Below 50		LV; RO	LT
		Below 75	75–82	Above 82
		Modal split passenger cars		

Source: http://ec.europa.eu/eurostat/web/transport/data/database, accessed on 5 August 2018.

some of the countries concerned closer to the EU average (76.4%). This applies to Croatia, Poland, Hungary and Slovenia, where the share of road transport exceeds 65% (Table 12.2).[10]

The decline in the role of railways is evident from the change in the number of passengers using this means of transport. In the years 2005–10, in most CEE countries, there was a decrease in the number of passengers in rail transport. In the following period (2010–15), thanks to the allocation of more funds to railways (especially as part of the support from EU funds for rail transport), there was an increase in rail passenger transport. Nevertheless, in seven CEE countries, the number of passengers travelling by rail in 2015 was lower than in 2005 (Figure 12.5).[11]

As a result, these countries are experiencing extensive development of roads, which is leading not only to the loss of biologically active areas, but also to an increase in landscape fragmentation, growing emissions of air pollutants, especially greenhouse gases, and an increase in the number of people exposed to traffic noise.

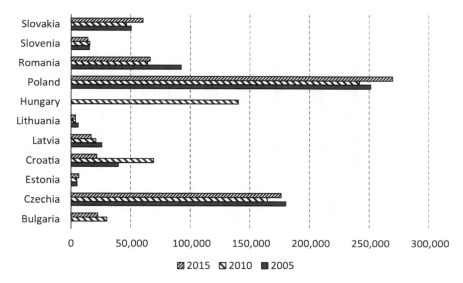

Figure 12.5 Total annual passenger transport by rail 2005–15 (in thousands) in CEE countries

Source: https://ec.europa.eu/eurostat/tgm/table.do?tab=table&init=1&language=en&pcode=t2020_rk310&plugin=1, accessed on 5 August 2018.

Pollution discharge

As a consequence of the economic and political changes that have taken place in the analysed countries, the amount of pollutants discharged into the environment has changed. In almost all of them, after 1990, there has been a significant reduction in the emission of pollutants to the air and water. On the other hand, the growth of individual consumption has resulted in a greater amount of municipal waste.

Air pollution (excluding greenhouse gases (GHG)). Emissions of basic pollutants discharged into the air (SO_2, NO_x) from CEE countries decreased significantly after 1990 (Figures 12.6 and 12.7). This was a result of both the economic transformation and the modernisation of industry (as evidenced by a greater decrease in emissions before 2005; see Figure 12.6), as well as environmental protection investments. In the case of SO_2 emissions, reductions in CEE countries in the period 1990–2016 ranged from 78% to 97% (with a EU-28 average of 90%); only four countries reduced their emissions to a lesser extent than the EU average.

In the case of NO_x emissions, reductions between 1990 and 2008 ranged from 19% to 65% (the EU-27 average was 39%), with 5 CEE countries achieving lower than the EU average reduction (Figure 12.7) (EEA 2010).

A much lower reduction was achieved in the case of pollutants produced mainly by road transport and inefficient heating equipment using poor quality

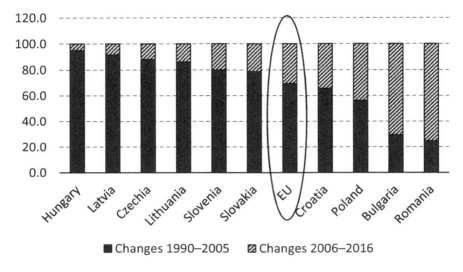

Figure 12.6 Changes in SO$_2$ emissions in CEE countries 1990–2016 (in %) (1990 = 100)

Source: http://appsso.eurostat.ec.europa.eu/nui/show.do?dataset=env_air_emis&lang=en, accessed on 10 August 2018.

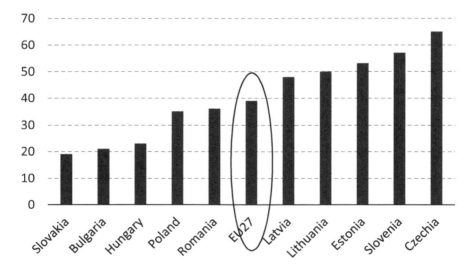

Figure 12.7 Reductions of NO$_x$ 1990–2008 in selected CEE countries

Source: European Union emission inventory report 1990–2008 under the UNECE Convention on Long-range Transboundary Air Pollution (LRTAP). EEA. Copenhagen 2010.

fuel (both local boiler-houses and individual heaters). An example of this is the change in emissions of particulate matter (see Figure 12.8). Emissions from these sources are currently the main factor causing poor air quality in many countries of the region.

The changes that have taken place in the economies of the analysed countries can be clearly seen if one looks at the significant decrease in greenhouse gas emissions between 1990 and 2016. This varies from nearly 12% in Slovenia to 73% in Lithuania (Figure 12.9). If we go back to an earlier period, the decreases in these emissions are even greater, as these countries' GHG emissions peaked in the 1980s.[12]

The situation is similar with regard to emissions per capita, although here the reductions have been slower. In 2015, only in Czechia and Poland were emissions per capita higher than the EU28 average (8.8 tons CO_{2eq} per capita). Meanwhile, countries such as Croatia, Latvia, Romania, Hungary and Lithuania belong to the group of Member States with the lowest GHG emissions per capita (7 tons CO_{2eq} per capita or less) (Figure 12.10). However, even in these countries, the emission levels are too high to meet the Paris Agreement commitments, i.e., limiting the growth of average temperature in the world to a level below 2°C.

In almost all the analysed countries, in the years 1990–2016, GHG emissions per national income unit fell by more than 50%. Slovakia, Romania, Lithuania, Estonia and Poland experienced a particularly fast reduction, with an average

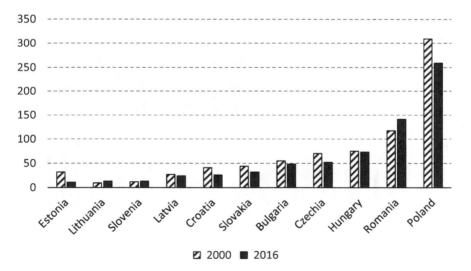

Figure 12.8 Emission of PM_{10} in selected CEE countries in 2000–2016 (in Gg)

Source: European Union emission inventory report 1990–2016 under the UNECE Convention on Long-range Transboundary Air Pollution (LRTAP). EEA Report No 6/2018.

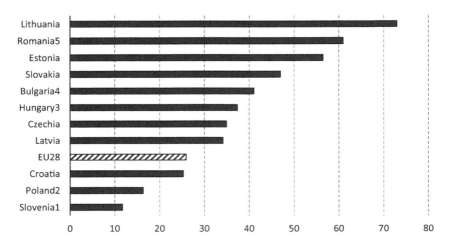

Figure 12.9 Reduction of GHG emissions in CEE countries 1990–2016 (in %)

Source: http://appsso.eurostat.ec.europa.eu/nui/show.do?dataset=env_air_gge&lang=en, accessed on 15 August 2018.

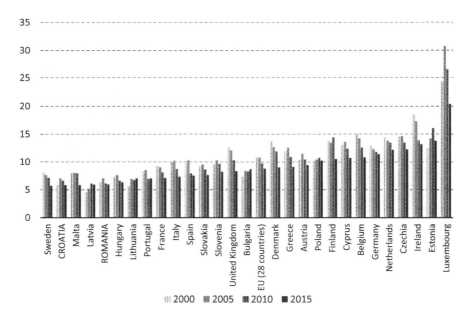

Figure 12.10 GHG emissions per capita in the EU 2000–2015 (Mg CO_{2eq})

Source: http://ec.europa.eu/eurostat/tgm/table.do?tab=table&init=1&language=en&pcode=t2020_rd 300&plugin=1, accessed on 15 August 2018.

annual decrease of over 4%. However, the values of these indicators are still higher in CEE countries than in almost all other EU Member States. This shows that there is considerable potential for reduction of GHG emissions in the countries of the region (Report . . ., 2017).

Despite the progress made towards more efficient use of water resources, the amount of wastewater discharged by the CEE countries into surface waters is still significant (Figure 12.11). A positive development is the significant reduction in the amount of untreated wastewater discharged in the region. However, there is still a need to improve the efficiency and effectiveness of wastewater treatment.

Figure 12.12 clearly shows differences between the European regions in terms of the population served by urban wastewater treatment and how effective the treatment is. In the period 1995–2015, the central parts of the EU (Austria, Belgium, Denmark, Germany, Luxembourg, the Netherlands, Switzerland and the United Kingdom) and northern parts (Finland, Iceland, Norway and Sweden) managed to provide a high percentage of the population with access to urban sewage systems (over 85%) where wastewater is fully treated. The third degree of waste treatment prevails. A similar process took place in the countries in the eastern part of the EU (Czechia, Estonia, Hungary, Latvia, Lithuania, Poland and Slovakia), although the share of the population using the sewage system is lower (about 75%). In the countries of this region, almost all wastewater covered by the sewage system is subject to treatment, including

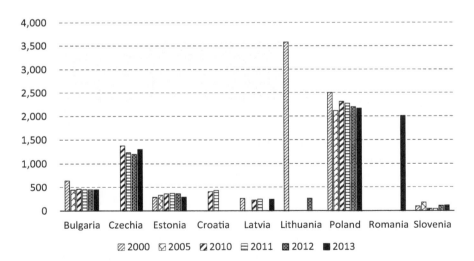

Figure 12.11 Generation of wastewater in CEE countries in million m³ (point sources 2000–2013)

Source: http://appsso.eurostat.ec.europa.eu/nui/show.do?dataset=env_wwgen_r2&lang=en, accessed on 15 August 2018. No data available for Hungary and Slovakia.

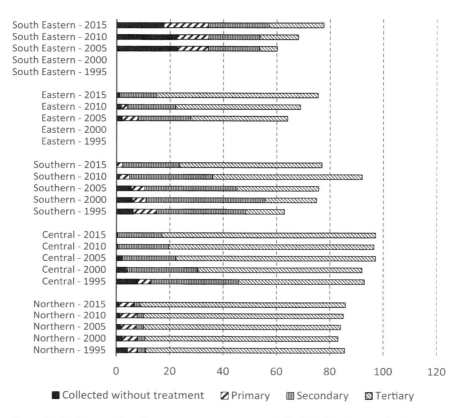

Figure 12.12 Changes in urban waste water treatment in the EU (% of population)

Note:

Northern Europe: Finland, Iceland Norway and Sweden.

Central Europe: Austria, Belgium, Denmark, Germany, Luxembourg, the Netherlands, Switzerland and United Kingdom.

Southern Europe: Greece, Italy, Malta and Spain.

Eastern Europe: Czechia, Estonia, Hungary, Latvia, Lithuania, Poland and Slovenia.

South-eastern Europe: Bulgaria, Romania and Turkey.

Source: www.eea.europa.eu/data-and-maps/daviz/changes-in-wastewater-treatment-in-8#tab-chart_3, accessed on 4 September 2018.

increased nutrient removal in a significant number of treatment facilities. The situation is different in the south-eastern region (Bulgaria, Romania and Turkey), where still about 20% of wastewater is not treated at all and the majority of wastewater is treated only mechanically or biologically. The same is true for the countries in the southern region (Greece, Italy, Malta and Spain), where a relatively high percentage of waste water is treated in second degree (biological) installations.[13]

In CEE countries, significantly more waste (than in other regions of the EU) is produced and deposited in landfills. Only Slovenia represents the average EU28 level (Figure 12.13 and 12.14). Croatia, Romania and Slovakia landfill more than three times the EU–28 average, while other countries landfill twice the EU average.[14]

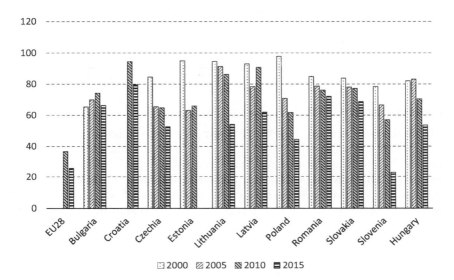

Figure 12.13 Volume of municipal waste generated in CEE countries 2000–2015, kg/inhabitant

Source: Eurostat Database cited for *Ochrona Środowiska 2017*. Główny Urząd Statystyczny. Warszawa.

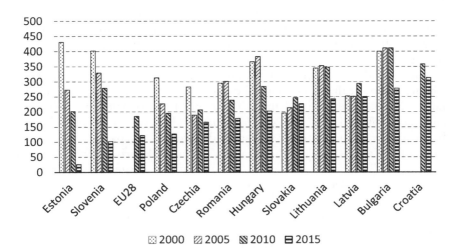

Figure 12.14 Landfilled municipal waste in CEE countries 2000–2015, kg/inhabitant

Source: Eurostat Database cited for *Ochrona Środowiska 2017*. Główny Urząd Statystyczny. Warszawa.

Condition of the natural environment

The level of the pressure exerted by socio-economic processes is vital for the quality of the environment in the countries of the region. A lowering of this pressure – especially in comparison with the period before the transformation – contributed to the improvement of the quality of the natural environment in many aspects. However, this process is not permanent, as the impact of negative phenomena (such as the development of road transport described above or excessive individual consumerism) may, in the short term, reverse the positive trends improving the quality of the environment of Central and Eastern Europe.

Ecological footprint

The difference between the biological capacity[15] of a country's environment and the size of its ecological footprint[16] is a synthetic indicator of the condition of the environment in individual countries and the effectiveness of their environmental policies. The biological capacity depends, in part, on the effectiveness of the environmental policy of a given country, and changes in the ecological footprint are a good reflection of the level of pressure exerted on the environment by the selected development model. These data, for the analysed countries, are presented in Table 12.3.

Despite significant differences in the value of individual indicators, there are similarities between the analysed countries which allow us to assign them to one of three groups.[17] The first group includes those countries where a significant increase in the ecological footprint after the transformation period has not been offset by an improvement in biocapacity. This group includes Croatia and Slovakia. In both countries, at the beginning of transformation (in Slovakia until 1994, in Croatia until mid-1996) the ecological footprint was lower than the value of their biocapacity, but later it started to grow strongly, which resulted in it significantly exceeding the value of biocapacity.

The second group consists of countries where the pressure on the environment is lower than its biological capacity, thanks to which a certain natural reserve has been created there. These are the two Baltic states (Estonia and Latvia) as well as Bulgaria and Romania. However, there is a difference between them. While in the Baltic states the biological capacity exceeded the value of ecological pressure throughout the analysed period (1992–2014), in the case of Bulgaria and Romania the surplus was created only at the end of the period under analysis (in 2013) as a result of a significant reduction in environmental pressure and increase in biocapacity; this shows the positive effect of Europeanisation on the level of environmental pressure in these countries.

The remaining countries (the third group – Czechia, Estonia, Hungary, Lithuania, Poland and Slovenia) are those where the biocapacity of the environment

Table 12.3 Biocapacity and ecological footprint indicators (per capita) and the difference between them in CEE countries

Country, period of analysis	Biocapacity	Ecological footprint	Difference	GDP per capita in 2014 000' USD	Comments
	per person (gha in 2014)				
Bulgaria, 1997–2014	3.3	3.2	+0.1	7.9	Biocapacity grew from 2.3 (in 1997) to 3.3 (in 2014). Reduction of footprint between 2008 (4.3) and 2014 (3.6). The two lines crossed in 2013.
Croatia, 1992–2014	3.0	3.7	−0.7	13.5	Until mid-1996, biocapacity (2.5–2.6) was higher than footprint. Later, the footprint began to grow (max. 4.7 in 2007).
Czechia, 1993–2014	2.7	5.6	−2.0	19.6	Reduction of footprint while biocapacity generally remained at a similar level throughout the whole period from 1993 (although in the early 2000s, the footprint exceeded 6.0); in 1993 the difference was −3.2.
Estonia, 1992–2014	9.7	7.0	+2.7	19.7	Biocapacity grew from 8.0 (in 1992). In 2002–04 the difference approached 0.0 (because the footprint grew to 8.7–8.8), but its value remained positive throughout the period.
Hungary, 1992–2014	2.6	3.5	−0.9	13.9	The difference decreased from 1992 (when it was −1.1), but generally remained at a similar level throughout the whole period.
Latvia, 1992–2014	8.0	5.6	+2.4	15.7	Throughout the whole period biocapacity was higher than footprint. Biocapacity grew from 5.6 but the footprint also grew from 3.6 in 1992.
Lithuania, 1992–2014	4.9	5.7	−0.8	16.4	Generally the difference remained at the same level throughout the whole period. Both biocapacity and footprint grew.
Poland, 1961–2014	2.1	4.4	−2.3	14.4	Footprint reduced from approx. 5.4 in 1989 to 4.4 in 2014 (in 1970s and 1980s it reached 6–6.2). Biocapacity stable since 1960s (1.9–2.2).
Romania, 1961–2014	2.9	2.8	+0.1	10.0	Considerable improvement (reduced footprint from 4.8 in 1988 and 4.6 in 1990). Biocapacity remained at a similar level. Since 2013 the difference is positive.
Slovenia, 1992–2014	2.3	4.7	−2.4	24.0	In 1992 the difference was −1.0 because footprint was lower. The footprint grew considerably after 2010.
Slovakia, 1993–2014	3.0	4.2	−1.2		Footprint grew from 2.4 in 1993 to 4.2 in 2014. Biocapacity remained at a similar level throughout the whole period. Since 1995, the footprint value significantly exceeds the value of biocapacity.

Source: http://data.footprintnetwork.org/#/, accessed 25 July 2018.

was below the ecological footprint throughout the analysed period and where the increase or decrease in the ecological footprint was generally accompanied by an increase or decrease in biocapacity. Therefore, the value of the difference indicator was negative throughout the period.

What is common to all analysed countries is that their ecological footprint was higher in 2014 than at the beginning of the analysed period.[18] Moreover, the ecological footprint in CEE countries was higher in 2014 than the global average (2.84 gha/person). However, there is no clear correlation between the size of the ecological footprint and biocapacity.

The high level of the ecological footprint in the analysed countries, higher than the global average, as well as the fact that the footprint is higher than biocapacity (in 7 countries out of 11 surveyed), shows that, despite significant progress in environmental protection and reduction of the pollutant load, the condition of the environment in many CEE countries is still not satisfactory. This is confirmed by a more detailed analysis of water status and air quality.

Water quality

The share of surface water bodies (SWBs) with good and insufficient ecological status of water in Central European countries is presented in Table 12.4. The data show that the majority (58%) of surface water bodies in these countries have insufficient quality status (although this is slightly better than the EU average). The worst situation is in Hungary (90% of SWBs with insufficient status) and Czechia (80%). In Hungary, 86.97% of surface water bodies with known ecological status/potential are affected by significant pressures. The dominant pressure type is water flow regulation (56.06% of SWBs). As a result, measures to improve the efficiency of municipal and industrial wastewater treatment (point sources are responsible for 19.2% of the pressure on SWBs in Hungary) and to reduce waste discharge from agriculture into water (the share of agricultural pressure is 25.5%) are not sufficient to ensure good surface water quality (WRc+ 2015a).

The example of Bulgaria may also indicate how difficult it will be to improve surface water quality in CEE countries. The main pressures on the water bodies identified in this country are: diffuse sources of pollution (42%) and point sources of pollution (34%) (WRc+ 2015b). After joining the EU, Bulgaria took a number of measures to implement the EU legal requirements for water protection, but due to limited financial means (only about 15% of water protection investments were financed from EU funds), huge investment is still needed to ensure a sufficient level of protection. Out of 108 agglomerations[19] above 10,000 population equivalent (p.e.), only 24 meet the requirements for wastewater treatment. In 48 agglomerations, wastewater treatment plants have to be built, and in 36 the existing treatment plants need to be modified. Investment in the development of water supply networks is also necessary: in 101

Table 12.4 Share of surface water bodies (SWBs) of good and insufficient ecological status in CEE countries

Country	% SWBs with the status	
	Good	Insufficient
Bulgaria	51	49
Croatia	42	58
Czechia	20	80
Estonia	60	40
Hungary	10	90
Latvia	21	79
Lithuania	nd	nd
Poland	31	69
Romania	66	34
Slovakia	56	44
Slovenia	60	40
CEE average	42	58
EU average	41	59

Source: Based on second River Basin Management Plan (RBMP) submitted in 2015 by those countries. WISE-SoW database: *Surface water bodies: Ecological status or potential group.* https://tableau.discomap.eea.europa.eu/t/Wateronline/views/WISE_SOW_SurfaceWaterBody/SWB_EcologicalStatusGroup?:embed=y&:showShareOptions=true&:display_count=no&:showVizHome=no, accessed 22 August 2018.

agglomerations, the extension of the sewage systems must be completed. The situation is even worse in smaller locations (between 2,000 and 5,000 p.e.). Out of 256 such agglomerations in Bulgaria, only 25 have a wastewater collection and treatment system meeting EU requirements. In 226 agglomerations of this size, new wastewater treatment plants have to be built, and in five the existing treatment plants have to be modified. In addition, 250 of these locations need their sewage systems to be expanded. The scale of this challenge is apparent (WRc+ 2015a).

It is therefore not surprising that surface water quality in the CEE countries has not improved between the middle of the first decade and the first half of the second decade of the 21st century. Comparing the data presented by the analysed countries in River Basin Management Plans (the first for the years 2009–15 and the second for the years 2016–21), the share of surface water bodies with good ecological status decreased by 6 percentage points (the average decrease in the entire EU at that time was 3 percentage points).[20] In five countries of the region, the share of SWBs with good status decreased. The biggest decline was observed in Latvia, at 28 percentage points. The greatest improvement was recorded in Poland, where the share of SBWs with good water status increased by 16 percentage points[21] in the period under discussion (Figure 12.15).

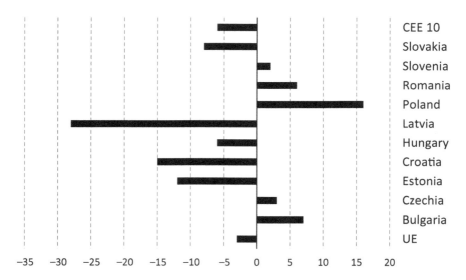

Figure 12.15 Changes in the share of SWBs with good status in selected CEE countries between the first and the second RBMP

Source: Own assessment based on analyses of the first and second River Basin Management Plans (RBMP) submitted by MS. WISE-SoW database: *Surface water bodies: Ecological status or potential group.*

The increase in the share of SWBs with insufficient water status in Latvia results both from better awareness of water quality in the country, as well as from other causes (e.g. insufficient development of municipal wastewater treatment systems; only 59% of the Latvian population use treatment plants). However, the main reason seems to be the lack of international cooperation on water protection with Belarus and Russia, which means that many rivers flow into the Latvian territory that are already seriously polluted (WRc+ 2015c).

Groundwater status in CEE countries, both in terms of quality and quantity, is significantly better than surface water. The information included in the second River Basin Management Plans, which these countries submitted to the European Commission in 2015, shows that groundwater resources are in good quantitative condition on more than 92% of the area of these countries (the average for the whole EU is 90.7%). The worst situation in this respect is in Hungary, where a poor quantitative status of water resources was reported on an area of 25.5% (which corresponds to 20% of groundwater bodies (GWBs)). The best situation is in Latvia, Romania and Slovenia, where the quantitative resources of all groundwater are in good condition.[22]

The chemical quality of groundwater is slightly worse: 82.4% of groundwater is of good status in the analysed CEE countries (however, this is still much better than the EU average of 74.9%). Groundwater is most polluted in Czechia (with 62.7% of water of insufficient status) and Bulgaria (44.7%). One hundred percent of Latvia's groundwater has good chemical status.[23]

Air quality

Despite a significant reduction in the load of pollutants discharged into the air from CEE countries, the air quality in the region is not good. However, this problem applies to the whole of Europe. Countries in the western part of the continent generally have higher concentrations of ozone and nitrogen oxides in the air than in central Europe. Insufficient air quality in CEE countries is primarily the result of high air pollution with suspended particulates and their compounds – including in particular the toxic benzo[a]pyrene. However, in reality, the situation in CEE countries may be worse than the monitoring results indicate, due to a much less developed network of monitoring stations in these countries. For example, ozone concentrations in Croatia are only tested at five monitoring stations, two of which recorded exceedance of the daily eight-hour limit values (EU standard: 120 $\mu g/m^3$) (European Environment Agency 2017). It is therefore likely that an expansion of the network of monitoring stations in CEE countries would show that air quality in this region is worse than the current surveys indicate.[24]

In 2015, concentrations above the daily limit value for PM_{10} were found in 19% of monitoring stations located in 20 EU Member States (the stricter value of the WHO AQG for PM_{10} annual mean (20 $\mu g/m^3$) was exceeded at 54% of the stations and in all Member States except Estonia and Ireland; see also Figure 12.17). The largest number of stations with excess concentration levels were located in Poland, Bulgaria and Italy. CEE concentrations above the daily limit value for PM_{10} were also very frequent in other countries: in Croatia they were found at two out of five measurement stations; in Slovakia at four out of eight; in Hungary at four out of ten; and in Latvia at one out of four. In 2015, 95% of the stations where the daily limit value for PM_{10} was exceeded were located in urban areas. This increases the risk to health caused by particulate matter air pollution.[25]

In 2015, the $PM_{2.5}$ concentrations were higher than the limit value in three Member States (Figure 12.16). The World Health Organization (WHO) recommended value for $PM_{2.5}$ annual mean (10 $\mu g/m^3$) was exceeded at 75% of the stations, located in 24 Member States. Estonia, Finland and Sweden did not report any exceedance of the WHO AQG (Air Quality Guidelines) for $PM_{2.5}$.[26] Bulgaria and Hungary did not submit the $PM_{2.5}$ monitoring results for 2015; in 2014 the annual mean $PM_{2.5}$ concentration in Bulgaria was higher that the limit allowed in the EU, whereas in Hungary it was lower than the EU limit, but higher than the level recommended by WHO (Map 12.1).[27]

The data presented in Figure 12.19 show the severity of the problem of pollution by suspended particulate matter in CEE countries. The AEI (average exposure indicator) is an average of concentration levels (over a three-year period) measured at urban background stations (representative of general urban

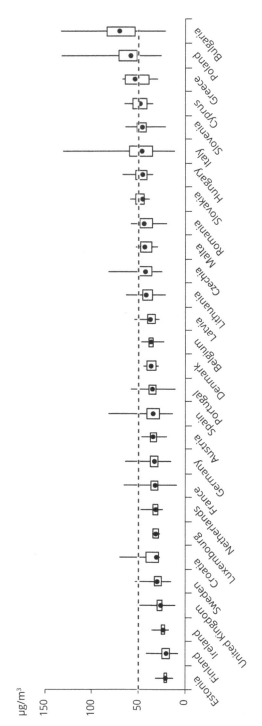

Figure 12.16 PM$_{10}$ concentrations in relation to the daily limit value in 2015 in the EU-28

population exposure) selected for this purpose by every national authority. For the 25 Member States for which the AEI could be calculated with the stations designated for this purpose, the AEI was above the exposure concentration obligation in Croatia (the AEI 2015 was 21 μg/m³), Hungary (22 μg/m³ for the AEI 2014 (the average for 2012–14, since Hungary did not report $PM_{2.5}$ data in 2015)) and Poland (the AEI 2015 was 23 μg/m³). Furthermore, based on the average of $PM_{2.5}$ concentrations measured at urban background stations, Bulgaria was also above the exposure concentration obligation with an estimated AEI of 26 μg/m³.[28]

The progress in the reduction of PM concentration in Bulgaria, Czechia, Slovenia, Croatia, Romania, Hungary and Slovakia has been considered insufficient.[29] Concentration of BaP (benzo[a]pyrene) in EU in 2015 is presented in Figure 12.17. It shows that the values above 1.0 ng/m³ were recorded at 32% of the reported BaP measurement stations, mainly at urban and suburban stations (94 % of all stations with values above 1.0 ng/m³ were in urban and suburban locations). Annual concentrations exceeded 1.0 ng/m³ in 2015 in 14 Member States. The figure shows that the values above 1.0 ng/m³ are predominant in Central and Eastern Europe. The concentrations measured at Polish stations continue to be very high, well above the target value.[30]

As regards other air pollutants, the situation in CEE countries does not generally differ from the EU average, and sometimes (e.g. with regard to

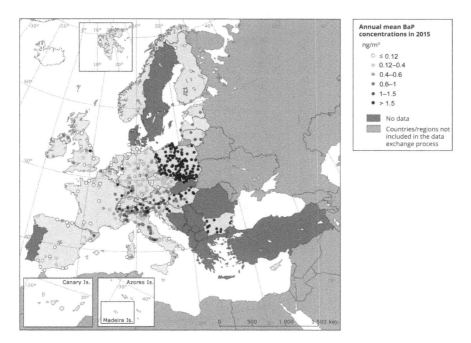

Map 12.1 $PM_{2.5}$ concentrations in the EU in 2015

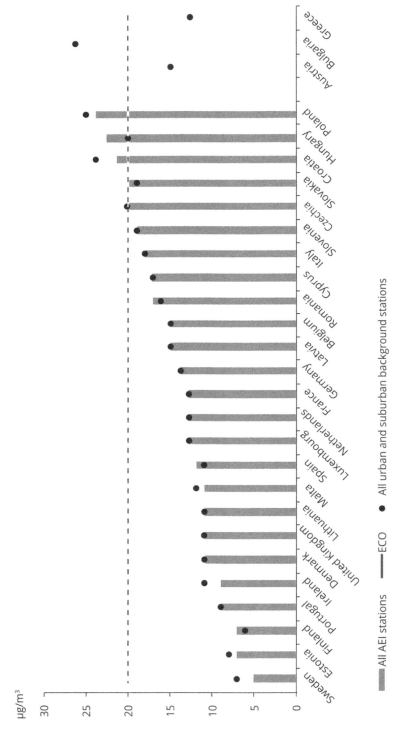

Figure 12.17 Average exposure indicator in 2015 and exposure concentration obligation in the EU

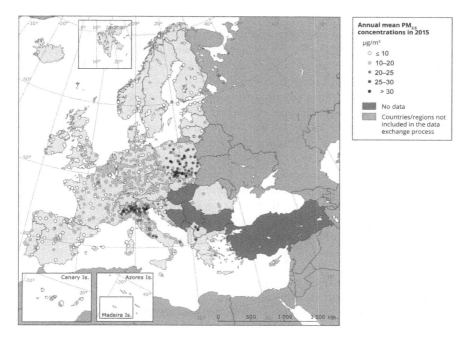

Map 12.2 Concentrations of BaP in EU in 2015

concentrations of nitrogen dioxide or ozone) is better than the EU average. Nevertheless, poor air quality is the source of the greatest environmental threat to the health of the inhabitants of Central and Eastern Europe.

Biodiversity

The region of Eastern and Central Europe has a high level of biodiversity, which can be attributed both to the natural conditions and to a lower level of urbanisation and industrialisation of agriculture (than in the 'old' EU Member States) until the 1990s. The social and economic transformation of the early 1990s, together with European integration have brought both negative and positive effects for the biodiversity of the region. According to research carried out in Poland, the privatisation process, although contributing to a reduction of the environmental pollution load, was not used to strengthen the environmental potential and to steer development processes in the direction of sustainable development (Karaczun and Grześkiewicz 1995). In retrospect, it seems obvious that the transformation processes tended to solve problems in the short term rather than to lay the foundations for long-term sustainable development. In many cases, the protection of nature under a democratic order proved to be more difficult than in the previous period – it was no longer enough for the government to order that new nature protection areas be created or new species be protected by law, but it was necessary to find a consensus between the conflicting interests of the parties concerned. What is more, the people of the CEE countries, 'starved' after the years of communism, desired new assets and often agreed to obtain them at the expense of natural resources. The situation began to change only after several years, when enriched communities began to notice the importance of good environmental conditions for the quality of life. On the other hand, the opening of markets – especially after the accession of CEE countries to the European Union – forced producers and farmers to compete not only with their neighbours but also with producers from other countries. This made it necessary to intensify production and search for methods to reduce production costs, often at the expense of landscape and environmental degradation, and increasing pressure on biodiversity.

Despite these negative phenomena, the impact of the transformation process on biodiversity protection in CEE countries should be assessed positively. European integration has introduced many new, effective tools for its protection – first of all, it has enforced the protection of the most valuable habitats within the Natura 2000 system; it has also introduced agro-environmental programmes, provided funds for nature protection and improved the way in which biodiversity protection is managed. The ability of the authorities of individual countries to use these tools has been of key importance for the effectiveness of biodiversity protection in these countries.

The common farmland bird index is a good indicator of changes in biodiversity (especially in rural areas). Changes in the value of this indicator after 2006 in selected CEE countries are presented in Table 12.5. Only in Latvia did the value of this indicator exceed the 2000 level; in other countries it decreased by 15.6–22 percentage points.

This decrease may be a result of low utilisation of pro-environmental CAP (Common Agricultural Policy) instruments in the CEE countries, as shown in Figure 12.18; only in four of these countries is the share of agricultural land on which instruments supporting biodiversity have been introduced higher than

Table 12.5 Common farmland bird index in selected CEE countries 2006–15

	2006	2007	2008	2009	2010	2011	2012	2013	2014	2015
Czechia	85.5	82.9	100.2	91.9	81.0	74.8	74.6	78.0	81.2	:
Estonia	91.5	89.5	81.7	68.9	69.8	68.2	70.7	73.8	78.1	75.4
Hungary	96.1	83.8	79.8	77.9	75.0	71.2	73.2	86.0	83.2	:
Latvia	98.9	115.4	112.0	98.7	121.3	103.1	119.3	123.0	116.3	:
Lithuania	78.1	68.6	70.8	77.7	83.1	74.9	69.7	72.2	78.0	:
Poland	90.9	88.3	99.3	93.7	87.8	87.2	84.5	85.1	84.4	:

Value of the index in 2000 = 100.

Source: https://ec.europa.eu/eurostat/tgm/table.do?tab=table&init=1&language=en&pcode=t2020_rn130&plugin=1, accessed 22 August 2018.

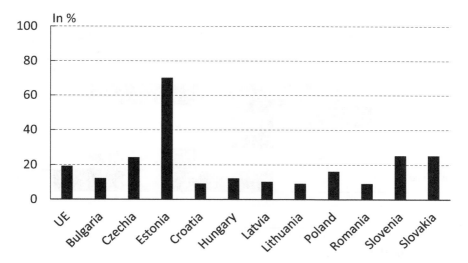

Figure 12.18 Percentage of agricultural land in CEE countries under management contracts supporting biodiversity and/or landscape protection (as of 25 August 2015)

Source: European Commission, 2015: Commission Staff Working Document: EU Assessment of Progress in Implementing the EU Biodiversity Strategy to 2020. Accompanying the document: Report from the Commission to the European Parliament and the Council. The Mid-Term Review of the EU Biodiversity Strategy to 2020 [COM(2015) 478 final] Part 2/3.

the average for the entire EU. However, the example of Estonia, where around 70% of agricultural land is covered by these instruments and yet the value of the Common Farmland Bird index has declined since 2000, may indicate that this is not sufficient to ensure effective protection of biodiversity.

A detailed analysis of the implementation of EU legislation aimed at protecting biodiversity (i.e. the Birds and Habitats Directives) in 19 EU Member States was carried out in 2018 by four non-governmental organisations (WWF, FoEE, EEB and Birdlife International). The results of the research carried out in five CEE countries revealed a low level of implementation of the directive requirements and the need to intensify efforts to protect biodiversity (Figure 12.19). Nevertheless, the results obtained in the CEE countries did not differ significantly from the results of studies carried out in the 'old' EU Member States.[31]

Areas included in the Natura 2000 network are of particular importance for the protection of Europe's biodiversity. Studies have shown that there are significantly more animal species in these areas, both from Annex I and from outside this Annex (Sluis et al. 2016). Rare plant species (including the Red List) are also more frequently found in areas included in the Natura 2000 network than in areas outside the network. The report also shows that among the eight Member States with the highest proportion of protected areas in the

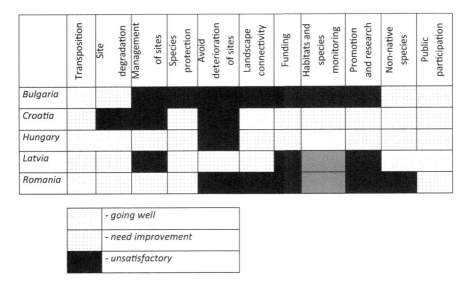

Figure 12.19 The state of implementation of the Birds and Habitats Directives in selected CEE countries

Source: http://wwf.panda.org/knowledge_hub/all_publications/?326895/The-State-of-Implementation-of-the-Birds-and-Habitats-Directives-in-the-EU, accessed on 27 August 2018.

network (Bulgaria, Croatia, Slovakia, Hungary, Slovenia, Romania, Greece and Spain), as many as six are from central Europe. As the information presented in Table 12.6 only three countries from the region have designated areas of Natura 2000 on an area smaller than the average for the entire EU (Latvia, Lithuania and Czechia). This increases the chance for effective protection of the region's biodiversity.

Quality of the environment and health

The insufficient quality of the natural environment in CEE countries degrades the quality of life of the inhabitants of this part of Europe, has an adverse impact on their health and may result in premature mortality. Although the share of households in these countries exposed to the negative impact of pollution or other environmental problems has been decreasing since 2005 (although in Poland, Slovenia and Lithuania this share has been increasing since 2010), the percentage is still higher than the EU average in more than half of the countries in the region (Table 12.7).

As stated earlier, the greatest environmental threat to the health of Central and Eastern European citizens is air pollution. Figure 12.20 shows urban populations in CEE countries exposed to air pollutant concentrations above selected air quality standards.

Table 12.6 Share (% of country's territory) of areas protected under Natura 2000 (habitats protection) in selected CEE countries 2008–17

	2008	2009	2010	2011	2012	2013	2014	2015	2016	2017
European Union	14	15	18	18	18	18	18	18	18	18
Bulgaria	30	30	34	34	34	34	34	34	34	34
Czechia	9	10	14	14	14	14	14	14	14	14
Estonia	17	17	18	18	18	18	18	18	18	18
Croatia	:	:	:	:	:	37	37	37	37	37
Latvia	11	11	11	12	12	12	12	12	12	12
Lithuania	10	13	12	12	12	12	12	12	12	12
Hungary	15	15	21	21	21	21	21	21	21	21
Poland	8	11	19	20	20	20	20	20	20	20
Romania	13	13	18	23	23	23	23	23	23	23
Slovenia	31	31	36	36	36	38	38	38	38	38
Slovakia	12	12	29	30	30	30	30	30	30	30

Source: https://ec.europa.eu/eurostat/data/database/, access 22 August 2018.

Table 12.7 Pollution, grime or other environmental problems in household survey 2005–17

	2005	2010	2015	2016	2017
European Union	18.8*	14.8	14.2	14.0	nd
Bulgaria	22.7	16.2	15.3	15.1	14.8
Czechia	19.8	18.5	13.8	13.5	11.6
Estonia	20.6	11.3	9.3	9.9	8.7
Croatia	nd	9.0	6.0	7.0	nd
Latvia	28.0	28.5	17.9	17.2	18.4
Lithuania	14.0	12.2	15.0	15.6	nd
Hungary	17.2	11.1	14.8	12.8	12.5
Poland	13.8	9.3	10.5	11.4	12.6
Romania	nd	19.9	15.3	14.5	14.6
Slovenia	20.2	18.6	15.8	15.9	16.8
Slovakia	18.7	20.3	11.2	9.3	nd

* Average value of 19 'euro' Member States.

Source: http://appsso.eurostat.ec.europa.eu/nui/show.do?query=BOOKMARK_DS-056144_QID_ C79B101_UID_-3F171EB0&layout=TIME,C,X,0;GEO,L,Y,0;HHTYP,L,Z,0;INCGRP,L,Z,1;UNIT, L,Z,2;INDICATORS,C,Z,3;&zSelection=DS-056144UNIT,PC;DS-056144INCGRP,TOTAL;DS-056144INDICATORS,OBS_FLAG;DS-056144HHTYP,TOTAL;&rankName1=HHTYP_1_2_-1_2&rankName2=TIME_1_0_0_0&rankName3=UNIT_1_2_-1_2&rankName4=GEO_1_2_0_1&rankName5=INDICATORS_1_2_-1_2&rankName6=INCGRP_1_2_-1_2&sortC=ASC_-1_ FIRST&rStp=&cStp=&rDCh=&cDCh=&rDM=true&cDM=true&footnes=false&empty=false&wai =false&time_mode=ROLLING&time_most_recent=false&lang=EN&cfo=%23%23%23%2C%23%23 %23.%23%23%23&lang=en, accessed 22 August 2018.

The data presented show significant differences between CEE countries. While in the Baltic states air quality does not in principle pose a risk to human health, in the Balkan countries, all (Slovenia) or almost all (Croatia) residents of urbanised areas are exposed to the excessive influence of particulate matter and ozone.

	PM$_{10}$ (daily limit value)	O$_3$ (target value)	NO$_2$ (annual limit value)
UE	<u>19</u>	<u>30</u>	<u>9</u>
Bulgaria	78	0	< 1
Croatia	81	94	3
Czechia	19	89	1
Estonia	0	0	0
Hungary	27	100	2
Latvia	4	0	4
Lithuania	2	0	0
Poland	81	38	1
Romania		12	1
Slovenia	100	100	0
Slovakia	6		5

Notes:

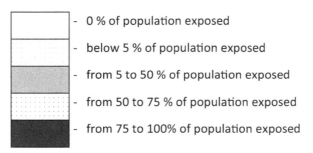

- 0 % of population exposed
- below 5 % of population exposed
- from 5 to 50 % of population exposed
- from 50 to 75 % of population exposed
- from 75 to 100% of population exposed

Figure 12.20 Urban population exposed to air pollutant concentrations above selected air quality standards

Source: www.eea.europa.eu/data-and-maps/figures/urban-population-exposed-to-air-1, accessed 22 August 2018.

Table 12.8 Premature deaths attributable to $PM_{2.5}$, NO_2 and O_3 exposure in CEE countries and the EU-28 in 2015

	Population	$PM_{2.5}$		NO_2		O_3	
		Annual mean*	Premature deaths	Annual mean*	Premature deaths	Annual mean*	Premature deaths
Bulgaria	7,246,000	24.0	13,620	16.5	740	2,519	200
Croatia	4,247,000	15.6	4,430	15.7	300	4,503	180
Czechia	10,512,000	18.6	10,810	16.8	550	3,822	310
Estonia	1,316,000	8.7	750	9	10	1,991	20
Hungary	9,877,000	17.3	11,970	17.1	1,210	3,620	350
Latvia	4,606,000	14.1	2,190	12.3	60	2,213	50
Lithuania	2,943,000	15.5	3,350	12.5	60	2,457	70
Poland	38,018,000	23.0	46,020	15.1	1,700	3,425	970
Romania	19,947,000	17.5	23,960	16.5	1,860	1,842	350
Slovakia	5,416,000	19.1	5,160	15.2	100	4,344	160
Slovenia	2,061,000	15.1	1,710	15	60	5,086	80
CEE-11	98,943,000	17.3	123,970	14.8	6,650	3,257	2,740
EU-28	502,351,000	14.0	399,000	18.7	75,000	3,507	13,600

* The annual mean (in $\mu g/m^3$) expressed as population-weighted concentration.

Source: European Environment Agency 2017: Air quality in Europe – 2017 report. Publications Office of the European Union, Luxembourg.

Table 12.8 shows the impact of air pollution by selected pollutants on the number of premature deaths in CEE countries. Although the population of CEE countries represents less than 20% of the EU population, as many as 31% of those dying prematurely due to particulate matter pollution come from the region. In the case of ozone pollution, this percentage is 21%, while for NO_2 it is only 8.9% (European Environment Agency 2017).

As regards $PM_{2.5}$, the highest numbers of premature deaths are estimated for the countries with the largest populations (Germany, Italy, Poland, the United Kingdom and France). However, in relative terms, when considering premature death per 100,000 inhabitants, the largest impacts can be observed in the central and eastern European countries where the highest concentrations are also observed (i.e. Bulgaria, Poland and Hungary). Slovenia and Croatia (along with Greece, Italy and Malta) are the countries with the highest percentage (per 100,000 inhabitants) of premature deaths due to too high ozone concentrations (European Environment Agency 2017).

Environmental protection governance

The environmental management system has a large impact on the quality of the natural environment, influencing, among other things, the amount of pressure exerted on its elements. The transformation process that the countries of Central and Eastern Europe have undergone has had a significant impact on the effectiveness of this system. Although, as mentioned above, the formation of the institutional system of environmental protection in the CEE countries began back in the 1970s and 1980s, until the transformation, the environmental policy of these countries was passive and completely subordinated to economic policy. An example of this might be the 'National Programme for Environmental Protection by 2010', adopted by the Polish government in 1988 (MOŚZNiL 1988). Despite huge environmental pollution and very high emissions, this programme not only did not provide for its reduction, but even expected it to increase because of the need to maintain a high rate of economic growth. A similar approach was followed in other countries of the region. Changes in the approach to environmental policy did not take place until after the beginning of the transformation process.

Since then, three periods of development and implementation of environmental policies can be distinguished. The first is the period from the transformation to the commencement of the accession negotiations. This was the period of defining new social and economic objectives within the emerging democratic system. Tasks in the field of policy protection were specified both in strategic documents (as in Poland, where the First Environmental Policy of the State was adopted in 1991) and in legal regulations (in 1991, provisions defining the principles of environmental protection were introduced into the Bulgarian Constitution). At that time, an institutional system for environmental protection management was created and instruments of environmental policies typical for democratic countries with market economies were introduced.

This initial period was also a time of support for the development and implementation of environmental policy, provided to CEE countries by the international community. The assistance included advice, education, institutional strengthening as well as financial support. An example of the latter is the Polish EcoFund Foundation established in 1992, whose activities were financed by the debt-for-environment swap of part of the Polish foreign debt. In 1992–2010, from this source, the EcoFund received about PLN 2.5 billion[32] (about EUR 630 million). However, the actual financial impact of the Foundation's work was much greater. Thanks to the efforts made to cooperate with other public institutions active in the field of environmental protection and the involvement of the beneficiaries' own resources, a leverage effect was achieved, the value of which can be estimated at 4.5. This means that approximately PLN 13 billion (i.e. about EUR 3.3 billion)[33] was spent in Poland on environmental protection in the years 1993–2008 thanks to the use of the debt-for-environment swap funds (E&Y, InE 2010). Support in the form of the Swiss debt conversion was also granted to Bulgaria, which in 1995 established the National Trust EcoFund.[34]

However, most of the institutions financing environmental protection were established without foreign support. The creation of an effective system of financing environmental protection was extremely important, as it enabled medium-term planning of pro-environmental investments, created a stable system for their financing and facilitated the implementation of priority programmes and investment projects. In 1989, the first institution of this type in CEE, the National Fund for Environmental Protection and Water Management, was established in Poland. In the following years, such institutions were also established in other countries (Table 12.9). The funds at their disposal came both from environmental charges and environmental penalties (Bulgaria, Czechia, Estonia, Hungary, Poland), fuel charges (Bulgaria, Hungary), state budget payments (Slovakia) and World Bank loans (Slovenia). In Bulgaria, Czechia, Estonia, Slovenia and Hungary, part of the resources raised by the state budget in the process of privatisation was also used as income for environmental funds (Francis et al. 1999).

The importance of creating a system of institutions financing environmental protection in CEE countries can be shown by comparing the amount of funds available for environmental protection in the seven CEE countries listed in Table 13.9 and in the countries that emerged after the collapse of the Soviet Union: in 1997 such funds amounted to about USD 735 million (about USD 9.44 per capita) in CEE countries against USD 36 million (about USD 0.16 per capita) in Russia and the Newly Independent States (NIS). Thanks to the establishment of institutional systems, in the years 1993–97 alone, the amount of funds available for environmental protection in the CEE countries in question increased by more than 70% (Francis et al. 1999).

Therefore, it is highly probable that without these systems, no progress in environmental protection in the CEE countries would have been possible.

The second period in the development of environmental management in CEE countries began with the opening of accession negotiations between the CEE countries and the European Commission. This was a time of enormous effort for most countries in the region. In a relatively short time, they not only had to adapt their environmental protection laws to the requirements of the EU, amending and adopting dozens of new legal acts and creating environmental protection administration systems adapted to the requirements of the EU, but they also had to ensure that the new regulations and obligations would be fulfilled. This stemmed from the concern of the European Commission that, in the event of excessive delays in the implementation of the new regulations in CEE countries, the so-called Mediterranean syndrome would occur – a substantial discrepancy between legal obligations and their actual implementation, which was the case, for instance, in Spain, Greece and Portugal after their accession to the EU (Jordan 1999). How difficult and costly that process was can be demonstrated by the example of Poland: the screening process showed that only 30% of national environmental legislation complied with the EU requirements, and the cost of implementing the new obligations was estimated at between EUR 30 billion and even EUR 60 billion (Jentzen et al. 1998). Although the EU tried to support these efforts financially – through pre-accession assistance programmes (support for environmental protection in Poland from the Instrument for Structural Policies for Pre-Accession (ISPA) amounted to about EUR 1.3 billion[35] between 2000 and 2003), the main effort had to be borne by the candidate countries.

Table 12.9 Key characteristics of selected environmental funds (established in 1989–94) in CEE countries

Country	Name of the fund Established in (year)	Income in million USD		Expenditure in million USD		Major fields of expenditure in 1997	Primary disbursement mechanism in 1997
		in 1993	in 1997	in 1993	in 1997		
Bulgaria	National Environmental Protection Fund 1993	3.60	9.49	2.18	4.38	Water (43.7%) Monitoring (20.5%) Waste (16.8%) Air (9.3%) Soil (8.3%)	Grants (76.8%) Equity investment (15.6%) Interest-free loans (7.7%)
Czechia	State Environmental Fund 1992	94.94	167.15	98.41	103.97	Water (57.4%) Air (36.5%) Nature/landscape protection (4.2) Waste (1.8)	Grants (55.4%) Soft and interest-free loans (7.6%) Interest subsidies (0.6%)
Estonia	Central Environmental Fund 1990	0.93 (in 1994)	7.69	1.08 (in 1994)	8.78	Water (33.3%) Building program (19.3%) 'Supervision' (11.9%) Waste (10.1%)	Grants (89.6%) Interest-free loans (approx. 22%) Soft loans (approx. 3%)
Hungary	Central Environmental Protection Fund 1993	29.90	80.99	17.19	84.56	Air (21.6%) Water (15.4%) Waste (13.9%)	Grants (approx. 75%) Interest-free loans (approx. 22%) Soft loans (3%)
Poland*	National Fund for Environmental protection and Water Management 1989	266.70	418.6	204.94	389.7	Water (39%) Air (33.2%) Soil (8.9%) Nature protection (3.4%)	Soft loans (61.2%) Grants (30.9%) Equity investment (5.1%) Interest subsidies (2.5%)
Slovakia	State Environmental Fund 1991	31.89	30.99	34.94	28.94	Water (55%) Air (26.9%) Waste (9.5%)	Grants (100%)
Slovenia	Environmental Development Fund 1994	2.02 (in 1994)	20.43	0.6 (in 1995)	17.81	Nature protection (2.3%) Air (73.5%) Water (21.7%) Waste (4.8%)	Soft loans (100%)

* In 1997, Poland also had 49 provincial environmental funds as well as community funds.

Source: Francis P., Klarer J., Petkova N. (eds), 1999: Sourcebook on environmental funds in economies in transition. A regional overview and survey of selected Environmental Funds in CEE and NI countries. OECD. Paris.

The third period began when individual countries became members of the EU. However, the investment effort did not come to an end – in the initial period, all countries had to continue the investments necessary to implement the EU rules, for which derogations for implementation had been obtained in the Accession Treaty. At the same time, these countries faced the need to comply with new obligations arising from the EU's adoption of new environmental legislation and the development of EU environmental policy. It should therefore come as no surprise that spending on environmental protection was (and still is) higher than the EU average in most CEE countries (Figure 12.21).

The share of environmental spending in recent years has been the lowest in the Baltic states (Latvia has been below the EU average for the whole period), the highest in Romania and Slovenia (in 2013 at about 1.2% of GDP) and in Czechia (about 1% of GDP). In six countries, the proportion of environmental protection expenditure to GDP after 2005 is steadily increasing, in two countries (Lithuania and Slovakia) it is on a downward trend.[36]

The high level of expenditure on environmental protection translates into an increase in the number of jobs related to the provision of environmental products and services. The data are shown in Table 12.10. Although they are of a random nature, they clearly indicate that the number of jobs in the sector in the countries that invest most in environmental protection is growing faster than the EU average.

However, the high level of spending on environmental protection has no correlation with the readiness and capability to implement EU requirements. Between 2007 and 2017, the European Commission pursued hundreds of cases against Member States for lack of harmonisation of EU law and/or for

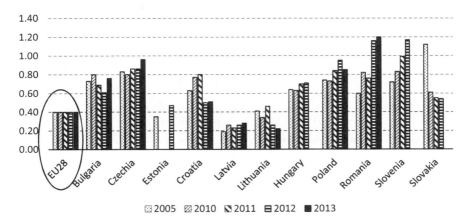

Figure 12.21 Environmental protection expenditure in CEE countries 2005, 2010–13 (% of GDP)

Source: http://appsso.eurostat.ec.europa.eu/nui/show.do?dataset=env_ac_exp2&lang=en, accessed on 13.07.2018.

Table 12.10 Employment in the environmental goods and services sector in CEE countries

Country	Period	Increase in %
EU–28	2007–15	22.0
Bulgaria	2011–15	34.6
Croatia	2015–16	1.8
Czechia	2012–15	23.9
Estonia	2014–15	18.9
Latvia	2008–15	16.6
Lithuania	2010–15	34.2
Poland	2007–15	49.3
Romania	2014–15	5.7
Slovenia	2013–15	1.5

No data available for Hungary and Slovakia.

Source: http://appsso.eurostat.ec.europa.eu/nui/show.do?dataset=env_ac_egss1&lang=en.

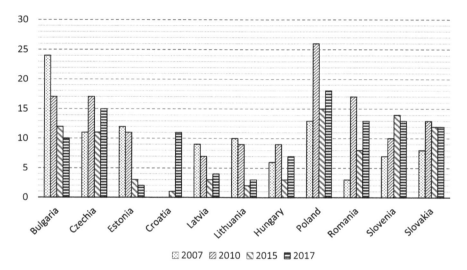

Figure 12.22 Number of proceedings for infringement of EU environmental law in CEE countries in the years 2007, 2010, 2015 and 2017

Source: http://ec.europa.eu/environment/legal/law/statistics.htm, accessed 8 August 2018.

insufficient implementation. The largest number of proceedings (481) were conducted in 2013; it is estimated that about one-third of these cases were instituted against countries from the CEE region (Figure 12.22). In 2017, the share of proceedings against CEE countries amounted to 33.2%, with the European Commission having the largest number of objections against Poland (18 cases) and Czechia (15 cases). However, Spain (30 cases) and Greece (27 cases)[37] accounted for the largest number of cases of this type among all EU countries.

The gravity and relevance of environmental issues in the overall policy of individual countries depends largely on the opinion of citizens on the importance of these problems in their lives. Figure 12.23 shows the results of the 2017 Eurobarometer survey on the assessment of the impact of environmental issues on the lives of people. Only in two CEE countries (Czechia and Estonia) was the percentage of respondents acknowledging that these issues have an impact on their lives lower than the EU average (Figure 12.23). Compared to the previous surveys in 2008, the opinion of Poles and Lithuanians has changed the most: in 2008, the percentage of respondents from these countries considering that environmental protection affects their lives was lower than the EU average (33% and 25%, respectively; Special Eurobarometer 468 2017).

On the other hand, residents of CEE countries, more than residents of other EU regions, believe that environmental problems should be tackled primarily at the national level (and not in cooperation with the EU) and point to the government as the authority responsible for these actions. Only in Estonia and Latvia was the share of respondents claiming that decisions in this respect should be taken jointly – by the government and the EU – higher than the average for the whole EU. This is surprising, because respondents generally acknowledged the role of the EU in implementing environmental policy objectives, and in most countries in the region (except Slovakia, Czechia, Romania and Estonia) support for more EU funding of environmental protection was stronger than the EU average (Special Eurobarometer 468 2017).

Eurobarometer surveys, on the other hand, showed that there is a difference between the perception of environmental priorities by residents of CEE and the rest of the EU. Respondents from CEE identified traditional problems as being the most important: air pollution (Bulgaria, Poland, Romania, Croatia), growth of waste volumes (Lithuania, Latvia, Hungary, Slovakia, Czechia, Estonia, Slovenia) or protection of nature and landscape, while for the inhabitants of the 'old' EU countries the first priority is fighting climate change (Special Eurobarometer

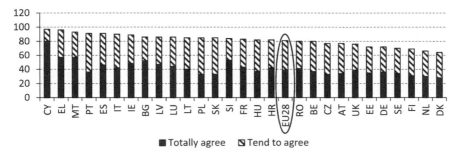

■ Totally agree   ◨ Tend to agree

Figure 12.23 Percentage of respondents declaring that environmental issues have an impact on their lives ('totally agree' and 'tend to agree') in the EU countries in 2017

Source: Special Eurobarometer 468, 2017: Attitudes of European citizens towards the environment. Summary. European Union.

468 2017). This has not changed significantly since 2008 and may explain the low priority given to climate protection in some CEE countries.

Conclusion

The impact of the systemic and socio-economic transformation on the quality of the environment in Central and Eastern Europe, and on the environmental policy of the countries of the region as well as its effectiveness, was undeniably positive (with the reservation that this assessment only applies to the 11 EU Member States in the region). After 1989, an extensive environmental management system was created in all the countries analysed, the environmental protection infrastructure was developed, and emissions of many pollutants discharged into the environment were reduced. Environmental policy was developed, and in most countries this policy is actively pursued (although only in some countries it involves proactive measures, in many others it is reactive). The high share of environmental protection spending in the GDP, which is higher than the EU-28 average in most countries of the region, shows that these countries are trying to bridge the gap in environmental protection between themselves and those EU Member States in which active measures to protect the environment have been pursued since the 1970s. It is worth remembering that when assessing the changes that have taken place in the analysed countries and the effects of these changes, we should compare them to those countries from the region which have not become members of the EU (Russia, Ukraine, NIS, other Balkan countries), rather than to the 'old' EU Member States. This also applies to environmental protection spending. Although the analysed countries spend more in terms of GDP than other Member States, in absolute terms (due to the significantly lower GDP of these countries) the funds allocated for these purposes are usually lower than in the 'old' Member States.

The analysis also seems to confirm the validity of the approach adopted at the end of the 1990s and the beginning of the 21st century by the European Commission and the Member States regarding environmental issues in the EU candidate countries. This included the expectation that they would not only adapt their laws and procedures to the EU requirements, but that they would also physically comply with the new obligations. Although in most cases this was not achieved before the date of membership (it was necessary to negotiate transitional periods for the implementation of certain directives), in the pre-accession period significant progress was achieved in the implementation of EU requirements. As a result, in the following years, the countries of the region did not become an 'impediment' to the development of EU environmental policy, and the number of proceedings initiated by the European Commission for lack of harmonisation or implementation of EU environmental regulations is generally lower in the case of CEE countries than in the case of the countries that became EU members in the 1980s (Greece, Spain and Portugal). This conclusion seems to hold even with regard to Poland, which blocked the development of EU climate policy three times between 2008 and 2014. However, this was primarily an attempt to protect the domestic mining sector and its own vision of energy policy rather than to oppose the development of the EU's environmental policy.

This general, positive assessment does not mean, however, that the countries of the region have effectively solved all their environmental problems. It rather indicates that the situation in this respect has somehow normalised and is typical of developed countries. The countries in question are still trying to catch up with more developed economies. This applies not only to environmental protection, but also to quality of life and standards of living, social welfare, the competitiveness and innovation of the economy or the level of individual incomes. The achievement of some of these objectives, if pursued without care for natural resources, may endanger the quality of the region's environment. The new challenges faced by these countries require further improvement of environmental policy and linking it with social and economic policies. Counteracting excessive consumption, creating sustainable mobility, sustainable approaches to waste management, protecting ecosystem services and focusing on nature-based solutions are key challenges.

This is all the more important because, although the countries in question have made significant progress in environmental protection, it is difficult to say that their development is in line with the principles of sustainable development. This is reflected, for example, in the low level of transforming the economy towards a circular economy. Only two countries in the region (Poland and Estonia) have a circular material use rate higher or similar to the EU-28 average, while the remaining countries have a much lower rate (although Slovenia and Czechia as well as Croatia and Latvia are making rapid progress; see Figure 12.24).

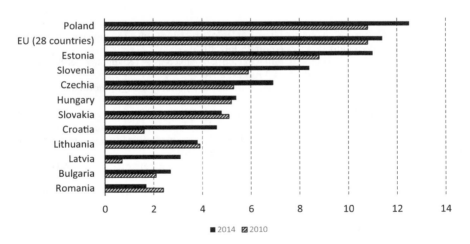

Figure 12.24 Circular material use rate in CEE countries (in %)

Source: http://ec.europa.eu/eurostat/tgm/table.do?tab=table&init=1&language=en&pcode=cei_srm030&plugin=1, accessed on 7 August 2018.

Today, almost 30 years after the beginning of the transformation process in CEE, it must be said that, although the starting point was similar for all the countries concerned (except for Croatia, which participated in the Balkan War in the 1990s), it is difficult to speak of a uniform experience or significant similarities between them. Each country has chosen its own path, and has used the opportunities offered by the process of transformation and European integration in different ways and with different effects. Some countries (Slovenia, Slovakia, Estonia, Latvia, Lithuania and Latvia) have decided to adopt the euro and thus to be at the centre of the EU decision-making process. Others, like Hungary and Poland (from 2015), have been increasingly contesting the values and principles of the European Union, including those concerning environmental protection. Therefore, the directions in which environmental policies in the analysed countries will develop, and whether their development will be consistent with the principles of sustainable development, will depend more and more on their own preferences and decisions.

Notes

1 The analysis covers 11 EU Member States: Bulgaria, Croatia, Czechia, Estonia, Hungary, Latvia, Lithuania, Poland, Romania, Slovakia and Slovenia.
2 www.un-documents.net/aconf48-14r1.pdf, accessed 5 September 2018.
3 www.europarl.europa.eu/atyourservice/pl/displayFtu.html?ftuId=FTU_2.5.1.html, accessed on 5 September 2018
4 Consolidated versions of the Treaty on the European Union and on the functioning of the European Union (2010/c 83/01). https://eur-lex.europa.eu/legal-content/PL/TXT/PDF/?uri=OJ:C:2010:083:FULL&from=PL, accessed on 22 August 2018.
5 http://appsso.eurostat.ec.europa.eu/nui/show.do?dataset=nrg_100a&lang=en, accessed on 3 August 2018.
6 http://ec.europa.eu/eurostat/tgm/table.do?tab=table&plugin=1&language=en&pcode =sdg_07_30
   http://ec.europa.eu/eurostat/tgm/table.do?tab=table&init=1&language=en&pcode =sdg_12_20&plugin=1, accessed on 25 July 2018.
7 https://ec.europa.eu/eurostat/tgm/table.do?tab=table&init=1&language=en&pcode=t 2020_31&plugin=1, accessed on 3 August 2018.
8 http://appsso.eurostat.ec.europa.eu/nui/show.do?dataset=road_if_motorwa&lang=en, accessed on 3 August 2018.
9 http://ciekaweliczby.pl/172-lata/, accessed on 5 August 2018.
10 http://ec.europa.eu/eurostat/web/transport/data/database, accessed on 5 August 2018.
11 https://ec.europa.eu/eurostat/tgm/table.do?tab=table&init=1&language=en&pcod e=t2020_rk310&plugin=1, accessed on 5 August 2018.
12 http://appsso.eurostat.ec.europa.eu/nui/show.do?dataset=env_air_gge&lang=en, accessed on 15 August 2018.
13 www.eea.europa.eu/data-and-maps/indicators/urban-waste-water-treatment/urban-waste-water-treatment-assessment-4, accessed on 4 September 2018.
14 Ibid.
15 Biological capacity:

> the capacity of ecosystems to regenerate what people demand from those surfaces. Life, including human life, competes for space. The biocapacity of a particular surface represents its ability to renew what people demand. Biocapacity is therefore the ecosystems' capacity to produce biological materials used by people and to absorb waste

material generated by humans, under current management schemes and extraction technologies. Biocapacity can change from year to year due to climate, management, and also what portions are considered useful inputs to the human economy. In the National Footprint Accounts, the biocapacity of an area is calculated by multiplying the actual physical area by the yield factor and the appropriate equivalence factor. Biocapacity is usually expressed in global hectares.

(source: www.footprintnetwork.org/resources/glossary/
#biocapacity, accessed on 25 August 2018)

16 Ecological footprint – a measure of the area of biologically productive land and water an individual, population, or activity requires to produce all the resources it consumes and to absorb the waste it generates, using prevailing technology and resource management practices. The ecological footprint is usually measured in global hectares. Because trade is global, an individual or country's footprint includes land or sea from all over the world. Without further specification, ecological footprint generally refers to the ecological footprint of consumption. Ecological footprint is often referred to in short form as footprint (source: http://data.footprintnetwork.org/#/, accessed on 25 August 2018).

17 All data on biocapacity and ecological footprint based on http://data.footprintnetwork.org/#/, accessed on 25 August 2018.

18 The analysed period is different for different countries and depends on the availability of reliable source data. The analysed period is indicated in Table 12.3.

19 The definition of 'agglomeration' is given in Article 2(4) of the Urban Waste Water Treatment Directive (91/271/EEC): 'Agglomeration means an area where the population and/or economic activities are sufficiently concentrated for urban waste water to be collected and conducted to an urban waste water treatment plant or to a final discharge point'.

20 There are no unequivocal conclusions about the reasons for the increase of the share of water with insufficient status. The reasons may include both insufficient implementation of the Framework Water Directive by the Member States and the steady increase in the volume of water subject to EU monitoring.

21 Own assessment based on analyses of first and second River Basin Management Plans (RBMP) submitted by MS. Source: WISE-SoW database: *Surface water bodies: Ecological status or potential group.*

22 Results based on WISE-SoW. *Groundwater bodies: Number or Size, by Quantitative status.* https://tableau.discomap.eea.europa.eu/t/Wateronline/views/WISE_SOW_Ground-WaterBody/GWB_QuantitativeStatus?:embed=y&:showShareOptions=true&:display_count=no&:showVizHome=no, accessed on 27 August 2018.

23 Results based on WISE-SoW. *Groundwater bodies: Number or Size, by Chemical status.* https://tableau.discomap.eea.europa.eu/t/Wateronline/views/WISE_SOW_Ground-Water_Statistics/GWBbyChemicalstatus?:embed=y&:showShareOptions=true&:display_count=no&:showVizHome=no, accessed on 27 August 2018.

24 Own assessment based on the data published in: European Environment Agency (2017): *Air quality in Europe – 2017 report.* Publications Office of the European Union, Luxembourg.

25 Own assessment based on the data published in: European Environment Agency (2017): *Air quality in Europe – 2017 report.*

26 Ibid.

27 Ibid.

28 Ibid.

29 Ibid.

30 Ibid.

31 http://wwf.panda.org/knowledge_hub/all_publications/?326895/The-State-of-Implementation-of-the-Birds-and-Habitats-Directives-in-the-EU, accessed on 27 August 2018.

32 In 2008 fixed prices.
33 Factoring to the adopted parity EUR/PLN for the entire period of the Foundation's operation (i.e. PLN 3.9463).
34 This institution is still functioning, its income is generated from the sale of GHG emission reduction units (see http://ecofund-bg.org/en/about-us/, accessed on 30 August 2018).
35 www.bcgconsulting.pl/fundusze_przedakcesyjne.php, accessed on 13 July 2018.
36 http://appsso.eurostat.ec.europa.eu/nui/show.do?dataset=env_ac_exp2&lang=en, accessed on 13 July 2018.
37 http://ec.europa.eu/environment/legal/law/statistics.htm, accessed on 25 July 2018.

References

Bowman, M., & Hunter, D. (1992). Environmental reforms in post-communist Central Europe: From high hopes to hard reality. *Michigan Journal of International Law*, 13(4), 921–980.

Carson, R. (1962). *Silent Spring*. Boston: Houghton Mifflin Harcourt.

E&Y, InE (2010). Report on the assessment of the eco-conversion programme implemented by the EcoFund Foundation. *Ernst & Young and Institute for Sustainable Development*. April 2010.

EEA, 2010: *European Union Emission Inventory Report 1990–2008 Under the UNECE Convention on Long-range Transboundary Air Pollution (LRTAP)*. EEA. Copenhagen.

European Environment Agency, 2017: *Air Quality in Europe – 2017 Report*. Publications Office of the European Union, Luxembourg.

Francis, P., Klarer, J., & Petkova, N. (eds.) (1999). *Sourcebook on Environmental Funds in Economies in Transition. A Regional Overview and Survey of Selected Environmental Funds in CEE and NI countries*. Paris: OECD.

Hill, P.J. (1992). Environmental problems under socialism. *Cato Journal*, 12(2), 321–335.

Jancar-Webster, B. (1991). Environmental politics in Eastern Europe in 1980. In: J. DeBartelaban (ed.), *The Breathe Free. Eastern Europe Environmental Crisis*. Washington, DC: The Woodrow Wilson Centre Press, Baltimore and London: The J. Hopkins University Press, pp. 25–55.

Jentzen, J., Schelleman, F., Karaczun, Z., Indeka, L., & Przepiera, A. (1998). *Costing and Financial Analysis of Approximation in Environment*. Agriconsulting Europe. Vol. 1 (p. 67), Vol. 2 (p. 68). Phare POL 96–0863.00.

Jordan, A. (1999). The implementation of EU environmental policy: A policy problem without a political solution? *Environment and Planning C: Government and Policy*, 17, 69–90.

Karaczun, Z.M., & Grześkiewicz, R. (1995). *Ownership transformation in Agriculture vs Environmental Protection*. Report 2/95. Warsaw: Institute for Sustainable Development.

Lang, I. (2003). Sustainable development – A new challenge for the countries in Central and Eastern Europe. *Environment, Development and Sustainability*, 5, 167–178.

MOŚZNiL. (1988). *Narodowy program ochrony środowiska do 2010 roku*. Warszawa: Ministerstwo Ochrony Środowiska, Zasobów Naturalnych I Leśnictwa.

Report from the Commission to The European Parliament and the Council (2017). *Two Years after Paris – Progress towards Meeting the EU's Climate Commitments*. Brussels, 7.11.2017 COM(2017) 646 final. (based on European Environment Agency data).

Sluis, T., Foppen, R., Gillings, S., Groen, T., Henkens, R., Hennekens, S., Huskens, S., Noble, D., Ottburg, F., Santini, L., Sierdsema, H., van Kleunen, A., Schaminee, J., van Swaay, C., Toxopeus, B., Wallis de Vries, M., & Walters, L. (2016). *How much Biodiversity is in Natura 2000?; The 'Umbrella Effect' of the European Natura 2000 protected area network*. Alterra Wageningen UR (University & Research centre), Wageningen.

Special Eurobarometer 468, 2017: *Attitudes of European Citizens Towards the Environment. Summary.* European Union.

U Thant, S. (1969). The Problems of Human Environment. Report by the UN Secretary General, 26.05.1969, *Newsletter of the Polish National Commission for UNESCO.* 1/1969.

WRc+ (2015a). *Assessment of Member States' progress in the implementation of Programmes of Measures during the first planning cycle of the Water Framework Directive Member State Report: Hungary (HU).* Available at: http://ec.europa.eu/environment/water/water-framework/pdf/4th_report/country/HU.pdf Accessed on 20 August 2018.

WRc+ (2015b). *Assessment of Member States' progress in the implementation of Programmes of Measures during the first planning cycle of the Water Framework Directive Member State Report: Bulgaria (BG).* Available at: http://ec.europa.eu/environment/water/water-framework/pdf/4th_report/country/BG.pdf Accessed on 26 August 2018.

WRc+ (2015c). *Assessment of Member States' progress in the implementation of Programmes of Measures during the first planning cycle of the Water Framework Directive Member State Report: Latvia (LT).* Available at: http://ec.europa.eu/environment/water/water-framework/pdf/4th_report/country/LT.pdf Accessed on 26 August 2018.

Part IV

The future challenges of the CEE countries within integrated Europe

13 Cohesion Policy in Central and Eastern Europe

Is it fit for purpose?[1]

John Bachtler and Martin Ferry

Introduction

The accession of the Central and Eastern European (CEE) countries presented the EU with its most formidable integration challenges since the formation of the European Economic Community. Much of the heavy lifting was done during the pre-accession period with political, institutional, economic and social reforms in the CEE Candidate Countries that were initiated or accelerated by the conditionalities involved in meeting the requirements of the acquis communautaire. The subsequent progress in terms of economic growth and convergence can be attributed to trade and investment, as outlined in the chapters by Orłowski and Capello in this volume. However, the gains and losses associated with accession and integration have not been distributed equally: some parts of Central and Eastern Europe have benefited more than others. As discussed in the chapter by Gorzelak and Smętkowski in this volume, a key feature of the post-accession period has been the widening of economic and social disparities – mainly between capital cities and other major urban areas, and other regions, and, in some countries, also between western and eastern regions. Peripheral, rural areas have often gained least from transformation and the accession process.

EU Cohesion Policy has been the major policy tool for providing EU funding for regional and local development to Central and Eastern European countries and regions, intended to fulfil the EU's Treaty commitment to economic, social and territorial cohesion. The policy is regarded as a significant benefit of EU membership and is always a central focus of negotiations on the EU's Multiannual Financial Framework (MFF). Over the period 2000–2020, some EUR 550 billion has either been paid out or is projected to be spent under Cohesion Policy funds to programmes and projects in Central and Eastern Europe. A central strategic and operational challenge for CEE countries is how to deploy these funds to best effect, a challenge that has been met with mixed success across time and between countries.

This chapter examines the record of Cohesion Policy in Central and Eastern Europe. It first charts the evolution of EU funding from the pre-accession period through successive MFF periods until the present (as well as projections for the future) and provides an overview of where the funding has been allocated. The chapter then explores the impact and 'added value' of Cohesion Policy for regional and local development in CEE, concluding with some reflections on the lessons learned.

Enlargement and preparations for Cohesion Policy

The enlargement of the EU in 2004 to include eight countries of Central and Eastern Europe, together with Cyprus and Malta, was one of the most important 'turning points' in Cohesion Policy since the 1988 reform of the Structural Funds. From the earliest discussions about enlargement in the early 1990s, it was evident that the accession of much poorer countries would have significant implications for Community policies and finances, with the need for sizeble transfers under Cohesion Policy and the Common Agricultural Policy (CAP – the agricultural policy of the European Union which implements a system of agricultural subsidies and other programmes) (Manzella and Mendez 2009; Bachtler et al. 2013).

Eurostat data in the mid-1990s showed a big disparity in development between the then EU15 and accession countries. Slovenia and the Czech Republic had levels of GDP per head (PPS) of 59% and 57% of the EU15 average; Slovakia was at 41%, Hungary at 37%, and Poland at 31%. Regional disparities were low by EU15 standards but were quickly widening; outside the capital cities, many regions were estimated to be between 15% and 40% of the EU15 average (Bachtler and Downes 1995; Gorzelak 1996; Weise et al. 2001; Gorzelak et al. 2010).

The accession process was protracted. Initially, it was not clear which countries would join and when. The EU15 Member States had concerns about the implications for their budgetary contributions and receipts, and the case for accession had to be made to the public – both in the EU15 and the accession states. The EU had to conduct parallel negotiations with 12 applicants, which were at different stages in the political, economic and social reforms undertaken as part of post-socialist transitions, combined with the institutional and administrative adaptations required to meet the demands of the acquis (Grabbe 2001; Bachtler et al. 2013).

Among the chapters of the acquis were obligations relating to EU Cohesion Policy. These principally required an institutional framework and adequate administrative capacity to ensure 'sound and cost-effective' programming, implementation, monitoring and evaluation of Structural and Cohesion Funds, as well as compliance with EU legislation in areas such as public procurement, competition and environment in the selection and implementation of EU-funded projects.

Preparation for these tasks was supported by the PHARE programme, intended (from 1994 onwards) to support the integration of Central and Eastern European countries into the EU and utilising the Structural Funds approach to multi-annual funding – although managed by DG Enlargement rather than DG

Regio. Further EU assistance was provided over the 2000–2006 period under the pre-accession instruments ISPA (Cohesion Fund type actions) and SAPARD (Rural Development type actions). For those countries that acceded to the EU in 2004 or 2007, some EUR 18.7 billion was allocated in grants over the 1990–2006 period under PHARE, ISPA and SAPARD, as well as through the 2007 Transition Facility funding for Bulgaria and Romania (B&S Europe 2015).

Subsequent research and evaluation found that PHARE (the main pre-accession instrument) was effective in supporting reforms, especially institutional and regulatory reforms, capacity-building of public services at different levels, investment in physical infrastructure and support to enterprises, NGOs and individuals. However, the reforms were often slow and incomplete, and the institutionalisation of assistance was constrained by weak coordination, high staff turnover, skill shortages, lack of ownership or resistance from stakeholders (SIGMA 1998; OECD 2001; Bossaert and Demmke 2003; Bachtler and McMaster 2008; Bachtler et al. 2014; B&S Europe 2015). It was argued that the lack of a 'formal conditionality' in the acquis meant that many countries did not give sufficient priority to regional policy in their accession planning (Hughes et al. 2003). Consequently, at the time of the first wave of enlargement in 2004, there was considerable concern as to whether the accession countries had the administrative capacity to manage EU funding effectively.

The financial framework for Cohesion Policy in the new Member States was also a difficult area. The Commission first put forward a proposal for the 2000–2006 Multiannual Financial Framework in the 1997 Agenda 2000 paper (European Commission 1997), trying to steer a path between EU15 concerns about the cost of enlargement and the development needs of the prospective new Member States. The EU budget ceiling was kept at 1.27% of EU GDP (and structural policy spending of 0.46%), proposing resources of EUR 275 billion, of which EUR 45 billion would be for the accession countries. Crucially, a limit on Structural Funds allocations was proposed – what became known as the 'absorption cap' – with transfers restricted to 4% of national GDP. Agreement was very difficult to achieve among the EU15, with arguments pitting net contributors concerned with 'budget discipline' against net beneficiaries (particularly Spain, Portugal and Greece) resisting cuts in their Cohesion Policy receipts to fund enlargement. Although an agreement on the MFF was reached at the Berlin European Council in March 1999, it was clearly only an interim solution, since the provision made for acceding countries was much lower than for the poorer members of the EU15 (Wishlade 1999; Bachtler et al. 2013).

Over the subsequent three years, as the accession negotiations moved into their final stages, it became clear that a larger number of Candidate Countries than anticipated would be acceding. The Commission's initial proposal for a financial package for the Candidate Countries (for 2004–06) was lower than had been agreed at the Berlin Council and would need to be shared between ten rather than six new Member States (European Commission 2002). Disagreement among the EU15 at successive Councils under the Spanish and Danish presidencies during 2002 were compounded by strenuous objections from

Table 13.1 Maximum enlargement-related appropriations for commitments 2004–06 (ten new Member States) (in EUR million, 1999 prices)

Commitment appropriations	2004	2005	2006
Heading 1: Agriculture	1,897	3,747	4,147
Heading 2: Structural actions	7,067	8,150	10,350
Heading 3: Internal policies and additional transitional expenditure	1,457	1,428	1,372
Heading 5: Administration	503	558	612
Total commitment appropriations	9,927	12,640	14,901
Heading X (for ten new Member States)	1,273	1,173	940
• Special cash-flow facility	1,011	744	644
• Temporary budgetary compensation	262	429	296

Source: Council of the EU (2002).

the Candidate Countries, notably Poland, foreshadowing arguments that would also become features of subsequent MFF negotiations (Mulvey 2002; Bachtler et al. 2013).

The final deal contained appropriations for commitments of EUR 37.5 billion, of which EUR 25.6 billion were for structural operations (see Table 13.1). At Poland's insistence, an additional heading of EUR 3.4 billion was included to provide a special cash-flow facility (to allow early release of funding) and temporary budgetary compensation for the new Member States. Although the allocations were essentially an 'interim arrangement' for three years, the funding for Structural and Cohesion Funds did account for 1.4% of the GDP of the new Member States, and 2% or more in Latvia (2.84%), Lithuania (2.4%) and Estonia (2.0%) (Applica et al. 2009b).

Accession and implementation of Cohesion Policy, 2004–06

The accession of the Czech Republic, Estonia, Hungary, Latvia, Lithuania, Poland, Slovak Republic and Slovenia (EU8), along with Cyprus and Malta, to the EU on 1 May 2004 constituted a major milestone in the development of the EU. However, as the Council noted at the time (Council of the EU 2003a), 'making a success of enlargement remains the key priority for the years to come'. In its Third Cohesion Report, the European Commission (2004) forecast that many new Member States would have to achieve sustained economic growth of 2.5% above the EU15 average for 20–30 years in order to reach a GDP per capita level of 75% of the EU15. It was acknowledged that major difficulties lay ahead in building up the necessary administrative capacity in the new members, as well as integrating them into the Lisbon Strategy, the Schengen acquis, economic policy coordination, the Stability and Growth Pact and the Eurozone. These challenges would grow as even poorer countries joined the EU; Bulgaria and Romania were expected to join the Union in January 2007 (Bachtler and Wishlade 2004).

Developing the first generation of Cohesion Policy programmes after accession was a demanding exercise for all new Member States. Despite the investment in capacity-building through the pre-accession funds (Figure 13.1), there was limited experience in strategic planning and coordination in line with EU rules and practice (EGO 2013). All of the Structural and Cohesion Policy programmes for 2004–06 in the EU8 were national ones, drawn up by central government ministries with limited involvement of subnational and nongovernmental bodies. Four of the eight new Central and Eastern European Member States had a single, national Structural Funds operational programme, the exceptions being Poland (seven programmes), Czech Republic (five), Hungary (five) and Slovakia (five). The programmes were also simpler than those in the EU15, with a smaller number of measures, a heavy concentration on basic infrastructure (see Table 13.2) and low levels of private co-financing. Ex ante appraisal found that several lacked a clear strategic basis, particularly in Estonia, Hungary, Lithuania and Slovakia, but all of the programmes were negotiated and adopted by the Commission by Summer 2004 (Applica et al. 2009a; Bachtler and McMaster 2008).

Notwithstanding the programming difficulties, the implementation of the 2004–06 programmes was relatively efficient. In advance of programme launch, all CEE countries made considerable efforts to publicise the funding and develop a project pipeline. At the end of the 2004–06 payment period in 2008, the CEE countries had absorbed 93% of Structural Funds allocations, much better than the EU25 average (see Table 13.2). However, there were problems in some countries in the implementation of RTDI (Latvia, Slovakia),

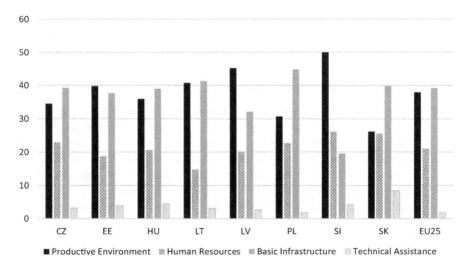

Figure 13.1 Allocation of Structural Funds by priority in CEE countries, 2004–06 (in %)

Source: Applica et al. (2009b).

Table 13.2 Financial absorption, decommitments and corrections for CEE Structural Funds programmes, 2004–06

Member State	Allocations 2004–06		% paid out 2004–08	Decommitments 2004–06 (%)	MS corrections (EUR mill)		Commission Corrections (EUR mill)
	EUR mill	% of EU8			Withdrawals	Recoveries	
CZ	1,584.35	10.5	90.64	−0.21	0	4.12	
EE	371.36	2.5	94.95	−1.84	2.15	0	
HU	1,995.72	13.2	94.11		11.45	0.02	0.04
LV	625.75	4.1	95.00	−1.57	1.07	0.26	3.08
LT	895.17	5.9	95.00		1.20	0.21	
PL	8,275.81	54.8	93.05		0	13.00	37.41
SK	1,115.19	7.4	93.31	−0.01	0.88	2.70	1.07
SI	237.51	1.6	91.82		0	1.54	1.89
EU8	**15,100.86**	**100.0**	**93.18**	**−0.13**	**16.77**	**21.85**	**43.49**
EU25	**211,923.20**		**90.80**	**−1.10**	**1,854.74**	**101.70**	**3,156.24**

Source: Bachtler et al. (2014) based on European Commission (2009) and Applica et al. (2009b).

human resource support (Czech Republic, Slovenia), and aid to large businesses (Poland) (Applica et al. 2009b). The level of decommitment was relatively good, with a minor level of decommitment for the EU8 as a whole; much of the loss of funds was accounted for by two countries, Estonia and Latvia. Levels of financial corrections in the form of withdrawals and recoveries were also low, although assessments by the European Court of Auditors found some concerns with the effectiveness of management and control systems. These and other empirical measures of performance suggested that 'EU8 administrative capacity for implementing Cohesion Policy developed faster and better than policy-makers and academic commentators predicted' (Bachtler et al. 2014: 752).

Substantial Cohesion Policy resources: 2007–13

While the implementation of the 2004–06 programmes was still in progress, the attention of Central and Eastern European policymakers was focused on the more important potential funding being negotiated for the subsequent period. In February 2004, the Commission put forward its proposals for the MFF for the 2007–13 period, envisaging annual Cohesion Policy spending (excluding rural development) increasing by 31%, from EUR 38.8 billion in 2006 to EUR 51 billion in 2013, as part of an overall EU budget involving an average of EUR 146 billion per year in 2007–13 (European Commission 2004). For the Central and Eastern European countries, the key issue was 'fair treatment' of the new Member States to ensure their receipts were comparable with EU15 countries like Spain and Portugal. In this context, the proposal for an absorption limit, capped at 4% of national GDP was regarded as highly disadvantageous. The budget negotiations took almost two years, and the European

Council agreement in December 2005 concluded with a significant reduction (of almost one-sixth) in the overall budget ceiling to EUR 864.3 billion (at 2004 prices) but with an increase in Cohesion Policy's share of the budget and an allocation of EUR 308.4 billion.

The MFF negotiations were marked by a high degree of solidarity among the ten new Member States (EU10 – the eight countries that acceded in 2004 plus Bulgaria and Romania) under Polish leadership. Although they were unable to prevent a reduction in the budget ceiling, they did influence the construction of the final deal on the budget, notably more emphasis on less developed countries and regions and a more progressive application of the absorption cap. They also affected the way that the regulatory debate evolved on co-financing, the n+3 rule and eligibility rules (Bachtler et al. 2013).

The outcome gave 43.7% of the Cohesion Policy budget (EUR 134.4 billion) to the EU10, over 40% of which was accounted for by the allocation to Poland (see Table 13.3). The EU8 were, as a group, to get more than double the annual allocations in the 2004–06 period. However, the influence of the allocation formula meant that the increases were more substantial in the Czech Republic and Slovenia (over 200%) compared to Poland and the Baltic states (50%–80%) because of the influence of capping (Bachtler et al. 2006). Bulgaria and Romania, acceding to the EU at the start of 2007 and receiving Structural and Cohesion Policy funds for the first time, were again accorded an 'interim arrangement' with around a fifth of the EU10 allocation between them.

The change in aid intensity also varied across the CEE countries (see Figure 13.2). All of the new Member States saw a significant increase in aid per head to levels ranging from EUR 223 per head in the case of Poland to EUR

Table 13.3 Indicative financial allocations for CEE Member States, 2007–13 (EUR million, 2004 prices)

	Convergence regions	Cohesion Fund	Phasing-out regions	Phasing-in regions	RCE regions	Terr. Coop	Total
Czech Rep	15,149	7,830	–	–	373	346	**23,698**
Estonia	1,992	1,019	–	–	–	47	**3,058**
Latvia	2,647	1,363	–	–	–	80	**4,090**
Lithuania	3,965	2,034	–	–	–	97	**6,096**
Hungary	12,654	7,589	–	1,865	–	343	**22,451**
Poland	39,486	19,562	–	–	–	650	**59,698**
Slovenia	2,407	1,239	–	–	–	93	**3,739**
Slovak Rep	6,230	3,433	–	–	399	202	**10,264**
Bulgaria	3,873	2,015	–	–	–	159	**6,047**
Romania	11,143	5,769	–	–	–	404	**17,316**
EU10	**85,025**	**44,514**	**0**	**2,228**	**772**	**1,896**	**134,435**
EU27	**177,081**	**61,559**	**12,521**	**10,387**	**38,743**	**7,750**	**308,041**

Source: European Commission (2006).

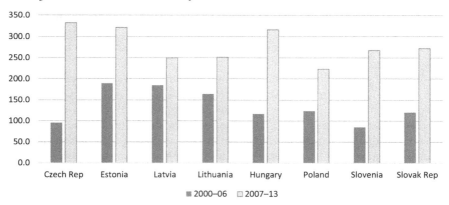

Figure 13.2 Aid per head per year 2004–06 and 2007–13 for EU8 (2004 prices)

Source: Bachtler et al. (2006) based on data in European Commission (2006).

332 in the Czech Republic. In several cases (Czech Republic, Hungary, Slovakia, Slovenia), the EU funding allocated for 2007–13 was three times the per capita allocation in 2004–06, but for others (Estonia, Latvia) the increase was more modest.

Implementing a much greater volume of funding in 2007–13 was a more challenging task for the EU10, allied to the greater prescriptiveness of the regulatory framework regarding thematic priorities (voluntary earmarking), national strategic reference frameworks, and strategic reporting. Bulgaria and Romania were implementing Cohesion Policy programmes for the first time, as was Croatia (for one year after its accession in 2013). Although significant proportions of funding were still allocated to physical infrastructure (principally roads) and environmental projects in the EU10 programmes, a higher proportion of the Funds was allocated to RTDI (especially in Poland), information and communications technology (ICT), entrepreneurship and broadband – some of which proved to be difficult to implement.

Further, implementation of the Funds involved a much larger number of programmes, in some cases with regionalised programming for the first time. The most complex implementation structure was in Poland where three national programmes for infrastructure and environment, human capital, and innovative economy (also Technical Assistance and European Territorial Cooperation) were complemented by 16 regional Operational Programmes (OPs) managing one quarter of the budget, and a programme for eastern Poland. Hungary had seven regional OPs, one for each of its NUTS2 regions, and six sectoral OPs. The Czech Republic had four sectoral OPs, seven regional OPs (one for each NUTS2 region), an OP for the Competitiveness region of Prague and two multi-objective OPs. Slovakia had two regional OPs and seven sectoral OPs.

Financial absorption was less efficient in many countries than in 2004–06 – although this also applied to many EU15 countries, which had a slower time

Table 13.4 Financial absorption and decommitments and EU funding corrections for CEE Structural Funds programmes, 2007–13

Member States	Allocations (EUR million)	Commitments (% of allocations)	Decommitments (% of allocations)	
			n+3	closure
Bulgaria	6,722.3	94.1	1.43	2.48
Croatia	845.3	96.7	0.12	0.03
Czech Republic	26,161.6	93.4	2.76	0.89
Estonia	3,313.6	100.0	0.00	0.00
Latvia	24,244.7	96.7	0.12	0.03
Lithuania	4,655	95.0	0.00	0.00
Hungary	6,826.8	95.0	0.00	0.00
Poland	67,309.8	95.9	0.00	0.00
Romania	18,852.8	91.0	2.57	6.43
Slovakia	11,242.6	97.1	0.15	2.70
Slovenia	4,084.4	95.9	0.00	0.03
EU11	**174,258.9**	**95.1**	**0.78**	**1.15**

Note: Commitments are cumulative net interim payments plus advance payments.

Source: Inforegio, Open Data platform.

profile of payments in 2007–13 compared to the previous period (Applica et al. 2016). Nevertheless, by the deadline for final interim payments in 2016, the CEE countries had committed some 95% of funding (see Table 13.4) across all the EU funds, with figures as high as 100% in the case of Estonia. Decommitment was low across the EU11 as a whole, bearing in mind that they were subject to making payments on commitments within three years (n+3) rather than the two years in other parts of the EU. However, some countries still experienced problems, notably Romania, which had 9% of funding decommitted: 2.57% because of the decommitment rule (particularly because of problems with implementing ESF and EFF); and the remainder due to irregularities identified during closure, especially associated with Cohesion Fund projects. Bulgaria and Slovakia also had relatively high levels of decommitment. Poland, Hungary, Lithuania and Estonia had very low levels of decommitment, remarkably so in the case of Poland given the very large volume of funding that had to be spent.

Tightening economic and budgetary context: 2014–20

For several CEE countries, the 2007–13 funding allocations under Cohesion Policy were the high point of EU funding receipts. Preparations for the 2014–20 period were dominated by the effects of the economic crisis affecting much of the EU, with major political differences between Member States on the EU's response to the Eurozone crisis as well as the squeeze on public finances in many countries. The Commission's initial proposals for the next

MFF in 2011 already indicated that, for the first time, spending on Cohesion Policy would begin to fall. In addition, the maps of regional disparities were becoming more complex. Differential regional growth meant that some Convergence Regions (notably the capital cities of Poland and Romania) would lose eligibility, while the Commission's proposal to introduce a new category of Transition Regions would provide preferential help for regions in difficulty in the EU15.

The conclusions of protracted negotiations, not achieved until early 2013, meant that the overall EU budget (total appropriations for commitments in the MFF) for 2014–20 fell by more than EUR 35 billion, representing a reduction of 3.5%. With more funding shifted to so-called Competitiveness policies, the allocation for Cohesion Policy fell by 8.4% to EUR 325.149 billion (2011 prices) for the 2014–20 period. The CEE countries accounted for about 59% of the allocations to Member States (see Table 13.5), with Poland by far the largest recipient with 40% of the EU11 total (EUR 77.6 billion).

The algorithm used for determining allocations (revised Berlin formula) produced gains and losses for different EU11 countries in 2014–20 compared to 2007–13 (see Figure 13.3). Poland gained most, with a 5.4% increase yielding an additional EUR 3.7 billion, and Romania, Slovakia and (to a limited extent) Bulgaria also increased their allocations. Croatia also was allocated a substantial budget of EUR 8.6 billion of Cohesion Policy funding for the first time. All other EU11 countries experienced a reduction in allocations, especially Slovenia whose funding fell by a third, with large cuts for the Czech Republic (−25%) and Hungary (−20%) also (Mendez and Bachtler 2014).

The 2013 reform of Cohesion Policy was also notable for a major 'turn' in the regulatory framework involving a stronger performance orientation with

Table 13.5 Cohesion allocations in 2014–20

	Cohesion Fund	Less-Developed Regions	More Developed Regions	Terr. Coop.	Youth Empl. Initiative	Total
Bulgaria	2,278.3	5,089.3	0	165.6	55.2	7,588.4
Czech Republic	6,258.9	15,282.5	88.2	339.7	13.6	21,982.9
Estonia	1,073.3	2,461.2	0	55.4	0	3,590.0
Croatia	2,559.6	5,837.5	0	146.1	66.2	8,609.4
Hungary	6,025.4	15,005.2	463.7	361.8	49.8	21,905.9
Lithuania	2,048.9	4,628.7	0	113.7	31.8	6,823.1
Latvia	1,349.4	3,039.8	0	93.6	29.0	4,511.8
Poland	23,208.0	51,163.6	2,242.4	700.5	252.4	77,567.0
Romania	6,935.0	15,058.9	441.4	452.7	106.0	22,993.8
Slovenia	895.4	1,260.0	847.3	62.9	9.2	3,074.8
Slovakia	4,168.3	9,483.7	44.2	223.4	72.2	13,991.7

Source: DG Regional Policy.

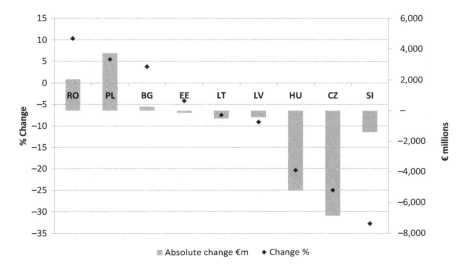

Figure 13.3 Changes in allocation for CEE countries, 2007–13 and 2014–20

Source: EPRC calculations in Bachtler et al. (2014).

requirements for programmes to have more clearly specified objectives, intervention logics and results targets. Conditionality provisions sought to ensure that the pre-conditions for effective implementation of the Funds were put into place, while a new performance framework and reserve were intended to incentivise the achievement of targets with sanctions for under-achievement. Accountability at EU level was to be reinforced by requiring the Council to discuss the implementation and results of the funds every two years. The principle of thematic concentration required more focus on specific objectives.

The combination of a delayed conclusion to the budget negotiations and decisions on the regulations, combined with a more demanding programming process, meant that many of the 2014–20 programmes started late. By the end of 2017, the payment rate was significantly slower than in the previous period, especially in the Baltic states, Poland, Slovenia and the Czech Republic (Bachtler, Ferry and Gal 2018). Absorption did, however, accelerate in the course of 2018. By the end of the year, most CEE countries were close to or above the EU average in terms of commitments and payments, the main exceptions being Romania and the Czech Republic.

Losing Cohesion Policy funds? Prospects for 2021–27

Looking forward to the 2021–27 period, the negotiations have already begun on the future EU budgetary and policy frameworks against the background of Brexit and the loss of the UK as a net contributor. The Commission's proposals, published in May 2018, provide for a budget of EUR 1,135 billion in commitments (2018 prices) for 2021–27, equivalent to 1.11% of EU27 GNI. Compared to 2014–20, the Commission proposes a significant shift away from Cohesion Policy and market-related expenditure and direct payments towards other areas of spend, notably the single market innovation and digital heading. Overall, the new proposals envisage that 'other' policies would account for almost half of spend, rather than just over a third in 2014–20. Taking account only of the ERDF, the Cohesion Fund and the ESF+, the proposed Cohesion Policy budget is around EUR 331 billion for 2021–27 compared with EUR 374 billion for 2014–20.

Within the Cohesion Policy heading, there are major implications for individual Member States. Although the Commission has proposed changes to the Berlin formula, the allocations are primarily determined by 'adjustments': a safety net (to limit cuts); and a reverse safety net capping (to limit increases). Increases in Cohesion Policy allocations are concentrated in southern Europe – especially Greece, Italy and Spain – which would see gains of over 10% relative to 2014–20. Among the CEE countries (see Figure 13.4), only Romania and Bulgaria would have modest increases. Seven countries would see decreases in Cohesion Policy allocations exceeding

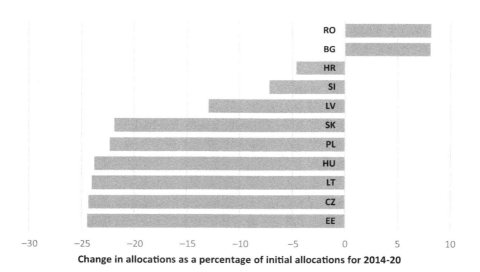

Change in allocations as a percentage of initial allocations for 2014-20

Figure 13.4 Impact of Commission proposal on Cohesion Policy allocations for 2021–27 in CEE

Source: Bachtler, J., Mendez, C. and Wishlade, F. (2019).

20% of initial 2014–20 allocations – mainly in Central and Eastern Europe (especially Poland, in absolute terms).

Overview of Cohesion Policy expenditure

Over the period 2000–2020, it is estimated that the CEE countries will have received over EUR 550 billion in Cohesion Policy funding under different funds.[2] As Figure 13.5 shows, these started off from small allocations through the pre-accession fund, ISPA, rising initially with the allocations for 2004–06 and the increasing steeply with the major allocations in the 2007–13 period and the rate of increase slowing (except for Croatia) in the 2014–20 period.

The regional distribution of funding over the 2000–2013 period is shown in Figures 13.6 and 13.7. Figure 13.6 shows the aggregate figures for payments through Cohesion Policy over the entire period. The urban focus of spending is evident in Poland with the Polish regions of Mazowieckie (Warsaw region) and Śląskie (which has 12 of the about 100 largest urban areas in Poland) receiving the most support of any NUTS2 region in Central and Eastern Europe, apart from Lithuania (which is a single NUTS2 unit).

A different picture emerges from Figure 13.7, which presents the distribution of funding on a per capita basis. Here it is clear that in many

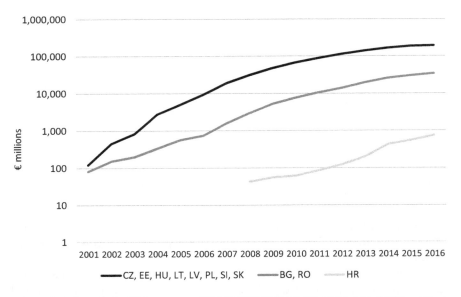

Figure 13.5 Cumulative EU payments (ERDF, CF, ESF, EAFRD (2001–16)) (EUR million)

Source: Based on data from the ESIF Open Data platform.

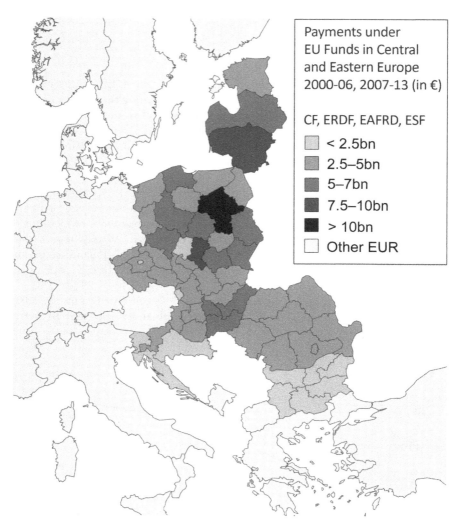

Figure 13.6 EU funding paid out in CEE by NUTS2 region, 2000–2013

countries (Poland, Hungary, Czech Republic, Slovenia, Bulgaria, Romania), the more disadvantaged areas – often eastern regions – are some of the biggest recipients.

A comparison of total payments by country is shown in Figure 13.8, where the dominant share allocated to Poland is clear, with Romania, Hungary and the Czech Republic also being major recipients. The European Regional Development Fund and the European Social Fund account for the greater part of the allocations to each country, although there are also substantial receipts

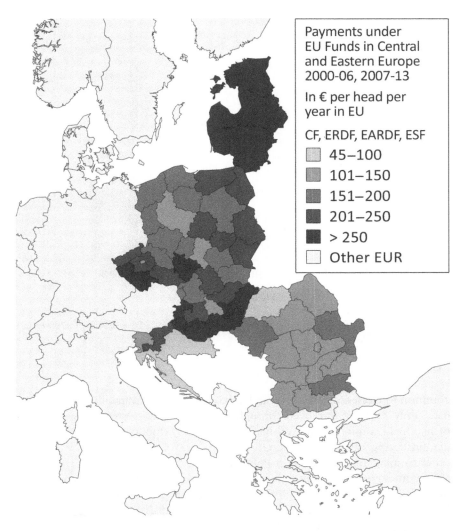

Payments under
EU Funds in Central
and Eastern Europe
2000-06, 2007-13

In € per head per
year in EU

CF, ERDF, EARDF, ESF

  45–100
  101–150
  151–200
  201–250
  > 250
  Other EUR

Figure 13.7 EU funding paid out per head in CEE by NUTS2 region, 2000–2013

under the European Agricultural Fund for Regional Development (especially
in Poland and Romania) and Cohesion Fund.

Assessing the achievements of Cohesion Policy in CEE Member States

Turning now to the effectiveness of spending, assessments of the achievements
of Cohesion Policy in CEE must acknowledge certain constraints. Some are

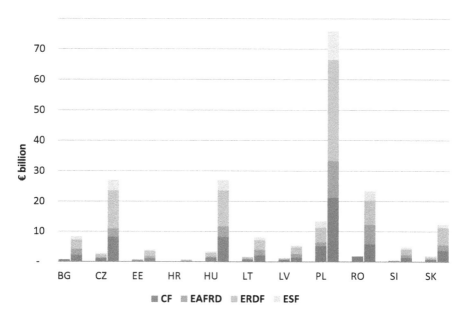

Figure 13.8 Cumulative EU payments for 2000–06 and 2007–13 – ERDF, CF, ESF and EAFRD (EUR billion)

Source: Based on data from the ESIF Open Data platform.

common to Cohesion Policy research across the EU: the availability of EU-level data (only recently improved through the Open Data platform); weaknesses of national monitoring and evaluation systems; methodological challenges of demonstrating causality; measurement error; and controlling for variables in order to disaggregate Cohesion Policy effects (Mohl and Hagen 2010). In the CEE context, a further limitation is the shorter timescale of Cohesion Policy implementation and evidence of impacts in the EU11 compared to the EU15. Further, while CEE is often discussed in general terms, the experiences of individual countries differ significantly, reflecting levels of economic development, country size, economic structure, national and regional politics, administrative traditions and, most recently, the impact of the economic crisis. Bearing in mind these caveats, Cohesion Policy's achievements in Central and Eastern Europe can be assessed in terms of contribution to growth and the reduction of regional disparities, achievements in specific policy fields, and governance.

Contribution of Cohesion Policy to economic growth and convergence in CEE

The first issue in assessing Cohesion Policy impact concerns its role in stimulating economic growth. Some of this work has involved evaluation studies and econometric modelling, carried out on behalf of the European Commission and based on different methodological approaches: ex ante, with macroeconomic or input–output models (e.g. Hermin, Quest, Beutel, RHOMOLO); and ex post, via econometric research (Brandsma et al. 2013; Davies 2017). For CEE Member States, these models largely indicate a positive effect of Cohesion Policy in raising GDP. These countries receive a large amount of financial aid, relative to other Member States and their own domestic funding for development.

One of the most recent studies of the impact of Cohesion Policy in Visegrád and partner countries[3] noted the much faster rate of economic growth compared to the EU average in 2007–15 (2.4%, compared to 0.72%). It concluded that Cohesion Policy funds had enhanced the process of convergence of GDP per capita growth rates in these countries against the EU average (Ministry of Economic Development 2017a). The study noted macroeconomic simulations showing that EU funds in the MFF 2007–13 added 4.5 percentage points to the real GDP per capita in these countries compared to the baseline scenario excluding EU funds. According to this, in 2006–15, the V4 countries[4] closed 14.3 percentage points of the gap in economic development and reached 72.3% of the EU's average GDP per capita.

Other studies have pointed to the particularly important role of Cohesion Policy in mitigating the effects of the financial crisis in these countries (Becker et al. 2018). The contribution of EU funds to investments of public authorities in these countries is high. Their share in total investments of the public sector exceeded 30% in most V4 + 4 countries and accounted for more than a half of all investments in Hungary and Slovakia (Ministry of Economic Development 2017a). The inflow of EU funds boosted aggregate demand in the V4 + 4 economies, stimulated investment and alleviated the sharp decrease in economic activity.

Nevertheless, as already noted, there are methodological caveats in these assessments. The role of Cohesion Policy in strengthening economic convergence is still open to debate: the results of macroeconomic modelling vary significantly depending on the method, time period or countries/regions analysed and there are many other factors that could contribute to the convergence of these economies, such as the economic integration of EU membership, business cycles and other factors (Dall'Erba and Fang 2017).

The role of Cohesion Policy in regional convergence has obvious significance for CEE Member States. In CEE, the shift to a market economy and economic integration into the EU have fuelled national economic growth and convergence since 1990 but also an increase in interregional and interpersonal income disparities, as some areas and individuals have benefitted more than others from increased growth opportunities. While capital cities and metropolitan areas have typically seen dynamic economic growth, expanding services and high FDI inflows, old industrial regions are undergoing major restructuring, and eastern regions are less likely to benefit from FDI and production oriented towards core EU markets (Chapman and Meliciani 2018).

Looking at the average annual growth rate of CEE regions between 2007–13, the performance of all regions rose while EU-15 regions rose at a slower rate or even declined (for instance regions in Greece, Spain, Italy and the United Kingdom). However, as noted elsewhere in this volume, regional disparities within CEE Member States have remained entrenched or have grown over the period. Moreover, recent studies have confirmed that regional disparities inside some CEE countries decreased during the years of crisis but have since returned to pre-crisis levels (Matkowski et al. 2016). The decrease in regional disparities occurred because the crisis affected the export- and construction-oriented regions, while self-reinforcing agglomeration effects took the regional disparities to the same level as before the crisis (Davies et al. 2015). The entrenchment of CEE regional disparities over time is demonstrated by the fact that of 66 regions with incomes classifying them as Less Developed Regions in 2005, just six 'graduated' to Transition Region status (three in the Czech Republic, one each in Poland and Bulgaria, along with Estonia) and remained there through to 2015 (Farole et al. 2018).

Again, it is challenging to provide a definitive account of Cohesion Policy's role in this process. On the one hand, there are arguments that by allocating a steady flow of funding to less developed regions, Cohesion Policy investment has been crucial in mitigating against increasing disparities in the economic development of sub-regions in CEE (Ministry of Economic Development 2017b). However, several studies have noted the tendency for Cohesion Policy funding allocations to concentrate in metropolitan areas and particularly the capital regions as compared to all other regions.

For instance, up to the end of 2016, Mazowieckie (the region with the capital city of Poland) had been allocated over 15% of the country's funding for 2007–13. Śląskie, another of Poland's most developed regions, was the second largest recipient with just below 8%, as shown clearly in Figure 13.6 above. Within Polish regions, there are significant internal differences in the level of funding per inhabitant, with funding concentrated in large towns and cities (GUS 2018). In general, more developed (urbanised) local units receive relatively more Cohesion Policy funds (Gorzelak 2017).

This variation can be explained by different factors. Policymakers have in several cases chosen to focus Cohesion Policy on major urban centres as drivers of national economies, anticipating the diffusion of benefits to less developed territories (Davies et al. 2015). Major projects tend either to be funded in these large centres or are managed from there. There is also territorial variation in the quality of projects put forward by local beneficiaries and in implementation capacity. Research has highlighted the limitations in institutional endowments and administrative capacity in less developed areas and the impact this can have on the returns of public investment (Rodriguez-Pose and Garcilazo 2015). Limitations in relevant skills and expertise in developing applications, the lack of co-financing funds, issues with searching for project partners have been noted as barriers for absorbing EU funds in disadvantaged CEE regions (Jaliu and Radulescu 2013). This is particularly the case in more progressive thematic areas such as research and innovation (Novosak et al. 2017).

Achievements in specific policy fields

The impact of Cohesion Policy has also been assessed through bottom-up analyses of specific policy sectors. These are usually based on programme and project data provided by Cohesion Policy monitoring systems and primary research. General information includes data on products rather than impacts (e.g. numbers of projects supported, jobs created or safeguarded and the development of basic infrastructure). However, there has been a growing focus on achievements in specific sectors, notably in research, technological development and innovation (Applica et al. 2013). The study on the impact of Cohesion Policy 2007–13 in Visegrád Group countries and partner states provides a succinct summary of some key inputs and headline results (see Table 13.6).

A basic weakness of this approach to assessing Cohesion Policy impact is dependence on often incomplete or not fully reliable data sets. Identifying

Table 13.6 Policy results from Cohesion Policy intervention in CEE

Policy field	'Headline' results
Support for competitiveness and innovativeness of the economies of the V4 + 4 countries went to about 143,000 SMEs (3.2% of all SMEs used CP).	Stimulated innovation, increased research and development initiatives in enterprises, helped close the financing gap for firms struggling to access commercial financing.
V4 + 4 countries invested about 13.8% of the Cohesion Policy funds in human capital and labour market interventions, ca. EUR 24.5 billion in the financial perspective 2007–13.	1.5 million participants of projects in the V4 + 4 countries found employment, one in five participants of human capital projects acquired or certified their qualifications.
V4 + 4 countries invested more than EUR 52 billion in transport. Support for road transport accounted for 64% of the allocation.	Marked improvement compared to 2007; however, the V4 + 4 countries did not develop their infrastructure up to the EU-15 level.
EUR 23.6 billion invested in environmental projects, EUR 6 billion in energy.	Major support to environmental investments but minor results in the energy sector. In some areas, including the sanitation infrastructure, some V4 + 4 countries approached the EU-15 average.

Source: Ministry of Economic Development (2017a) *The Impact of Cohesion Policy 2007–2013 in Poland, Visegrád Group Countries and Partner States*, conducted by Imapp, Warsaw.

achievements from the funding provided by the EU funds is challenging as the quantitative indicators included in monitoring reports are in many cases not adequately explained, not sufficiently related to the end goals of policy and not consistent across programmes – which makes aggregation even of core indicators hazardous. Moreover, the qualitative information contained in the reports in most cases is not clearly linked to the quantitative data and does not enable them to be meaningfully interpreted in terms of policy objectives.

Questions remain concerning the impact of these investments. To take one heading as an example, EU Cohesion Policy has a significant part to play in addressing the challenge of strengthening RTDI in CEE. The EU12[5] allocated an average of 20% of total Cohesion Policy funding to innovation (i.e. around EUR 34.7 billion). This included investment in entrepreneurship, research and development, ICT and human capital. On the one hand, recent analyses have noted increases in GDP expenditure on R&D (GERD)/GDP ratios for CEE Member States from below 0.8% in 2006 to 1.2% in 2012 or by 0.4 percentage points of GDP. GERD/GDP did not increase during the period of economic growth before 2008, but they did after 2008 when GDP had fallen in many CEE Member States as a result of the crisis. A potential explanation for this anti-cyclical trend is EU support for R&D and innovation through Cohesion Policy (Radosevic 2015). The Commission's ex post evaluation has gathered examples where Cohesion Policy support has had this vital impact on levels of innovation investment (European Commission 2016).

However, evaluation evidence indicates that across CEE, EU innovation support in the period 2007–13 was largely related to 'hard' capital investments (the purchase of technology, new machines, new infrastructure, etc.) rather than investment in the development of indigenous innovation capacities. For instance, ex post evaluation of the EU funded Economy Growth OP in Lithuania 2007–13 found that objectives concerning business-science collaboration and related policy challenges were not transformed into more substantial policy instruments. Instead, large investments were made in public R&D infrastructure (EUR 364 million from the ERDF) (European Commission 2015). In the Czech Republic, the strongest demand for support from the OP Enterprise and Innovation 2007–13 was for the purchase of new technology and equipment. Various support centres for start-ups and innovation-oriented entrepreneurs were created (business incubators, science and technology parks, innovation centres, hubs and clusters, etc.). In Poland, a World Bank study found that more than 40% of funds from the OP Innovative Economy 2007–13 went to large companies for technology upgrading through fixed capital investments into plant machinery (Kapil et al. 2013). Other evaluations of OPs have indicated that spending under infrastructure-related categories were substantially higher than those related to objectives supporting innovation and R&D activities: funds had not significantly impacted on cooperation between firms and research and development units which still prioritised investments in fixed assets (PSDB 2012).

Of course, investment in RTDI infrastructure has a crucial role to play in parts of CEE where this base is missing or worn down. Absorbing EU investment is beneficial in boosting 'demand side' growth and higher consumption. Nevertheless, many evaluations have been critical of the strong focus in EU-funded innovation investment on RTDI infrastructure and technology absorption (see the chapter by Radosevic, Yoruk and Yoruk in this volume). The link between investment in infrastructure and technology absorption and increased productivity growth based on innovation and R&D activities is uncertain. In some cases, this approach has proven weak in leveraging private sector investments into research and innovation (R&I) and fostering public research commercialisation. Studies of innovation policies in CEE confirm that a fundamental weakness is the lack of a corporate sector that actively uses links with science to innovate (Veugelers and Schweiger 2016). Such problems are particularly pronounced in the lagging regions, mostly in the east of the CEE countries where regional innovation systems are underdeveloped: lack of human capital and poor institutional quality has been found to constrain competitiveness and investment decisions (European Commission 2017a).

These findings have implications for Cohesion Policy's impact on long-term sustainable development in CEE. Research from previous EU enlargements distinguishes between 'demand' side effects and impacts on the 'supply side' in Member State economies (Bradley et al. 2007; Gorzelak 2017). 'Demand side' growth driven by CP spending on infrastructure investment creates higher investment, higher consumption and higher levels of imports. However, its impact can be transitory, lasting only as long as there are significant amounts of Cohesion Policy funding available. There are longer term costs for maintenance and there is a danger that a dependency culture develops, where in the name of generating 'structural change', less developed regions come to rely on transfers and experience convergence in consumption but persistent divergence in productive output and potential (Farole et al. 2011). There is a strong argument that CEE Member States will need to divert EU-funded investment from absorption to innovation to maintain sustainable growth in the long term (Kapil et al. 2013).

The governance of Cohesion Policy in Central and Eastern Europe

More qualitative approaches to assessing Cohesion Policy achievements have focused on governance and implementation, sometimes invoking the concept of 'added value'. The Commission interprets 'added value' as the 'value resulting from the Community assistance that is additional to that which would have been secured by national and regional authorities and the private sector' (European Commission 2001). Contributions to the debate on this added value have been provided over the past two decades in both the policy and academic literatures. Collectively, these contributions point to ways though which the Cohesion Policy can influence policy and practice in regional and local development in CEE Member States (Polverari et al. 2017).

One area of perceived added value is the leverage of additional public and private resources for regional economic development. Cohesion Policy constitutes a significant proportion of development spending in CEE, and it has contributed to changing the balance of priorities on national development agendas. As noted above, EU funds in CEE have played an important part in maintaining public investment and safeguarding jobs during economic downturns. They acted as an important 'buffer' during the economic recession, allowing national authorities to fund investment in areas which constrained domestic budgets were not able to support, to the same scale or as promptly. In the EU as a whole, public investment declined by 20% in real terms between 2008 and 2013. In the CEE countries, public investment (measured as gross fixed capital formation) fell by a third and Cohesion funding came to play a fundamental role (see Figure 13.9).

On the other hand, whereas in older Member States the availability of Cohesion Policy has been found to have encouraged 'financial pooling' from private partners (ÖIR 2007), this leverage effect on private investment is limited in CEE. The level of co-financing required for Cohesion Policy is constrained in comparison to older Member states. It is also clear from OPs and implementation reports that this additional funding is almost exclusively leveraged from the public sector and investment from the private sector is very low. The economic crisis has had an impact in this respect as public sector budget cuts have made finding match funding very challenging across programmes. Financial engineering instruments are anticipated to play an increasingly important role in accessing new sources of investment funding but these are only gradually emerging in CEE.

The implementation of Cohesion Policy programmes can also have an impact on regional development objectives and activities, such as the overall

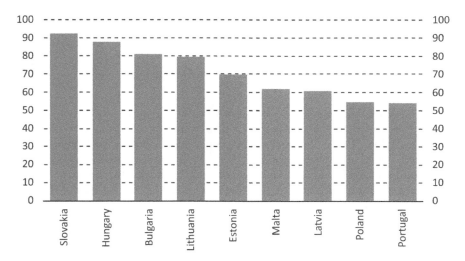

Figure 13.9 Cohesion policy funding and national co-financing as % of total public investment, 2010–12

strategic framework and objectives of regional and local development policies. The organisation of funding in seven-year programme periods has been lauded as providing a stable policy environment, allowing longer-term planning. As a result, programmes have promoted a more strategic, long-term conceptualisation of regional development in these countries (Misiąg and Tomalak 2008). The way that national regional policy objectives are expressed is often modelled on EU Cohesion Policy (operational programmes, a logic of objectives-priorities-measures, etc.), suggesting that there has been a substantial EU impact (EPRC and EUROREG 2010). This impact is also apparent in the strategic focus of development initiatives, in the enhanced concentration on SME competitiveness and innovation, alongside the new themes such as low-carbon and poverty reduction (CSIL, CSES and ZEW 2016). From the mid-2000s onwards, the Structural Funds promoted a focus on measures to foster competitiveness, entrepreneurship and innovation in line with the priorities set out in the EU's Lisbon Agenda (Mendez 2011).

More recently, the thematic concentration requirements further emphasised innovation and SME competitiveness, and also expenditure on transition to a low-carbon economy (energy, climate change) and on social inclusion and poverty relief measures (Altus 2016; Fargion and Profeti 2016; Lenschow and Baudner 2016). In doing so, Structural Funds programmes shifted national policy interventions away from the traditional narrow focus on infrastructure and business aid, and broadening the regional policy agenda (Bachtler et al. 2016). This has been particularly apparent in CEE where the language of development policy has changed, reflecting policy emphasis on innovation-related themes. There is awareness of new approaches beyond infrastructure support in strategic thinking. This suggests a potential impact of Cohesion Policy strategies on institutional settings in the longer term (Ferry and McMaster 2013).

One area is the strengthening of capacities within government administrations (especially at regional and local levels) to design and implement economic development interventions and projects (Pellegrin et al. 2009). The application of specific EU legal requirements in the implementation of Cohesion Policy programmes has mobilised Member States to improve policy frameworks which serve not only the EU Funds but also other sources of public investment (concerning public procurement systems, environmental impact assessments etc.) (European Commission 2017b). Although variable across CEE Member States and regions, progress has been made especially during the 2007–13 period: programme design has become more professional, with more analysis, strategic reflection and partner consultation; increased 'partnership-working' – greater involvement of regional/local bodies, economic and social partners – although usually not in funding decisions; investment in project generation – working with applicants to get 'good projects'; more sophisticated project selection systems – competitive calls, scoring criteria and so forth (Ferry 2017). Policy monitoring and evaluation approaches developed in response to Cohesion Policy obligations have led to increased accountability and transparency in CEE Member States, for example in the Baltic states (Muravska et al. 2016) and influenced evaluation approaches to national policies in CEE Member States which have limited traditions in this field (Ministry of Infrastructure and Development 2014).

Cohesion Policy has strengthened participation of different actors in regional policy, opening the field to a range of sectors and private and voluntary spheres. This is most notable in the involvement of regional and local authorities in regional development in CEE – albeit with variable impact in terms of actual influence on decision-making (Yanakeiv 2010). The implementation of Cohesion Policy programmes, through the principle of subsidiarity, is credited with having increased the involvement of regional and local authorities in the administration of EU programmes and even stimulated the creation of regional-level frameworks in domestic administrative systems. This has been the case for example in Poland, where regional and local authorities have played increasingly prominent roles in the management and implementation of Cohesion Policy in 2007–13 and in so doing have developed substantial capacity and experience (Dąbrowski 2013). Indeed, the ongoing development of technical skills and management capabilities at sub-national levels in some CEE countries (notably in Poland and the Czech Republic) is apparent in their commitment to introducing new ideas or approaches and encouraging experiments with new forms of governance, such as urban policy governance through EU-funded Integrated Territorial Investments in 2014–20 (van der Zwet et al. 2018; Ferry and Borkowska-Waszak 2018; Koppitz 2018). The inclusion of such actors through Cohesion Policy has encouraged new forms of dialogue, collaboration and networking among local governments and local stakeholders (Dobre 2010).

Developing and sustaining these types of added value is, however, challenging. Thus far, most progress in capacity-building has been made in the strengthening of capacity for procedural or operational compliance with Commission regulations and requirements, especially financial management and control. Cohesion Policy management and implementation systems in CEE Member States were designed to ensure procedural correctness rather than to facilitate access to EU funds by applicants; double and triple sets of checks were required for payment requests, slowing down the disbursement of grants (Oraže 2009; Bachtler et al. 2013). The cost of good performance in absorption and compliance is often weak performance in strategic results and impacts. As noted above in the case of research and innovation, Cohesion Policy funding has often been spent according to short-term considerations, either responding to urgent problems, political considerations or the need to absorb funds quickly, rather than long-term strategic development. This undermines the opportunities for development that CP offers (Balás and Kiss 2011).

While the need for administrative capacity-building has been increasingly recognised as an important pre-condition for effective implementation of Cohesion Policy (Gorzelak and Ferry 2014; European Commission 2017a, 2017c), this is dependent on the wider domestic institutional environment which – in some countries – is not supportive of good performance (Surubaru 2017a). Political patronage has undermined the development of expertise and managerial continuity, and political clientelism has been problematic for effective project selection (Bloom and Petrova 2013; Surubaru 2017b). Resources have been 'misallocated', with policy preferences not aligned with thematic or spatial development needs (Bruszt and Vukov 2015; Medve-Bálint 2017, 2018). The scale of investment combined with formalistic administrative compliance mechanisms and a lack of transparency in public procurement have contributed to corruption in the allocation of funds (European Commission 2017c; Fazekas and King 2018).

Structural reforms to enhance growth in CEE are considered to be incomplete. The European Commission has argued that unfavourable macroeconomic and structural conditions may undermine the effectiveness of investment and the potential benefit for citizens (European Commission 2017a, 2017c). However, there is no agreement on the institutional preconditions for coordinated EU policy in this area, and the optimal trade-off between changes to EU economic governance and industrial policy, and convergence and equity (Duszczyk 2014; Kalman and Tiits 2014; Borsi and Metiu 2015; Karo et al. 2017; Bachtler, Oliveira Martins et al. 2018).

Further, EU policy development (and academic assessment) with respect to Cohesion Policy in CEE often take as a starting point the government and policy experience of more developed economies. They take insufficient account of legacy constraints; and they overestimate the scope for institutional emulation – for example with respect to strategy development in areas like smart specialisation (Karo and Kattel 2015; Serbinica and Constantin 2018) or implementation processes such as the partnership principle (Demidov 2017). Of particular importance is the degree of centralisation of Cohesion Policy decision-making, increasingly so in some CEE countries, the limited powers and resources of subnational government authorities (apart from Poland), and the weak position of the non-governmental sector (Raagma et al. 2014). Lastly, assumptions about how EU policy 'should' be implemented are being challenged by what have been variously termed 'partial backsliding' on democracy (Börzel and Frank Schimmelfennig 2017) or 'de-Europeanisation' and 'de-democratisation' (Ágh 2016) in some Central and Eastern European countries, and the controversial use of conditionalities linked to Cohesion Policy in areas such as the rule of law (Bachtler and Mendez 2019).

Conclusions

EU Cohesion Policy played an important part in the economic transformation of Central and Eastern Europe. Significant funding has been allocated to the CEE countries from 2000 onwards as they acceded to the EU, and with some exceptions the new Member States have been able to absorb the funding efficiently. Romania and to a lesser extent Bulgaria are the countries that have struggled most to commit and spend money on time and without irregularities.

Although the conclusions of research and evaluation studies are mixed, there is broad evidence that Cohesion Policy has contributed significantly to economic growth and convergence of the CEE countries. As in some EU15

Member States in the past, much of the funding in the early programme periods was committed to physical infrastructure: improvements in transport, water supply and sewage systems, environmental projects and broadband. Over time, a more diverse set of priorities have been supported, but implementing projects in areas like RTDI, low carbon, and entrepreneurship has not always been easy. This reflects continuing deficits in administrative capacity in terms of the skills, systems and tools needed for effective analysis of regional and local development problems, strategic planning and project implementation.

A wider concern is the incomplete state of institutional reforms and, in some countries, the politicisation of investment decisions. Some progress has been made with the greater emphasis on administrative capacity-building and support by the European Commission, and the use of ex ante conditionalities to encourage the necessary pre-conditions for investment to be put in place. The creation of a Structural Reform Service Programme, and the potential obligation for structural reforms to be required as part of the evolving changes to European economic governance should also improve the investment context.

The big challenge facing CEE countries are growing territorial disparities and the degree to which people and places feel 'left behind' – which is economically damaging, socially unjust and politically detrimental especially with the rise of populist and Eurosceptic parties across Europe. At the same time, the high point of funding through EU Cohesion Policy has passed for most CEE Member States, and it appears that the EU is determined to prioritise other spending priorities through the EU budget. This requires the CEE countries to place more emphasis on developing domestic regional development policies and strategies – with a conceptual and institutional basis that reflects the needs and possibilities of the Central and Eastern European 'region' – and ensure they are properly resourced. A more regionally differentiated, place-based approach to territorial development would potentially require CEE Member States to reverse the centralisation of economic development policy and (re)build regional and local government structures as credible, capable actors. Lastly, they will need to maximise the use of (declining) Cohesion Policy resources for more effective strategic investment priorities.

Acknowledgements

The authors would like to thank Dr Wilbert van Hoed (EPRC) for assistance with the preparation of several of the maps and charts in this chapter.

Notes

1 This chapter was partly prepared within the project No. 2017/27/B/HS5/01906, 'The role of EU funds in Poland's regional and local development in light of international experiences', financed by The National Science Centre, Poland.
2 The data in this section and the charts and maps in Figures 13.5–13.8 are based on the ESIF Open Data platform available through Inforegio.eu. The accuracy of the data depends on Member State reporting systems and may not be fully comparable across countries and regions.

3 Poland, Czech Republic, Hungary, Slovakia, Bulgaria, Romania, Slovenia and Croatia (V4 + 4).
4 Visegrád 4: Poland, Czech Republic, Hungary and Slovakia.
5 Bulgaria, Czech Republic, Estonia, Cyprus, Latvia, Lithuania, Hungary, Malta, Poland, Romania, Slovenia and Slovakia.

References

Ágh, A. (2016). The deconsolidation of democracy in easy-Central Europe: The new world order and EU's geopolitical crisis. *Politics in Central and Eastern Europe*, 12(3), 7–36.

Altus (2016). The Use of New Provisions during the Programming Phase of the European Structural and Investment Funds, *Final Report to the European Commission (DG Regio)*, Altus Framework Consortium.

Applica, Ismeri Europa & WIIW (2009a). Ex Post Evaluation of Cohesion Policy Programmes 2000–2006 Co-financed by ERDF – Synthesis Report, *Report to the European Commission (DG Regio)*, Applica, Ismeri Europa, WIIW.

Applica, Ismeri Europa & WIIW (2009b). Ex Post Evaluation of Cohesion Policy Programmes 2000–2006 Co-financed by ERDF – Financial Implementation of Structural Funds, *Report to the European Commission (DG Regio)*, Applica, Ismeri Europa, WIIW.

Applica, Ismeri Europa & CEA (2016). Ex post evaluation of Cohesion Policy programmes 2007–2013, focusing on the European Regional Development Fund (ERDF) and the Cohesion Fund (CF), *Report to the European Commission (DG Regio)*.

B&S Europe (2015). Evaluation of PHARE financial assistance to Bulgaria (BG), Cyprus (CY), Czech Republic (CZ), Estonia (EE), Hungary (HU), Latvia (LV), Lithuania (LT), Malta (MT), Poland (PL), Romania (RO), Slovakia (SK), Slovenia (SI), *Final Report to the European Commission (DG Enlarge)*, Business & Strategies Europe, Brussels.

Bachtler, J., & Downes, R. (1995). *Regional Disparities in the Visegrad States*. Report to the European Commission (DG XVI), published in Fifth Periodic Report on the Social and Economic Situation and Development of the Regions of the Community. Brussels: Office for Official Publications of the European Communities.

Bachtler, J., & McMaster, I. (2008). EU cohesion policy and the role of the regions: Investigating the influence of structural funds in the new member states. *Environment and Planning C: Government and Policy*, 26(2), 398–427.

Bachtler, J., & Mendez, C. (forthcoming, 2019). Cohesion and the EU budget: Is conditionality undermining solidarity? In: R. Coman, A. Crespy & V. Schmidt (eds.), *Governance and politics in the post-crisis European Union*. Cambridge: Cambridge University Press.

Bachtler, J., & Wishlade, F. (2004). *Searching for Consensus: The Debate on Reforming EU Cohesion Policy*, EoRPA Paper 04/4, European Regional Policy Research Consortium, European Policies Research Centre, University of Strathclyde, Glasgow.

Bachtler, J., Begg, I., Charles, D., & Polverari, L. (2016). *EU Cohesion Policy in Practice*. London: Rowman & Littlefield International.

Bachtler, J., Ferry, M., & Gal, F. (2018). Research Paper on the Implementation of European Structural and Investment Funds, *Report to the European Parliament (Policy Department on Budgetary Affairs)*, Brussels.

Bachtler, J., Mendez, C., & Oraže, H. (2014). From conditionality to Europeanization in Central and Eastern Europe: Administrative performance and capacity in cohesion policy. *European Planning Studies*, 22(4), 735–757.

Bachtler, J., Wishlade, F., & Mendez, C. (2006). *New Budget, New Regulations, New Strategies: The Reform of EU Cohesion Policy*, EoRPA Paper 06/3, European Regional Policy Research Consortium, European Policies Research Centre, University of Strathclyde, Glasgow.

Bachtler, J., Mendez, C., & Wishlade, F. (2013). *EU Cohesion Policy and European Integration: The Dynamics of EU Budget and Regional Policy Reform.* Aldershot: Ashgate.

Bachtler, J., Oliveira Martins, J., Wostner, P., & Zuber, P. (2018). *Towards Cohesion Policy 4.0: Structural transformation and inclusive growth*, RSA Europe, Brussels.

Bachtler, J., Mendez, C. and Wishlade, F. (2019). Reforming the MFF and Cohesion Policy 2021–27: pragmatic drift or paradigmatic shift? *European Policy Research Paper No. 107*, University of Strathclyde Publishing 2019.

Balás, G., & Kiss, G. (2011). *Expert Evaluation Network Delivering Policy Analysis on The Performance of Cohesion Policy 2007–2013 Year 1–2011 Task 2: Country Report on Achievements of Cohesion Policy Hungary*, Report to the European Commission, Directorate-General Regional Policy.

Becker, S.O., Egger, P.H., & von Ehrlich, M. (2018). Effects of EU regional policy: 1989–2013. *Regional Science and Urban Economics*, 69, 143–152.

Bloom, S., & Petrova, V. (2013). National subversion of supranational goals: 'Pork-barrel' politics and EU regional aid. *Europe-Asia Studies*, 65(8), 1599–1620.

Borsi, M.T., & Metiu, N. (2015). The evolution of economic convergence in the European Union. *Empirical Economics*, 48(2), 657–681.

Börzel, T.A., & Schimmelfennig, F. (2017). Coming together or drifting apart? The EU's political integration capacity in Eastern Europe. *Journal of European Public Policy*, 24(2), 278–296.

Bossaert, D., & Demmke, C. (2003). *Civil Services in the Accession States, New Trends and the Impact of the Integration Process*, Maastricht: European Institute of Public Administration.

Bradley, J., Untiedt, G., & Mitze, T. (2007). *Analysis of the Impact of Cohesion Policy A note explaining the HERMIN-based simulations* Project-No. 2006 CE.16.0.AT.035, Dublin, 14 May 2007.

Brandsma, A., Kancs d'A., Monfort, P., & Rillaers, A. (2013). *Rhomolo: A Dynamic Spatial General Equilibrium Model for Assessing the Impact of Cohesion Policy*. European Commission, Brussels.

Bruszt, L., & Vukov, V. (2015). Transnationalizing states in Europe's peripheries: European integration and the evolution of economic state capacities in the Southern and Eastern peripheries of Europe. *The Journal of Comparative Economic Studies*, 10, 69–91.

Chapman, S., & Meliciani, V. (2018). Explaining regional disparities in Central and Eastern Europe: The role of geography and of structural change. *Economics of Transition* (online at https://doi.org/10.1111/ecot.12154).

Council of the EU (2002). *Brussels European Council – Presidency Conclusions*, 24–25 October 2002.

Council of the EU (2003b). *Presidency Conclusions of the Informal Ministerial Meeting for Regional Policy and Cohesion*. Hellenic Presidency of the Council of the European Union, Halkidiki, 16 May 2003.

Council of the EU (2003a). *Multiannual Strategic Programme of the Council 2006–2006*, Council of the European Union, Brussels, POLGEN 85, 8 December 2003.

CSIL, CSES and ZEW (2016). European Commission (2016). *Support to SMEs, increasing research and innovation in SMEs and SME development, Ex post evaluation of Cohesion Policy programmes 2007–2013, focusing on the European Regional Development Fund (ERDF) and the Cohesion Fund (CF)*, Final report to the European Commission (DG Regio), Work Package 2, Brussels.

Dąbrowski, M. (2013). Europeanizing sub-national governance: Partnership in the implementation of European Union structural funds in Poland. *Regional Studies*, 47(8), 1363–1374.

Dall'Erba, S., & Fang, F. (2017). Meta-analysis of the impact of European Union structural funds on regional growth. *Regional Studies*, 51(6), 822–832.

Davies, S. (2017). Does Cohesion Policy work? Meta-analysis of Research on the Effectiveness of Cohesion Policy, *European Policy Research Paper*, No. 99, European Policies Research Centre, University of Strathclyde, Glasgow.

Davies, S., Ferry, M., & Gross, F. (2015). Policy Reform under Challenging Conditions: Annual Review of Regional Policy in Europe. *European Policy Research Paper* No.90, European Policies Research Centre, University of Strathclyde, Glasgow.

Demidov, A. (2017). Europeanization of interest intermediation in the Central and Eastern European member states: Contours of a mixed model. *East European Politics*, 33(2), 233–252.

Dobre, A.M. (2010). Europeanization and new patterns of multi-level governance in Romania. *Southeast European and Black Sea Studies*, 10(1), 59–70.

Duszczyk, M. (2014). Poland under economic crisis conditions. *Perspectives on European Politics and Society*, 15(3), 370–384.

EGO (2013). Ocena systemu realizacji polityki spójności w Polsce w ramach perspektywy 2004–2006.

EPRC and EUROREG (2010). *The Objective of Economic and Social Cohesion in the Economic Policies of Member States*, Final Report to the European Commission, (DG Regio), n.d. University of Warsaw, 91.

European Commission (2001). *Community Value Added: Definition and Evaluation Criteria.* Unpublished paper. DG REGIO, Commission of the European Communities, Brussels.

European Commission (2004). Communication from the Commission to the Council and the European Parliament *Building our common future: Policy challenges and budgetary means of the enlarged Union 2007–2013*, COM(2004) 101 final, Brussels, 10 February 2004.

European Commission (2006). *The Growth and Jobs Strategy and the Reform of EU Cohesion Policy: Fourth progress report on cohesion*, COM(2006) 281, 12 June 2006.

European Comission (1997). *Agenda 2000 – For a Stronger and Wider Union,* Communication of the Commission DOC 97/6.

European Commission (2002). *Information Note - Common Financial Framework 2004-2006 for the Accession Negotiations*; SEC (2002) 102 final of 30 January 2002.

European Commission (2009). *20th Annual Report on the Implementation of the Structural Funds (2008)*, European Commission, Brussels, COM(2009) 617 final.

European Commission (2015). *Ex post evaluation of Cohesion Policy programmes 2007–2013, focusing on the European Regional Development Fund (ERDF) and the Cohesion Fund (CF), Lithuania Case Study: OP Economic Growth.*

European Commission (2016). *Strategic Plan 2016–2020*, DG Regional and Urban Policy, May 2016, Brussels.

European Commission (2017a). *Competitiveness in Low-income and Low-growth regions: The Lagging Regions Report*, Commission Staff Working Document, Brussels, SWD(2017) 132 final, 10 April 2017.

European Commission (2017b). *The Value Added of Ex ante Conditionalities in the European Structural and Investment Funds*, Commission Staff Working Document, Brussels, SWD(2017) 127 final, 31 March 2017.

European Commission (2017c). *My Region, My Europe, Our Future: Seventh Report on Economic, Social and Territorial Cohesion.* Luxembourg: Publications Office of the European Union.

Fargion, V., & Profeti, S. (2016). The social dimension of Cohesion Policy. In: S. Piattoni & L. Polverari (eds.), *Handbook on Cohesion Policy in the EU*. Cheltenham: Edward Elgar, pp. 285–301.

Farole, T., Rodríguez-Pose, A., & Storper, M. (2011). Cohesion policy in the European Union: Growth, geography, institutions. *Journal of Common Market Studies*, 49, 1089–1111.

Farole, T., Goga, S., & Ionescu-Heroiu, M. (2018). Rethinking Lagging Regions, *World Bank Other Operational Studies* 29823, World Bank, Washington, DC.

Fazekas, M., & King, L.P. (2018). Perils of development funding? The tale of EU Funds and grand corruption in Central and Eastern Europe. *Regulation and Governance*. https://doi.org/10.1111/rego.12184

Ferry, M. (2017). The Role of EU Funds in Enhancing the Development Potential of CEE economies. In: *Condemned to be left behind? Can Central and Eastern Europe emerge from its low-wage model?* ETUI edited book, Brussels.

Ferry, M., & Borkowska-Waszak, S. (2018). Integrated territorial investments and new governance models in Poland. *European Structural and Investment Funds Journal*, 1/2018.

Ferry, M., & McMaster, I. (2013). Cohesion policy and the evolution of regional policy in Central and Eastern Europe. *Europe-Asia Studies*, 65(8), 1502–1528.

Gorzelak, G. (2017). Cohesion policy and regional development. In: J. Bachtler, P. Berkowitz, S. Hardy & T. Muravska (eds.), *EU Cohesion Policy: Reassessing Performance and Direction*. London and New York: Routledge, pp. 220–240.

Gorzelak, G. (1996). *The Regional Dimension of Transformation in Central Europe*. London: Jessica Kingsley Publishers

Gorzelak, G., & Ferry, M. (2014). Future Cohesion Policy Suggestions, *GRINCOH Working Paper Series – Policy Paper 4*, EUROREG, University of Warsaw.

Gorzelak, G., Bachtler, J., & Smętkowski M. (2010). *Regional Development in Central and Eastern Europe. Development Processes and Policy Challenges*. New York: Routledge.

Grabbe, H. (2001). How does Europeanization affect CEE governance? Conditionality, diffusion and diversity. *Journal of European Public Policy*, 8(6),1013–1031.

GUS (2018). *Rocznik Statystyczny Województw 2017*.

Hughes, J., Sasse, G., & Gordon, C. (2003). EU enlargement, Europeanisation and the dynamics of regionalisation in the CEECs. In: M. Keating & J. Hughes (eds.), *The Regional Challenge in Central and Eastern Europe. Territorial Restructuring and European Integration*. Brussels: P.I.E.-Peter Lang, pp. 69–88.

Jaliu, D., & Radulescu, C. (2013). Six years in managing structural funds in Romania. Lessons learned. *Transylvanian Review of Administrative Science*, 9(38), 79–95.

Kalman, J., & Tiits, M. (2014). Coordinated Policies and Cohesion Policies: Their Relationship and Impact on the Member States, *GRINCOH Working Paper 7.04*, Institute of Economics, Centre for Economic and Regional Studies of the Hungarian Academy of Sciences, and Institute of Baltic Studies.

Kapil, N., Piątkowski, M., Radwan, I., & Gutierrez, J.J. (2013). Poland enterprise innovation support review: From catching up to moving ahead, *World Bank, Enterprise Innovation Support Review*.

Karo, E., & Kattel, R. (2015). Economic development and evolving state capacities in Central and Eastern Europe: Can 'smart specialization' make a difference? *Journal of Economic Policy Reform*, 18(2), 172–187.

Karo, E., Kattel, E., & Raudla, R. (2017). Searching for exits from the great recession: Coordination of fiscal consolidation and growth enhancing innovation policies in Central and Eastern Europe. *Europe-Asia Studies*, 69(7), 1009–1026.

Koppitz, D. (2018). *Post 2020 Regional Policy in the Czech Republic as a stepping stone to future territorial dimension of ESI Funds*, presentation given in Brussels by Deputy Minister, 18 January 2018.

Lenschow, A., & Baudner, J. (2016). Cohesion Policy and the green economy. In: S. Piattoni & L. Polverari (eds.), *Handbook on Cohesion Policy in the EU*. Cheltenham: Edward Elgar.

Manzella, G-P., & Mendez, C. (2009). The Turning Points of EU Cohesion Policy, Working Paper for the Barca Report, Brussels. https://ec.europa.eu/regional_policy/archive/policy/future/pdf/8_manzella_final-formatted.pdf

Matkowski, Z., Prochniak, M., & Rapacki, R. (2016). Real income convergence between Central Eastern and Western Europe: Past, present, and prospects. *Ekonomista*, 24, 853–892.

Medve-Bálint, G. (2018). The cohesion policy on the EU's Eastern and Southern periphery: Misallocated funds? *Studies in Comparative International Development*, 53, 218–238.

Medve-Bálint, G. (2017). Funds for the wealthy and politically loyal? How EU Funds may contribute to increasing regional disparities in East Central Europe. In: J. Bachtler, P. Berkowitz, S. Hardy & T. Muravska (eds.), *EU Cohesion Policy: Reassessing Performance and Direction*. London and New York: Routledge, pp. 220–240.

Mendez, C., & Bachtler, J. (2014). *Prospects for Cohesion policy in 2014–20 and Beyond: Progress with Programming and Reflections on the Future*, EoRPA Paper 14/4, European Regional Policy Research Consortium, European Policies Research Centre, University of Strathclyde, Glasgow.

Mendez, C. (2011). The Lisbonization of EU cohesion policy: A successful case of experimentalist governance? *European Planning Studies*, 19(3), 519–537.

Ministry of Economic Development (2017a). *The Impact pf Cohesion Policy 2007–2013 in Poland, Visegrad Group Countries and Partner States*, study commissioned by the Ministry of Economic Development, Warsaw, Poland, conducted by Imapp.

Ministry of Economic Development (2017b). *Strategia na rzecz Odpowiedzialnego Rozwoju*, Warsaw, Poland.

Ministry of Infrastructure and Development (2014). *The Process of Evaluation of Cohesion Policy in Poland 2004–2014*, report by National Evaluation Unit, Ministry of Infrastructure and Development, Warsaw, Poland.

Misiąg, W., & Tomalak, M. 2008. Wpływ wydatków z funduszy strukturalnych i Funduszu Spójności na stan finansów publicznych w latach 2004–2006, ekspertyza dla Ministerstwa Rozwoju Regionalnego (presented in the Ministry of Regional Development, Warsaw on 22 April 2008).

Mohl, P., & Hagen, T. (2010). Do EU structural funds promote regional growth? New evidence from various panel data approaches. *Regional Science and Urban Economics*, 40, 353–365.

Mulvey, S. (2002). *Euro leaders prepare to make history*. BBC News. Available at: http://news.bbc.co.uk/1/hi/world/Europe/2563791.stm

Muravska, T., Aprāns, J., & Dahs, A. (2016). Cohesion Policy in the sparsely populated countries. In: Piattoni, S., & Polverari, L. (eds.), *Handbook on Cohesion Policy in the EU*. Cheltenham: Edward Elgar, pp. 285–301.

Novosák, J., Hájek, O., Horváth, P., & Nekolová, J. (2017). Structural funding and intrastate regional disparities in post-communist countries. *Transylvanian Review of Administrative Sciences*, 13(51), 53–69.

OECD (2001). *Public Sector Leadership for the 21st Century*. Executive Summary. Online publication. Available at: www.oecd.org/dataoecd/0/34/2434104.pdf

ÖIR (2007). *The leverage effect of the European cohesion policy under the SF*, Final Report, commissioned by the Committee of the Regions.

Oraze, H. (2009). *Ex post evaluation of Cohesion Policy programmes 2000–2006: The effectiveness, continuity and spillovers of management and implementation systems in the EU10*, Final Report to the European Commission (DG Regio), EPRC, Glasgow and Metis, Vienna.

Pellegrin, J., Sartori, D., Valenza, A., Koutsokos, S., & Shutt, J. (2009). *An analysis of the Added Value of European Structural Funding*, study requested by the European Parliament's Committee on Regional Development, CSIL and Leeds Metropolitan University, Brussels.

Polverari, L, Ferry, M., & Bachtler, J. (2017). The structural funds as 'agents of change': New forms of learning and implementation. *IQ-Net Thematic Paper*, 40(2), European Policies Research Centre, University of Strathclyde, Glasgow.

PSDB (2012). *Wstępna ocena realizacji i efektów Regionalnego Programu Operacyjnego Województwa Śląskiego na lata 2007–2013.* www.ewaluacja.gov.pl/Wyniki/Documents/Wstepna_ocena_realizacji_i_efektow_RPOWS_14022013.pdf.

Raagmaa, G., Tarmo, K., & Kasesalu, R. (2014). Europeanization and De-Europeanization of Estonian regional policy. *European Planning Studies*, 22(4), 775–795.

Radosevic, S. (2015). R&D and technology upgrading in the CEEC: Issues and policy implications, presentation at *GRINCOH Final Conference*, University of Warsaw, 26–27 February 2015.

Rodríguez-Pose, A., & Garcilazo, E. (2015). Quality of government and the returns of investment: Examining the impact of cohesion expenditure in European regions. *Regional Studies*, 49(8), 1274–1290.

Serbanica, C., & Constantin, D.L. (2016). EU cohesion policy and innovation support in Central and Eastern Europe: A critical review. *CESifo Forum*, 1, 24–31, 19 March 2018.

SIGMA (1998). *Sustainable Institutions for European Union Membership.* SIGMA Papers No 26. United Nations Online Network in Public Administration and Finance.

Surubaru, N-C. (2017a). Administrative capacity or quality of political governance? EU Cohesion Policy in the new Europe, 2007–13. *Regional Studies*, 51(6), 844–856.

Surubaru, N-C. (2017b). Revisiting the role of domestic politics: Politicisation and European Cohesion Policy performance in Central and Eastern Europe. *East European Politics*, 33(1), 106–112.

Van Der Zwet, A., & Bachtler, J. (2018). New implementation mechanisms for integrated development strategies in ESIF. *European Structural and Investment Funds Journal*, 6, 1, 3–12.

Veugelers, R., & Schweiger, H. (2016). Innovation policies in transition countries: One size fits all? *Economic Change and Restructuring*, 49, 241.

Weise, C., Bachtler, J., Downes, R., McMaster, I., & Toepel, K. (2001). The Impact of Enlargement on Cohesion, Final Report to the European Commission (DG Regio), Berlin and Glasgow.

Wishlade, F.G. (1999). *Eligible Areas and Financial Allocations under the New Structural Funds: Quarts, Pint Pots and Half-Measures?* Report to the European Regional Policy Research Consortium, European Policies Research Centre, University of Strathclyde, Glasgow.

Yanakiev, A. (2010). The Europeanization of Bulgarian regional policy: A case of strengthened centralization. *Southeast European and Black Sea Studies*, 10(1), 45–57.

14 Structural changes and future perspectives of CEE economies

Roberta Capello

Introduction

The devastating effects of the recent economic crisis – the worst since the Second World War – are well known, measured by decreasing GDP and employment growth rates in all advanced economies in the world. Revision of public expenditure allocation criteria was a 'must' in those countries where the stability and growth pact exerts strong pressures on national debts and deficits (Reinhart and Rogoff 2010), with the consequence of limiting Keynesian growth mechanisms and of concentrating fewer public resources in the most efficient areas of advanced economies. A decrease in all other components of aggregate demand was registered in the crisis period; international trade fell, as well as private investments, hit hard by the credit crunch which came as a consequence of the financial intermediaries' decision to prefer the public to the private sector, when guarantees existed on sovereign default.

The general decrease in productivity growth, which had already started before the crisis, was exacerbated during the economic slowdown period; and this negative trend has not changed so far, making the official international institutions worried about the 'future of productivity' (OECD 2017), which is not showing any reverse trends even through the digitalization revolution that is diffusing through all industries, opening the way for the new 'Industry 4.0' revolution paradigm.

Central and Eastern European Countries are not exempt from such trends, even if exhibiting some peculiarities. The crisis was less severe, but nevertheless changes took place in macroeconomic trends, and imposed structural adjustments of economic systems which were destined to reshape the nature and sources of the competitive advantages of these countries; price competitiveness partially vanished because of an increase in labour cost higher than the increase in productivity, with the consequence that FDI attractiveness was reduced (Hagemejer and Tyrowicz 2012; Dell'Anno and Villa 2013). These tendencies seem to persist even in the period of recovery from the economic slowdown, questioning the future of one of the main sources of growth in these countries.

On top of these trends, structural gaps exist that distinguish these countries from the rest of Europe. One of the most important is the innovation gap that

Central and Eastern European countries register with respect to other European regions; in a period of digitalization of all industries and the launching of the Industry 4.0 technological paradigm, this situation could impact negatively on the competitiveness of these economies. The future of this part of Europe remains rather unclear, with a consequence for Europe as a whole.

This contribution aims to highlight the challenges that Central and Eastern European economies are going to face, by describing the structural changes mentioned above. In particular, attention will be paid to the innovation patterns that characterize Central and Eastern European countries (CEECs) in relation to the European average. The second aim of this chapter is to present some future perspectives, in the form of scenarios, that have been recently predicted by the author, based on the conditions ensuing from the way these challenges are faced (Capello and Caragliu 2016).

Structural adjustments in CEECs

The economic crisis hit Central and Eastern European countries at the moment when they were adjusting their structure towards that of the Western countries. One of these adjustments was the increase of labour costs in line with Western levels, to rightly guarantee a convergence in per capita income levels. Figure 14.1 shows that after 2001, most CEE countries had a higher growth rate in the compensation per employee than the EU average (Bachtler and Gorzelak 2007), a trend that continued during the crisis. After 2012, when the period of

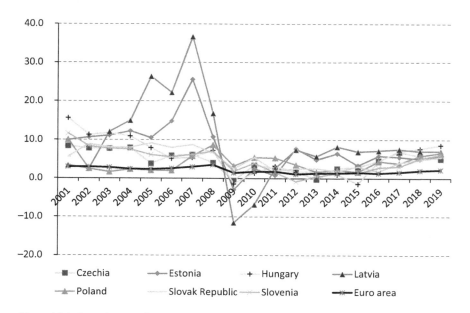

Figure 14.1 Growth rate of compensation per employee, 2001–19 CEECs

recovery started, this trend did not change, but has increased since 2016 and is even predicted to reinforce itself in the next few years.

The positive trend in compensation per employee has not been accompanied, however, by a proportional increase in labour productivity; the latter registered a more instable trend (Figure 14.2), and even a drastically lower growth relative to the growth in wages; this resulted in a loss of cost-competitiveness, one of the major sources of growth for such countries.

The loss of external competitiveness is witnessed by the trend in the real effective exchange rates which, in fact, show a higher than EU average trend in all Central and Eastern countries (Figure 14.3). The exceptions to this trend are Poland, Czechia and Hungary, where price-competitiveness levels have been clearly maintained through the devaluation of the national currencies. This trend is predicted to remain stable over the next two years (Figure 14.3).

A second change in a new trend, which seems to have continued after the end of the big recession, is the decisive slowdown of FDI inflows; after a constant higher level of attractiveness compared to the European Union average, peaking at the outbreak of the crisis in 2008, the situation changed drastically, with CEECs losing attractiveness with respect to both Europe and the United States (Figure 14.4).

Intangible investments seemed to be somewhat more resilient to the crisis. In the European Union, in fact, there has been a steady increase in R&D over GDP investments, which probably reflects the long term nature and the large

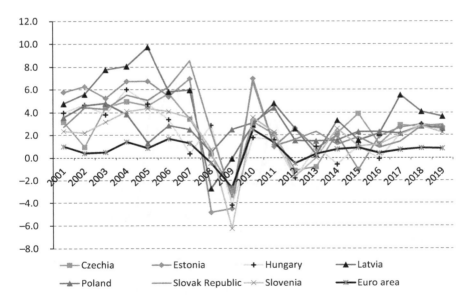

Figure 14.2 Growth rate of labour productivity, 2001–19 CEECs

Source: OECD Economic Outlook, 2017.

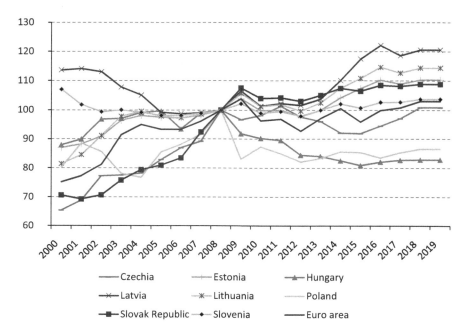

Figure 14.3 Real effective exchange rates – CEECs

Source: OECD Economic Outlook, 2017.

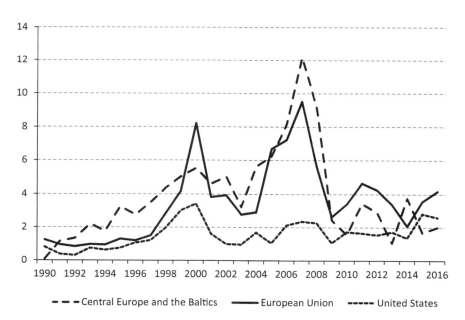

Figure 14.4 FDI inflows over GDP in the United States, EU and CEECs in the period 1990–2016

Source: World Bank, 2017.

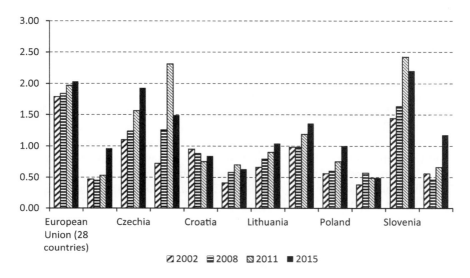

Figure 14.5 R&D over GDP in CEECs, 2002–15

sunk costs that might be borne at the initial stages of investments, possibly acting as buffers to the transmission of cycles (OECD 2017). Some of the CEECs reflect the same tendencies, while others like Estonia, Romania and Croatia register a decline (Figure 14.5). Meanwhile, what is clear in looking at these trends, is that CEECs have suffered a constant gap in R&D investments over GDP with respect to Europe as a whole, which does not seem to have changed irrespective of all policies recommendations suggested by the EU in its official documents such as the Europe 2020 Agenda (European Commission 2010a).

This last issue is not trivial. A new paradigmatic jump is predicted to occur thanks to the digitalization process and the consequent rise of the Industry 4.0. Even if this line of thought does not envisage any significant sources of increased productivity, as was the case with electrification in the 20th century (Gordon 2012), there is a techno-optimistic approach that digitalization will reinforce productivity growth, and therefore competitiveness. This issue calls for more investigation into the innovation trends in CEECs, which will be the subject matter of the next section.

Patterns of innovation in CEECs

In the face of the knowledge creation gap that existed between Europe and the most advanced economies, the Lisbon Agenda and the Europe 2020 Agenda recommended policy makers to achieve a target of 3% R&D investments over

GDP (European Commission 2010a). At the same time, a large debate was launched as to whether R&D investments were the right innovation tools to stimulate innovation.

A unanimous reply came from different scholars, suggesting that each nation and region had their own mode of innovation by which to develop their innovation policies. At the regional level, DG Regio launched the 'smart specialization strategy' suggested by the 'Knowledge for Growth' expert group advising the former European Commissioner for Research, Janez Potocnik (Foray 2009; Foray and David 2009); this advocated consistent matching of investments in knowledge and human capital, with the current industrial and technological 'vocations' and competences of territories. 'Strategies have to consider the heterogeneity of research and technology specialization patterns' (Giannitsis 2009: 1). The EU official document *Regional Policy Contributing to Smart Growth in Europe* (European Commission 2010b) was the first official move in this direction, calling for the need to identify sectors and technological domains on which regional policies should be tailored to promote local innovation processes in these specialization fields.

In those years, the author of this chapter and her research team developed a study on 'Knowledge, Innovation and Territory (KIT)', with the aim of developing a conceptual framework able to identify different regional innovation patterns (Capello and Lenzi 2013). This term is used to indicate the way in which knowledge and innovation are produced according to the presence/absence of certain contextual conditions that allow for the creation and/or the adoption of knowledge and innovation (Capello and Lenzi 2013). Conceptually, the different innovation patterns are obtained by breaking down, separating, demarcating in time and space, and finally recomposing the different stages of the knowledge-innovation chain following a relational logic of interregional cooperation and exchange (Camagni 2015). By reasoning in such a way, three main 'archetypal' innovation patterns were conceptualized, namely (Capello and Lenzi 2013):

1   *A science-based pattern*: in this pattern, thanks to the presence of contextual conditions favouring knowledge creation, knowledge is primarily created locally, by firms, universities and R&D centres, and exchanged and enriched through interregional cooperation with selected external partners, as highlighted in most of the literature dealing with knowledge and innovation creation and diffusion (Jensen et al. 2007; Mack 2014). In this pattern, contextual conditions, such as the presence of entrepreneurs and collective learning mechanisms, easily guarantee the translation of knowledge into innovation.

2   *A creative application pattern*: in this pattern, regions lack the conditions for generating new knowledge from within, and knowledge is primarily sourced outside the region. However, these regions are characterized by the presence of entrepreneurial creativity and collective learning processes that

allow external knowledge to be sought, found, brought into the area, and turned into innovation (Foray et al. 2009). Knowledge exchanges are nourished more by cognitive and sectoral proximity (i.e. shared cognitive maps) than by belonging to the same local community (Asheim and Isaksen 2002).

3   *An imitative innovation pattern*: in this pattern, regions lack the contextual conditions that allow knowledge and innovation to be produced internally. Innovation is the result of imitation processes, frequently dependent on relationships between local firms and dominant firms (typically multinationals), as described in the literature dealing with innovation diffusion (Pavlínek 2002).[1]

The empirical application of the innovation archetypes provided an interesting picture, where the three theoretical patterns split into six types. The first and second patterns each split into two, on the basis of distinct processes of knowledge accumulation and knowledge acquisition for innovation discovery. The imitative innovation pattern split between passive and active imitative attitudes. Six different groups of regions characterised by six different patterns are in this way obtained, namely (Capello and Lenzi 2018):

*   The European science-based area, where knowledge in general purpose technologies is generated;
*   The applied science area, where codified technological, engineering-based knowledge is produced;
*   A smart technological application area, where knowledge brought into the area is contained in codified technologies;
*   A smart and creative diversification area, where knowledge brought into the region is embedded in technological and engineering skills;
*   An active imitative innovation area, where innovation is creatively imitative, since it is adjusted to the needs of the local area;
*   A passive imitative innovation area, where innovation is just applied as it is in the local context.

The distribution of Central and Eastern European (NUTS2) regions among five patterns (keeping the imitative regions all together) over the period 2002–04 is reported in Table 14.1. None of the Central and Eastern European regions belongs to the European regional science-based pattern, while most of them (78%) are present in the imitative innovation pattern. Moreover, only 3.92% of the NUTS2 regions are in the applied-science area, concentrated in Czechia and Estonia. Less than 9% of regions belong to the smart technological application area, mostly concentrated in Czechia, with a few in Slovenia.

The situation in Table 14.1 is stable over time. The same empirical exercise of identifying regional patterns of innovation was done with data in 2004–06; the result was rather interesting, showing a persistence of all regions in CEECs to remain in their pattern (Capello and Lenzi 2018).

Table 14.1 Distribution of CEECs NUTS2 regions in the different innovation patterns in the period 2002–04

	BG	CZ	EE	HU	LT	LV	PL	RO	SI	SK	Total Central and Eastern Countries	Total Western C	EU
European science-based area											0.00	100	20
Applied science area		1.96	1.96								3.92	96.08	51
Smart technological application area		7.46							1.49		8.96	91.04	67
Smart and creative diversification area		2.30			1.15		10.34	3.45	1.15	1.15	19.54	80.46	87
Imitative innovation area	16.22			18.92		2.70	18.92	13.51		8.11	78.38	21.62	37
Number of regions	6	8	1	7	1	1	16	8	2	4	54	208	262

The lack of patterns based on R&D in general purpose technologies and in the capacity to change patterns over time generates a certain feeling of pessimism regarding the outlook for knowledge growth in this part of Europe.

Some descriptive analyses can be useful in understanding the economic performance of such innovation areas. When one looks at the economic performance of regions across patterns of innovation in Western and Eastern Europe, the result is interesting, even if no cause-effect relationship is measured: before the crisis, labour productivity was growing more in smart technological application areas than in smart and creative diversification areas: in fact, in the former areas, employment growth was less than GDP growth (Figure 14.6a), while the opposite was registered in the latter areas (Figure 14.6b). The two trends were more pronounced in Eastern regions than in the West. But what is even more striking is that labour productivity was worse in the imitative innovation regions of Western Europe than in the East (Figure 14.6c).

If we look at the economic performance of regions belonging to different patterns of innovation in different periods of time, other interesting results emerge. Figure 14.7 shows the annual average GDP growth rate in three periods of time, representing the period just before the crisis (2005–07), during the crisis (2008–12), and in the post-crisis period (2012–15), for regions belonging to the three less complex innovation patterns, where innovation is not linked to R&D activities.

Even if no cause-effect relationships can be assumed, the picture shows that the highest GDP growth is associated with regions belonging to the smart and creative diversification areas in all periods. Areas belonging to the imitative innovation patterns show a similar economic performance to the smart technological application areas: in the post-crisis period, the imitative innovation areas show an even higher recovery capacity than the smart technological application areas.

Without claiming a cause-effect chain, these descriptive results show that the imitative innovation patterns demonstrate relatively better economic outcomes than other patterns in Central and Eastern regions, and that, in general, each pattern of innovation can have a positive performance. This is in line with the findings of previous quantitative econometric studies, where clear cause-effect relationships were controlled for: no pattern is by definition worse than another in terms of economic performance. In particular, regions belonging to imitative innovation patterns do not gain any advantage from R&D investments, since this type of innovation is not based on R&D (Capello and Lenzi 2013). Instead, they obtain more advantage from innovation policies dedicated to the reinforcement of their own innovation pattern: incentives to maximize the returns on imitation in the case of imitative innovation patterns, incentives to maximize the application of existing knowledge, in the case of creative application patterns, and incentives to maximise R&D investments in the case of science-based patterns (Camagni and Capello 2015).

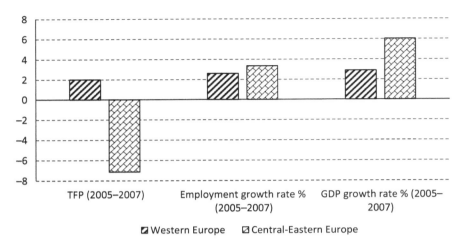

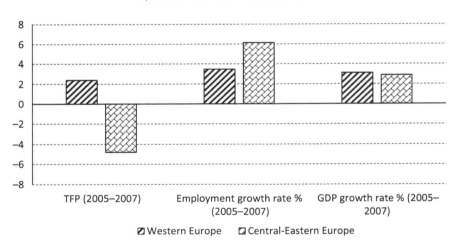

Figure 14.6 Economic performance across territorial patterns of innovation: Western vs. Eastern Europe

All this brings us to the suggestion that, even if CEECs do not drive the Industry 4.0 revolution, being followers rather than pioneers in radical innovation processes, their innovative structure will not confine them to a losing position. Their mode of innovation is able to take advantage from an imitative pattern, on the condition that a creative process accompanies the imitative activity.

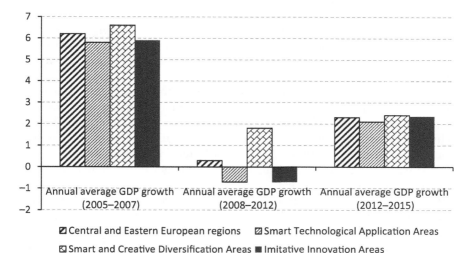

Figure 14.7 Annual average GDP growth rate before, during and after the crisis

Future challenges and perspectives

Nowadays, CEECs are no longer a single and homogenous area: they are characterized by a clear eastern periphery and show differentiated patterns of growth, based on different assets and territorial structures, and calling for different strategies. Moreover, CEECs have to face specific economic and spatial challenges, which require appropriate policy responses (European Bank for Reconstruction and Development 2013; Camagni and Capello 2015).

The first challenge is to make wages converge with Western levels without losing cost-competitiveness. Careful monitoring of the trend of external competitiveness synthesized by the trend of real effective exchange rates is necessary. The means of achieving both results (increase in unit labour cost and external competitiveness) is to keep wage increases in line with productivity increases. This challenge should not be met by relying on currency devaluations, a tool that may be useful in very critical circumstances but which provides only short term advantages. Elements that should be strictly monitored are the transfer of high monetary wages from modern sectors (and regions) to traditional sectors (and regions); real estate bubbles due to excessive concentration of growth in a few urban areas; process and product innovation; and the productivity/wage equilibrium (Camagni and Capello 2015).

The second challenge for these countries is to put in place a renovating strategy, which relies less on FDI and more on endogenous investments, taking advantage of technological multipliers and technological spillovers from multinational companies (MNCs) into the local fabric. An effort should also be made to enhance local entrepreneurship; this could be achieved by relying on existing industrial relations and existing skills, competencies and specializations.

The third challenge is to control rent increases and monopolies, not only in real estate and in commercial activities, but also in industrial and financial sectors. Rents erode personal disposable incomes and industrial profits, lowering the endogenous growth potential of countries.

The fourth challenge, of a territorial nature, is to support development in second- (and third-)rank cities, so as to decrease the inflationary pressure from rent increases stemming from the concentration of activities in central areas. This strategy will strengthen the economic base of national economic systems, and make it possible to exploit the territorial capital of each country.

The way in which these challenges are met will generate different scenarios for these countries. In a recent work, the present author has developed two alternative scenarios, based on the way CEECs respond to the challenges just mentioned (Capello and Caragliu 2016): (1) a scenario of place-based competitiveness and (2) a scenario of political and social cohesion. The two scenarios are based on opposite, and rather extreme, assumptions regarding both macroeconomic trends and the rationale behind regional policies. Thus the two scenarios are guided by two different policy goals.

The first scenario assumes competitiveness to be the leading goal, obtained through the exploitation of a hugely differentiated and scattered endowment of 'territorial capital', mostly found in second and third rank cities, where untapped potential for development is mobilized; these cities will become particularly attractive for foreign investors, who will see them as a strategic location for gaining access to potentially growing markets. Following this perspective, R&D investments are expected to be concentrated in second-rank cities, thanks to the presence of new FDI flows and the efforts of national and local policy makers to release untapped potential in second-rank cities. Reinforcement of R&D and innovation will enable CEECs to increase productivity, gain competitiveness and re-launch industrial activities. In Western countries, a re-launch of innovation and R&D activities will be directed towards green technologies, which will favour the reindustrialization of Europe, facilitated by lower interest rates and private investments.

These assumptions are reinforced with hypotheses on macroeconomic trends: following the competitiveness logic of the whole scenario, the limited resources for public expenditure in the EU are assumed to be re-directed towards second-rank, medium-sized cities, the loci of most of the unexploited potential for growth, where agglomeration economies, due to limited urban size, can still produce growth advantages.

This scenario is compared to an alternative, contrasting, scenario, in which *political and social cohesion* is the main goal, with the aim of repairing the social costs inflicted by the crisis, without necessarily foregoing economic modernization. Social incentives are applied to fight high unemployment rates and to keep the increase in wages in line with the increase in productivity levels, so as to (re-)gain cost competitiveness. This approach calls for political cohesion between policymakers and trade unions.

Creation of employment opportunities are expected in the public sector thanks to the availability of public resources with a more relaxed austerity plan than in the previous scenario. In this scenario, the limited public expenditure is distributed to favour peripheral, mostly rural areas, where investments are concentrated in exploiting natural resources (mountains, forests, seas, rivers) and enhancing local identity, expressed through local handicraft activities, local food production and so forth. The most appealing fields for public investments are represented by health and social services. R&D and innovation will be used in order to re-launch peripheral and rural areas, through the reinforcement of broadband networks and its strategic use for business purposes (websites, e-commerce, e-tourism, etc.). In this scenario, EU smart specialization strategies will achieve their best results, being able to identify the innovative technological domain of each region, that is the technological fields in which regions are specialized and to which regional policies should be tailored to promote local innovation processes (Camagni et al. 2014; McCann and Ortega-Argilés, in 2014).

When translated into quantitative assumptions, and inserted as levers of a macro-econometric regional growth model, called MASST (Capello 2007; Capello et al. 2011, 2017), the two opposite scenarios give rise to two completely different and unexpected growth patterns for Europe. The political and social cohesion scenario shows, as expected, the lowest aggregate GDP growth. However, what is unexpected is that convergence is lower than in the competitive scenario. Meanwhile, the competitiveness scenario, achieved through the exploitation of under-exploited territorial resources present in second-rank areas, is able to achieve at the same time two important results: a lower increase in disparities and higher aggregate GDP growth.

Table 14.2 Scenario results by macro areas

Scenario	Reference: stuck in transition			Place-based competitiveness scenario – reference scenario			Social cohesion scenario – reference scenario		
Variable	EU27	Old15	CEECS	EU27	Old15	CEECS	EU27	Old15	CEECS
GDP growth	1.84	1.83	1.90	0.49	0.50	0.34	−0.11	−0.12	−0.05
Manufacturing employment growth	1.55	1.63	1.25	0.52	0.56	0.35	−0.57	−0.64	−0.30
Service employment growth	1.54	1.45	2.20	0.43	0.43	0.45	0.05	0.06	−0.02
Total employment growth	1.54	1.48	1.89	0.45	0.45	0.35	−0.07	−0.07	−0.10

Source: Capello and Caragliu (2016).

Conclusions

The brief picture sketched above shows clear structural changes in eastern countries' economies. Loss of cost-competitiveness, the concentration of activities in capital regions, and reduced attraction of FDI, along with the traditional weaknesses of this part of Europe in terms of limited innovation capacity, call for new competitive strategies in the future.

The way in which these countries are able to put in place such strategies will affect the future of the region. When alternative growth scenarios are analysed, interesting results emerge. The scenario in favour of social cohesion, with the aim of remedying the social costs produced by the crisis, predictably brings the lowest aggregate GDP growth. However, the results on convergence are not as high as expected. The competitiveness scenario, with the aim of reviving growth through the exploitation of untapped territorial resources, especially present in second rank cities, is at the same time more expansionary and cohesive. This is true for Europe as a whole, as well as for CEECs, whose growth rates are higher in the scenario where dispersed, un-exploited local excellence is identified and exploited, restoring economic growth and enhancing regional convergence trends.

These observations lead us to the conclusion that cohesion policies should favour local excellence and reinforce territorial specificities, rather than urge traditional social support, even if such support does not deny the importance of economic modernization (Bachtler and Gorzelak 2007).

Note

1 The regional patterns of innovation framework adopts a relative conception of innovation: regions are innovative insofar as local firms are able to do something new with respect to their past, and not with respect to a dominant paradigm present worldwide (Camagni 2015). In this respect, imitation can also represent innovations that are new to a region.

References

Asheim, B.T., & Isaksen, A. (2002). Regional innovation systems: The integration of local 'sticky' and global 'ubiquitous' knowledge. *The Journal of Technology Transfer*, 27(1), 77–86.

Bachtler, J., & Gorzelak, G. (2007). Reforming EU cohesion policy: A reappraisal of the performance of the structural funds. *Policy Studies*, 28(4), 309–326.

Camagni, R. (2015). Towards creativity-oriented innovation policies based on a hermeneutic approach to the knowledge-space nexus. In: A. Cusinato & A. Philippopoulos-Mihalopoulos (eds.), *Knowledge-creating Milieus in Europe: Firms, Cities, Territories*. Berlin: Springer Verlag, pp. 341–358.

Camagni, R., & Capello, R. (2015). Rationale and design of EU cohesion policies in a period of crisis. *Regional Science Policy and Practice*, 7(1), 25–49.

Camagni, R., Capello, R., & Lenzi, C. (2014). A Territorial Taxonomy of Innovative Regions and the European Regional Policy Reform: Smart Innovation Policies. *Scienze Regionali – Italian Journal of Regional Science*, 13(1), 69–106

Capello, R. (2007). A forecasting territorial model of regional growth: The MASST model. *The Annals of Regional Science*, 41(4), 753–787.

Capello, R., & Caragliu, A. (2016). After crisis scenarios for Europe: Alternative evolutions of structural adjustments. *Cambridge Journal of Regions, Economy and Society*, 9(1), 81–101, doi: 10.1093/cjres/rsv023

Capello, R., & Lenzi, C. (eds.) (2013). *Territorial Patterns of Innovation. An Inquiry on the Knowledge Economy in European Regions*. London: Routledge.

Capello, R., & Lenzi, C. (2018). Regional innovation patterns from an evolutionary perspective. An investigation of European regions. *Regional Studies*, 52(2), 159–171, doi: 10.1080/00343404.2017.1296943

Capello, R., Caragliu, A., & Fratesi, U. (2017). Modeling regional growth between competitiveness and austerity measures: The MASST3 model. *International Regional Science Review*, 40(1), 38–74.

Capello, R., Fratesi, U., & Resmini, L. (2011). *Globalisation and Regional Growth in Europe: Past Trends and Scenarios*. Berlin: Springer Verlag.

Dell'Anno, R., & Villa, S. (2013). Growth in transition countries BigBang versus Gradualism. *Economics of Transition*, 21, 381–417.

European Bank for Reconstruction and Development (2013). Stuck in transition?, Transition Report 2013, London.

European Commission of the European Communities (2010a). *Europe 2020. A Strategy for Smart, Suitable and Inclusive Growth*, Communication from the Commission, COM(2010)2020

European Commission of the European Communities (2010b). *Regional Policy Contributing to Smart Growth in Europe*, COM(2010)553, Brussels.

Foray, D. (2009). Understanding smart specialisation. In: D. Pontikakis, D. Kyriakou & R. van Bavel (eds.), *The Question of R&D Specialisation*. Brussels: JRC, European Commission, Directoral General for Research, pp. 19–28.

Foray, D., David, P., & Hall, B. (2009). Smart specialisation – The concept. *Knowledge Economists Policy Brief*, (9).

Giannitsis, T. (2009). Technology and specialization: Strategies, options, risks. *Knowledge Economists Policy Brief*, (8).

Gordon, R. (2012). Is U.S. Economic Growth Over? Faltering Innovation Confronts the Six Headwinds. *NBER Working Papers* No. 18315.

Gorzelak, G. (1998). Regional development and planning in East Central Europe. In: M. Keune (ed.), *Regional Development and Employment Policy. Lessons from central and eastern Europe*. Geneva/Budapest: ILO – CEET, pp. 62–76.

Hagemejer, J., & Tyrowicz, J. (2012). Is the effect really so large? Firm-level evidence on the role of FDI in a transition economy. *Economics of Transition*, 20, 195–233.

Jensen, M.B., Johnson, B., Lorenz, E., & Lundvall, B.A. (2007). Forms of knowledge and modes of innovation. *Research Policy*, 36(5), 680–693

Mack, E. (2014). Broadband and knowledge intensive firm clusters: Essential link or auxiliary connection? *Papers in Regional Science*, 93(1), 3–29

OECD (2017). *The Future of Productivity*. Paris: OECD.

Pavlínek, P. (2002). Transformation of central and east European passenger car industry: Selective peripheral integration through foreign direct investment. *Environment and Planning A*, 34, 1685–1709.

Reinhart, C.M., & Rogoff, K.S. (2010). Growth in a time of debt. *American Economic Review*, 100, 573–578.

Conclusions

The Central and Eastern European countries have become members of the European Union after a painful process of post-socialist transformation. The success of this unprecedented political, social, institutional, economic and technological (as well as environmental) restructuring has allowed them to become part of the world's largest common market and to become active participants in the development of the European Union's manifold policies to improve standards of living and to open their societies to the outside world.

In spite of the unquestionable successes in economic growth, social advancement, and political and institutional reforms, post-socialist transformation and the early years of EU membership did not enable the CEE countries to overcome several critical weaknesses in their overall socio-economic and institutional structures. In particular, there is a disjuncture between fast productivity growth and low rates of growth attributed to technological innovation. These countries still strive to achieve international competitiveness based more on low costs of production than through offering innovative commodities and services to demanding customers. Partly as a result of this development paradigm, most CEE countries were disproportionately affected by the 2008–09 crisis. It is arguable that they are not sufficiently prepared to meet the 'smart growth' goals of the Europe 2020 strategy, and many challenges for sustainable growth and development remain. In order to maintain further convergence momentum, the CEE countries have to increase their degree of value capture in the global value chains.

A second area of concern is that growth is territorially imbalanced in the CEE countries, more so than in most other parts of the EU. Economic, social and environmental territorial differences still persist among the more pronounced outcomes of the new Member States' accelerated growth and deep structural changes. The benefits of transformation in these countries have been unequally distributed among particular social groups and regions – with the emergence of highly educated and internationally successful professionals and entrepreneurs, on the one hand, but structural unemployment (recently overcome to a large extent as a result of massive outmigration), persistent poverty and social exclusion (in some countries with an ethnic flavour) on the other. Regional imbalances, furthermore, have been characterised by a rapid process of metropolisation, which has privileged a handful of dynamic urban centres while exacerbating the structural problems of old industrial regions, vast rural areas and regions located on borders, especially the EU's eastern borders. Only recently, some signs of diffusion of growth could be observed and territorial polarisation began to decrease slightly – but it is limited to areas with a favourable location (like those adjacent to metropolitan cores, stretching along major transportation corridors, and undergoing successful industrial restructuring). As different as they are in social, cultural and geographical terms, regions that are still declining (if not in absolute terms, at least in relation to successful ones) share general problems of economic peripherality and many negative impacts of structural change, such as rural de-population, 'brain drain', disinvestment and, frequently, below-average levels of socio-economic well-being. This polarised economic and territorial development within CEE clearly points to future challenges, not only for particular countries, but also for European cohesion.

Institutional progress has not been as successful as one might have assumed in the wake of accession to the EU. As research has revealed, this progress in fact ceased in 2004–07: after accession, the new Member States seemed to relax, having fulfilled the basic requirements of acquis communautaire and thereby receiving a stamp of 'institutional morality'. However, they subsequently abandoned further improvements of their administrative structures and procedures. Clientelism, low transparency in public procurement, corruption, and unclear mechanisms of political recruitment of cadres have not been eradicated and in some countries, even after accession, have influenced the mechanisms of public life.

A few years ago, the above paragraphs would have sufficed to describe and explain the transformation processes of the CEE countries. In 2004–07, the 'end of history' perspective in relation to CEE could have been justified: we tended to believe that the path to a mature democracy and efficient market economy was straight and even and that we would proceed along this path without major upheavals. However, all of a sudden, a new phenomenon emerged in some countries – the destruction of liberal democracy and limitation of the rule of law. Two countries lead in this negative tendency: Hungary and Poland, which has triggered the European Commission to begin the procedure under Article 7 of the Treaty of the European Union against these two Member States, as countries which persistently breach the EU's founding values such as freedom, democracy, equality, the rule of law and respect for human rights. One has to remember that the political parties in power which introduce such antidemocratic measures received popular support, in Hungary even enabling Fides to reach a constitutional majority in the parliament. In other CEE countries, several other misdoings in this respect can be encountered, although not to the extent observed in Hungary and Poland. However, in all of them, anti-immigration policies have been introduced which have received wide public support.

A fundamental question emerges: what are the reasons for this unexpected turn of political values in the CEE countries? Markowski is perhaps right in saying that linking this change with the remnants of *Homo Sovieticus* would be too simplistic and incorrect. Another plausible explanation relates to the shallow roots of democracy in this part of the continent and low-level attachment to formal procedures and institutions which are considered less effective than direct interpersonal relations and ad hoc decision-making. Still another explanation points to the fact that the CEE countries flow in the widening stream of anti-establishment attitudes and practices that is spreading around the world, including mature democracies like the United States and some Western European countries.

Some other analytics[1] indicate that the CEE societies have become tired of imitating the West, or that they have begun to doubt if western values suit Central and Eastern European societies. Although this may not be to the extent of rejecting these values – as is happening in Russia and partly in Ukraine – the CEE people may have come to the conclusion that they will never match the original standards and defend themselves by challenging these standards. Frustration and feelings of exploitation and humiliation may be the foundations of approval for authoritarian rule and agreement to breaching the rules of democracy.

In the title of the book there was a hidden question: what has changed in CEE after 1990 and what has remained stable? Without doubt, after the initial changes of borders at the beginning of the 1990s (the unification of Germany, collapse of the Soviet Union, velvet divorce of Czechoslovakia, and dreadful war in the former Yugoslavia) borders have been stable (with the exception of the secession of Kosovo in 2008). Will this continue in the future? Probably yes, although there have been some disputes between Kosovo and Serbia on some slight adjustment of frontiers. Hopefully, the state borders will not be further amended, and worries in the Baltic republics about their statehoods and independence will not materialize.

The spatial structures of the CEE countries definitely follow the principles of *longue durée*. These structures became even more pronounced due to the processes of metropolisation. The peripherality and stagnation of some less developed regions have not disappeared in spite of Cohesion Policy interventions. Major transportation routes have not changed and have been significantly upgraded due to massive investments in transportation infrastructure with high involvement of EU funds. However, the connections with western Europe to a great extent replace previous links with the post-Soviet republics and the Russian Federation. There are no strong arguments to foresee any deep changes of these spatial patterns in the future, though some signs of dissemination of growth may be noticed.

It was presumably not expected that the CEE countries would develop one of the most acute demographic problems in all Europe. Massive outmigration and low fertility have changed the age structures of their populations and made the future demographic prospects bleak and uncertain. This is definitely a reversal of traditional demographic trends and one of the greatest dangers for the future of labour markets, the vitality of pension systems and, therefore, for their systems of public finance. A possible remedy – opening to immigration – has been ruled out, at least temporarily, which represents a further change in traditional positive attitudes to the 'other' that were displayed by most CEE societies before the migration crisis in Europe and anti-immigration rhetoric of several CEE parties.

Certainly, de-industrialisation coupled with the inclusion of large parts of remaining industrial potential into the production chains of major transnational corporations has been an important process changing the socio-economic structures of the CEE countries and their regions. The emergence of a service economy – located mainly in large urban centres – has been a supplement to deindustrialisation allowing these centres to maintain their status quo as the most developed and affluent areas in CEE. These processes have maintained their momentum throughout the last 30 years and are very likely to proceed in the future – providing that the world economy does not enter a long and deep recession, which of course cannot be excluded. In such circumstances, the CEE countries would become a vulnerable part of the global system and recession could be deeper and longer for them than for the stronger, more advanced economies.

Volatile and shallow support for democratic procedures and mechanisms, and for the rule of law, seems to be an inherent feature of the CEE societies, which did not have much chance to develop fully fledged democratic systems in the past. The progress achieved after 1990 has been reversed, and future development remains unclear. It is doubtful if the CEE countries will become the European forerunners in reintroducing constitutional order and political stability, and abandoning populist rhetoric. It is more likely they will join the group of European 'troublemakers', either the states or their anti-establishment parties of both right- and left-wing orientation (*les extrêmes se touchent*).

Finally, accession to the EU has been a major event in the recent history of the CEE countries. With some exaggeration, for some of them this can be compared to the acceptance of Christianity from Rome more than a thousand years ago, which at that time meant joining the West. The first years of membership seemed to prove the benefits of the event for the two sides: the 'old' and the 'new' Member States. However, recent developments challenge this opinion. The CEE countries are ceasing to offer cheap labour and low costs of production and are becoming less attractive to external investors. Moreover, even within the 'old' EU, protectionist attitudes are emerging – several governments are beginning to disapprove of relocating production plants to CEE, even when it is still economically profitable. Net payers in the EU oppose transferring large sums of EU funds to poorer Member States which do not follow common European values. The largest CEE countries have not adopted the euro and some of them openly oppose this move, even in the more distant future. Moreover, if we compare the policy stands of several CEE countries on the main challenges for the future of the EU, as specified in the famous White Paper of Secretary-General Junker from March 2017, it is clear that the area of agreement is relatively narrow. Thus the future role of these countries in the EU is uncertain, and their current proposals for reforms lead rather to loosening the mutual ties between the Member States than tightening them and making the European Union more integrated.

In earlier writing, my observations of the developments in the 21st century and reactions to the global crisis led me to challenge the traditional division of Europe into East and West[2] suggesting that this perspective had become obsolete. On economic grounds – the ability for growth and financial stability – this might have been true, and perhaps still is true, even now. However, in 2019, in the sphere of values and attitudes towards European integration, this division, generally speaking, seems to be back.

The history of the CEE countries did not end in 2004–07, just as it did not end globally in 1990. On these both scales, the future is becoming more and more uncertain, and the longing for stability must be replaced by an awareness of unknown change.

Notes

1 Krastev I., & Holmes S. (2018). Explaining Eastern Europe: Imitation and its discontents. *Journal of Democracy,* 29(3), 117–128.
2 Gorzelak, G. (2010). The financial crisis in Central and Eastern Europe, in G. Gorzelak and Chor-Ching Goh (eds.). *Financial Crisis in Central and Eastern Europe: From Similarity to Diversity.* Warsaw: Scholar, pp. 236–252.

Index